S0-AIO-081

explore

one encyclopedia—
a world of knowledge

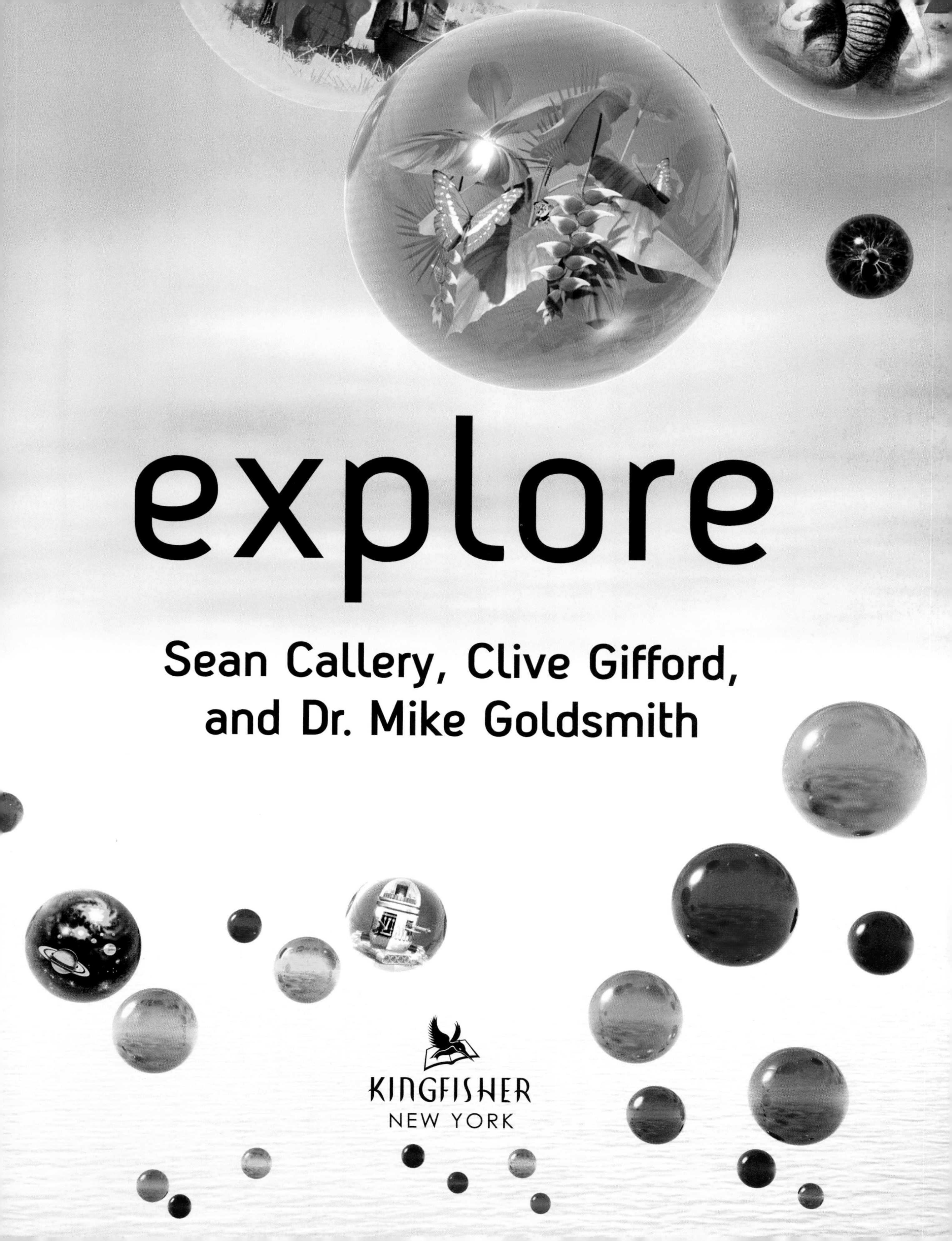

explore

Sean Callery, Clive Gifford, and Dr. Mike Goldsmith

KINGFISHER
NEW YORK

Contents

Planet Earth

Viewed from space, Earth looks like a swirling blue marble. It is the fifth-largest of the eight planets in the solar system and the third-closest planet to the Sun, orbiting at an average distance of 93 million mi. (150 million km). Together, Earth's water, atmosphere, and distance from the Sun help make it the only known body in space to support life.

Formation and structure

Earth is a planet that measures 7,883 mi. (12,714km) in diameter. Made out of rock, it has a core of very hot metal.

Earth is not perfectly round but is slightly flattened at the top and bottom, known as the poles. Earth also bulges at the equator—the imaginary line around the middle of the planet.

Mantle is 1,800 mi. (2,900km) thick, with a temperature of more than 2,300°F (1,300°C).
Inner core is around 1,600 mi. (2,600km) in diameter.
Crust varies in thickness from 4–19 mi. (6–30km).

Formation of Earth

Earth was formed around 4.5 billion years ago. Clouds of dust, rock, and gas were pulled together by gravity. Over millions of years, the outer surface cooled to form solid rock, while gases formed the atmosphere around it.

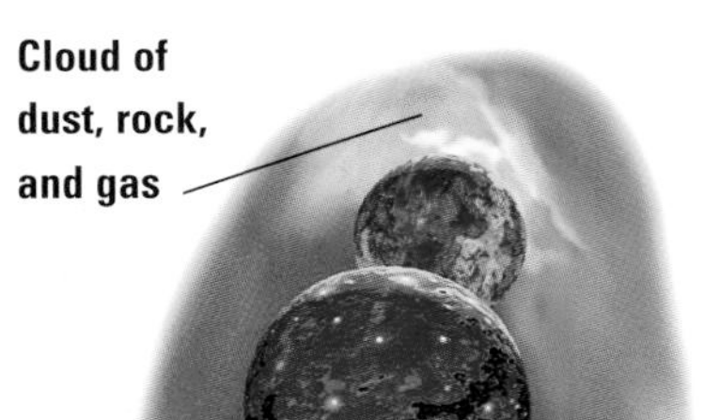

Cloud of dust, rock, and gas

Earth's crust

The crust is the planet's thin outer surface. It varies between 4 mi. (6km) and 19 mi. (30km) in depth and is made up of rocks and minerals such as silica and quartz. More than 70 percent of this crust surface is covered by the water of seas, oceans, rivers, and lakes.

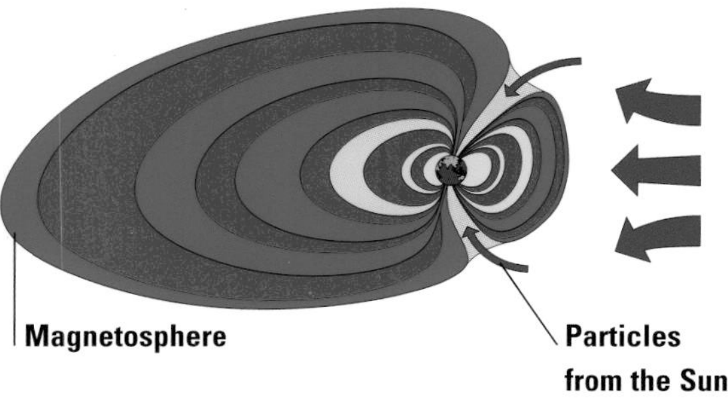

Earth's magnetism

Earth's outer core creates a giant magnetic field—the magnetosphere. This stretches around Earth and reaches out far into space. It helps prevent particles from the Sun and space from harming life on Earth.

Atmosphere

Outer core is 1,395 mi. (2,250km) thick.

Below the surface

Beneath Earth's crust is the mantle, which is composed of partially melted rock and metals. Beneath the mantle is Earth's core, made of two parts: a hot liquid metal outer core and a solid metal inner core.

Naturally hot

In the Valley of the Geysers in Russia, steam and boiling water pour out of holes in Earth's crust. Water is heated by hot rocks just below Earth's surface and escapes in different ways. Fountain geysers erupt in short bursts from pools of water. Cone geysers have steady, narrow jets.

SCIENTIFIC INPUT

GEOLOGICAL TIME

Geologists study Earth, its rocks, and their history. They also measure the age of rocks and fossils (*see p. 19*) using geological time. This calendar of Earth's history is divided into epochs and eras that lasted many millions of years. From the study of dinosaur fossils (above), geologists have established that dinosaurs lived during the Mesozoic Era, from 251 to 65 million years ago (m.y.a.).

Continents and mountains

A continent is a giant area of land. One third of Earth's surface is land, divided into seven continents: Asia, Africa, North and South America, Antarctica, Europe, and Australia.

CONTINENTAL DRIFT
These diagrams show how the continent Pangaea became today's continents.

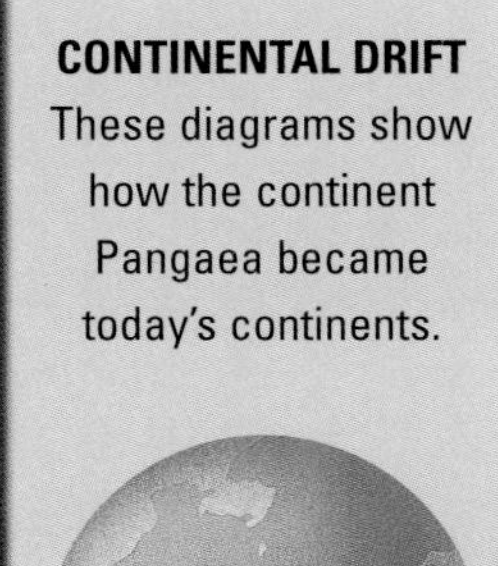

200 million years ago

110 million years ago

Today

Mountains are high peaks of land, often formed by movements in Earth's crust. They are found in groups called mountain ranges. The highest mountain, Mount Everest, is in the Himalaya Mountains.

Continental plates

Earth's crust is made up of several giant slabs of solid rock called continental plates. These float on Earth's mantle and move very slowly.

Fault lines

Faults or fault lines are cracks in Earth's crust. There are faults where two continental plates meet. Faults are often where volcanic activity and earthquakes occur.

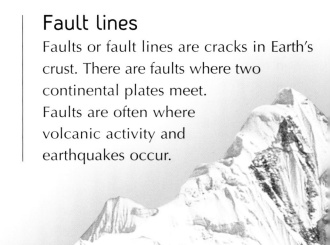

Continental drift

At first, there was only one giant continent, Pangaea. Over many millions of years, Pangaea slowly separated into today's continents. This movement is called continental drift, and it is still occurring.

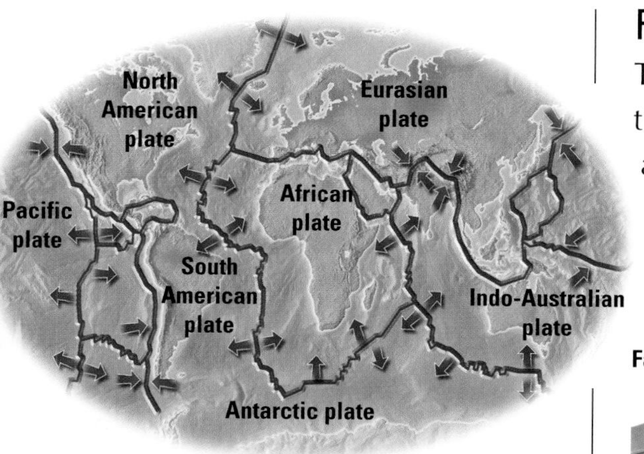

Plate activity

This map shows the world's major continental plates and the arrows show the direction in which they are currently moving. There are seven major continental plates and nine minor continental plates.

Forming mountains

The movement of the continental plates creates most of the world's mountains. Land is driven upward, buckles, and folds, often along faults. Volcanoes (*see pp. 16–17*) can also create mountains by spewing out large amounts of lava and ash, which harden as they cool to form rocks.

Fault-block mountain

Fold mountain

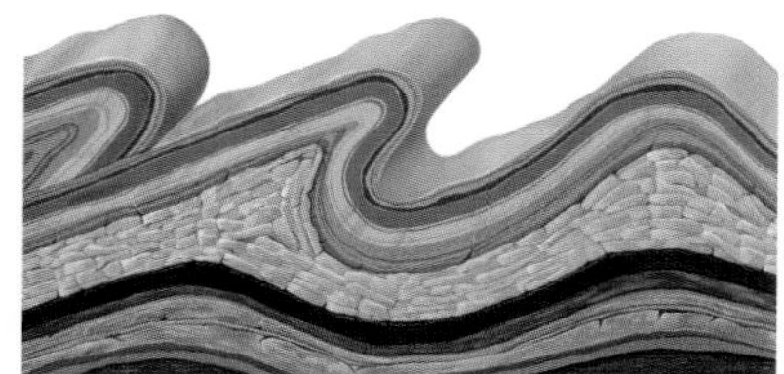

Types of mountains

A large block of land can be forced upward by plate movement to form a fault-block mountain. Other mountains, such as the Andes in South America and the Rockies in North America, are fold mountains. These are formed when softer rocks are bent into folds by immense pressure.

The Himalayas continue to move upward.

Making a mountain range

The Himalaya Mountains were formed millions of years ago by two continental plates pushing into each other. The mud and sediment on the seabed were squeezed together and pushed up to create the mountain range.

Earthquakes

Earthquakes are caused by movements of Earth's crust that trigger pressure in part of the crust to be released as energy.

As many as 500,000 earthquakes happen every year. The majority are small and harmless, but powerful earthquakes can cause enormous damage.

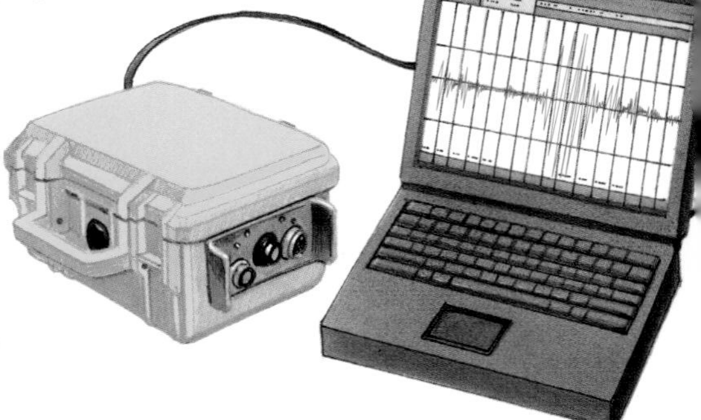
Mobile seismograph

TYPES OF SHOCK WAVES
There are three forms of shock waves generated by an earthquake.

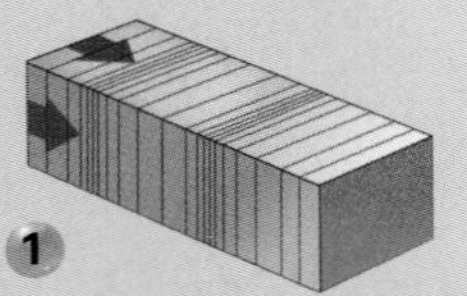
1 Waves travel deep under the ground, stretching and compressing rocks.

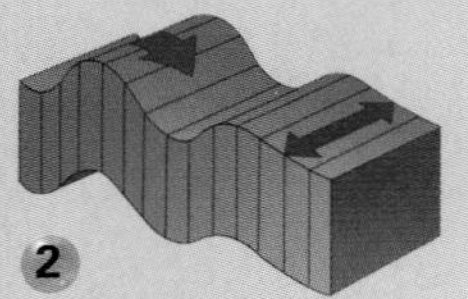
2 Waves also travel under the ground but shift rocks up and down and from side to side.

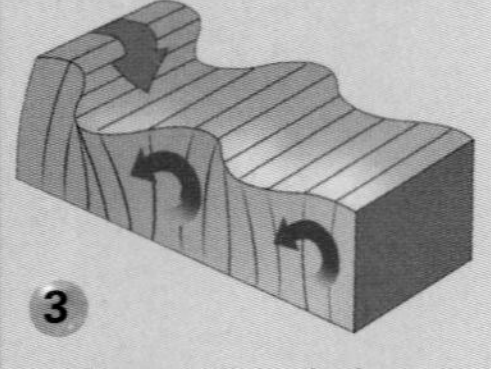
3 Waves travel along Earth's surface and cause the most damage.

Focus and epicenter

An earthquake begins at a point underground called the focus or hypocenter. The point on the surface directly above that is called the epicenter. This is usually where the greatest force is felt.

Shock waves

From the focus released energy spreads out quickly in the form of a series of rippling energy waves called shock waves. Their force weakens as they travel.

Tsunamis

Earthquakes can generate giant ocean waves called tsunamis. These can be devastating if they reach land. In 2004, a massive earthquake on the floor of the Indian Ocean resulted in the Asian tsunami. It killed more than 230,000 people.

Measuring earthquakes

Earthquake experts, or seismologists, study and measure earthquakes. They use a variety of scientific instruments, including satellites and seismographs, to chart Earth's vibrations.

Shock waves spreading out in all directions

The Richter scale

The Richter scale indicates the magnitude or strength of an earthquake. Earthquakes above 3.5 are strong enough to be noticed but do little damage. Major earthquakes register 7.0 or above. The earthquake that helped generate the Asian tsunami measured more than 9.0.

HISTORICAL DATA

EARTHQUAKE DAMAGE

Earthquakes in built-up areas can inflict a lot of damage. Roads, bridges, tunnels, and buildings collapse or are torn apart, while deadly landslides, fires, and explosions may be caused by broken cables and pipelines. In 1995, an earthquake measuring 7.3 on the Richter scale destroyed roads and buildings in the Japanese city of Kobe.

Epicenter directly above the focus

Fault between two plates of Earth's crust

Focus of earthquake deep underground

Earthquake zones

Certain parts of the planet are more likely to suffer earthquakes than others. This map shows where major earthquakes have occurred in the past. Most of these were along existing faults (green), because this is where Earth's crust is often under the most pressure.

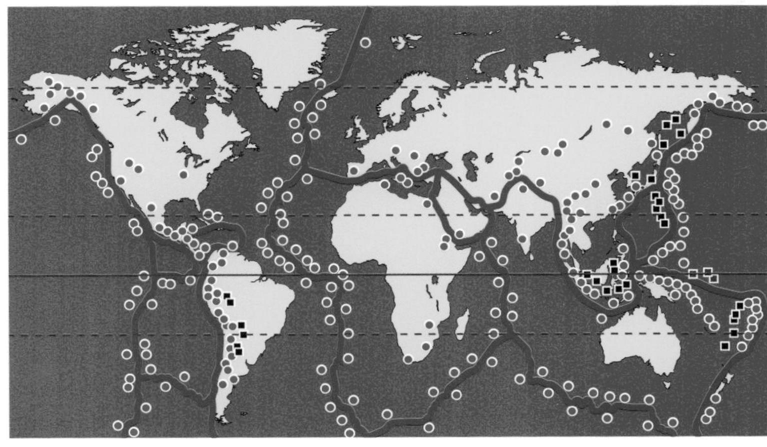

VOLCANOES

VOLCANOES ARE OPENINGS THROUGH WHICH RED-HOT LIQUID ROCK CALLED MAGMA FORCES ITS WAY TO THE SURFACE OF EARTH. MAGMA COMES FROM DEEP INSIDE EARTH, AND THESE ERUPTIONS OCCUR WHERE EARTH'S CRUST IS AT ITS WEAKEST.

EXPLOSIVE ERUPTIONS

On the Italian island of Sicily, Mount Etna stands 2,062 ft. (3,326m) high. It is the largest active volcano in Europe. Along its slopes, magma seeps and oozes out as lava through long cracks in the rocky crust called fissures. In the past, a buildup of gases under pressure has resulted in explosive eruptions, with lava, ash, and gases thrown high up into the air. The most explosive eruptions have blown away the top of the volcano, leaving giant craters.

A violent eruption throws out chunks of hot rock, lava, ash, and a massive cloud of gas, which can be poisonous.

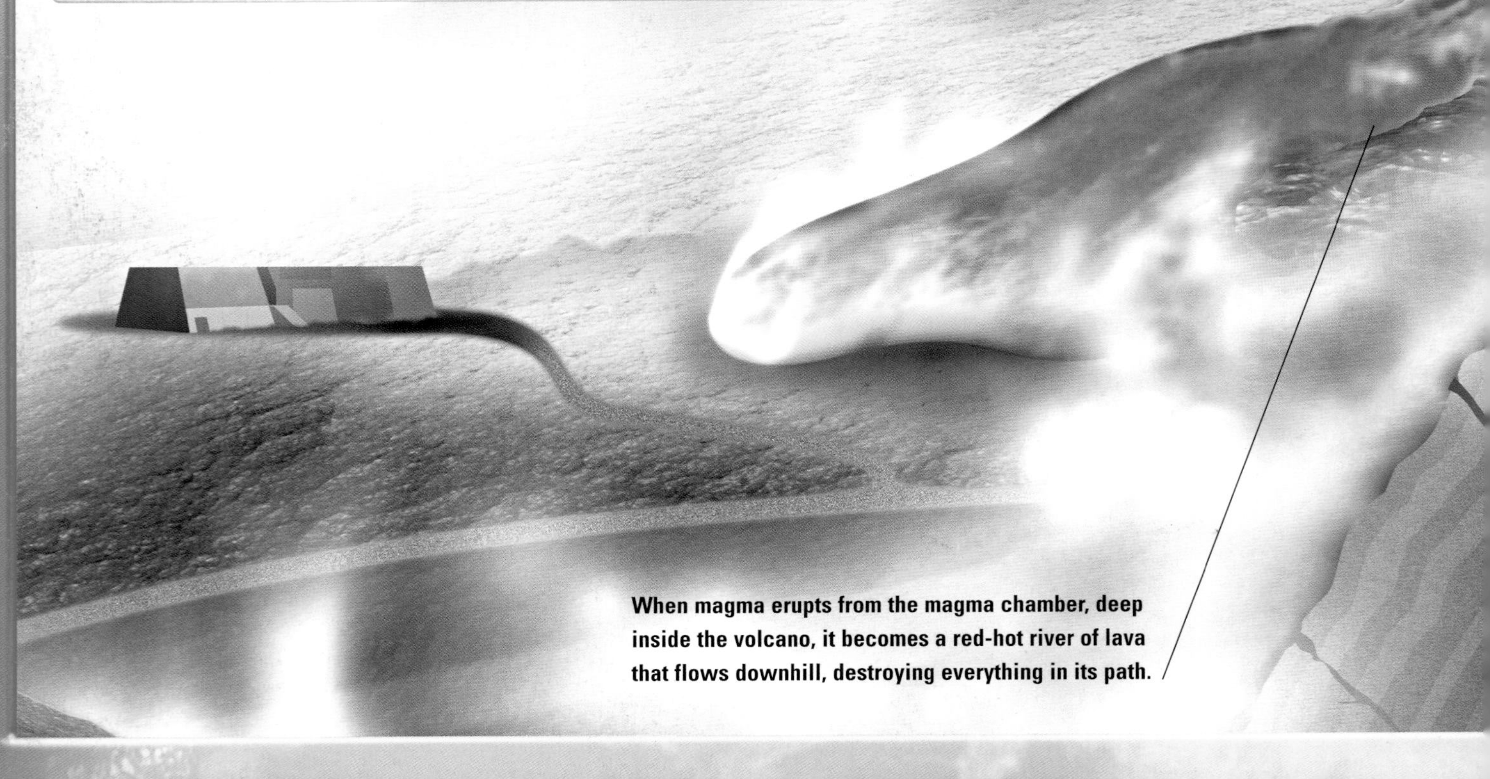

When magma erupts from the magma chamber, deep inside the volcano, it becomes a red-hot river of lava that flows downhill, destroying everything in its path.

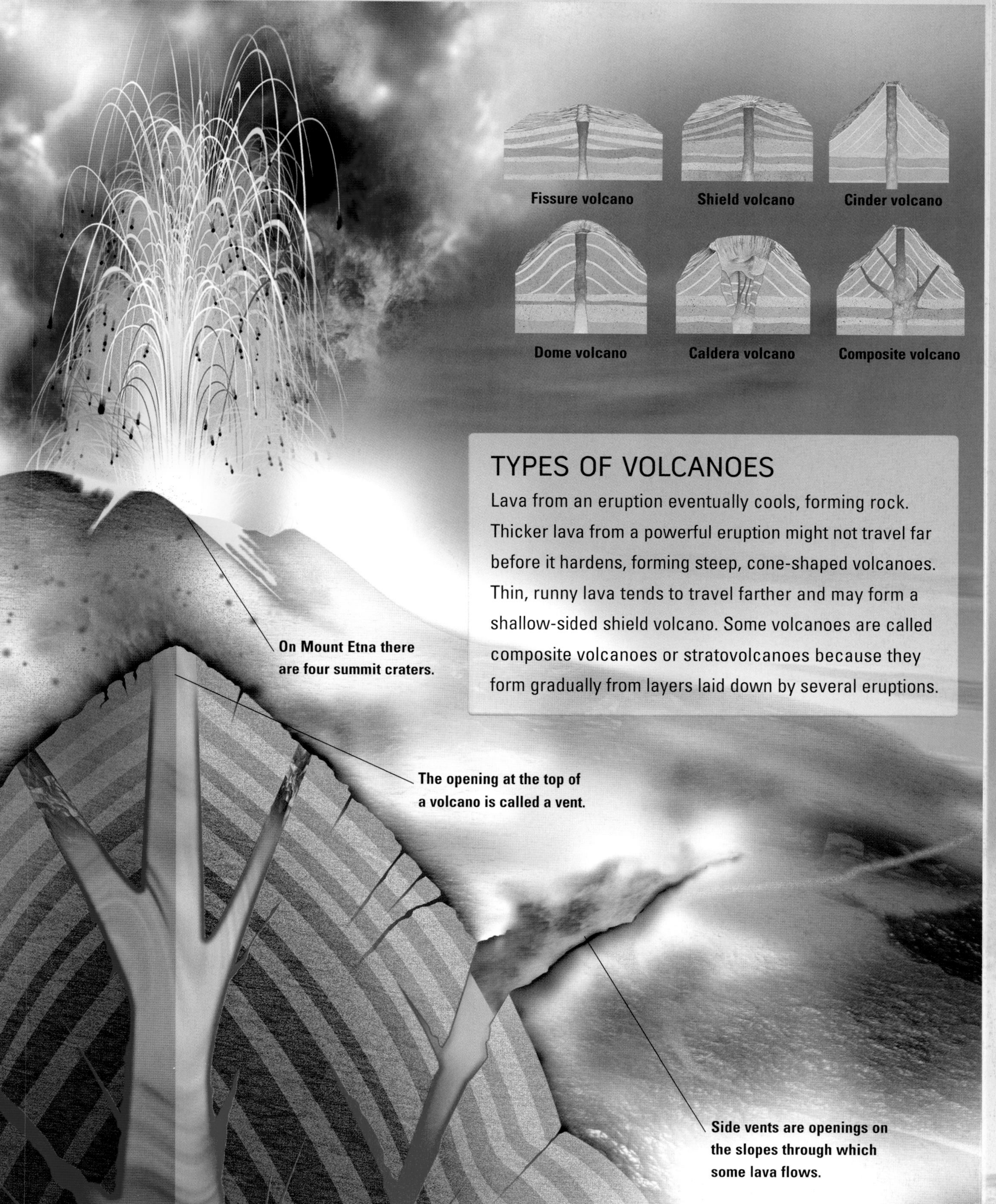

Fissure volcano
Shield volcano
Cinder volcano
Dome volcano
Caldera volcano
Composite volcano
On Mount Etna there are four summit craters.
The opening at the top of a volcano is called a vent.
Side vents are openings on the slopes through which some lava flows.

TYPES OF VOLCANOES

Lava from an eruption eventually cools, forming rock. Thicker lava from a powerful eruption might not travel far before it hardens, forming steep, cone-shaped volcanoes. Thin, runny lava tends to travel farther and may form a shallow-sided shield volcano. Some volcanoes are called composite volcanoes or stratovolcanoes because they form gradually from layers laid down by several eruptions.

Rocks and soil

Rocks are solid, nonliving materials. They are divided into three types: igneous, metamorphic and sedimentary.

MOHS SCALE

The Mohs scale rates ten minerals, from the softest to the hardest.

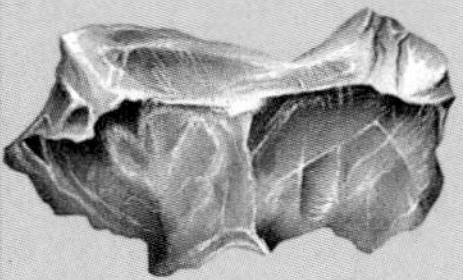

Talc is the softest mineral, rated as 1.

Gypsum is rated as 2 and can scratch talc.

Apatite is rated as 5 on the Mohs scale.

Quartz is rated as 7 on the Mohs scale.

Diamond is the hardest mineral, rated as 10.

Rocks are formed from chemical compounds called minerals. Minerals, such as copper, are single elements, while others, such as silicon, are made up of many elements.

Igneous rock

Igneous rock is formed from magma or lava that has cooled and hardened. Granite is an igneous rock that forms deep underground. The spectacular columns of Giant's Causeway in Northern Ireland are basalt, which is an igneous rock that is formed from lava that cooled above the ground.

Metamorphic rock

Metamorphic means changed, and intense heat or pressure transforms this rock. For example, heat and pressure have changed some types of the sedimentary rock limestone to form marble, a metamorphic rock.

Sedimentary rock

Over millions of years, tiny particles of worn-away rock, or the skeletons and shells of creatures, were compacted (pressed together) to form solid sedimentary rock. The sandstone and limestone of the Grand Canyon, Arizona, are good examples of this.

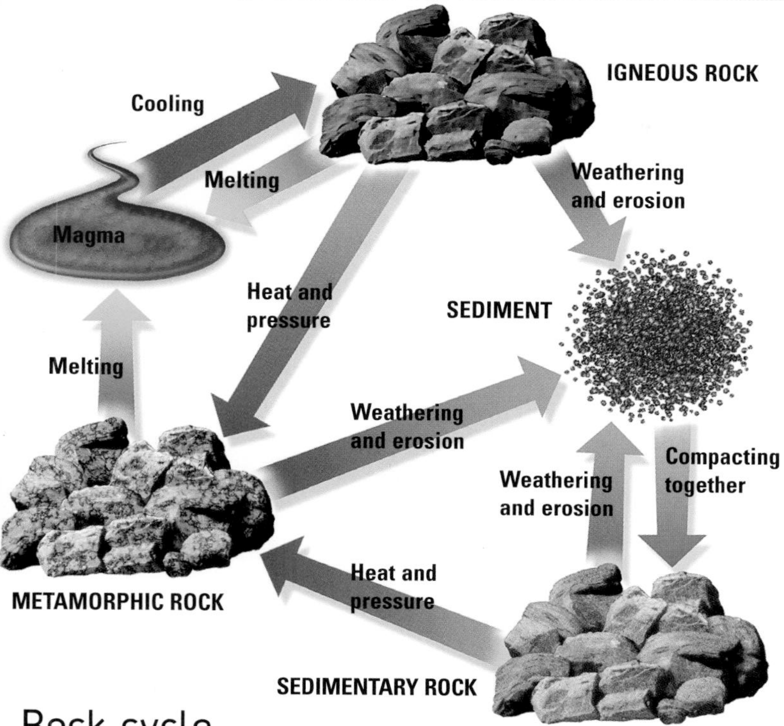

Rock cycle

The rock cycle is a way of showing the different ways in which rocks can change over long periods of time. An igneous rock, for example, can be worn away, with the particles forming a layer of sediment. Over time, these are compacted to form a sedimentary rock. This rock can then be changed again, by heat and pressure, into a metamorphic rock.

Minerals under pressure

When put under pressure and at certain temperatures, some minerals form gemstones. These can be cut and polished. Many gemstones—for example, rubies, opals, emeralds, and diamonds—shine with beautiful colors.

Rock strata

Geologists have discovered that many sedimentary rocks exist in layers, with the oldest rocks below layers of newer rocks. A layer of the same type of rock is called a stratum (*plural* strata). Scientists are able to examine strata to provide a record of rock formation over millions of years.

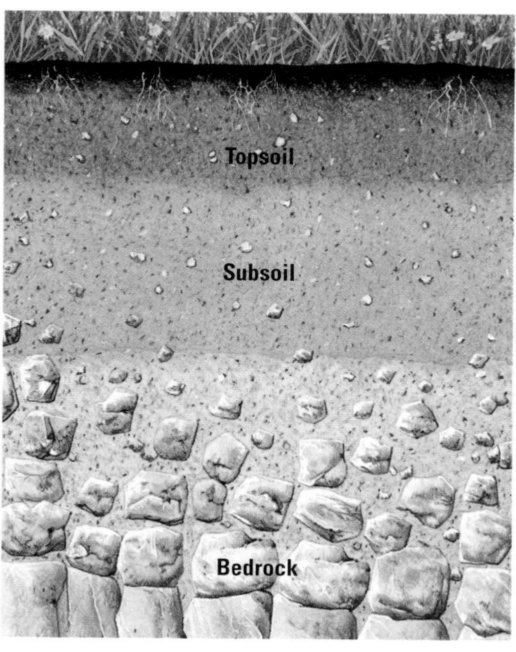

Soil composition

Soil is made up of broken particles of rock mixed with air, water, tiny holes called pores, and humus, which is old plant matter. There are different soil types. Sandy soil is loose and dry. It does not usually hold water as well as thick and sticky clay soils.

Weathering and erosion

Weathering is the gradual altering or breaking up of rocks at or very close to Earth's surface. Erosion happens when rocks and other material are worn or washed away.

FREEZE THAWING
Freeze-thaw action is an example of weathering that can shatter or break up pieces of rock.

1. Rain seeps into cracks in the rock. As the temperature drops, the water freezes.

2. Water expands when it becomes ice, so the frozen water widens the cracks in the rock.

3. Repeated freezing and thawing lead to the cracks breaking apart the rock.

Weathering can happen in different ways. Constant heating and cooling cause rocks to split, while chemicals in rain and the atmosphere create a chemical reaction, weakening or dissolving rocks.

Coastal erosion

Ocean waves can erode coastlines dramatically. The continual action of the waves hurls fragments of rocks at the land. These act as abrasives, wearing away cliffs and shores.

Waterfalls

The power of moving water erodes. Sometimes running water travels over rocks that are resistant to erosion but erodes softer rocks farther ahead. This creates a sharp ledge and a drop, which can form a waterfall.

Softer rock at the base of a cliff erodes easily.

Wind erosion

Wind erosion works most powerfully in dry regions with little water and few plants to bind soil and particles together. When carried by the wind, the particles erode rock formations.

Creating dunes

Sand dunes form along coasts and in dry desert regions. Wind blowing mostly from one direction creates a crescent-shaped sand dune with a shallow sloping side closest to the wind and a steeper slope on the far side.

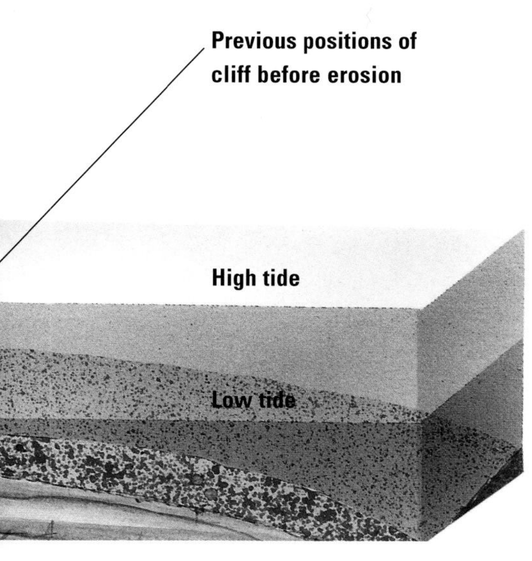

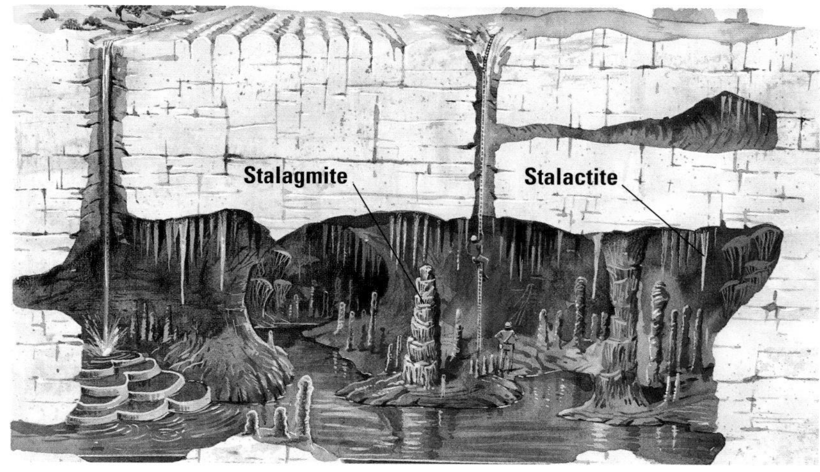

Caves and caverns

When rain combines with carbon dioxide in the air or with decaying plant matter in the soil, it forms carbonic acid. This flows through cracks and gaps in the ground and dissolves limestone rock, creating caves full of dramatic features such as stalagmites and stalactites.

SCIENTIFIC INPUT

ACID RAIN

When polluting gases in the atmosphere from motor vehicles and industry combine with rainwater or snow, this causes acid rain. Acid raid is very harmful. The chemicals in acid rain destroy lakes and forests and damage statues and buildings made of rocks such as sandstone and limestone.

Glaciers and ice

Ice is water that has frozen to become a solid. Ice covers more than ten percent of Earth's surface and contains around three fourths of the total amount of fresh water on the planet.

Ice is found as giant ice sheets around Earth's North and South poles. It is also found in the form of glaciers—giant rivers of ice that have shaped landscapes.

Movement and power

Large glaciers move slowly (less than 3 ft./1m per day) but with enormous force. They scour and wear away the landscape and pluck giant boulders off the land. Glaciers carry rocky debris called moraine with them.

Glaciation

Glaciers often start in mountain valleys where heavy snowfall does not melt. The snow is pressed together, forming solid ice that begins to creep down the mountainside. A glacier advances downhill when more snow builds up at its top than melts away at its front.

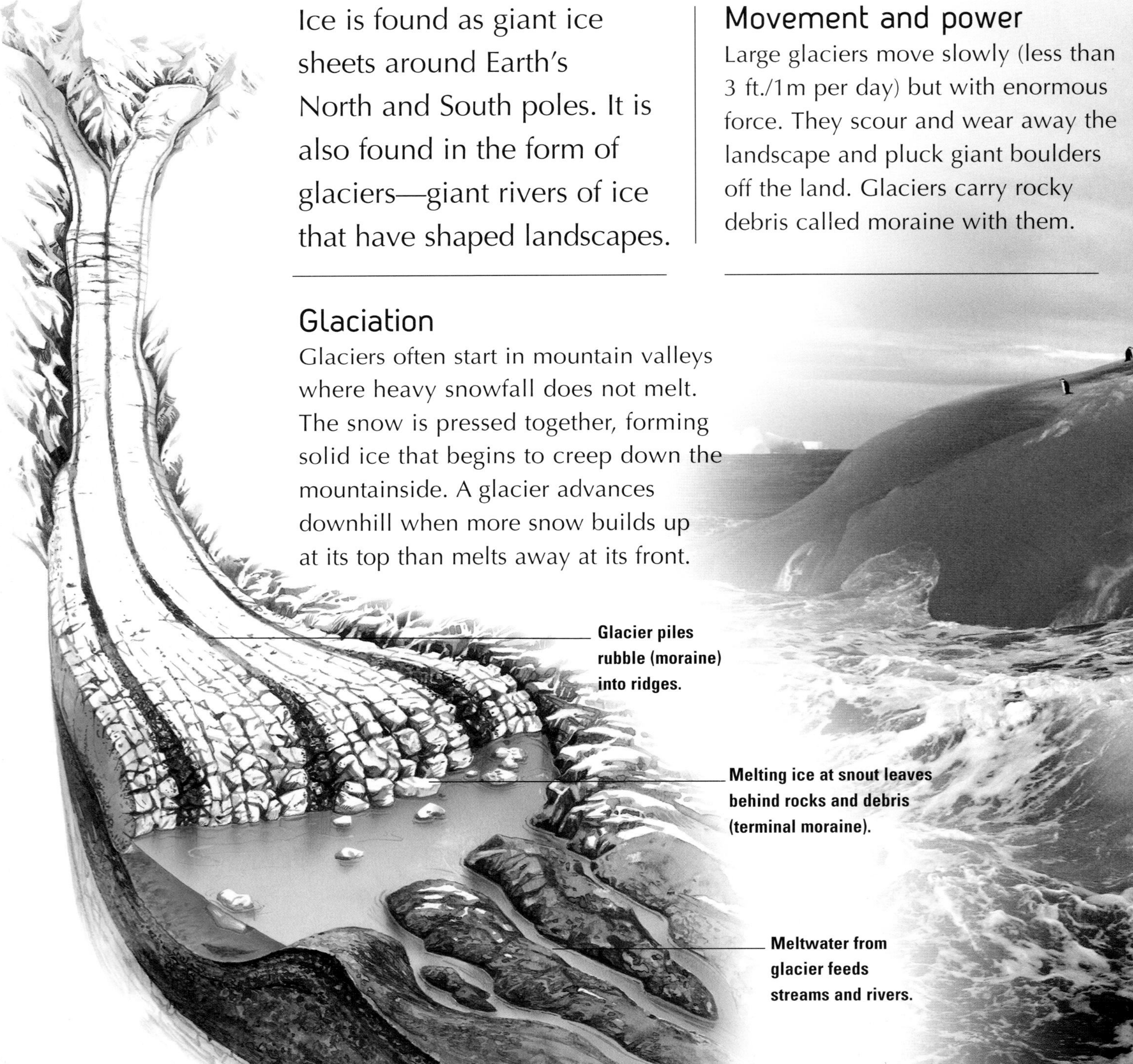

Glacier piles rubble (moraine) into ridges.
Melting ice at snout leaves behind rocks and debris (terminal moraine).
Meltwater from glacier feeds streams and rivers.

Glacial landscapes

Glaciers change the landscape. Bowl shapes called cirques can form high up, where the glacier begins. Lower down, broad U-shaped valleys are carved out, while the moraine carried by the glacier creates fertile farmland.

Ice sheets

Ice sheets are enormous ice masses of more than 31,000 sq. mi. (50,000km^2) in area. The emormous ice sheet that covers Antarctica is almost 9 million sq. mi. (14 million km^2).

Ice caves

An ice cave is any hollowed-out rock structure that has ice inside all year long. Large chambers in the ice of a glacier are called glacier caves. They are sometimes used by scientists to study the inside of a glacier.

Icebergs

An iceberg is a part of an ice sheet or a coastal glacier that breaks off in a process called calving. Ice is less dense than liquid water, so icebergs float in the ocean. Only around one eighth of an iceberg is visible on the water.

RIVERS AND LAKES

RIVERS ARE LARGE BODIES OF RUNNING WATER. THEY MAKE UP ONLY A TINY PORTION OF THE WATER ON EARTH BUT ARE INCREDIBLY IMPORTANT. RIVERS CARRY WATER TO DIFFERENT AREAS, SHAPING THE LAND THROUGH WHICH THEY RUN.

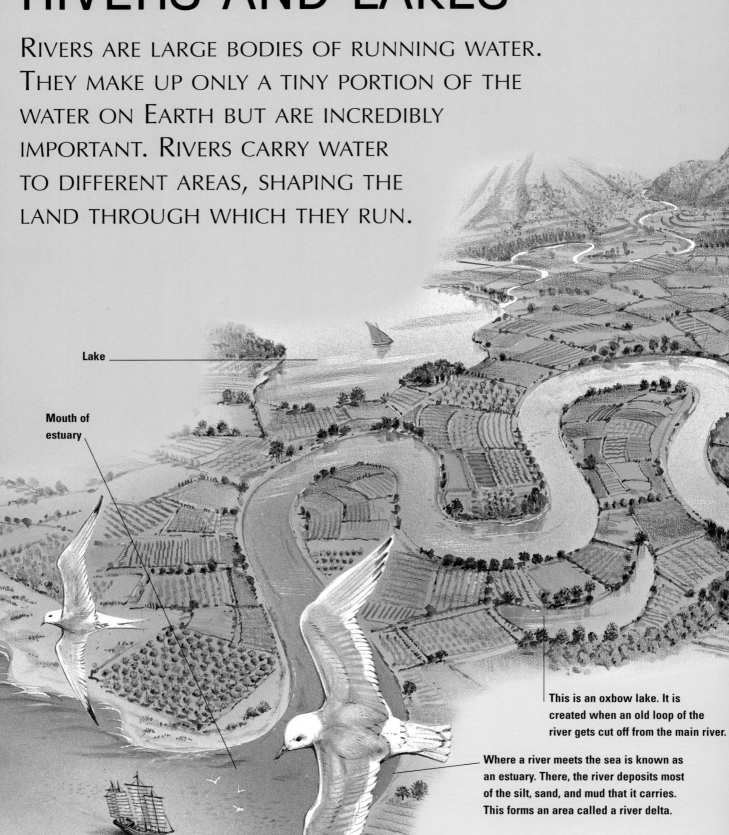

Lake

Mouth of estuary

This is an oxbow lake. It is created when an old loop of the river gets cut off from the main river.

Where a river meets the sea is known as an estuary. There, the river deposits most of the silt, sand, and mud that it carries. This forms an area called a river delta.

A RIVER'S SOURCE

Many rivers begin life high up in hills and mountains. Small streams are fed by water from underground springs, rain, or melting snow and ice. As they travel down slopes, they join to form a river. Smaller rivers, or tributaries, may also flow into the river.

This river begins life as small streams fed by melting snow and ice high up on the mountain.
In its young stage, the river water runs fast and cuts a V-shaped valley into the rock.
Waterfall
Tributary
In its mature stage, the water moves slowly and the river winds in large bends, called meanders, across the landscape.

EROSION AND LANDSCAPING

As the water in a river moves, it cuts into and wears away the rocks that it runs over. Some of the worn-away material is carried in the water. This process is called erosion. The material carried by a river, from pebbles to tiny sand and grit particles, can act as an abrasive, wearing away more rocks.

LAKES

Enclosed bodies of water are called lakes. They form wherever water collects, usually in holes or depressions in the ground. Lakes are fed by melting snow, rain, and sometimes rivers or streams. They provide homes for many plants and animals.

Seas and oceans

Ninety-seven percent of the water on Earth is found in the planet's seas and oceans. Seas are areas of the oceans that are partially cut off by land.

ATOLL FORMATION

An atoll is an island in the Indian or Pacific ocean that encircles a lake called a lagoon.

1

A volcanic eruption causes the peak to poke above the water to become an island.

2

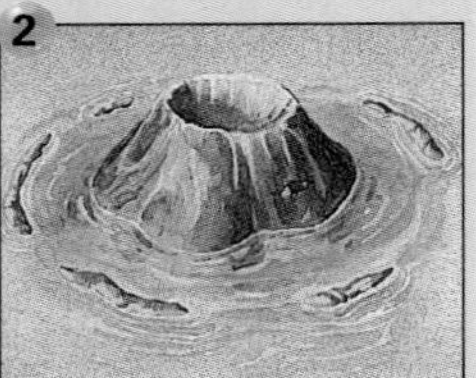

A coral reef develops around the island and then rises as the island gradually sinks.

3

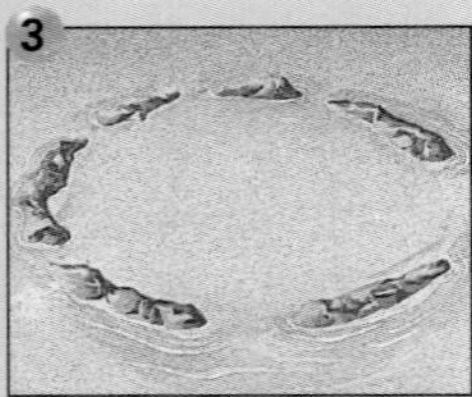

The island disappears completely, leaving only the coral atoll circling the lagoon.

There are four oceans: the Arctic, Indian, Atlantic, and Pacific. The Pacific Ocean is the largest and deepest. Salt water flows between the oceans, moved by waves, currents, and tides.

Ocean floor

Most of the ocean floor is made up of flat abyssal plains. However, in some places, giant mountains rise up thousands of feet. A few reach the surface, where they become islands. Where the continental plates meet underwater, giant trenches form.

Coastlines

The coast is where the land meets the sea or ocean. The action of waves and tides can erode softer rock, leaving a curved bay, while harder rock sticks out into the sea and is called a headland.

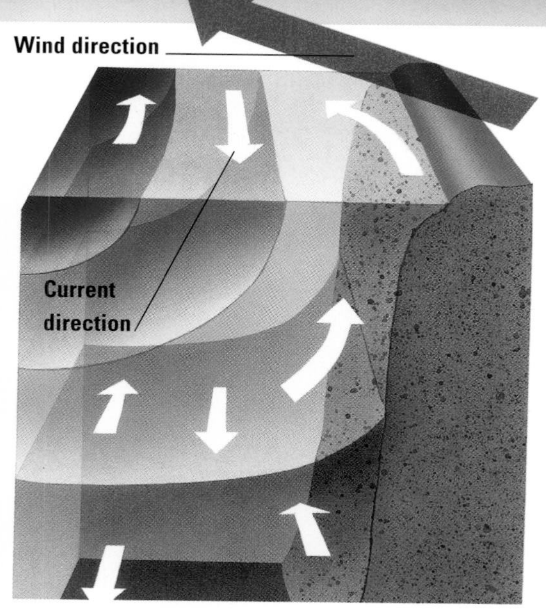

Currents

Wide bands of water called currents flow around the planet's oceans. They vary in temperature, travel thousands of miles, and can have a big influence on climate.

The mighty Pacific Ocean

The Pacific Ocean stretches from the Bering Strait in the Arctic Circle to the edge of Antarctica. It is so large that it covers one third of the entire surface of Earth and all the land of the world could fit inside it.

Tides

Tides are the regular rise and fall of the ocean's water. They are seen when water rises up a beach at high tide and retreats at low tide. Tides are caused by the Moon's gravity pulling on Earth (*see p. 39*).

Waves

Winds traveling across the ocean's surface create circular movements in the water known as waves. The highest part of a wave is called its peak or crest. Its lowest part is the trough. When they reach shallow water, waves topple forward and break.

Black smokers

Hydrothermal vents are openings in the ocean floor. They are nicknamed black smokers because the very hot waters that rise from them look like smoke. These waters are rich in minerals.

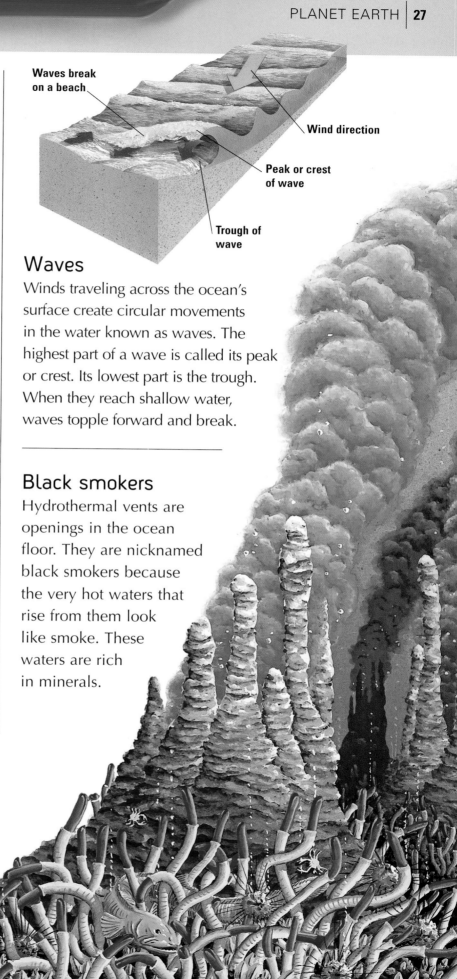

ATMOSPHERE

EARTH'S ATMOSPHERE IS A BODY OF GASES THAT SURROUNDS THE PLANET. IT PROVIDES OXYGEN TO BREATHE, TRAPS SOME OF THE SUN'S WARMING ENERGY, AND PROTECTS US FROM HARMFUL RADIATION AND PARTICLES FROM SPACE.

Jet airliners cruise in the lower stratosphere, just above the majority of the weather.

Small fragments of material in space burn up in the mesosphere, creating meteor showers when viewed from Earth's surface.

Clouds mostly form in the troposphere, where most of the world's weather is generated.

Air currents circulate through the troposphere.

THE COMPOSITION OF AIR

Air in the atmosphere is a mixture of different gases. These include nitrogen (78%), oxygen (21%), and argon (1%). Air also includes some carbon dioxide and water vapor, which vary in amount.

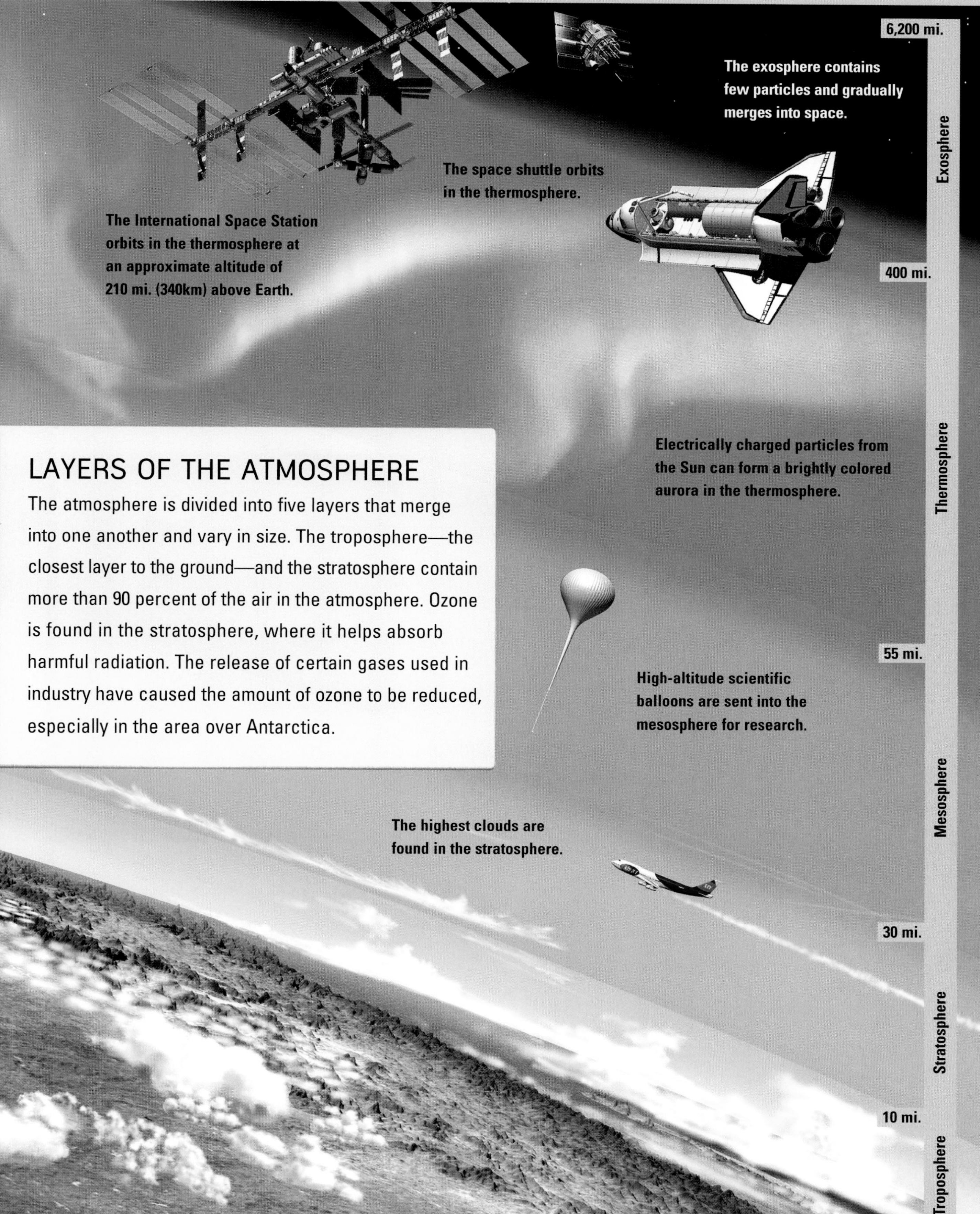

6,200 mi.
The exosphere contains few particles and gradually merges into space.
Exosphere
The space shuttle orbits in the thermosphere.
The International Space Station orbits in the thermosphere at an approximate altitude of 210 mi. (340km) above Earth.
400 mi.
Electrically charged particles from the Sun can form a brightly colored aurora in the thermosphere.
Thermosphere
55 mi.
High-altitude scientific balloons are sent into the mesosphere for research.
Mesosphere
The highest clouds are found in the stratosphere.
30 mi.
Stratosphere
10 mi.
Troposphere

LAYERS OF THE ATMOSPHERE

The atmosphere is divided into five layers that merge into one another and vary in size. The troposphere—the closest layer to the ground—and the stratosphere contain more than 90 percent of the air in the atmosphere. Ozone is found in the stratosphere, where it helps absorb harmful radiation. The release of certain gases used in industry have caused the amount of ozone to be reduced, especially in the area over Antarctica.

Earth's resources

Earth provides the human race with an incredible amount of different natural resources. These range from energy supplies to metals and raw materials.

MAKING ALUMINUM

Aluminum is used to make many things, from soda cans to aircraft parts.

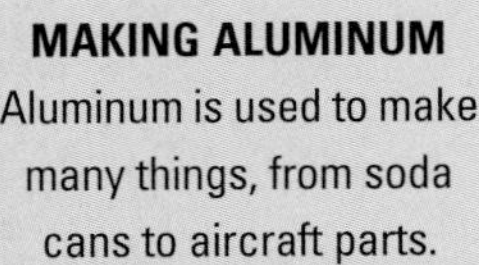

1 A rocky ore, bauxite, is mined from the ground.

2 Bauxite is processed to extract aluminum.

3 The aluminum is made into cans for food.

Many resources, including fossil fuels, are nonrenewable. This means that they cannot be replaced as quickly as the human population is currently using them.

Fossil fuels

Over thousands of years, ancient plant and animal matter has been compressed under layers of rock. It has formed three vital fossil fuels: coal, oil, and natural gas. These are all burned to create energy in order to generate electricity, provide heat, and power motor vehicles. In addition, oil in particular is used to make plastics and many other products.

Deforestation

Forests provide many valuable resources, from wood for building to paper and wood chips that are made into processed wood panels. Destroying forests without replanting them is called deforestation. Over the past 40 years, almost one half of the world's forests have disappeared, either cut down for their wood or cleared for new farmland or settlements.

Geothermal energy

The heat beneath Earth's surface is harnessed in certain places. Hot springs on the surface are bathed in (above) or used to pipe hot water into homes. Geothermal energy plants tap into reservoirs of hot water underground, using the hot water and steam to power turbines that in turn generate electricity.

Renewable energies

Some energy sources on Earth are renewable. This means that they cannot be used up. These sources include the energy in ocean waves and tides and the solar energy from the Sun, which can be converted into electricity by photovoltaic, or solar, cells. The power of the wind can also be harnessed to create electricity by wind turbines grouped together to create a wind farm (left).

Processing metals

Metals such as gold, iron, copper, and zinc exist in Earth's crust and can be mined and extracted. Some are heated until they melt. They are then poured into molds to make perfect metal parts.

Steel is made by mixing three parts melted iron to one part scrap steel.

Raw materials

Rocks and minerals provide raw materials for construction—from bricks made from clay that is used to build huts and houses to concrete made from sand, gravel, cement, and water. More than 100,000 tons of concrete were used in the construction of Sydney Opera House in Australia.

Earth facts

Earth has a diameter of around 7,883 mi. (12,714km) from North Pole to South Pole and a circumference around the equator of approximately 24,847 mi. (40,075km). It has a land area of 58 million sq. mi. (148 million km^2) and a water area of 141 million sq. mi. (362 million km^2).

HIGHEST MOUNTAINS

Mount Everest, Asia 29,071 ft. (8,863m)
Aconcagua, South America 22,866 ft. (6,959m)
Mount McKinley, North America 20,316 ft. (6,194m)
Mount Kilimanjaro, Africa 19,559 ft. (5,963m)
Mount Elbrus, Europe 18,476 ft. (5,633m)
Vinson Massif, Antarctica 16,062 ft. (4,897m)

LARGEST ISLANDS

Greenland 831,090 sq. mi. (2,131,000km^2)
New Guinea 312,000 sq. mi. (800,000km^2)
Borneo, Indonesia 296,400 sq. mi. (726,000km^2)
Madagascar, Africa 225,420 sq. mi. (578,000km^2)
Baffin Island, Canada 197,000 sq. mi. (507,000km^2)
Sumatra, Indonesia 165,750 sq. mi. (425,000km^2)
Honshu, Japan 88,530 sq. mi. (227,000km^2)

LONGEST RIVERS

Nile, Africa 4,135 mi. (6,670km)
Amazon, South America 3,998 mi. (6,448km)
Chang Jiang (Yangtze), Asia 3,906 mi. (6,300km)
Mississippi–Missouri, North America 3,732 mi. (6,020km)
Yenisey–Angara, Asia 3,435 mi. (5,540km)
Huang (Yellow), Asia 3,388 mi. (5,464km)
Ob-Irtysh, Asia 3,354 mi. (5,409km)
Paraná-Rio de la Plata, South America 3,026 mi. (4,880km)
Congo, Africa 2,914 mi. (4,700km)
Lena, Asia 2,728 mi. (4,400km)

LARGEST LAKES

Caspian Sea, Asia and Europe 145,002 sq. mi. (371,800km^2)
Superior, North America 32,117 sq. mi. (82,350km^2)
Victoria, Africa 27,105 sq. mi. (69,500km^2)
Huron, North America 23,244 sq. mi. (59,600km^2)

THE WORLD'S OCEANS

Pacific	166,240,000km^2
Atlantic	86,560,000km^2
Indian	73,430,000km^2
Arctic	13,230,000km^2

The Sun sets and rises over Earth.

USEFUL WEBSITES

www.geography4kids.com/index.html Earth's formation, rocks, and atmosphere.
http://quake.wr.usgs.gov/info/ Earthquake information from the U.S. Geological Survey.
www.geolsoc.org.uk/gsl/null/lang/en/page2673.html Fact sheets on geological topics.
http://nsidc.org/glaciers/ Glaciers, their formation, and effects.

Space and the Stars

Looking up at a starlit sky, it is possible to see stars trillions of miles away. The galaxy to which our Sun belongs extends many times farther than this, and it is only one of countless billions that make up the universe. Today, people have the technology to probe these distant galaxies with telescopes and to send robots to explore the solar system.

The solar system

Earth and other planets, in addition to many smaller bodies, orbit the Sun and form our solar system. There are eight planets, which vary greatly in size.

The solar system contains moons, comets, asteroids, dwarf planets, and meteoroids, as well as interplanetary gas and dust. Most of these objects move within a flat, round area of space that has a star, the Sun, at its center.

The solar system includes planets and comets that orbit around the Sun.

The birth of the Sun

The solar system formed from a cloud in space 4.6 billion years ago. Gravity pulled part of the cloud together until it was so crushed and hot that nuclear reactions began. This part of the cloud began to glow, and it became the Sun at the center of our solar system.

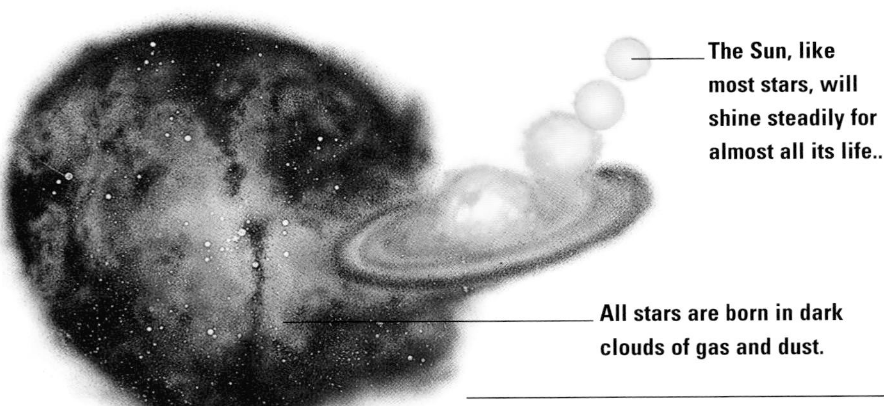

The Sun, like most stars, will shine steadily for almost all its life..

All stars are born in dark clouds of gas and dust.

Size of the solar system

The planets occupy an area around 5.6 billion mi. (9 billion km) across, but there are many smaller objects beyond. The width of the system is probably 19 trillion mi. (30 trillion km).

Formation of the planets

In other parts of the cloud, gravity gathered together dust and gases into spinning clumps. The clumps grew into giant rock chunks called planetesimals. These joined to form dozens of planets.

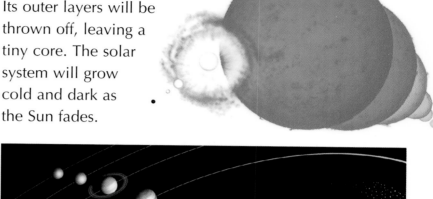

The Great Bombardment

For around 200 million years, enormous chunks of rock smashed continuously into the newly formed planets, destroying many of them. When the bombardment ended, around 3.8 billion years ago, only eight planets remained. Many huge craters from this assault can still be seen on the surface of the Moon, as well as on Mercury and Mars.

The end of the solar system

In around five billion years, the Sun will run out of fuel. It will turn red (right) and swell enormously. Its outer layers will be thrown off, leaving a tiny core. The solar system will grow cold and dark as the Sun fades.

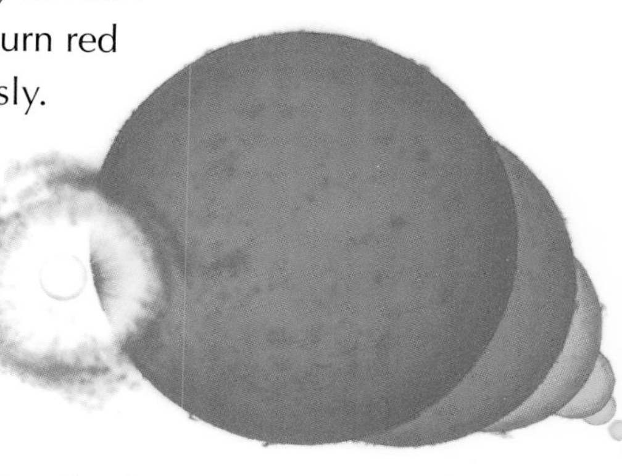

SCIENTIFIC INPUT

GRAVITY AND THE BALANCE OF THE SOLAR SYSTEM

All objects pull on one another with the force of gravity, but this pull can be felt only if one of the objects is massive. The Sun is an incredibly massive object, and its gravity holds the entire solar system together. If the planets did not orbit the Sun, it would pull them into it. The closer they are to the Sun, the faster they have to orbit in order to avoid this.

Other solar systems

Many stars have their own families of worlds orbiting around them. With so many billions of stars in the universe, it is almost certain that many of these worlds are similar to our own.

THE SUN

THE SUN IS OUR LOCAL STAR, AND EARTH AND OTHER MEMBERS OF THE SOLAR SYSTEM ALL MOVE AROUND IT. WITHOUT THE SUN'S LIGHT AND HEAT, THERE WOULD BE NO LIFE ON EARTH.

THE LIFE OF OUR SUN

More than one million objects the size of Earth would fit inside the Sun, which is 4.6 billion years old. It will last for around another five billion years. Its surface temperature is around 9,000°F (5,000°C), and the temperature of its outer atmosphere, the corona, is several million degrees Fahrenheit.

Storms on the Sun sometimes throw out huge masses of glowing gas called prominences high into space.

Sometimes the Moon passes directly between the Sun and Earth. This is called a solar eclipse. During eclipses, the Sun's corona can be seen. It is a thin outer atmosphere that is millions of degrees hotter than the photosphere.

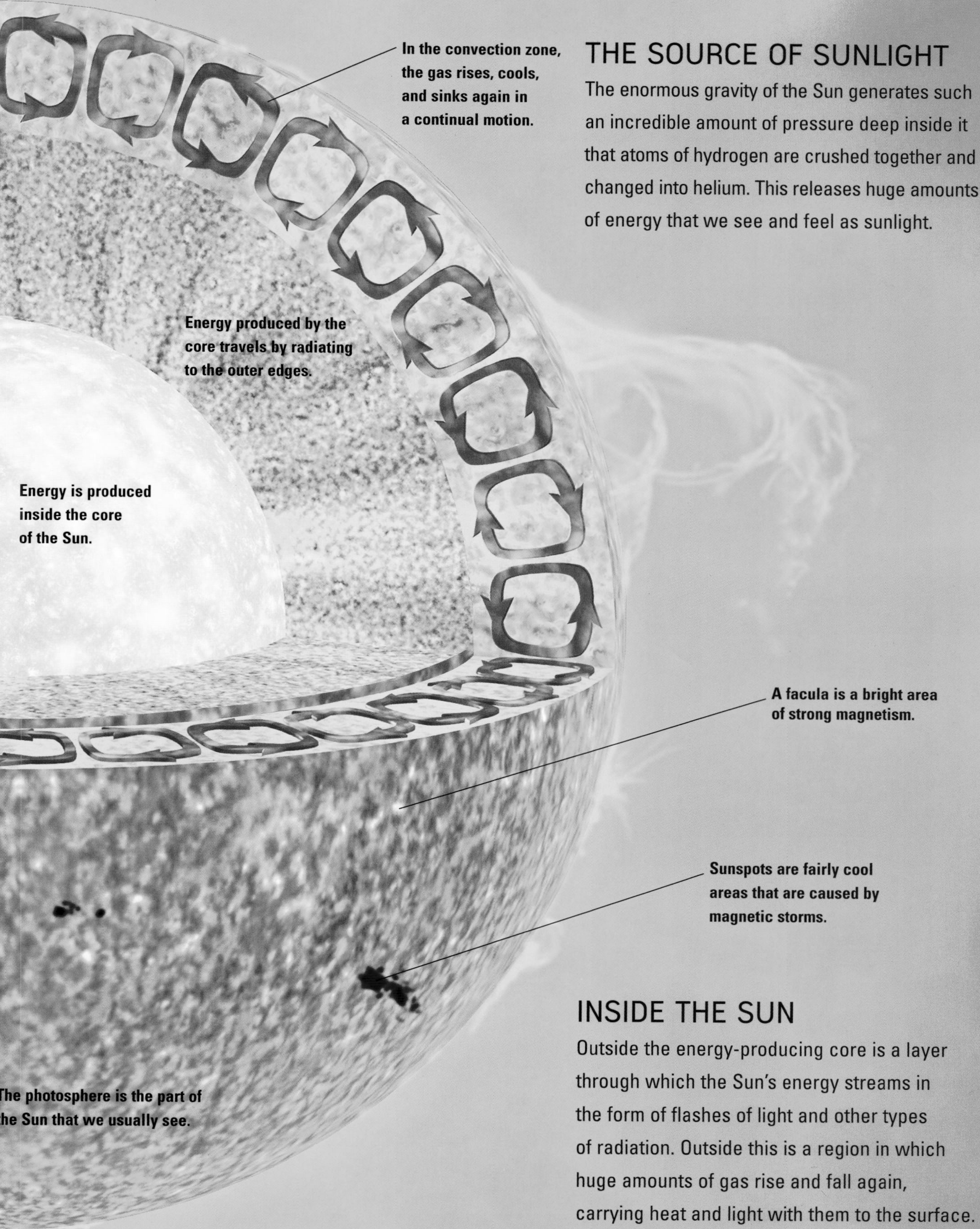

In the convection zone, the gas rises, cools, and sinks again in a continual motion.
Energy produced by the core travels by radiating to the outer edges.
Energy is produced inside the core of the Sun.
A facula is a bright area of strong magnetism.
Sunspots are fairly cool areas that are caused by magnetic storms.
The photosphere is the part of the Sun that we usually see.

THE SOURCE OF SUNLIGHT

The enormous gravity of the Sun generates such an incredible amount of pressure deep inside it that atoms of hydrogen are crushed together and changed into helium. This releases huge amounts of energy that we see and feel as sunlight.

INSIDE THE SUN

Outside the energy-producing core is a layer through which the Sun's energy streams in the form of flashes of light and other types of radiation. Outside this is a region in which huge amounts of gas rise and fall again, carrying heat and light with them to the surface.

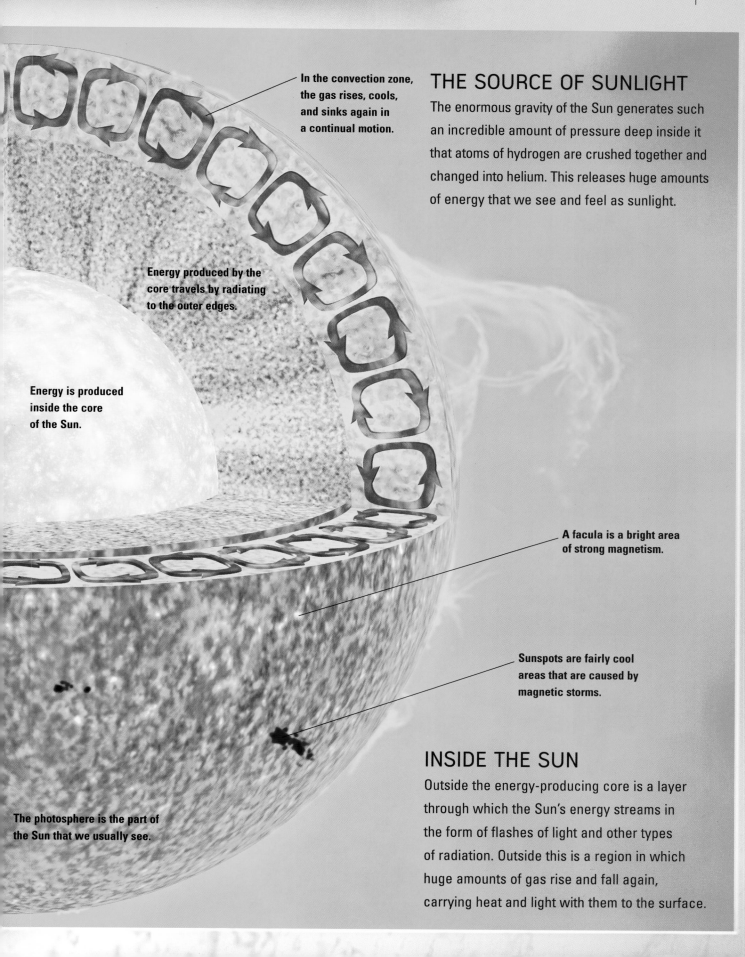

The Moon

The Moon is around 238,328 mi. (384,400km) away. It is by fa the closest world to Earth, the only one whose surface is clearl visible in the night sky, and the only one that humans have visite

Although it is close to us, the Moon is still a mysterious place. It takes the same amount of time to spin around as it takes to orbit Earth. This means that we always see the same area of the Moon and that some of it is always hidden.

The birth of the Moon

The Moon was born around 4.5 billion years ago. A body the size of Mars smashed into Earth, and some of the fragments formed the Moon.

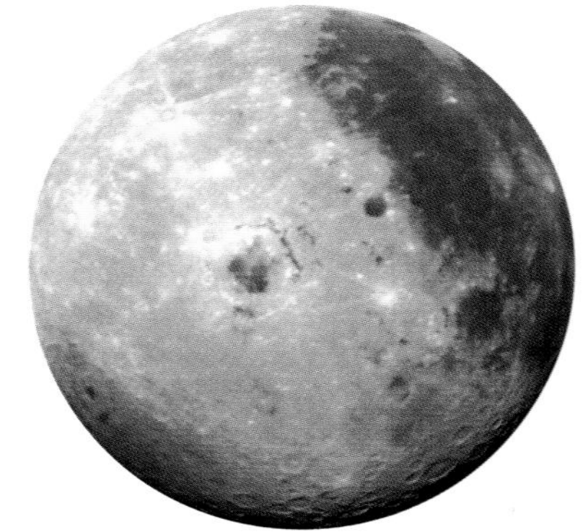

The far side of the Moon

Unlike the side we see, the far side of the Moon has no large "seas," which are actually plains of ancient lava. However, there are more craters on the far side.

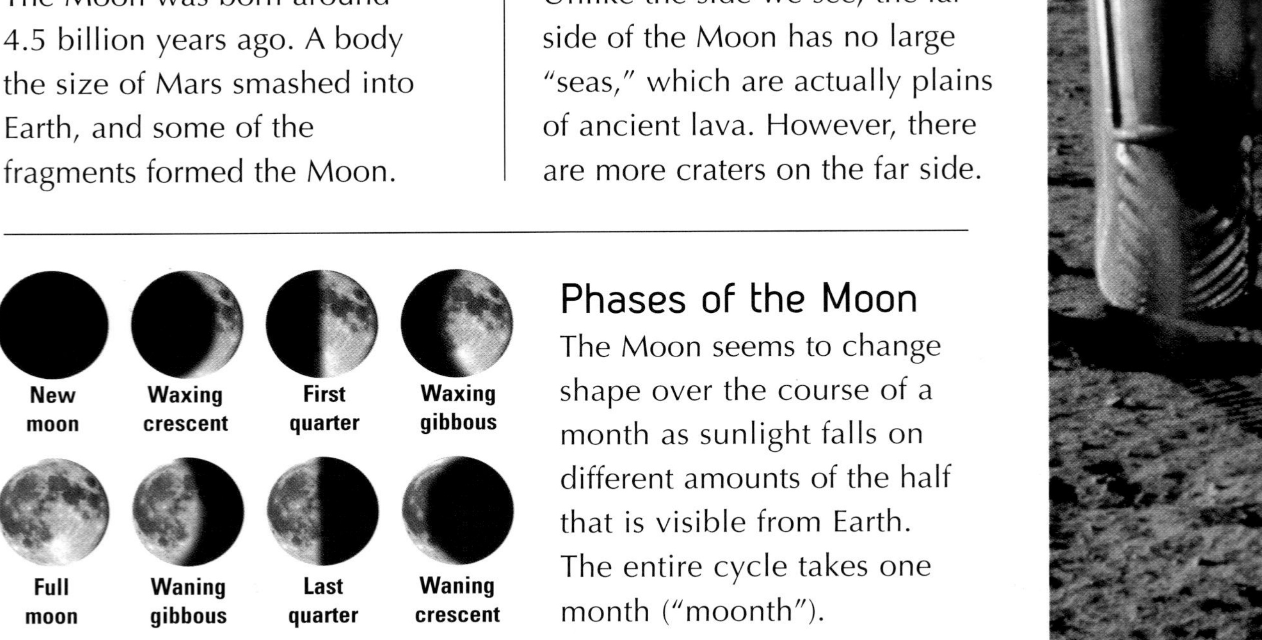

Phases of the Moon

The Moon seems to change shape over the course of a month as sunlight falls on different amounts of the half that is visible from Earth. The entire cycle takes one month ("moonth").

Astronauts on the Moon

Twelve astronauts landed on the Moon between 1969 and 1972. On some missions they took an electric car called a lunar rover, which meant that they were able to explore larger areas than they could on foot.

The Moon and the tides

As Earth turns under the Moon, the Moon pulls on Earth and its oceans. As a result, the oceans rise and fall on the world's coasts, and these motions are called tides. The Sun has a similar, but lesser, effect.

The rocky planets

Planet Earth is one of the four rocky planets. All of these have metal centers covered by thick layers of rock.

THE ROCKY PLANETS
The relative sizes of the rocky planets are shown below.

Mercury

Venus

Earth

Mars

The rocky, or "inner," planets all orbit close to the Sun. Mercury is almost airless, while Venus has a thick atmosphere, Earth has oceans, and Mars has a rust-colored surface.

Venus

Venus has a thick atmosphere that traps the Sun's heat, making it the hottest planet. Acid rain falls constantly from the clouds. These clouds hide the surface from view. Spacecraft have made radar maps of the landscape, like this one below.

Mercury

The sunlit side of Mercury is hot enough to melt metal, but the lack of a protective thick atmosphere means that the planet loses heat quickly at night. This means that the dark side is colder than anywhere on Earth.

Venusian weather

On Venus, the thick air is constantly moving. These two spinning hurricane-like shapes (above) have been seen at the north and south poles of the planet.

Mars

Martian soil contains iron, which rusts to give the reddish color that is seen from Earth. Like Earth, the planet has polar icecaps and many dormant volcanoes. Dry riverbeds show that water once flowed there.

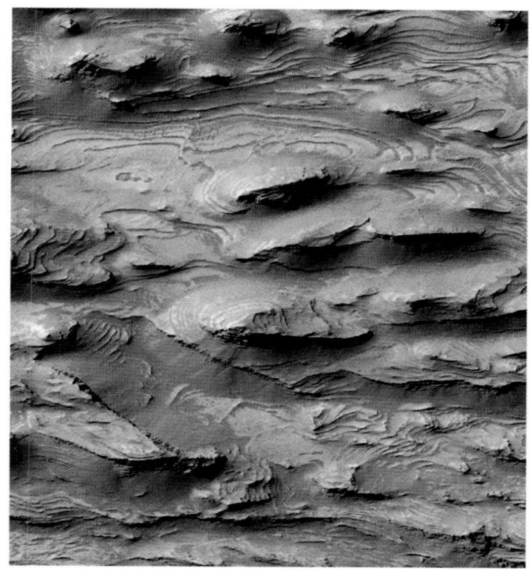

Martian rock layers

This satellite image of part of the surface of Mars shows a pattern of rock layers. Each layer is around 30 ft. (10m) thick, and there are more than 100 layers. These layers might be the bottoms of ancient seas that dried up billions of years ago.

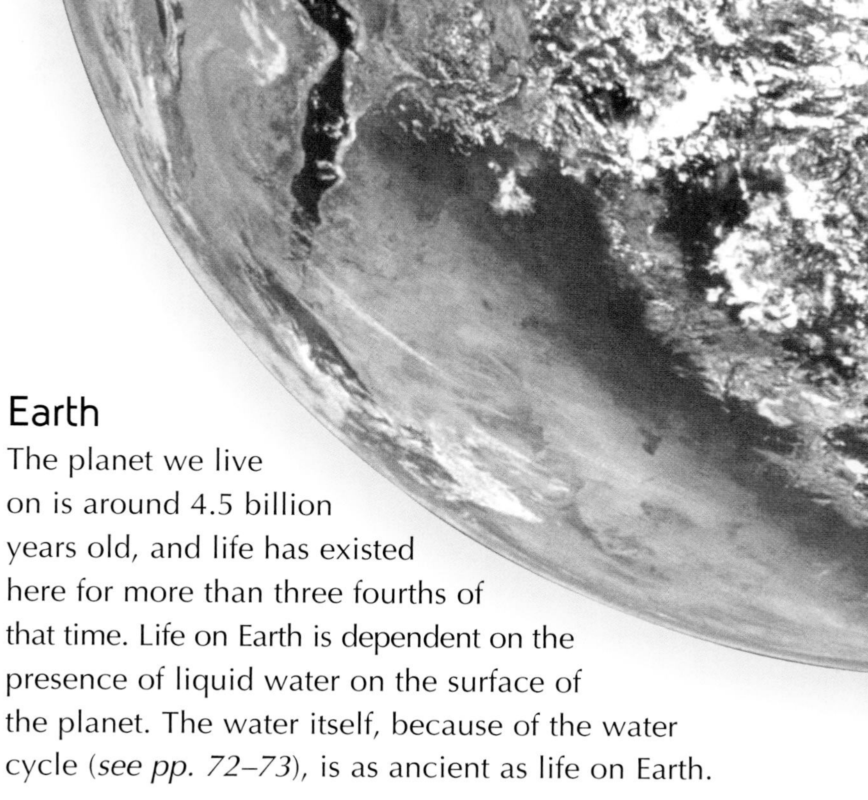

Earth

The planet we live on is around 4.5 billion years old, and life has existed here for more than three fourths of that time. Life on Earth is dependent on the presence of liquid water on the surface of the planet. The water itself, because of the water cycle (*see pp. 72–73*), is as ancient as life on Earth.

CULTURAL NOTE

PLANETARY GODS

The ancient Greek and Roman civilizations made connections between each one of the planets that they knew about and one of their gods or goddesses. In Roman mythology, for example, Venus (above left) was the goddess of love, while Mars (above right) was the god of war. Mercury was the fleet-footed messenger of the gods. Saturn was a god of farming, and Jupiter was the king of all the gods.

The giant planets

More than 360 million mi. (580 million km) from Earth, the giant planets of Jupiter, Saturn, Uranus, and Neptune slowly orbit the Sun.

The giant planets have deep, cold atmospheres, and each one is orbited by a system of rings and many moons. Jupiter and Saturn often shine brightly in the night sky, but Uranus and Neptune are too faint to see.

THE GIANT PLANETS
The relative sizes of the giant planets are shown below.

Neptune

Uranus

Saturn

Jupiter

Neptune

Neptune is the most distant planet. It is also the coldest and windiest planet in the solar system and has the longest year—165 Earth years. Huge white clouds move rapidly across its blue atmosphere.

Saturn's moons

Saturn has dozens of moons. Most are simply lumps of icy rock, but the largest of the moons, Titan, has a thick atmosphere and tarlike lakes.

Saturn

This planet is so light for its size that it would float in water—if there was an ocean large enough to contain it. Like the other giant planets, it has an atmosphere that is rich in hydrogen and a rocky center.

Io

Jupiter

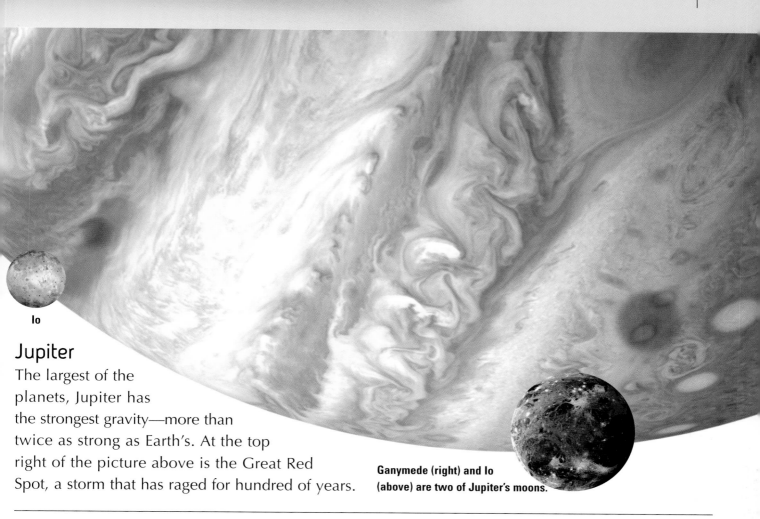

The largest of the planets, Jupiter has the strongest gravity—more than twice as strong as Earth's. At the top right of the picture above is the Great Red Spot, a storm that has raged for hundred of years.

Ganymede (right) and Io (above) are two of Jupiter's moons.

Uranus

Uranus has an atmosphere that contains methane, which gives it a blue-green color. It spins on its side, the result of a collision with another planet millions of years ago. Because of this, night on Uranus can last for more than 40 Earth years.

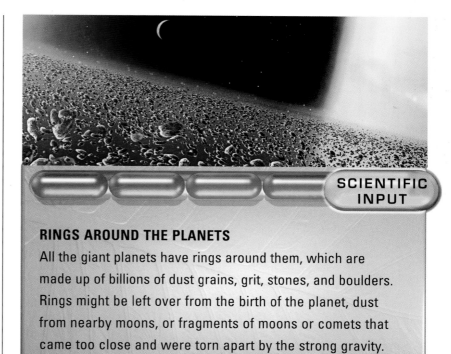

SCIENTIFIC INPUT

RINGS AROUND THE PLANETS

All the giant planets have rings around them, which are made up of billions of dust grains, grit, stones, and boulders. Rings might be left over from the birth of the planet, dust from nearby moons, or fragments of moons or comets that came too close and were torn apart by the strong gravity.

SPACE RUBBLE

IT IS NOT ONLY THE PLANETS THAT ORBIT THE SUN. THERE ARE BILLIONS OF OTHER OBJECTS, TOO—FROM TINY GRAINS OF DUST TO LUMPS OF ROCK THAT ARE MORE THAN 1,240 MI. (2,000KM) ACROSS. MOST OF THIS MATERIAL CANNOT BE SEEN FROM EARTH.

COMET

Comets are lumps of ice and grit that sweep toward the Sun on long orbits. As the sunlight warms them, twin tails of dust and gas form.

ASTEROID BELT

Asteroids are lumps of rock and metal that are left over after the planets formed. Some are 125 mi. (200km) across. Most orbit between Mars and Jupiter.

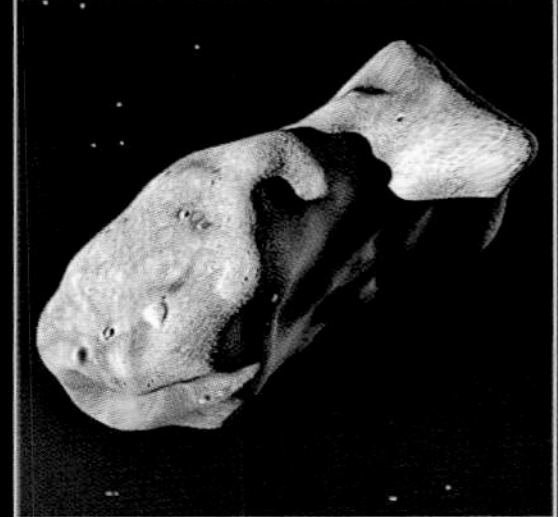

Neptune

Uranus

The Kuiper belt contains lumps of ice and other frozen materials called KBOs (Kuiper belt objects). Many of these objects are more than 60 mi. (100km) across.

The Oort cloud is spherical, or rounded. The asteroid belt, the Kuiper belt, and the orbits of the planets are all flat.

PLUTO AND CHARON

Pluto is a dwarf planet—a small, round world that orbits the Sun. Charon is the largest of its three known moons. The other two moons were first seen in 2005.

COMETARY NUCLEUS

Comets come from the outermost part of the solar system. There, they make up the Oort cloud. The cometary nucleus is the central part at the head of a comet.

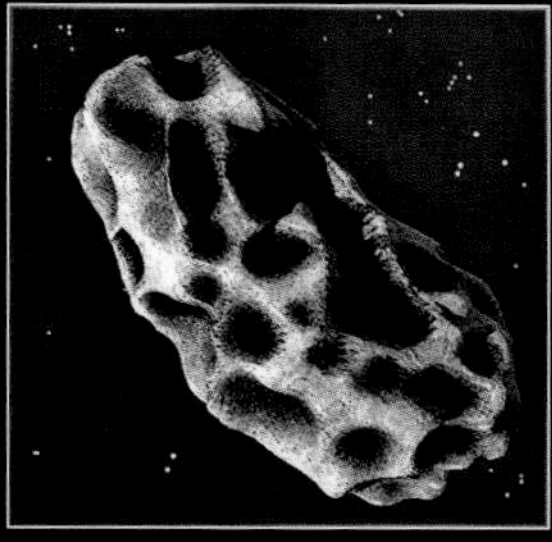

Satellites and space stations

Any object that orbits another object in space is called a satellite. Earth has one natural satellite, the Moon, and thousands of artificial ones.

The first artificial satellite, *Sputnik 1*, was launched from the U.S.S.R. and went into orbit in 1957. Its radio beep was heard all over the world and marked the beginning of the space age.

Types of satellites

The satellite above is called *Telstar* and was launched in 1962. It relayed TV and radio signals from one part of Earth to another. Today, satellites are used for many different activities, including spying, weather monitoring, space research, and navigation.

Space stations

A satellite that is designed to take people onboard is called a space station. The first space station was the Soviet *Salyut 1*, launched in 1961. Another Soviet space station, *Mir* (below), was used by both U.S. and Russian astronauts. American space shuttles could dock with and transfer crew to and from *Mir*.

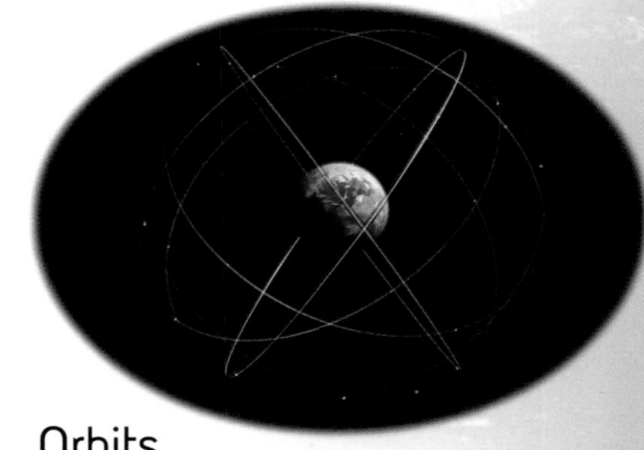

Orbits

A satellite—or any object—with the correct speed and direction will continue to orbit a planet or other large body in space without the need to use engines. Orbits can be either circular or elliptical (oval) in shape.

Astronauts at work on the International Space Station

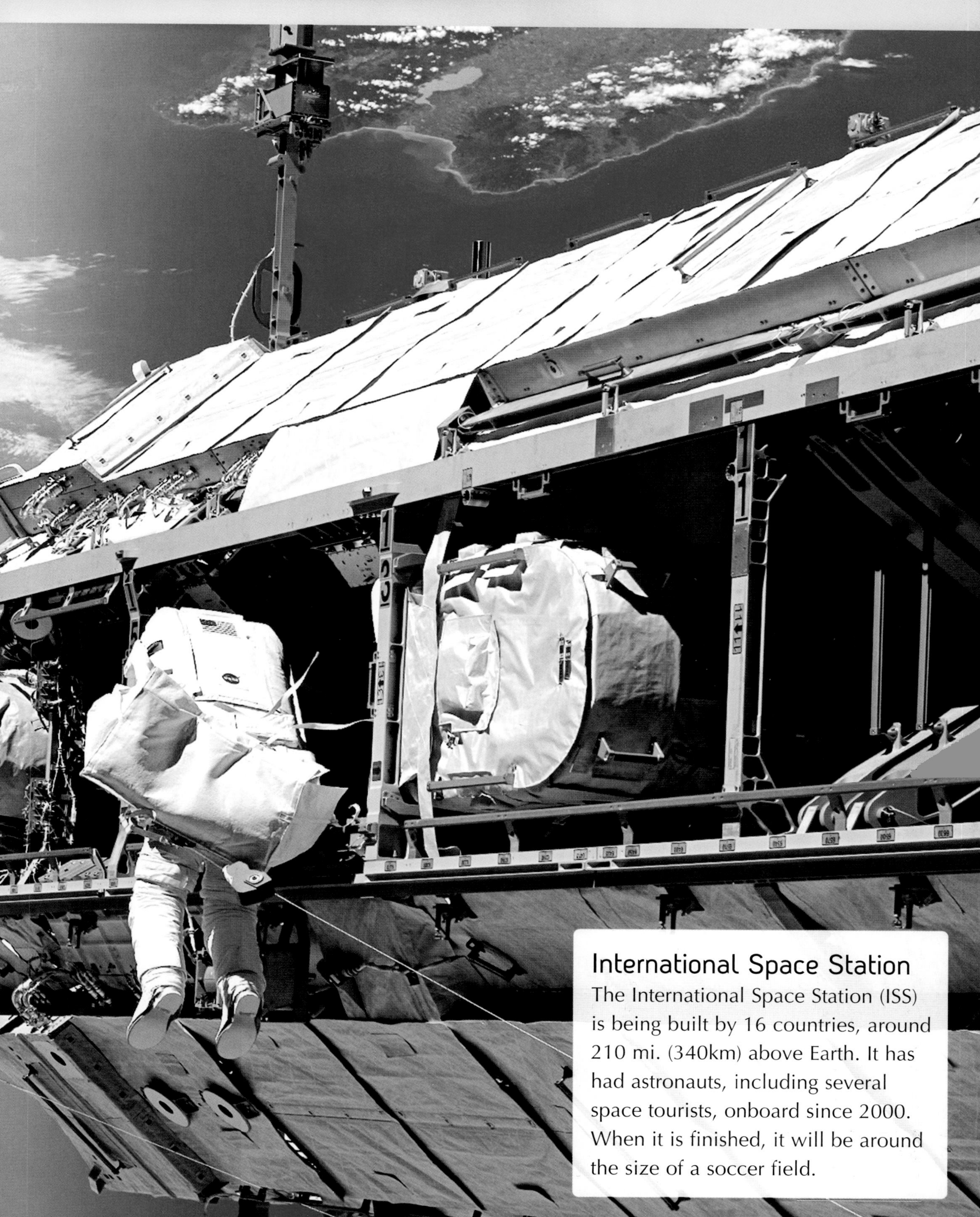

International Space Station

The International Space Station (ISS) is being built by 16 countries, around 210 mi. (340km) above Earth. It has had astronauts, including several space tourists, onboard since 2000. When it is finished, it will be around the size of a soccer field.

Space exploration

Space travel is one of our greatest achievements. It has many practical benefits, but it is driven by our urge to reach and study unknown worlds.

In order to escape Earth's gravity, survive in space, and return home safely, some of the most complex and powerful technology that people can build is required.

Rockets and space flights

To leave Earth, all spacecraft use powerful rockets. Burning gases rush out of a rocket, pushing the spacecraft in the opposite direction. Smaller rockets are used to change course.

HISTORICAL DATA

THE FIRST HUMAN IN SPACE

Yuri Gagarin became the first cosmonaut (the Soviet term for an astronaut) on April 12, 1961. The first person to travel into space, he orbited the Earth once in *Swallow*, his *Vostok-1* spaceship. He returned to Earth after 108 minutes in space.

Space shuttles

A space shuttle is an American spacecraft that takes off by rocket power but lands like a plane. The first shuttle blasted into space in 1981. Unlike other spaceships, space shuttles can be used again and again. They are used to launch and repair satellites and travel to the ISS.

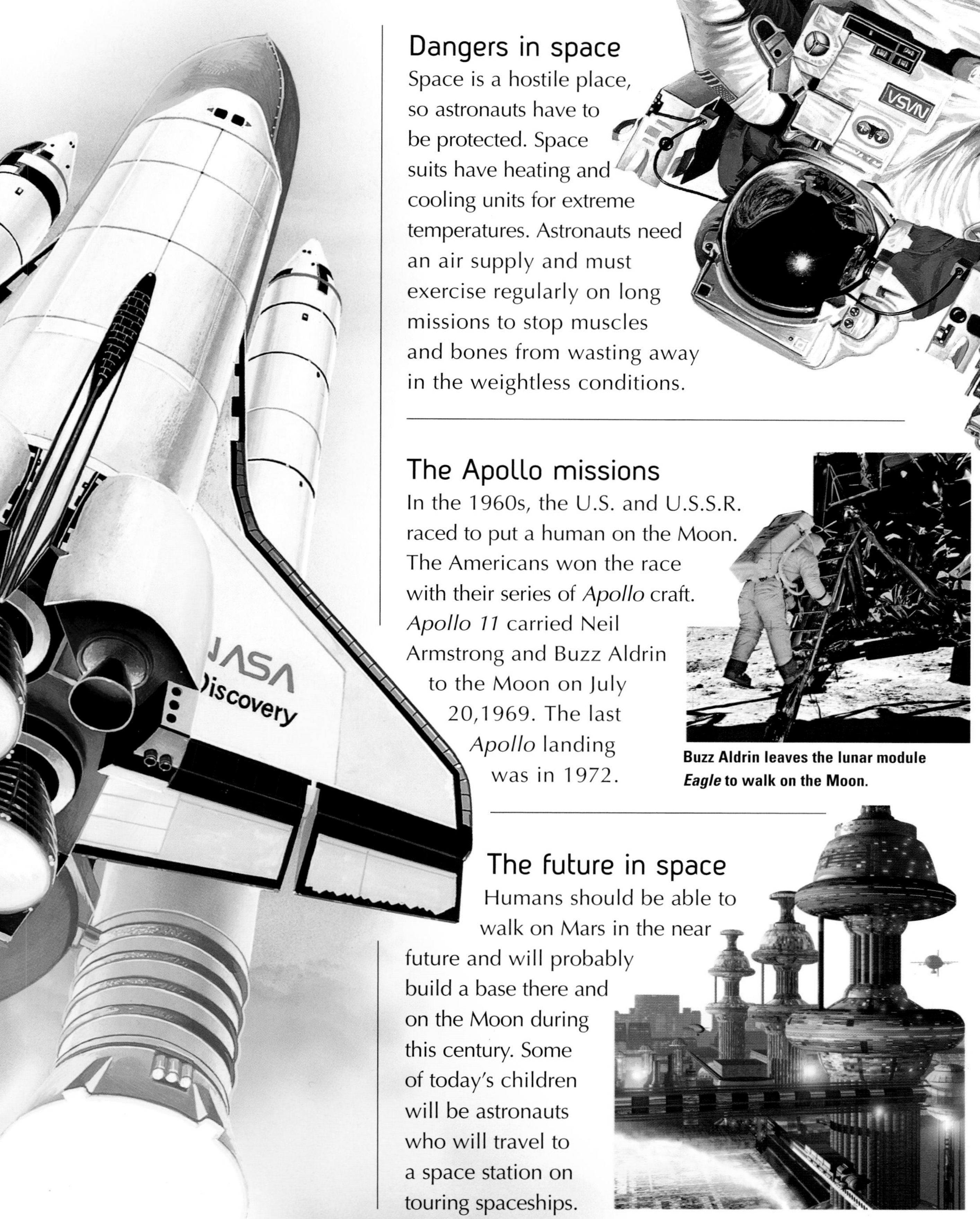

Dangers in space

Space is a hostile place, so astronauts have to be protected. Space suits have heating and cooling units for extreme temperatures. Astronauts need an air supply and must exercise regularly on long missions to stop muscles and bones from wasting away in the weightless conditions.

The Apollo missions

In the 1960s, the U.S. and U.S.S.R. raced to put a human on the Moon. The Americans won the race with their series of *Apollo* craft. *Apollo 11* carried Neil Armstrong and Buzz Aldrin to the Moon on July 20,1969. The last *Apollo* landing was in 1972.

Buzz Aldrin leaves the lunar module *Eagle* to walk on the Moon.

The future in space

Humans should be able to walk on Mars in the near future and will probably build a base there and on the Moon during this century. Some of today's children will be astronauts who will travel to a space station on touring spaceships.

Space robots

Humans have traveled only as far as the Moon. However, robots have explored every planet and voyaged even deeper into space.

Some robots are probes that fly past or crash onto other worlds, but more advanced robots can land safely and sometimes even move around.

***Mariner 10* travels toward Venus on its way to Mercury.**

Robot Moon probes

The Moon was the first destination for robot probes, and it was in 1959 that an orbiting robot probe sent back the first images of the far side of the Moon.

Probes to Mercury and Venus

Mercury was visited by *Mariner 10* in 1974–1975 and is currently being studied by the Messenger probe. The hostile atmosphere of Venus has destroyed all the probes that have landed there, but a few have managed to send signals back to Earth first.

Robots on Mars

Many robots have been sent to Mars, mostly to search for signs of life there. Advanced rovers like this *Exomars* have built-in intelligence that allows them to make simple decisions for themselves.

Probing asteroids and comets

Ten asteroids and four comets have been visited by probes. In 2004, a robot probe called *Stardust* collected samples from comet Wild 2 and returned them to Earth in 2006.

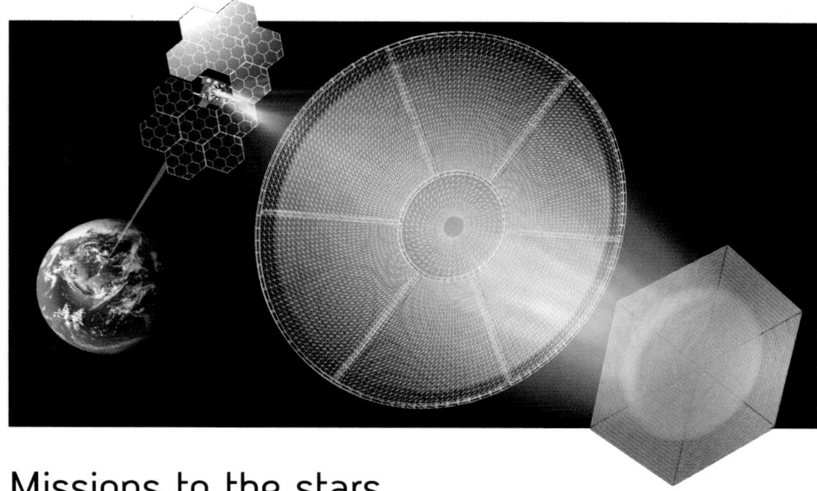

Missions to the stars

There are plans to use a powerful microwave beam to push a probe that weighs only a few ounces. This would accelerate it to an incredible speed and allow it to reach the closest star in outer space in only a few decades.

Fly-by missions

These missions send space probes past planets to take photos and measurements. In the 1970s and 1980s, the *Pioneer* and *Voyager* probes flew past the giant planets. All of them are now beyond the farthest planet and are still moving. Some fly-by probes use the gravity of the planets to increase their speed.

SCIENTIFIC INPUT

SPEED OF A SPACE PROBE

The *Pioneer* and *Voyager* probes are traveling at more than 7 mi. (12km) per second, but even so they will not approach any stars for more than 40,000 years. Scientists are puzzled because the probes are not moving as predicted. This might be because of an unknown force. This artist's picture shows *Voyager 2* approaching the planet Uranus on January 24, 1986.

Stars and stardust

Most of the points of light in the night sky are stars, which are vast balls of glowing gas. Many of them are bigger and brighter than the Sun.

Usually, the more massive a star is, the shorter its life span. The biggest stars shine for only a few million years.

LIFE CYCLE OF A STAR
Here are the stages in the life of a star that is much more massive than the Sun.

1

A star is born in a huge dark cloud.

2

The star shines for millions of years.

3

When it runs out of fuel, it explodes as a supernova.

4
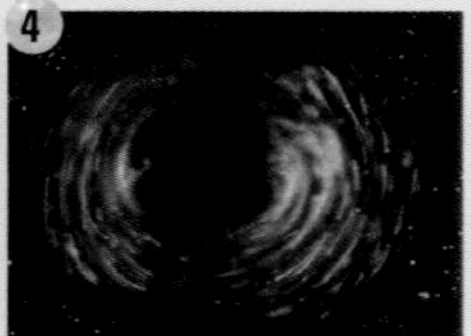
The dead core becomes a black hole.

Red giants and white dwarfs

When stars like the Sun run out of fuel, they swell and redden, turning into red giants. The outer layers of red giants drift, spread, and thin out, leaving behind a hot core called a white dwarf. This is a group of white dwarfs.

Giants and supergiants

When stars approach the end of their lives, they swell into giants (ten to 100 times brighter than the Sun) or supergiants (10,000 to 100,000 times brighter). This is Betelgeuse, a supergiant in the constellation Orion.

Variable stars

Many stars are called variables because they change in brightness or color, either gradually or suddenly. The variable star in the center of this dust cloud gave off a sudden brief flash of light only a few years ago.

Neutron stars and pulsars

A neutron star is a type of dead star that has been crushed by its own gravity. Some spinning neutron stars, called pulsars, send beams of radiation through space. When these beams sweep across Earth, they can be detected as a pulse of radio waves.

Stardust

The space between stars (the interstellar medium, or ISM) is not empty. The cloudy shapes in the image above are vast clouds of cosmic dust, thrown off by aging stars. One percent of the ISM in our galaxy is dust; the rest is gas.

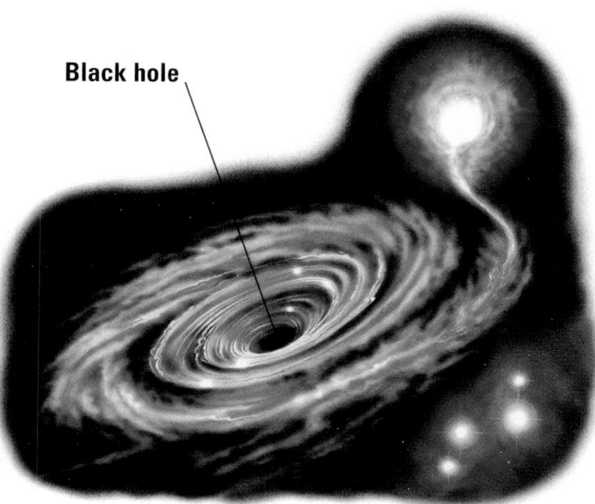

Black holes

The more massive a star is, the more it shrinks when it dies and the stronger its gravity becomes. The most massive stars become black holes, crushed so small that their gravity pulls in everything near them. Even light cannot escape.

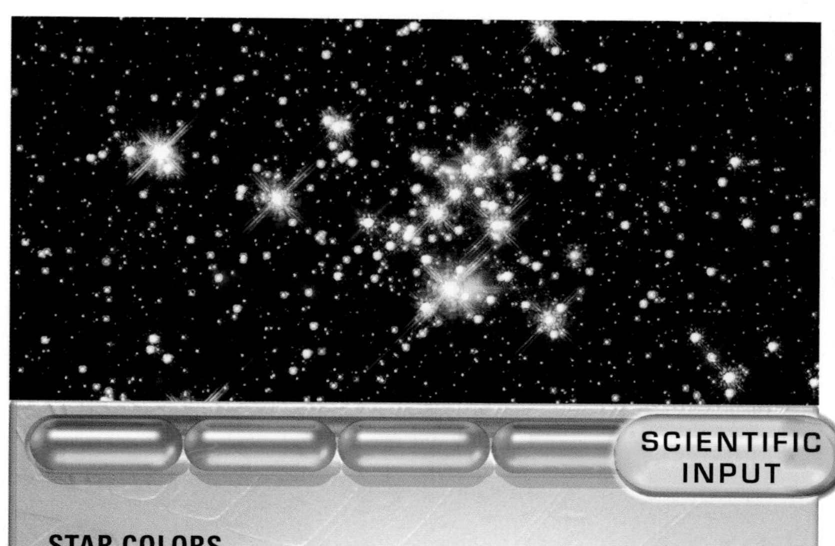

SCIENTIFIC INPUT

STAR COLORS

All stars look white to us because their distance makes them dim. In fact, many stars are colored; the hottest are blue white. Stars that are a little cooler than the Sun are yellow, and even cooler ones are orange or red. Some stars also look red because their light shines through dust clouds.

CONSTELLATIONS

ON A CLEAR, DARK, MOONLESS NIGHT, IT IS POSSIBLE TO SEE AROUND 2,000 STARS IN THE SKY. PEOPLE HAVE IDENTIFIED THE PATTERNS AND SHAPES THAT THEY MAKE AND CALL THEM CONSTELLATIONS.

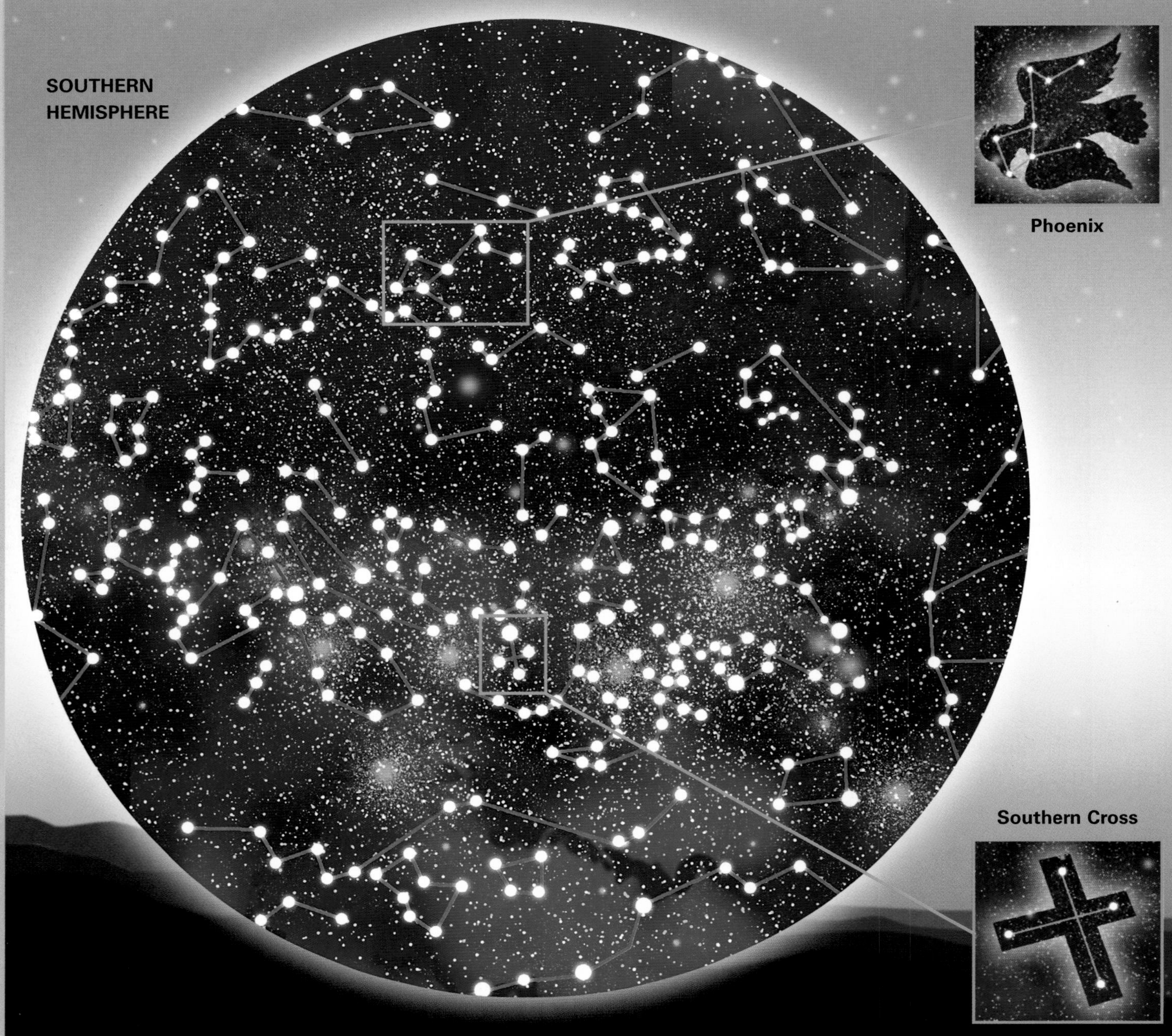

NAMING A CONSTELLATION

Today, there are 88 constellations. Some of them, such as Pegasus and Hercules, have the names that they were given thousands of years ago. Others, such as the Air Pump and the Telescope, were named only a few hundred years ago.

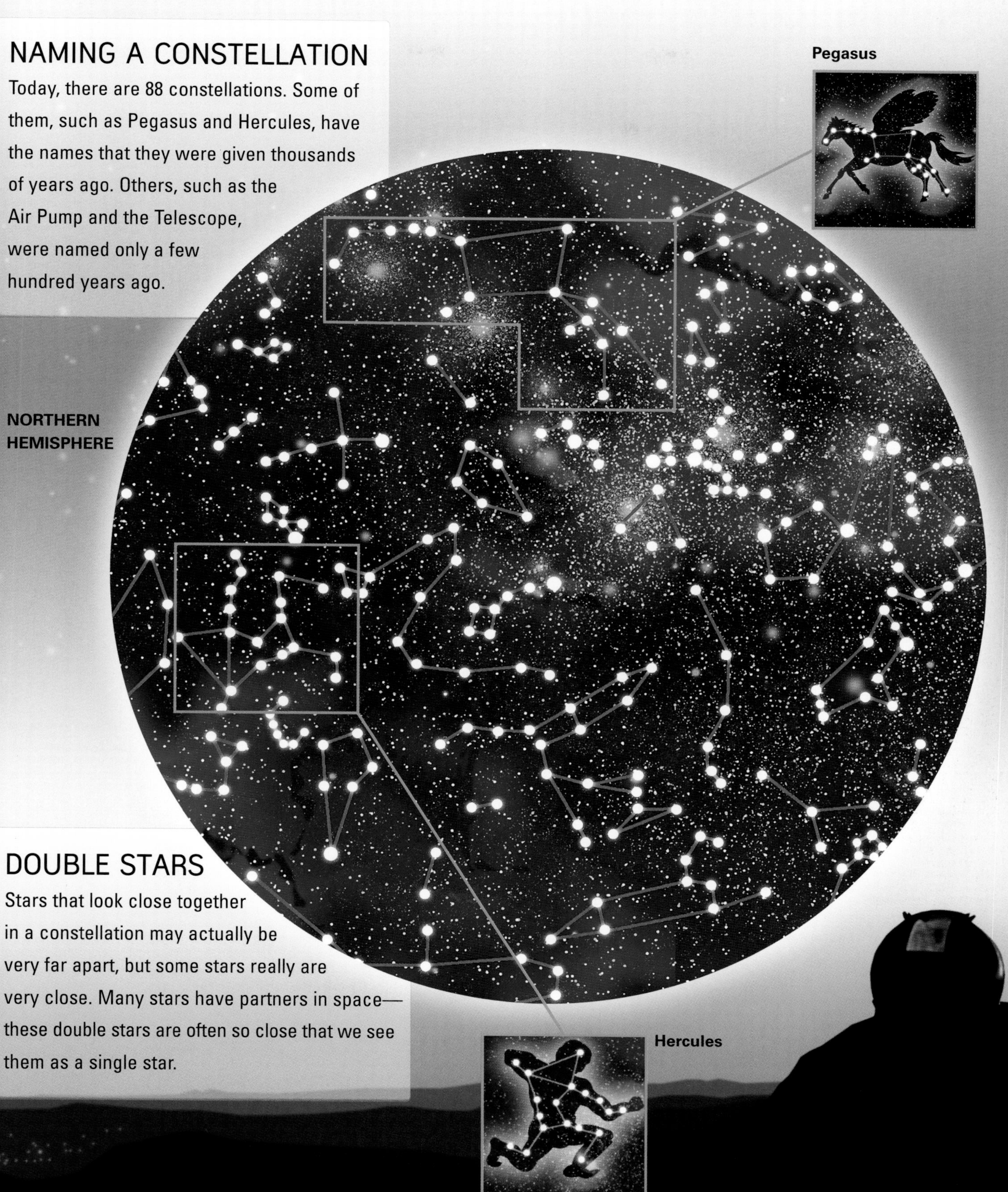

DOUBLE STARS

Stars that look close together in a constellation may actually be very far apart, but some stars really are very close. Many stars have partners in space—these double stars are often so close that we see them as a single star.

Space clouds

When people first used telescopes to look at the night sky, they saw many fuzzy shapes there. They called these shapes nebulae, which is Latin for "clouds."

TYPES OF GALAXIES
Galaxies are classified by their shape. The Milky Way galaxy is a barred spiral galaxy.

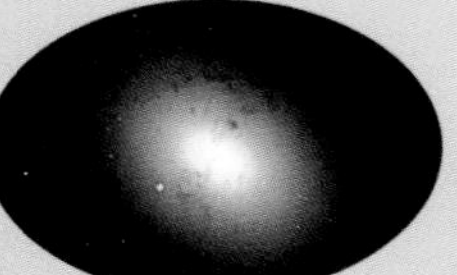

Elliptical galaxies are round or oval and contain mostly old stars.

Spiral galaxies have arms where many new stars are born.

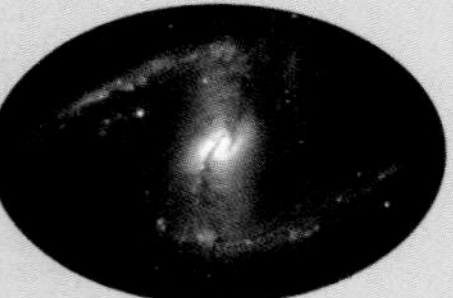

Barred spiral galaxies include a central bar shape made up of stars.

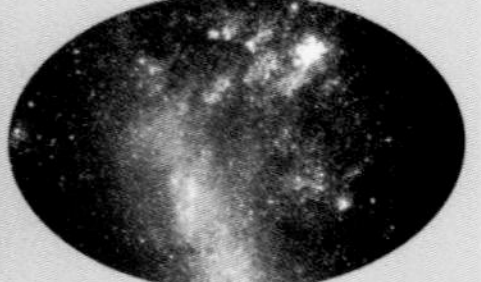

Irregular galaxies are many different shapes and sizes.

There are many types of nebulae. Some are formed of billions of distant stars (these are usually called galaxies), while others—much closer to Earth—are glowing masses of gas or dark sooty clouds.

The Milky Way galaxy

The Sun is grouped with at least 100 billion other stars to form a galaxy called the Milky Way. We see nearby stars as separate dots in the sky, but more distant stars in our galaxy merge together into a hazy band of light.

Other galaxies

Most stars in the universe are gathered into galaxies, and there are more than 100 billion of these galaxies stretching through space. The largest of these contain trillions of stars.

Types of nebulae

Emission nebulae shine with light of their own, while reflection nebulae are lit up by nearby stars. Planetary nebulae are balls of hot gas from dying stars, and supernova remnants are the glowing remains of dead stars.

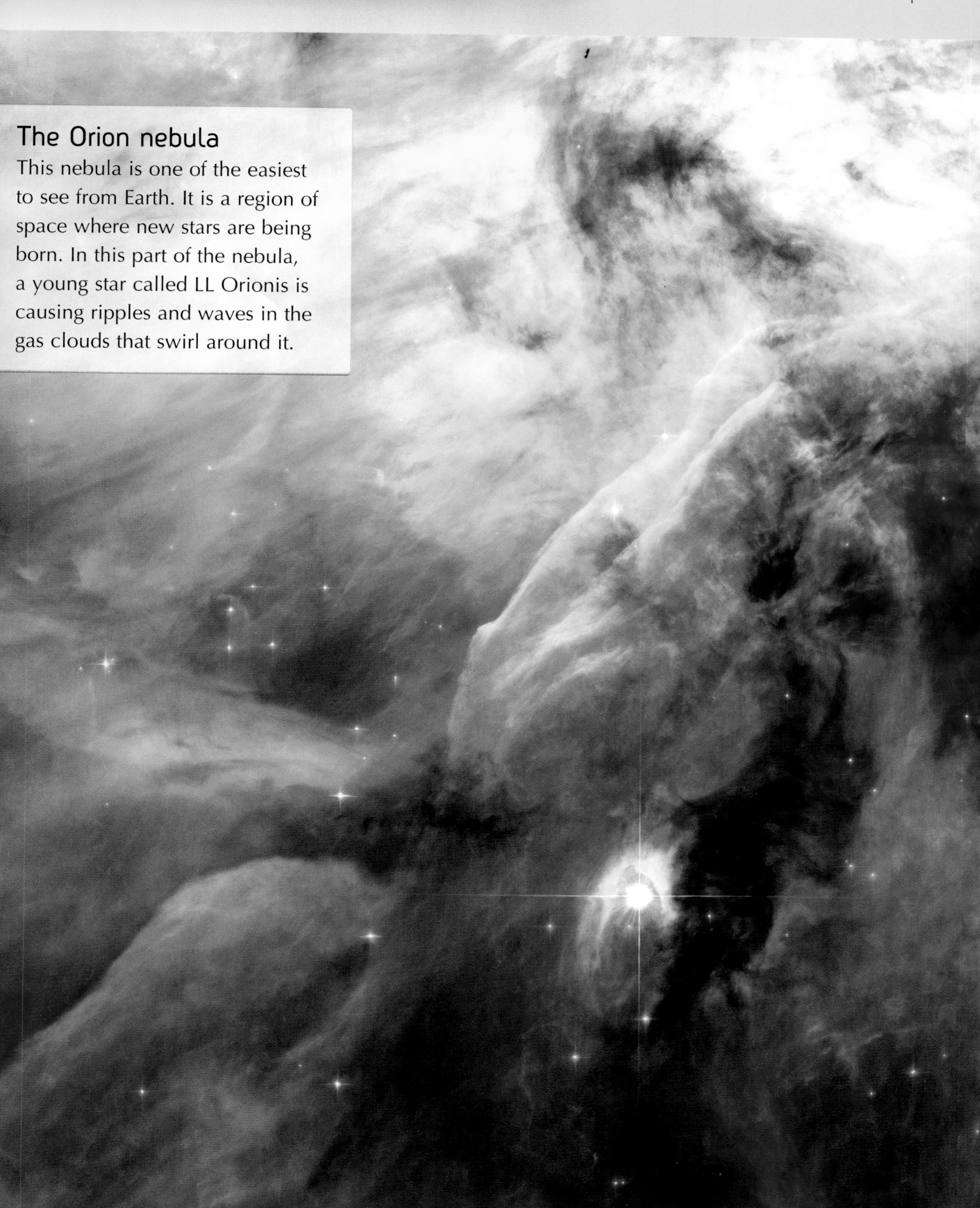

The Orion nebula

This nebula is one of the easiest to see from Earth. It is a region of space where new stars are being born. In this part of the nebula, a young star called LL Orionis is causing ripples and waves in the gas clouds that swirl around it.

THE UNIVERSE

EVERYTHING THAT EXISTS—OR EVER HAS OR EVER WILL—IS PART OF THE UNIVERSE. THE UNIVERSE IS AN UNIMAGINABLY VAST, ENDLESS SPACE, BUT MOST OF THIS SPACE IS ACTUALLY EMPTY.

THE EXPANDING UNIVERSE

In the 1920s, astronomers were amazed to discover that the galaxies are all rushing away from one another. They also found out that the farther apart the galaxies are, the faster they move. The astronomers realized that this meant that the entire universe is expanding.

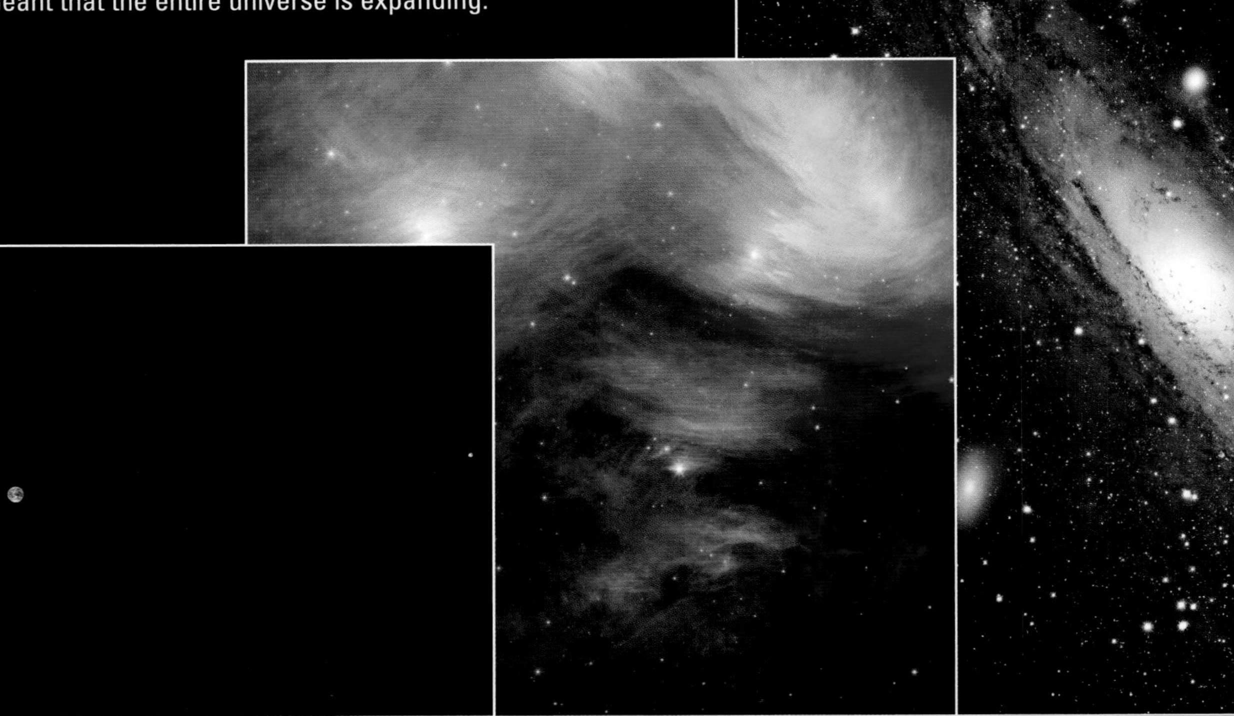

The solar system
The 238,300-mi. (384,400-km) (1.2 light-seconds) distance from Earth (left) to the Moon (right) is tiny compared to the scale of the universe in these images.

Local stars—the Pleiades
In our part of the universe, most stars are a few light-years (a few tens of thousands of billions of miles) apart.

Galaxies—Andromeda
Galaxies such as Andromeda contain around one trillion stars and are a few hundreds of thousands of light-years across.

THE BIG BANG

The expansion of the universe has been happening since it began in a sudden burst of energy called the big bang, 13.7 billion years ago. The faint remaining warmth of the big bang can still be measured.

THE END OF THE UNIVERSE

No one is certain how the universe will end, but it is most likely that it will continue expanding and cooling forever. All the stars will slowly burn out, until the universe is completely cold and dark.

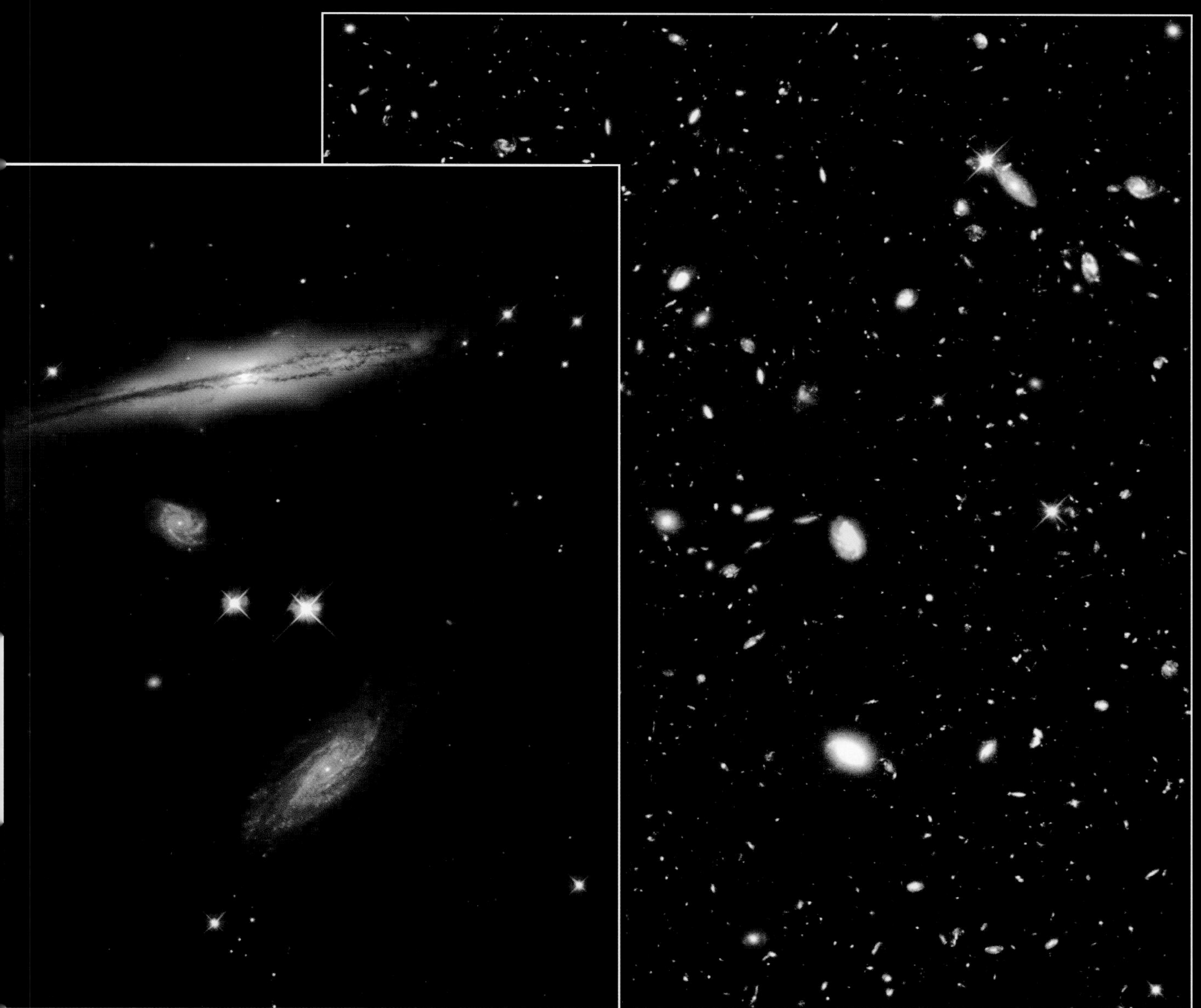

Clusters—Capricorn
Galaxies form clusters like this small one n Capricorn. Our own Milky Way galaxy s part of a cluster called the Local Group.

Distant galaxies
These are some of the most distant galaxies we can see, using pictures taken by the Hubble space telescope. They are billions of light-years away.

Life elsewhere

Are we alone in the universe? Searching for an answer to this question is one of the biggest projects in astronomy today.

The search for life elsewhere is being carried out in many ways. While space robots search for life in the sands of Mars, powerful signals are on their way to the stars and radio telescopes listen for messages from alien civilizations.

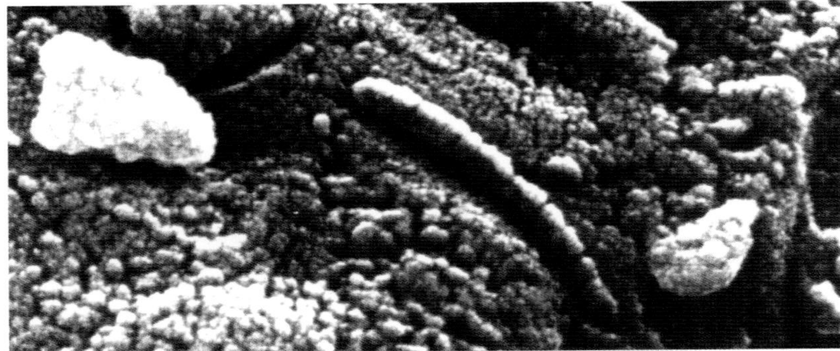

Is there life on Mars?

In 1984, a meteorite that came from Mars was found in Antarctica. In it, scientists found objects that look like bacteria, a very simple form of life. Many scientists now think that these structures were never alive.

The original pattern has been colored here to show the different parts of the message.

Searching for life

This pattern above was sent by radio into space in 1974 as a message to aliens. It includes the shape of a person and of the radio telescope that sent it, as well as a simple map of the solar system.

Life close to the giant planets

This is the frozen surface of Europa, one of the largest moons of Jupiter. Under these thick layers of ice, there is a sea that is at least 30 mi. (50km) deep, which is warmed by the effects of Jupiter's gravity. It is thought that living creatures might exist there.

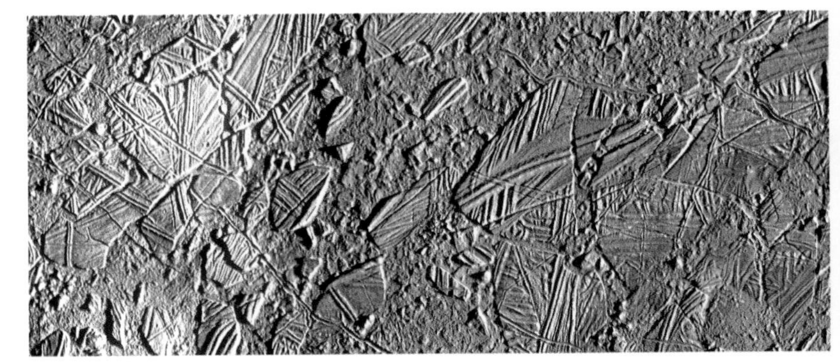

Signals from outer space

In 1977, a radio telescope in Ohio detected what is now known as the "wow" signal. This signal was a sudden, powerful burst of radio waves from space that lasted for 72 seconds. It has not been detected again, and no natural cause for it has been discovered.

CULTURAL NOTE

SCIENCE-FICTION ALIENS

For many years, people have written books and made movies about creatures from space—usually frightening and dangerous ones, unlike the friendly alien that appeared in the movie *Men in Black* (above). The more unlike Earth a planet is, the more different to us any intelligent creatures there are likely to be.

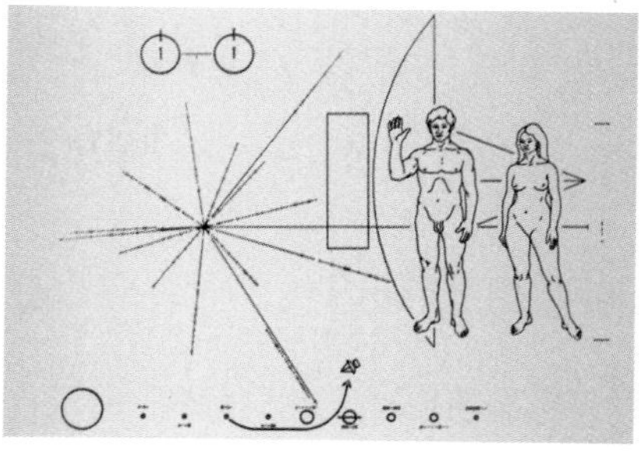

Post card to an alien

This image was drawn on metal plates and sent into space on the *Pioneer 10* and *Pioneer 11* space probes. It was intended as a message that would be easy to interpret by any intelligent aliens that might find it.

Life at the extremes

Alien life might be like nothing we know on Earth. Floating creatures like these (below) might live in the clouds of giant planets, which are known to exist close to many of the stars.

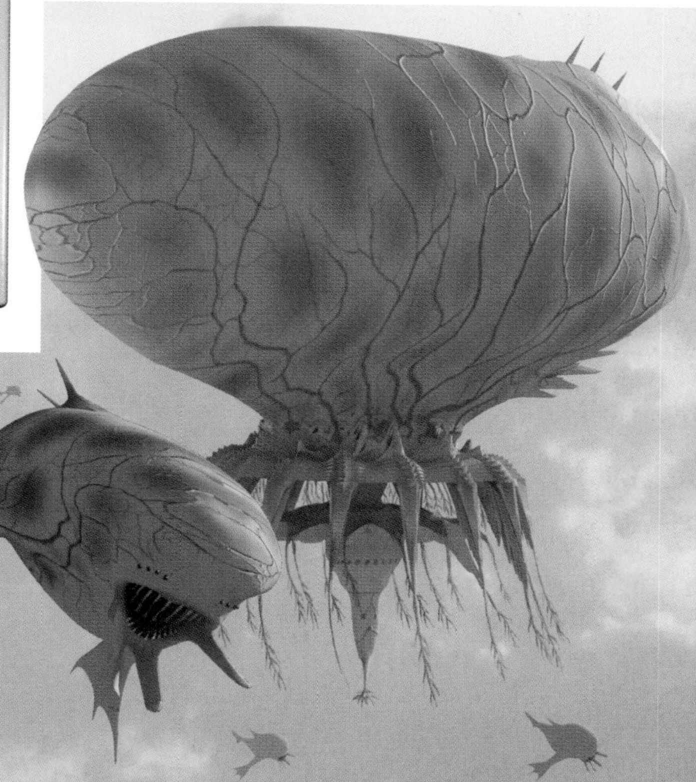

Astronomy

For thousands of years, people have gazed at the night sky. Their attempts to explain what they saw make astronomy a truly ancient science.

In 1609, Galileo made a telescope to study the stars. In 1687, Isaac Newton's mathematical laws of physics were published, explaining the motions of the Moon, planets, and comets.

Telescopes

Optical telescopes collect light to make distant objects look both larger and brighter. Reflecting telescopes use a bowl-shaped mirror, while refractors use glass lenses.

Radio telescope

Many objects in space send out radio signals, and radio telescopes pick these up and make them stronger. The dish of a radio telescope reflects the signals to a concentrated point, like the mirror in a reflecting telescope

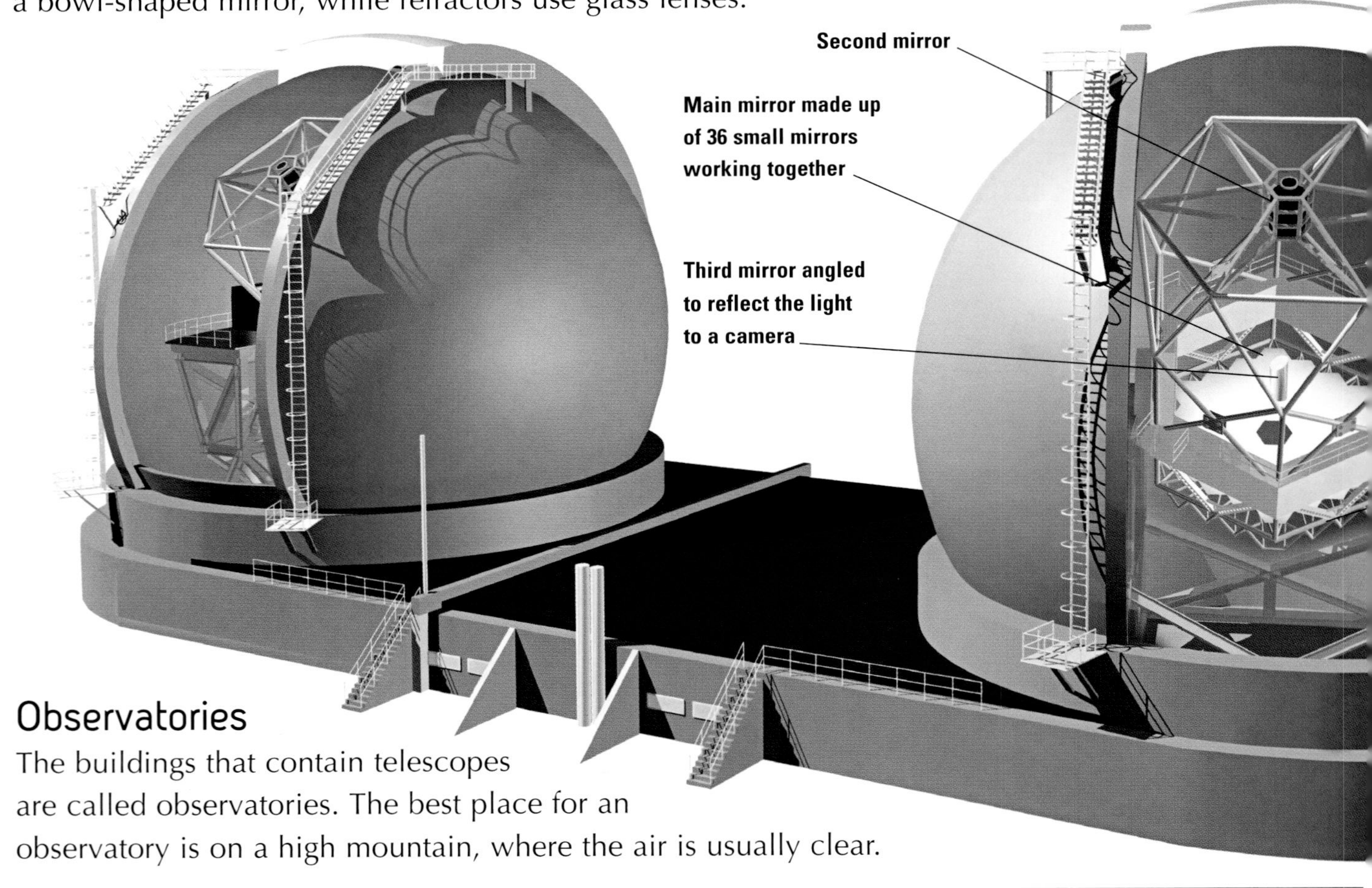

Observatories

The buildings that contain telescopes are called observatories. The best place for an observatory is on a high mountain, where the air is usually clear.

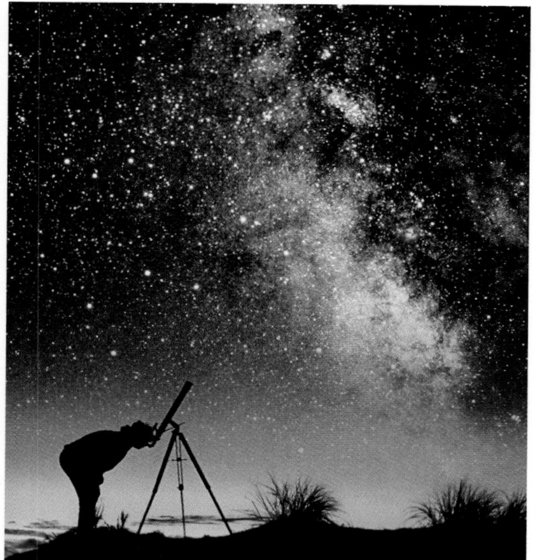

Stargazing

Anyone can be an astronomer, and amateur astronomers do important work such as finding new comets and studying variable stars. For everything except the smallest telescopes, a tripod is essential to keep images steady.

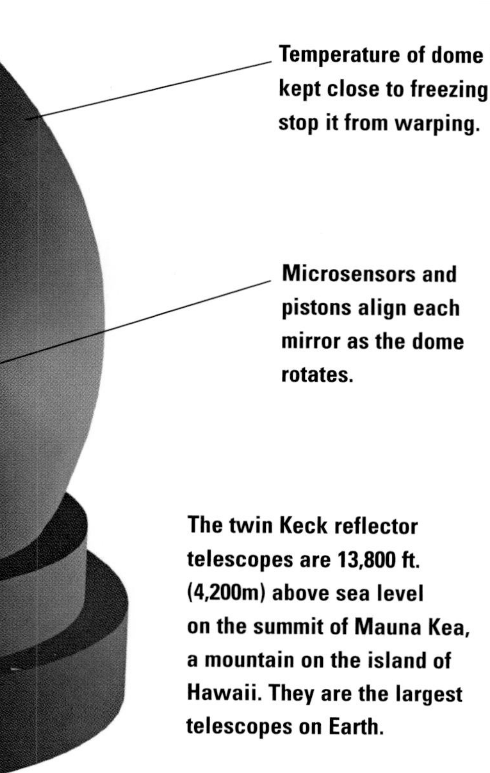

Temperature of dome is kept close to freezing to stop it from warping.
Microsensors and pistons align each mirror as the dome rotates.

The twin Keck reflector telescopes are 13,800 ft. (4,200m) above sea level on the summit of Mauna Kea, a mountain on the island of Hawaii. They are the largest telescopes on Earth.

Space telescopes

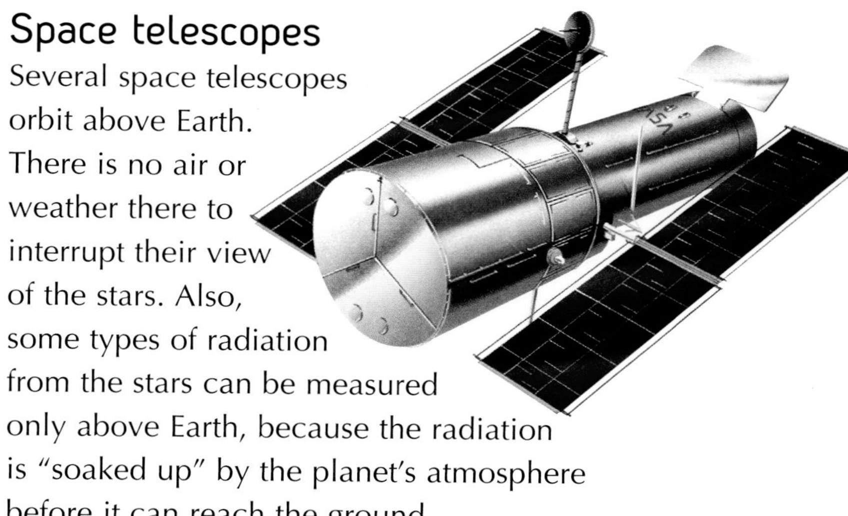

Several space telescopes orbit above Earth. There is no air or weather there to interrupt their view of the stars. Also, some types of radiation from the stars can be measured only above Earth, because the radiation is "soaked up" by the planet's atmosphere before it can reach the ground.

Stars from long ago

Stars are very far away, so their light takes years to reach Earth. If a star is described as 100 light-years away, that means its light takes 100 years to reach us and that we see that star as it used to be, 100 years ago.

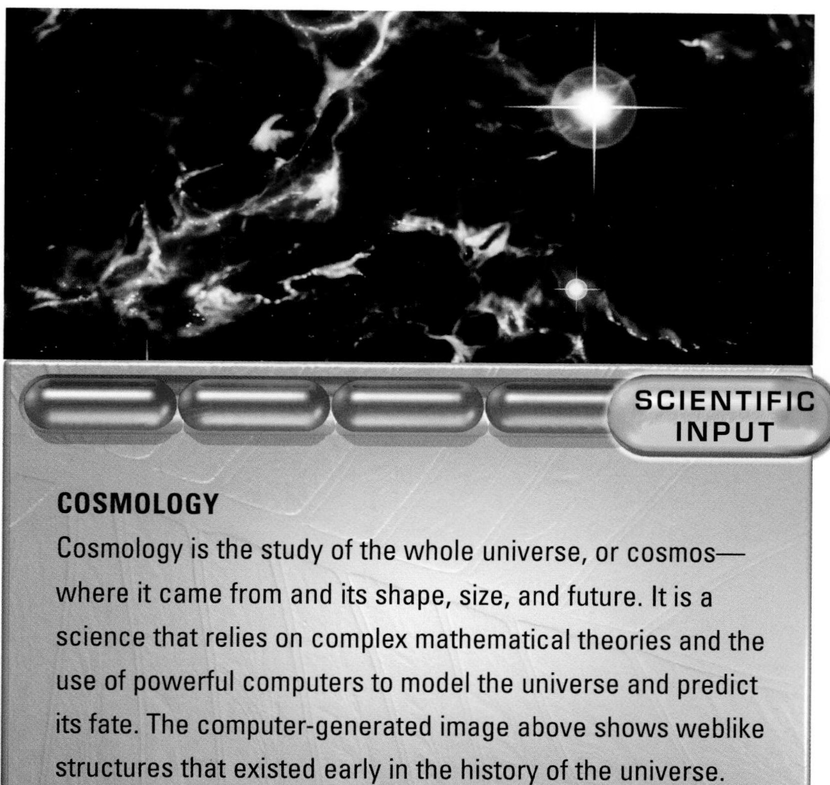

SCIENTIFIC INPUT

COSMOLOGY

Cosmology is the study of the whole universe, or cosmos—where it came from and its shape, size, and future. It is a science that relies on complex mathematical theories and the use of powerful computers to model the universe and predict its fate. The computer-generated image above shows weblike structures that existed early in the history of the universe.

Space facts

The distance between planets is given in astronomical units (AU), which are roughly equivalent to the distance from Earth to the Sun. Light-years are the distance traveled by light in one Earth year, or 5,878,625,373,183.6 mi. (9,460,730,472,580.8km).

PLANETS OF THE SOLAR SYSTEM

Mercury
Distance from Sun: 0.387 of Earth's
Radius: 0.382 of Earth's

Venus
Distance from Sun: 0.723 of Earth's
Radius: 0.949 of Earth's

Earth
Distance from Sun: 1 (92,955,807 mi./149,597,871km)
Radius: 1 (3,941 mi. /6,357km)

Mars
Distance from Sun: 1.524 of Earth's
Radius: 0.532 of Earth's

Jupiter
Distance from Sun: 5.203 of Earth's
Radius: 11.19 of Earth's

Saturn
Distance from Sun: 9.555 of Earth's
Radius: 9.41 of Earth's

Uranus
Distance from Sun: 19.22 of Earth's
Radius: 3.98 of Earth's

Neptune
Distance from Sun: 30.11 of Earth's
Radius: 3.81 of Earth's

KEY SPACE MISSIONS

1957 *Sputnik 1*: first artificial satellite
1961 *Vostok 1*: Yuri Gagarin, first human in space and in orbit
1962 *Mariner 2*: first spaceship to Venus
1965 *Mariner 4*: first spaceship to Mars
1969 *Apollo 11*: Neil Armstrong and Buzz Aldrin are first humans on the Moon
1971 *Salyut 1*: first space station
1973 *Pioneer 10*: first spaceship to Jupiter
1974 *Mariner 10*: first spaceship to Mercury
1979 *Pioneer 11*: first spaceship to Saturn
1981 Columbia shuttle: first reusable spaceship
1986 *Voyager 2*: first spaceship to Uranus
1989 *Voyager 2*: first spaceship to Neptune
2000 First humans living in the International Space Station

Earthrise from the Moon

USEFUL WEBSITES

http://apod.nasa.gov/apod/ Discover the cosmos with the astronomy picture of the day.
www.kidsastronomy.com/ Astronomy and the universe for kids of all ages.
www.bbc.co.uk/science/space/exploration/ Past, present, and future space exploration.
http://adc.gsfc.nasa.gov/adc/education/space_ex/index.html Space exploration fact sheets.

The Living World

Our planet is home to an incredible range of living things, from bacteria that can be seen only under a microscope to enormous blue whales that are 108 ft. (33m) long and can weigh more than 180 tons. More than 1.8 million species of plants and animals have been identified so far, but scientists estimate that up to 90 percent more remain to be discovered.

Habitats and biomes

Plants and animals live in habitats, or locations, that provide the food, water, and protection they need to survive.

A biome is a large general habitat such as a rainforest or a hot desert. Each biome contains a number of different habitats that can support a variety of species.

Communities

Living things that exist in one habitat are a community. Many depend on one another. Plants in a pond habitat might add oxygen to the water, which provides a place for insects and other creatures to lay their eggs. The plants and eggs provide food for fish and insects, which in turn might be food for birds.

Adaptation

Animals and plants have evolved to develop features that suit their habitats. This is called adaptation. Cacti in desert habitats have fleshy stems that swell so that they can store water. The elf owl, the smallest of all owls, uses this adaptation by making its nest in cacti in deserts in the U.S.

Specialized habitats

Some living things require specific places to live. The giant panda's habitat is cool, wet, mountain forests in China where bamboo—which is 99 percent of its diet—grows.

Biodiversity

Biodiversity describes the rich and varied forms of life on the planet. There are more than 1.8 million known species on Earth, but there might be millions more to discover.

In the sun

Some plants have evolved so that they can obtain sunlight. Bladder-wrack seaweed has air pockets that help it float on the water's surface.

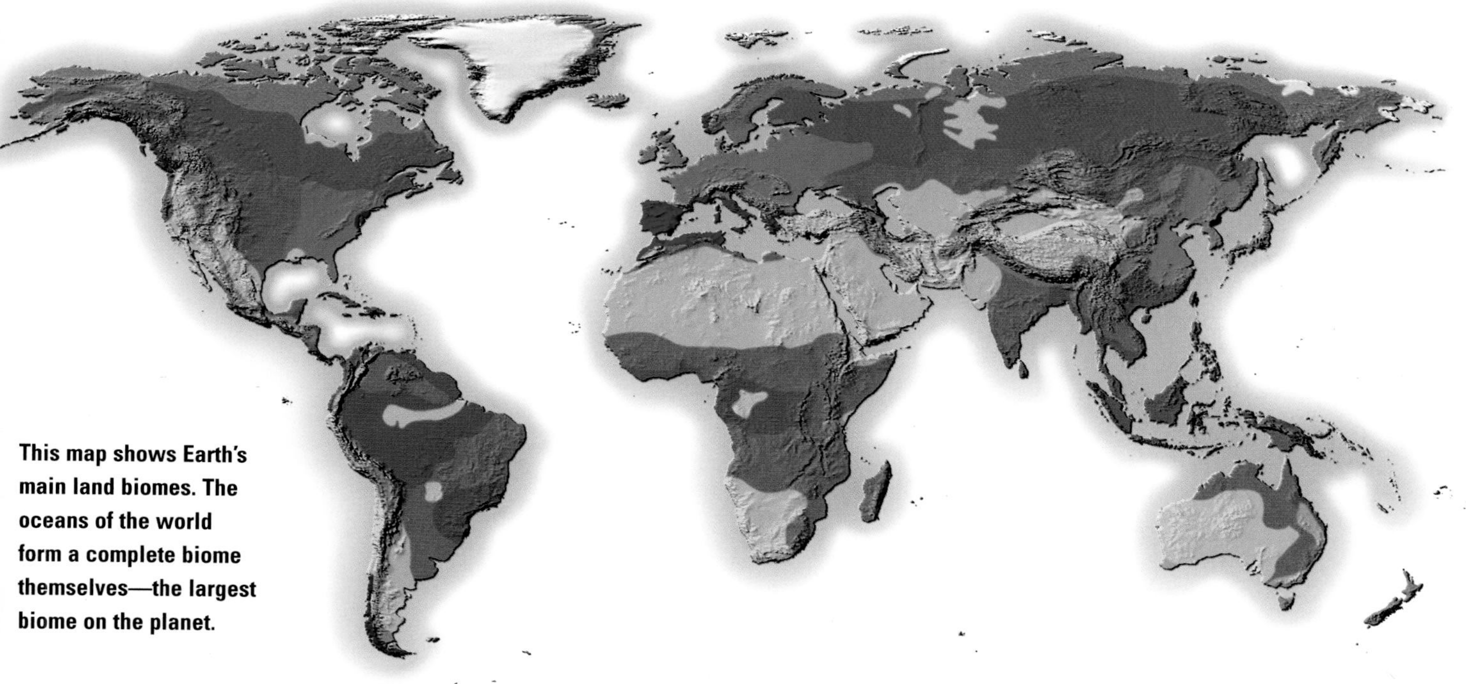

This map shows Earth's main land biomes. The oceans of the world form a complete biome themselves—the largest biome on the planet.

Polar
Tundra
Coniferous forest
Desert
Tropical rainforest
Mediterranean scrubland
Wetland
Temperate woodland
Grassland and savanna
Mountain

World biomes

Biomes are mostly shaped by climate because it influences which plants and animals can survive in a region. Some creatures, such as human beings, have been able to adjust and adapt to thrive in many different biomes throughout the world.

Alpine biome

In the alpine, or mountain, biome, harsh winters and strong winds mean that only plants that live close to the ground, such as mosses, lichens, and purple saxifrage, can survive. Because of the cold climate, no reptiles can live there, only warm-blooded vertebrates such as birds, mountain goats, and marmots (center).

Two mountain ibex fight in their habitat in the alpine biome.

Ecosystems and cycles

An ecosystem is a complete community of living things together with their environment. It can be as large as a complete coral reef or as small as a single tree.

Nutrients and resources, such as carbon, nitrogen, and water, help living things survive. They are used and reused by nature in a continual exchange of the nutrients. This is called a cycle.

A balanced system

No living thing exists on its own. Each is part of an ecosystem and has complex relationships with other living things and with its habitat.

In a food chain, each level gets energy by feeding on the level below.

Herons eat fish.

Fish eat water beetles.

Water beetles eat tadpoles.

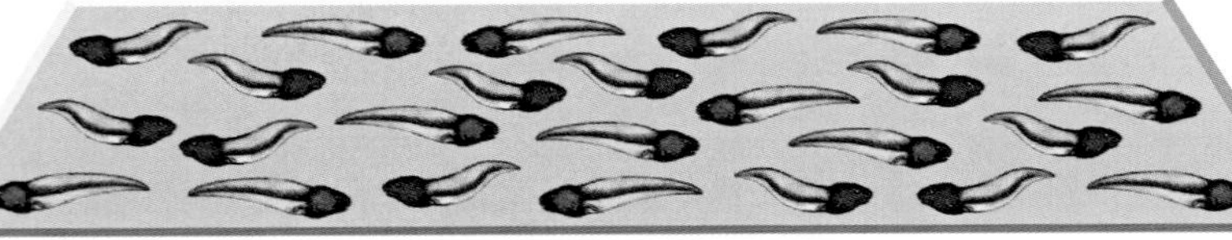

Tadpoles eat pondweed.

Pondweed uses energy from the Sun to grow.

Nitrogen cycle

Nitrogen is needed by all living things. It reaches the soil in rain, as well as in dead and rotting matter. Bacteria in the soil combines nitrogen with other substances to create nutrients that plants can absorb.

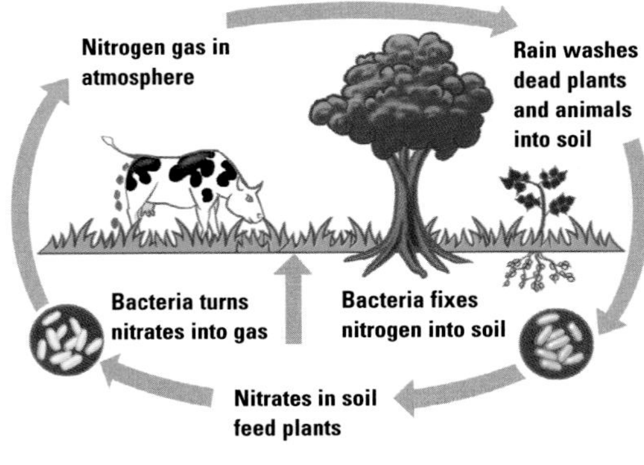
Nitrogen gas in atmosphere
Rain washes dead plants and animals into soil
Bacteria turns nitrates into gas
Bacteria fixes nitrogen into soil
Nitrates in soil feed plants

Food chains

A food chain is a way of showing how living things find food and then become food for others. The heron is the top predato this simple food chain (lef

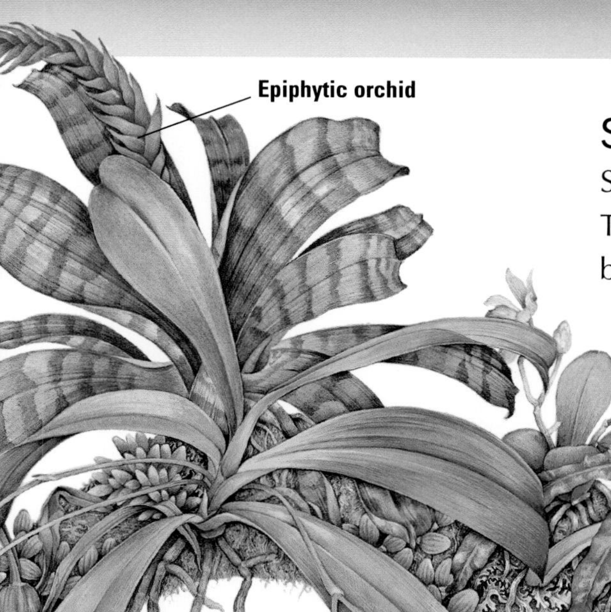

Symbiosis

Symbiosis is a relationship between two different species. This can benefit both—for example, the Egyptian plover bird gains food by cleaning the teeth of crocodiles. Epiphytic plants, including some orchids, live on other plants in order to get greater access to sunlight.

Carbon cycle

Carbon is found in every living thing. Plants take in carbon dioxide from the atmosphere to help their growth. Animals eat plants, releasing carbon dioxide by breathing, as well as when they die and rot.

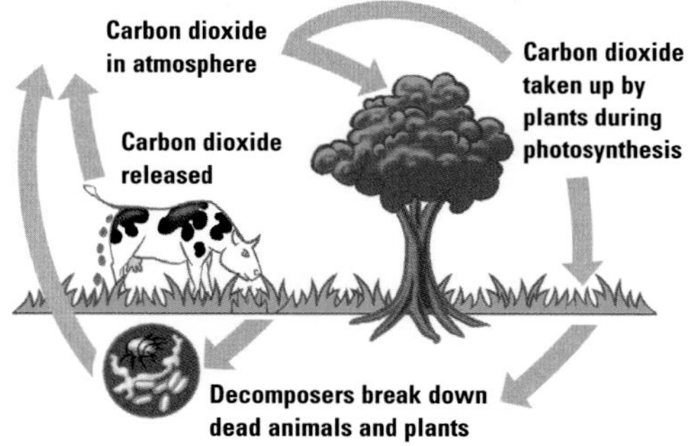

Producers and consumers

Plants are known as primary producers. They take sunlight and use it to help make food. Animals are consumers because they eat plants, other creatures, or a mixture of plants and animals.

EARTH EVIDENCE

FUNGI

Fungi lack chlorophyll and do not make food by photosynthesis. Instead, they break down and digest the food outside their bodies before they absorb it. There are more than 70,000 known species of fungi, including mushrooms, toadstools, yeasts, and molds. Fungi break down dead animals and plant matter, releasing chemicals and nutrients back into the soil.

CLIMATE ZONES

THE WEATHER PATTERN OF A REGION OVER A LONG PERIOD OF TIME IS CALLED ITS CLIMATE. CLIMATE ZONES ARE A WAY OF MAPPING THE VARIOUS MAJOR TYPES OF CLIMATES AROUND THE WORLD.

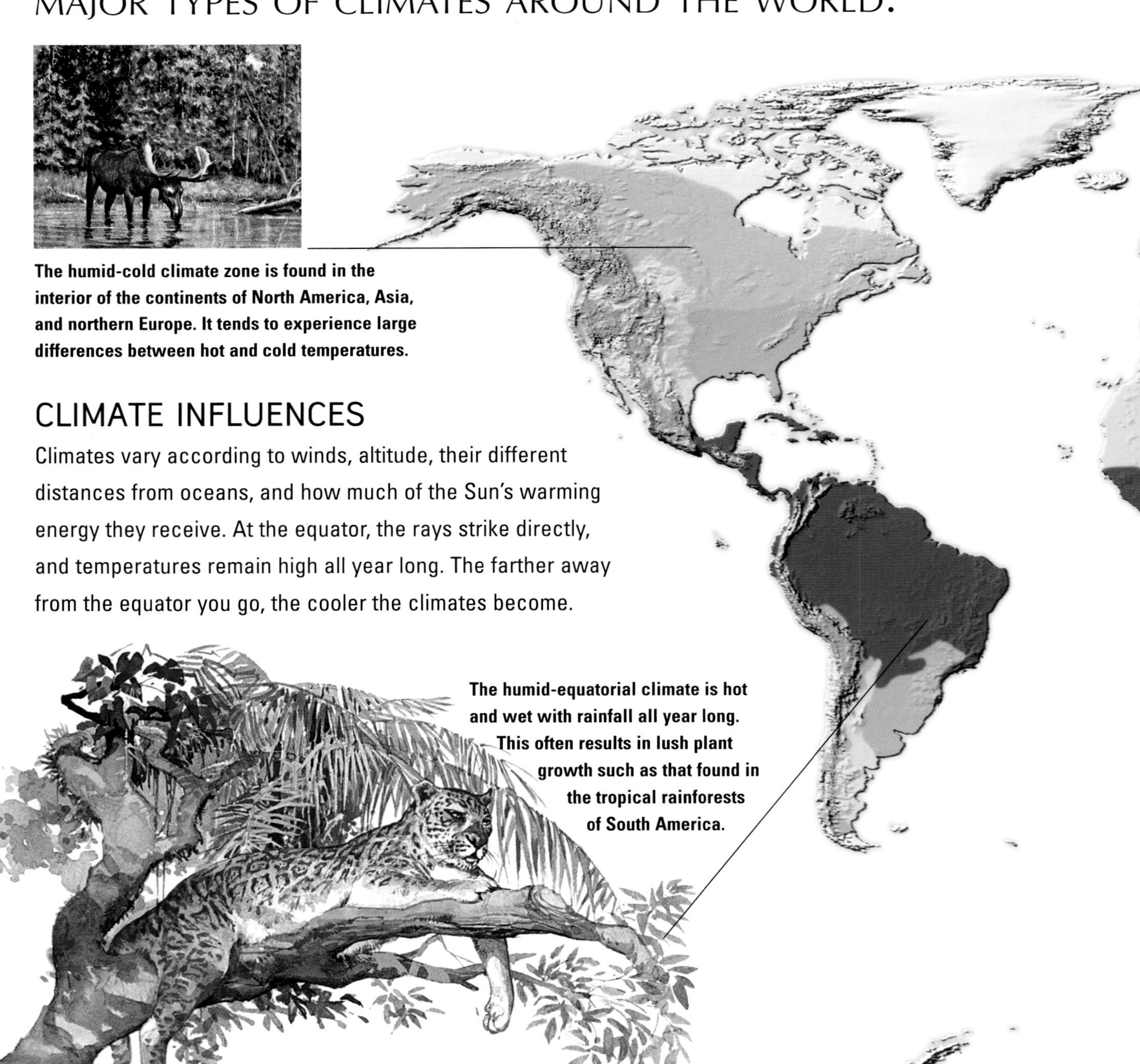

The humid-cold climate zone is found in the interior of the continents of North America, Asia, and northern Europe. It tends to experience large differences between hot and cold temperatures.

CLIMATE INFLUENCES

Climates vary according to winds, altitude, their different distances from oceans, and how much of the Sun's warming energy they receive. At the equator, the rays strike directly, and temperatures remain high all year long. The farther away from the equator you go, the cooler the climates become.

The humid-equatorial climate is hot and wet with rainfall all year long. This often results in lush plant growth such as that found in the tropical rainforests of South America.

In a highland climate, it is colder on the mountains than on the lower ground surrounding them. The rain and snowfall levels are higher on the mountains.

KEY TO WORLD MAP

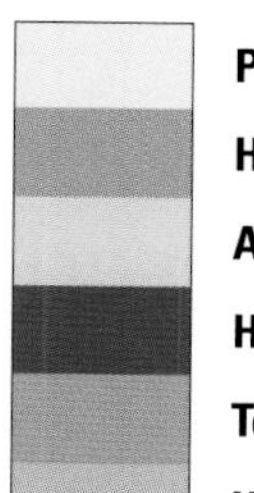

- Polar
- Highland
- Arid and semiarid
- Humid equatorial
- Temperate
- Humid cold

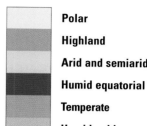

Arid and semiarid climates have very little rainfall. They are dry and usually hot all year long, although some areas have cold winters. They often result in desert biomes. This frilled lizard lives in an arid climate zone in the desert interior of Australia.

Temperate climate zones can have rainfall all year long—for example, in Europe. Or it can be warm and have only a short rainy season, as it does in the grasslands of the African savanna.

The polar climate around the farthest northern and southern parts of the planet is very cold and dry. These penguins in Antarctica live in subzero temperatures for most of the year.

Weather

Weather describes the conditions in the atmosphere that affect an area, including temperature, rain, wind speed, and the amount of sunshine.

CLOUD TYPES
Clouds can be classified by their shape.

Cumulonimbus threaten thunderstorms.

Nimbostratus can bring rain or sleet.

Low-level cumulus can cover hilltops.

Cirrus are high-altitude wisps of clouds.

Cirrostratus are rippled and at a high altitude.

The Sun heats Earth's surface and also its atmosphere, creating winds and areas of high and low air pressure. These areas interact, forming weather systems.

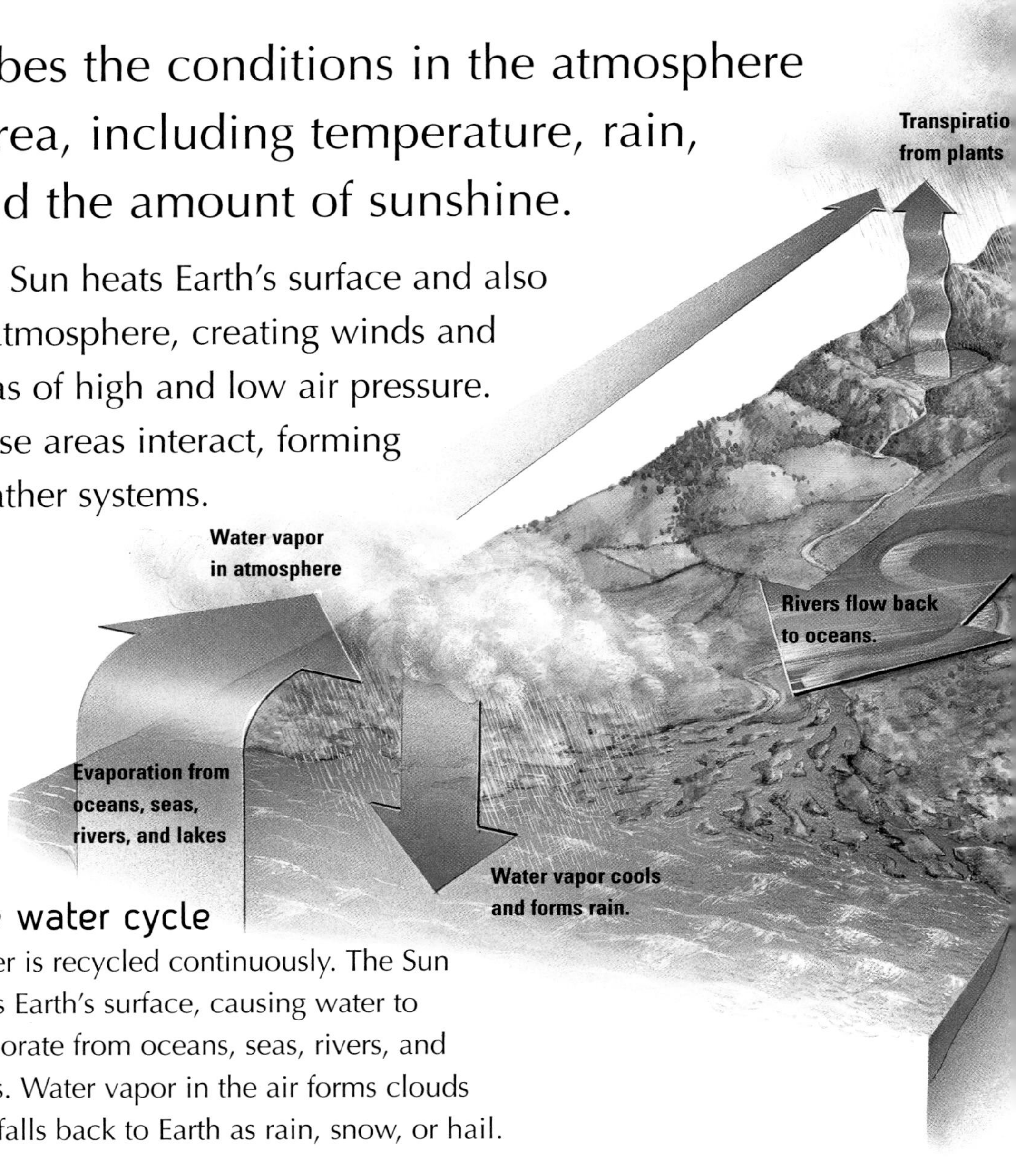

Transpiratio
from plants

Water vapor
in atmosphere

Rivers flow back
to oceans.

Evaporation from
oceans, seas,
rivers, and lakes

Water vapor cools
and forms rain.

The water cycle

Water is recycled continuously. The Sun heats Earth's surface, causing water to evaporate from oceans, seas, rivers, and lakes. Water vapor in the air forms clouds and falls back to Earth as rain, snow, or hail.

Clouds and rainfall

Warm, moist air cools as it rises over high land or meets cooler air, forming clouds. When the cooled air can no longer support all the water it holds as vapor, rain falls. Sunlight shining on water droplets can form rainbows.

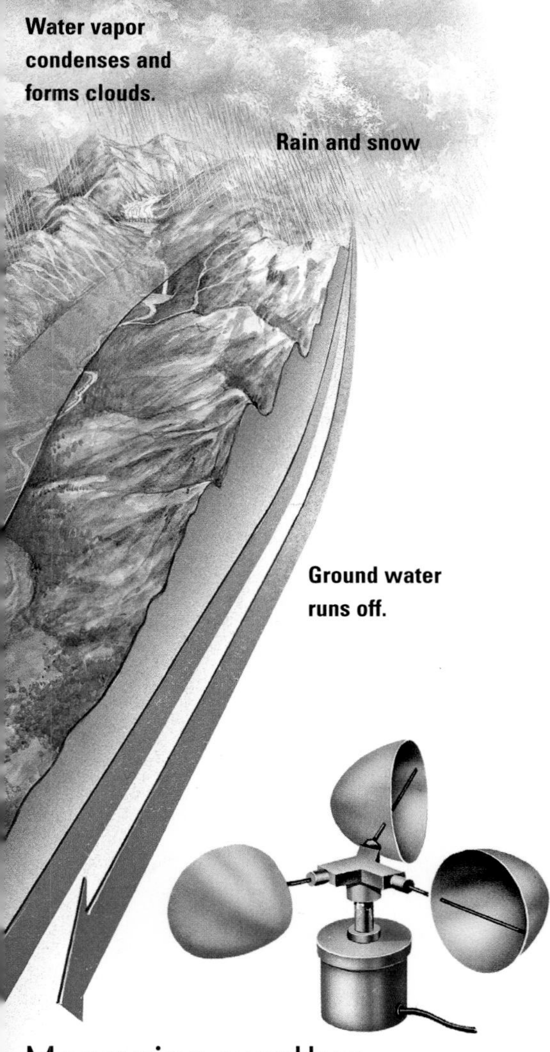
Water vapor condenses and forms clouds.
Rain and snow
Ground water runs off.

Measuring weather

Weather details are measured and recorded using different instruments. These include thermometers and rain gauges. Anemometers (above) are used to measure wind speed.

Forecasting

Weather forecasting uses space satellites and computers to track the conditions in the atmosphere. Forecasters try to predict patterns of weather, although weather can be unpredictable and change quickly.

Snow and hail

Water droplets can freeze into ice crystals inside clouds. The crystals join to form snowflakes, which fall in a snowstorm or are mixed with rain (sleet). Hailstones are balls of ice that fall mostly from storm clouds.

Humidity

The moisture in the air is called humidity. In general, the hotter the air, the more moisture it can hold. Humid conditions make animals feel sticky and hot, because sweat cannot evaporate quickly and easily.

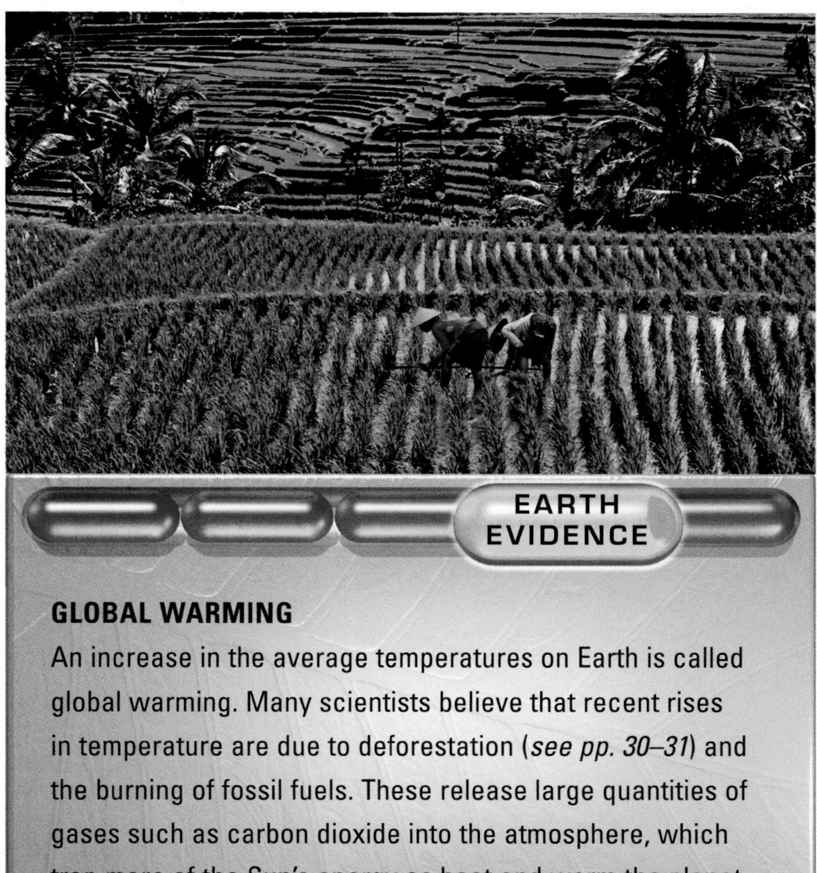

EARTH EVIDENCE

GLOBAL WARMING

An increase in the average temperatures on Earth is called global warming. Many scientists believe that recent rises in temperature are due to deforestation (*see pp. 30–31*) and the burning of fossil fuels. These release large quantities of gases such as carbon dioxide into the atmosphere, which trap more of the Sun's energy as heat and warm the planet.

WILD WEATHER

MORE THAN 1,500 THUNDERSTORMS HAPPEN AROUND THE WORLD AT ANY ONE TIME, AND THAT IS ONLY ONE EXAMPLE OF WILD WEATHER. STRONG WINDS, LIGHTNING, HEAVY RAIN, AND SNOW CAN ALL CAUSE HAVOC.

MONSOON RAINS

Monsoon is the name given to a wind that blows from one direction all winter long and then from another direction in the summer. The most notable is the Asian monsoon that brings very heavy rains during the summer months (usually April to October). These rains often cause massive floods in Bangladesh, India, and other parts of Asia.

HURRICANES

Also known as typhoons or cyclones, hurricanes begin over tropical oceans These windstorms can be more than 370 mi. (600km) in diameter, with winds up to 125 mph (200km/h). The hurrican calm center is called the eye.

TORNADOES

A tornado is a column or funnel of air that spins rapidly and violently. Tornadoes are usually less than 1,640 ft. (500m) wide where they reach the ground, but they appear quickly and can be very destructive. Speeds around the edges can reach 300 mph (480km/h), the fastest winds on Earth.

LIGHTNING

Lightning is electricity that is released from the atmosphere during a storm. Colliding water particles in storm clouds build up positive and negative electric charges. Lightning happens when these charges move to even themselves out. Lightning might be a large flash in the sky (sheet lightning) or jagged forks of light that reach the ground (fork lightning). Thunder is the sound of the hot air around the lightning expanding violently.

Plants

Aside from some bacteria and cyanobacteria, or blue-green algae, plants are the only living things that can make their own food. There are more than 300,000 different species

Plants are essential to other forms of life on Earth. They provide most of the planet's food and the oxygen found in the atmosphere.

Ferns are related to prehistoric vegetation that once covered Earth.

Nonflowering plants

Nonflowering plants include mosses, liverworts, horsetails, and more than 10,000 species of ferns. Instead of roots, mosses and liverworts have threadlike anchors called rhizoids.

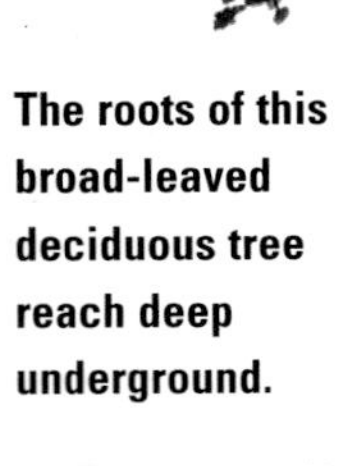

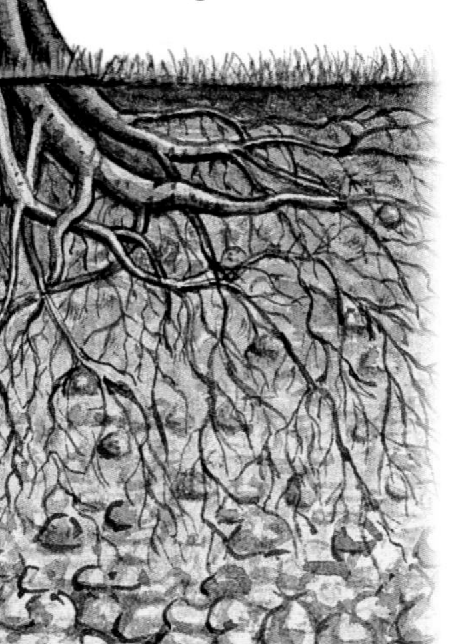

The roots of this broad-leaved deciduous tree reach deep underground.

Roots

The roots of a plant are the part that is usually beneath the soil. Roots can collect water and nutrients from the soil through fine root hairs. They also help anchor the plant in place, and some plant roots can spread out a long distance underground.

Photosynthesis

Plants make their food by a process called photosynthesis. A green pigment, chlorophyll, in the leaves absorbs energy from sunlight. This reacts with carbon dioxide gas (from the air) and water to create oxygen and carbohydrates such as glucose and starch. These are the plants' food.

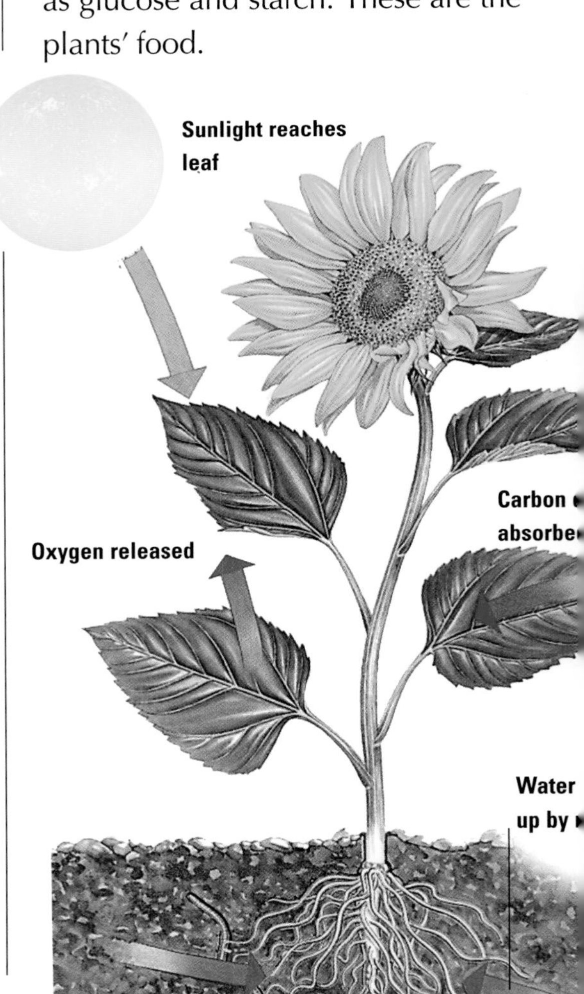

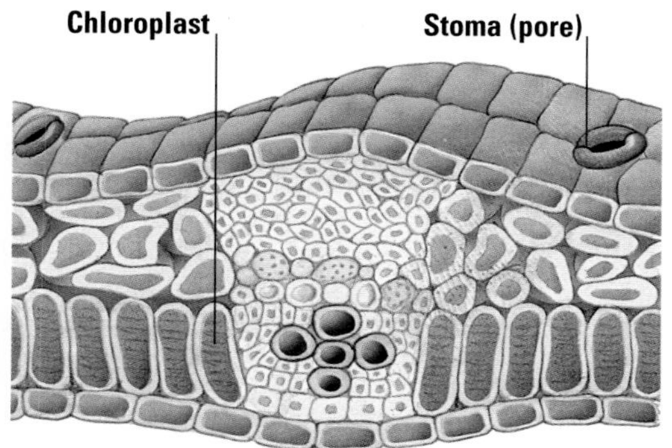

Anatomy of a leaf

Leaves vary in shape and size, but almost all have veins that carry water and food to and from the leaf. Leaves are packed with chloroplasts that contain chlorophyll. Gases pass in and out of tiny pores or holes in a leaf called stomata.

Stems

A stem supports the plant's leaves and flowers. A stem contains tubes called xylem and phloem. These transport water and food—nutrients—around the plant. In some plants, such as a cactus, food is made in the stem rather than in the leaves.

Stem

Roots take in water and minerals from the soil.

Storing nutrients

Some plants store nutrients, such as starch, in swollen growths for use during the growing season. They are usually underground in order to protect them from plant-eating animals. Bulbs, such as this onion, have fleshy leaves wrapped together. Tubers, such as a potato, are solid.

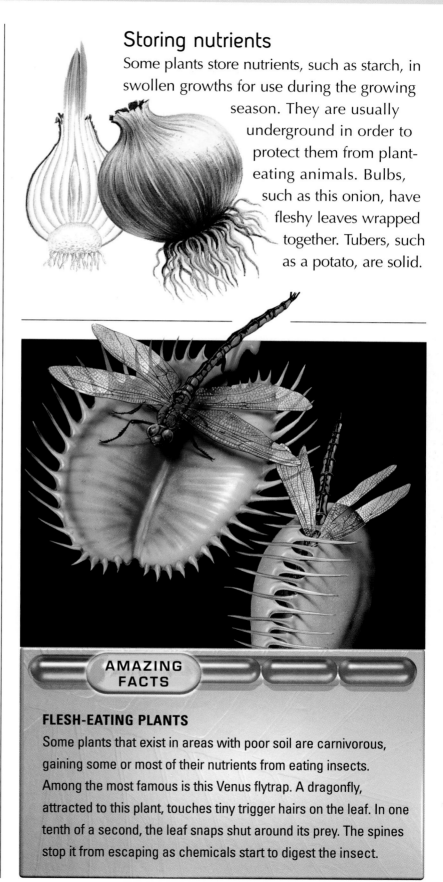

AMAZING FACTS

FLESH-EATING PLANTS

Some plants that exist in areas with poor soil are carnivorous, gaining some or most of their nutrients from eating insects. Among the most famous is this Venus flytrap. A dragonfly, attracted to this plant, touches tiny trigger hairs on the leaf. In one tenth of a second, the leaf snaps shut around its prey. The spines stop it from escaping as chemicals start to digest the insect.

PLANT REPRODUCTION

REPRODUCTION IS THE WAY NEW PLANTS ARE CREATED. MANY PLANTS HAVE FLOWERS THAT CONTAIN THEIR SEX CELLS AND ORGANS. THESE PRODUCE A SEED THAT CAN GROW INTO A NEW PLANT.

NO SEEDS OR FLOWERS

Mosses and ferns reproduce with tiny spores instead of from seeds. Ferns produce spores on the undersides of their fronds (feathery leaves). Sometimes a new plant is produced without either a seed or a spore. The strawberry plant produces long stems called runners that can grow into the soil and form a new plant. However, strawberries also produce seeds, so they can reproduce in two different ways.

FLOWERING PLANTS

Most plants produce flowers that contain separate male and female sex cells. Male sex cells are called pollen, and the process of them joining with female sex cells is called pollination. Some plants pollinate themselves, but most rely on their pollen being carried to another plant before a new plant can be formed.

An Australian birdwing butterfly sips nectar from a flower. Its legs are coated in pollen. When it lands on a different plant, it may pollinate it.

The pollen sticking to this bee's body will rub off on the next flower that the bee visits.

A poppy plant has bright red flowers. In the center is the nectar that bees collect and use to make honey.

A pollen sac where the bee stores pollen to take back to the hive for food

POLLEN DISPERSAL

Flowering plants need outside help in order to move pollen. Wind disperses the pollen of plants such as grasses, while some aquatic plants rely on water to carry their pollen. Other plants have bright flowers and a sweet food, called nectar, to attract insects or birds.

Pollen sticks to the feathers of this hummingbird as it uses its long bill to drink nectar.

Seeds and growing

Plants produce seeds that contain food supplies and the makings of a new plant. Most seeds are inside fruit. The seeds of conifers are found on the surface of cones.

TYPES OF SEEDS
Fruit contain different numbers of seeds—from one to dozens.

Seeds need to move away from the parent plant to find their own space in the soil in order to grow. This movement is called dispersal.

Seeds

Seeds form after a plant has been pollinated. They usually have a hard outer coating. Inside, there is a supply of food that they use when they start to germinate, or grow, into a plant. The largest seed, of the coco-de-mer palm, weighs more than 44 lbs. (20kg).

Apple seed

Fruit

Fruit contain seeds. The fruit can be dry like pea pods, hard like acorns, or juicy like cherries and tomatoes. The seeds inside these coffee berries (below) are the beans that are used to make coffee.

Plant growth

Plants grow throughout their lives. Some grow rapidly—bamboo can grow 12 in. (30cm) in a single day. As plants develop, they grow from their root and shoot tips. The roots grow downward toward moisture in the soil. Aboveground, a plant usually grows upward, although it will also bend its stems and grow toward sunlight—a process called phototropism.

Seed dispersal

Plants disperse their seeds in different ways. Some have fruit with hooks or burrs that catch onto an animal's fur. Some seeds are eaten and carried away. Many seeds are carried by the wind. Others, such as this squirting cucumber, explode, forcing out the seeds.

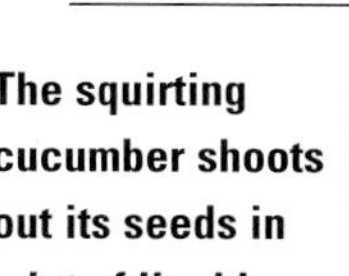

The squirting cucumber shoots out its seeds in a jet of liquid.

Germination

In soil, a seed germinates when the soil, water, and temperature conditions are correct. It splits, and a root is formed that then pushes downward. A shoot heads upward out of the soil and produces the first leaves.

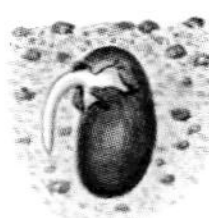

1. Root grows down

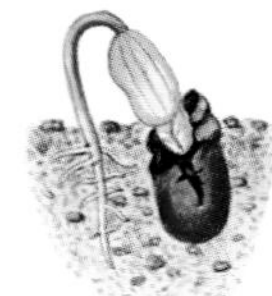

2. Seed case splits

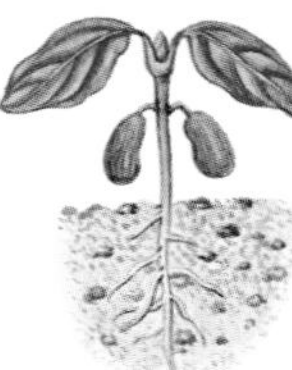

3. Seedling produces first leaves

Annuals and perennials

An annual plant germinates from a seed and then grows, flowers, produces a seed, and dies within one year. Perennial plants live longer. Their leaves and stem may die, but the roots survive. The plant will then flower again the next year.

Trees and forests

Trees are large plants that have solid, woody stems called trunks, and they can grow for many years. Forests of trees cover approximately 30 percent of the land on Earth.

TREES OF THE WORLD
Among the thousands of species of trees, there are some that are very unusual.

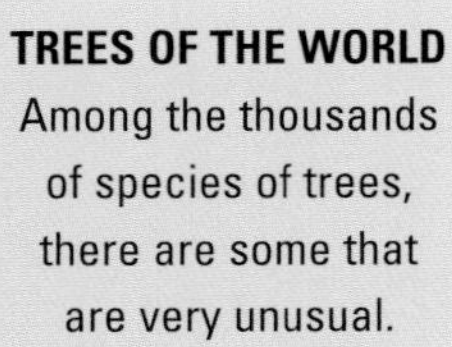

The African baobab's stout trunk can grow more than 30 ft. (9m) in diameter.

Palms have giant leaves growing out of a single point.

Bristlecone pines are the oldest living things on Earth.

The banyan tree has roots that hang in the air from its branches.

Trees are essential to the life of the planet because they release large amounts of oxygen into the air, create important habitats, and help protect soil from erosion.

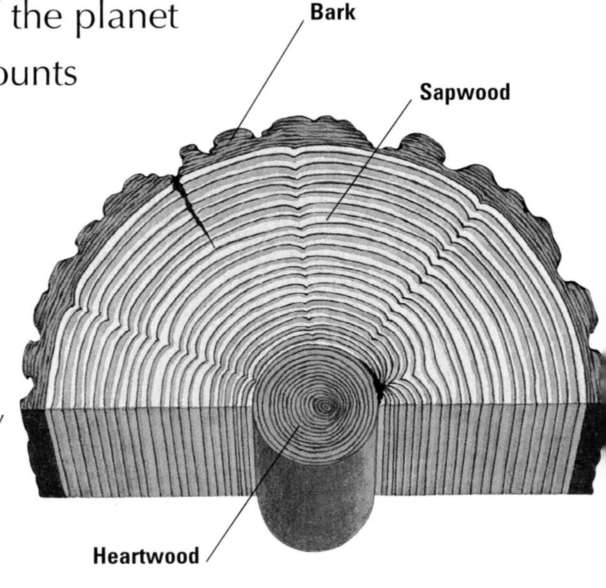

Tree anatomy

Trees have leaves, branches, roots, and a stem. The outside of the woody stem is covered in bark. This tough, waterproof layer protects the living, growing sapwood inside.

Deciduous trees

These trees include the oak, horse chestnut, elm, and sycamore. They all bear flowers and have fruit that house their seeds. In cooler climates, they shed their broad leaves in the fall to preserve food and water.

Coniferous trees

These trees have thin, needlelike leaves that they shed and regrow all year long, so they are evergreen in the winter. Their waxy leaves don't lose much water. This allows conifers such as pines to grow in cold regions.

Forest resources

Forests provide rich habitats. For humans, there is shelter, fuel, fruit and nuts to eat, and materials for building. Trunks of rubber trees can be tapped (above) to release a sticky liquid that forms natural rubber.

Temperate forests

Forests in temperate climates have mostly deciduous trees. In the fall, the leaves are drained of their chlorophyll, and they turn different shades of red, yellow, and brown.

AMAZING FACTS

RECORD-BREAKING TREE

The giant redwood, or sequoia, is a huge coniferous tree found in scattered clumps called groves in California. The tallest grow up to 300 ft. (93m) high, have trunks that are almost 30 ft. (9m) in diameter, and can weigh more than 6,000 tons. The oldest trees are around 3,200 years old, and a single mature tree disperses 300,000 seeds every year.

The taiga

The taiga or boreal forest is a broad band of coniferous forest that extends around the north below the tundra. Larger predators such as wolves hunt down moose and deer there.

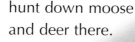

RAINFORESTS

RAINFORESTS ARE LUSH AREAS OF DENSELY PACKED TREES AND PLANTS FOUND IN WARM, WET REGIONS—TROPICAL RAINFORESTS—OR IN MILDER AREAS—TEMPERATE RAINFORESTS.

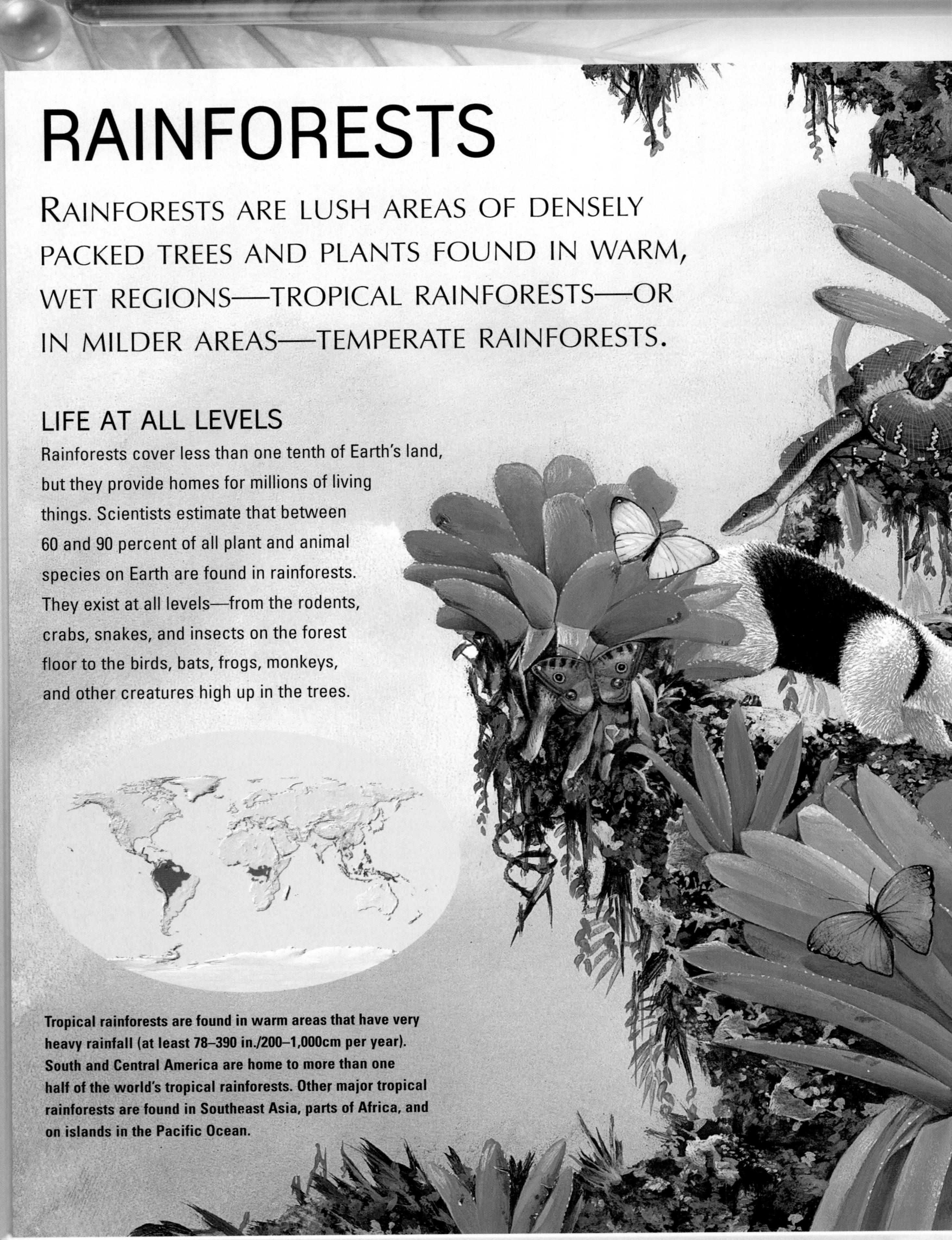

LIFE AT ALL LEVELS

Rainforests cover less than one tenth of Earth's land, but they provide homes for millions of living things. Scientists estimate that between 60 and 90 percent of all plant and animal species on Earth are found in rainforests. They exist at all levels—from the rodents, crabs, snakes, and insects on the forest floor to the birds, bats, frogs, monkeys, and other creatures high up in the trees.

Tropical rainforests are found in warm areas that have very heavy rainfall (at least 78–390 in./200–1,000cm per year). South and Central America are home to more than one half of the world's tropical rainforests. Other major tropical rainforests are found in Southeast Asia, parts of Africa, and on islands in the Pacific Ocean.

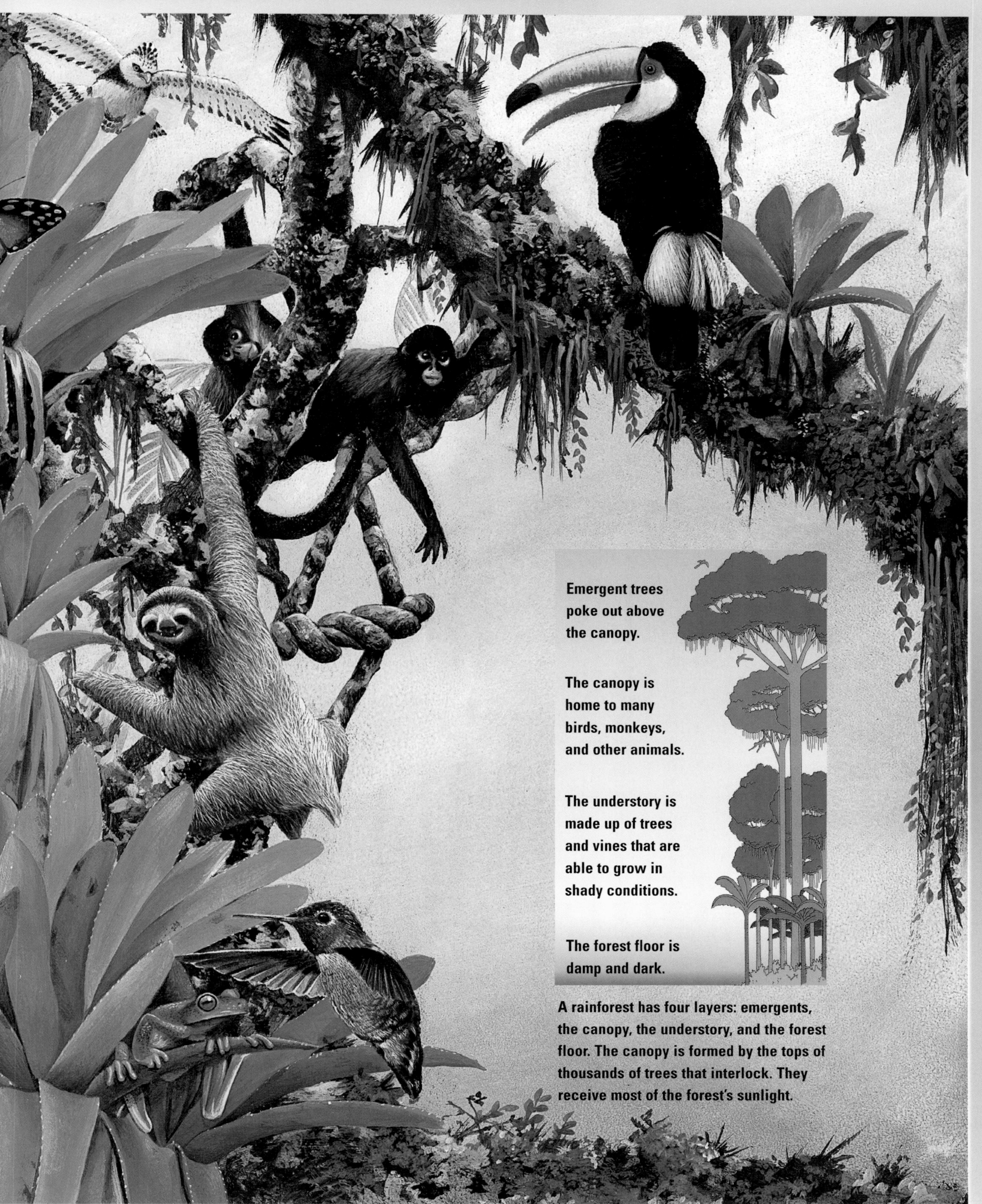

Emergent trees poke out above the canopy.
The canopy is home to many birds, monkeys, and other animals.
The understory is made up of trees and vines that are able to grow in shady conditions.
The forest floor is damp and dark.

A rainforest has four layers: emergents, the canopy, the understory, and the forest floor. The canopy is formed by the tops of thousands of trees that interlock. They receive most of the forest's sunlight.

Hot and cold deserts

Deserts cover around one fourth of the world's land and are the driest places on the planet. They are regions of the world where rainfall is less than 10 in. (250mm) per year.

Deserts are not always hot and sandy—cold deserts also exist. Whether they are hot or cold, deserts are difficult places for the hardy animals and plants that live there.

Finding water

For plants in hot deserts, collecting and storing water is crucial for survival. Some have long roots that go deep underground to seek out moisture. Others have fleshy stems that swell to store water, such as cacti, or collect water from fog, like the welwitschia plant.

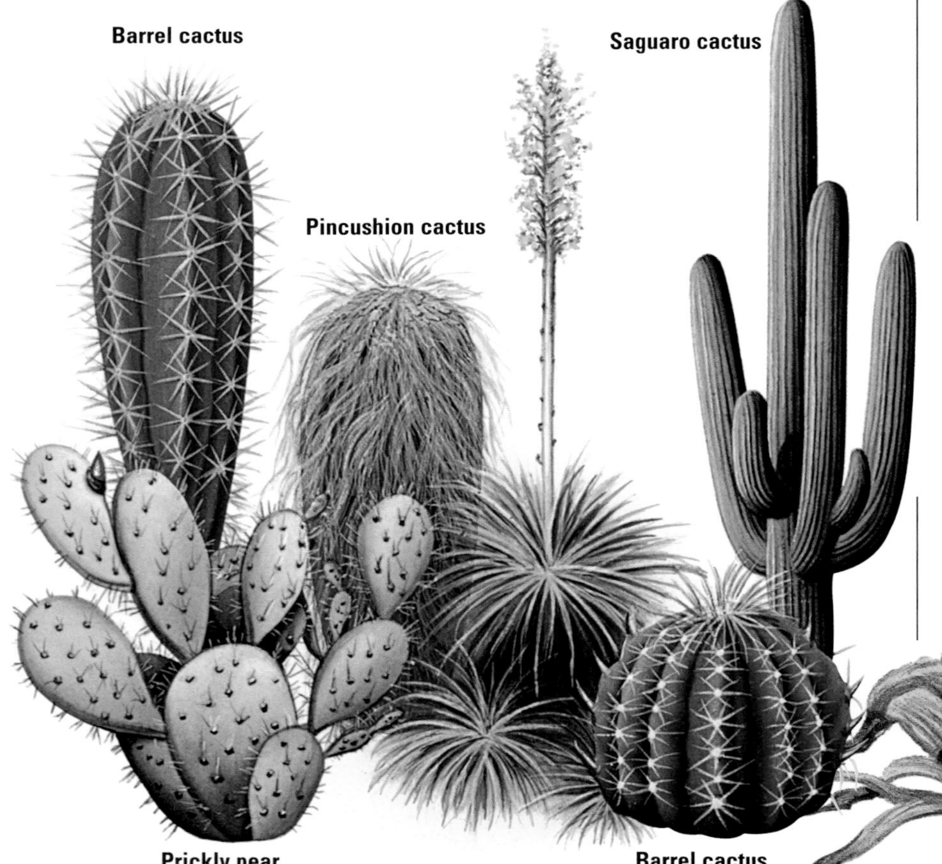

Desert creatures

Insects, reptiles, and some smaller animals get all their water from eating desert plants or seeking out water holes or oases. In hot deserts, many live underground in burrows, away from the searing heat. Many are nocturnal—sleeping during the day but active at night.

Welwitschia

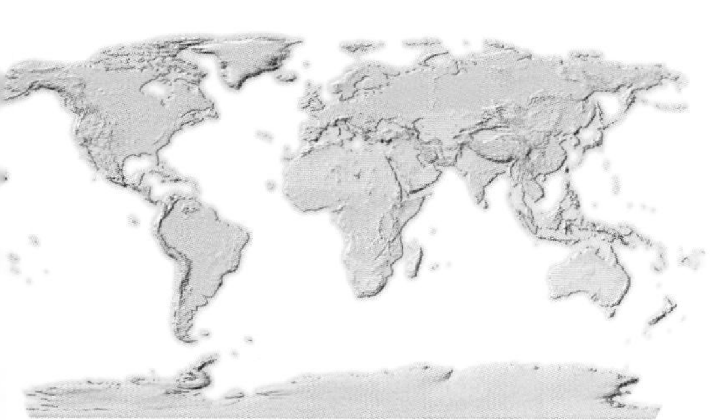

Desert regions

This map shows where the world's deserts are found. Hot deserts are on all of the continents except temperate Europe and frozen Antarctica. The largest desert is the Sahara, which covers most of North Africa. It is almost the same size as the United States and is growing each year.

The Arctic

The area called the Arctic encircles the North Pole and includes the Arctic Ocean. The ocean's high levels of fish provide food for Arctic peoples and some large mammals, including walrus and seals (above). Polar bears—the largest land meat eaters on Earth—also live there.

Antarctica

Antarctica is a mostly icy wasteland. Parts of the continent have less than 2.4 in. (60mm) of rain or snowfall each year. Average temperatures during the winter vary from –94°F (–70°C) to –4°F (–20°C). Penguins survive because of the thick layers of fat and feathers that help insulate them against the extreme cold.

The tundra

The tundra makes up around 15 percent of the planet's land. Only mosses, grasses, and some small bushes and trees can survive during its cold winter. In its short summer, plant life thrives, attracting millions of insects, birds, and some plant-eating animals such as lemmings and caribou. The soil beneath the ground surface remains frozen all year long.

OCEAN LIFE

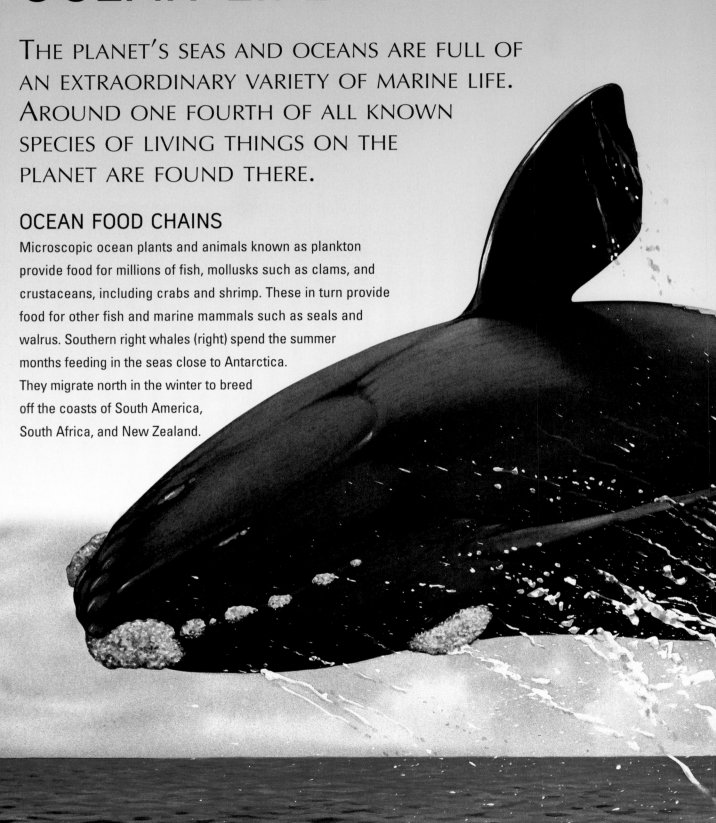

THE PLANET'S SEAS AND OCEANS ARE FULL OF AN EXTRAORDINARY VARIETY OF MARINE LIFE. AROUND ONE FOURTH OF ALL KNOWN SPECIES OF LIVING THINGS ON THE PLANET ARE FOUND THERE.

OCEAN FOOD CHAINS

Microscopic ocean plants and animals known as plankton provide food for millions of fish, mollusks such as clams, and crustaceans, including crabs and shrimp. These in turn provide food for other fish and marine mammals such as seals and walrus. Southern right whales (right) spend the summer months feeding in the seas close to Antarctica. They migrate north in the winter to breed off the coasts of South America, South Africa, and New Zealand.

CORAL REEFS

Corals live in warm, shallow waters and form reefs that provide a rich habitat for many plants, fish, and other creatures—reefs shelter more than one third of all marine life species. Corals are made up of animals called polyps. When they die, their hard skeletons help form a reef. Australia's Great Barrier Reef is the world's largest coral reef and is 1,240 mi. (2,000km) long.

SHALLOWS AND SEASHORES

While some creatures live in the ocean depths, most marine life exists much closer to the surface or in shallow water. Seashores, where a sea or ocean meets land, provide homes for many living things in rock pools, beaches, and cliff faces. Some animals have adapted to avoid being washed away by the tide. For example, clams dig deep in the sand, and limpets attach themselves to rocks.

Grasslands

Grasslands are biomes that feature gently rolling hills or flat land covered in grasses with some trees and bushes. These areas have distinct rainy and dry seasons during the year.

Grasses and other plant life grow very quickly during the rainy season. They provide plentiful food for rodents and birds, as well as for large herds of grazing animals and their predators.

North American plains

The North American plains, or prairies, were once home to huge herds of bison. Today, most of the land has been cultivated. It supports large herds of cattle and sheep or is planted with cereal crops such as wheat and corn.

African savanna

Savanna grasslands in Africa are hot and dry, but the rainy season triggers enough plant growth to support giant herds of antelope, zebras, wildebeests, and other grazing animals. The different animals graze in different ways and provide food for meat eaters such as lions, cheetahs, and hyenas. More than two million grazing animals follow the rainy season, migrating every year in October into an area of Tanzania known as the Serengeti Plain.

South American Pampas

The Pampas are large plains in South America that have rough grass or scrubs and very few trees. They cover an area of 292,500 sq. mi. (750,000km^2)—more than twice the size of Germany. They are home to many creatures, including cavies (below), which are wild guinea pigs.

Australian grasslands

Australia's grasslands provide homes for large numbers of insects, marsupials such as kangaroo, wallabies, koalas, and wombats, and birds such as emus and kookaburras. The land is covered in tough grasses and clumps of trees, including the wattle, eucalyptus, and thorny acacia.

Antelope on the Serengeti Plain

Natural resources

The natural world has many useful resources. These include food, energy, materials, and medicines that have been used by people for thousands of years.

NATURAL MATERIALS

Some plants provide valuable materials. People have learned to extract and use these.

Cotton is grown and woven into thread and millions of clothing items.

Fibers from the stem of the jute plant are processed to make twine, rope, and sacking.

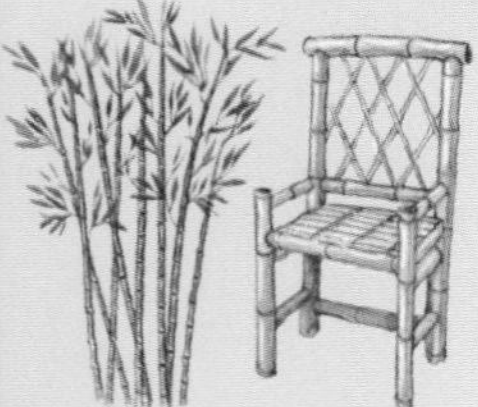

The flexible stems of bamboo plants are used to make furniture, fences, and other items.

Natural resources vary from country to country. Saudi Arabia, for example, has one fourth of the world's known reserves of oil.

Food and farming

Farming is the process of raising livestock animals and growing plant crops for food. Soil and climate help decide which crops are grown where. Corn (above) is the most common crop grown in North and South America.

Fishing

Around 200 million people work in the fishing industry. Most fish are caught in giant nets that trail from trawler ships. Fish and shellfish form a vital part of many people's diets.

Logging

Wood is one of the most useful and versatile of all natural resources. The logging industry chops down and transports trees. The wood is cut and processed to make many products. Wood fibers are used to make paper.

Materials for building

The natural world provides different materials for building. Many people live in huts made from bundled reeds (above), mud and grass, or clay bricks that have been left to dry and harden.

Renewable resources

These can be restocked or renewed over time. Some living things, such as trees, are renewable as long as they are not used up at a faster rate than they can be replaced. Solar, wind, and geothermal energy are also renewable resources.

Mining

Mining is the extraction of minerals from Earth's crust. These include metals such as aluminum, copper, and gold, gemstones, and coal. Marble and limestone, used for building, are dug out in quarries (right).

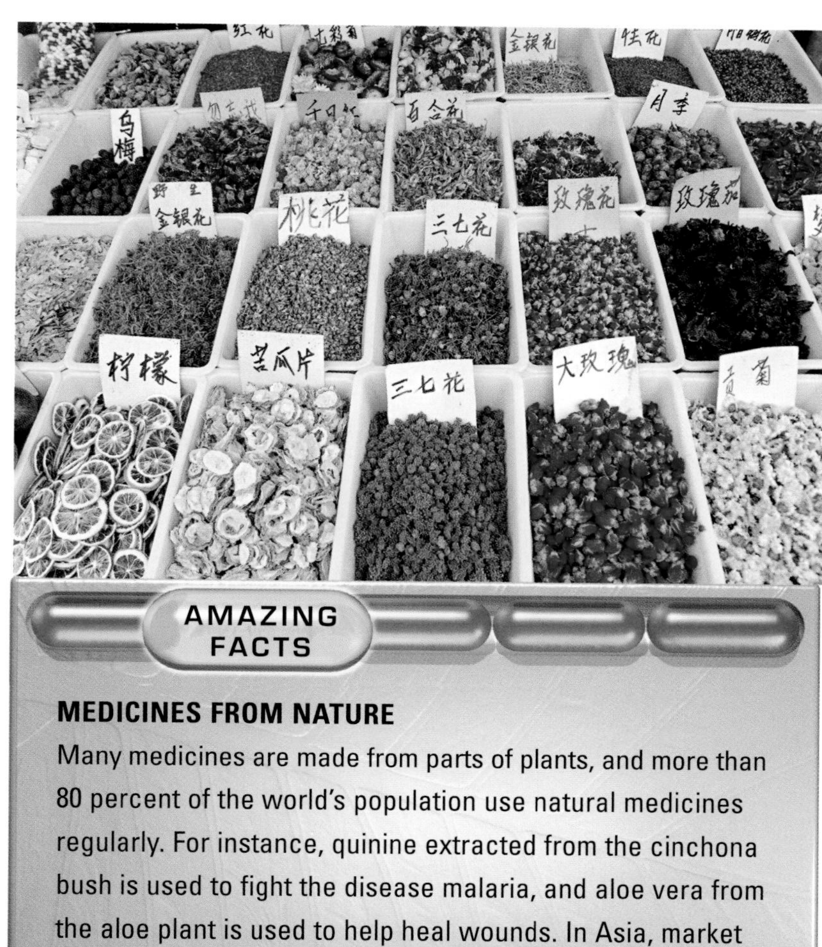

AMAZING FACTS

MEDICINES FROM NATURE

Many medicines are made from parts of plants, and more than 80 percent of the world's population use natural medicines regularly. For instance, quinine extracted from the cinchona bush is used to fight the disease malaria, and aloe vera from the aloe plant is used to help heal wounds. In Asia, market stands selling plant medicines are common (above).

Threats and conservation

Parts of the planet and many species of living things are under threat. This is mostly because of the growing numbers of people and the high demand for the planet's natural resources.

Conservation is about protecting and taking care of the natural world. Many projects try to reduce threats to habitats and ecosystems or look after threatened species.

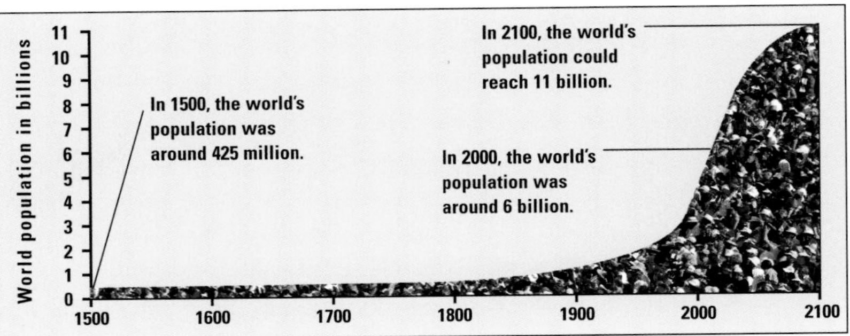

Population growth

The human population has boomed in the past 200 years. In just 40 years, from 1950 to 1990, it doubled. Today, more than 6.6 billion people live on Earth. And they all need food, water, shelter, and many other goods and services.

Pollution

If harmful substances are released, they can pollute the environment. They sometimes damage habitats, kill living things, and can be very hard to clean up. Pollution includes litter on land, oil spills in water (above), or smoke from factories and car exhausts in the air.

Three Gorges Dam

The giant Three Gorges Dam in China generates electricity from running water. The 607-ft. (185-m)-high, 1.4-mi. (2.3-km)-long dam is controversial because a large area of land had to be flooded in order for the dam to work. The flooding destroyed wildlife habitats.

Land clearance

Thousands of square miles of forests and other open land are cleared every year. People do this for fuel or wood to sell or to create farmland or space for settlements. This damages and destroys habitats for many animals and plants.

National parks

Many countries have set aside protected areas of their land and water as national parks. The goal is to preserve the natural environment and the species that live there. Most national parks receive large numbers of visitors.

Endangered species

More than 4,000 different species of plants and animals, including the tiger, are now very rare and under threat of extinction. Hunting, the destruction of habitats, and pollution are the main reasons for this.

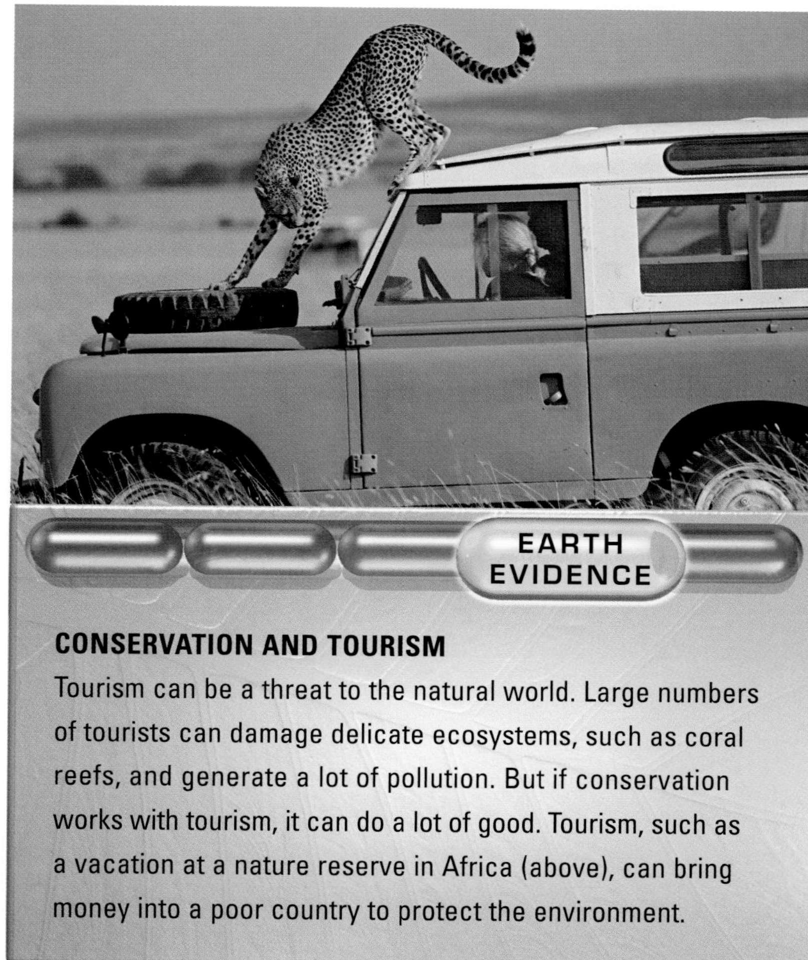

EARTH EVIDENCE

CONSERVATION AND TOURISM

Tourism can be a threat to the natural world. Large numbers of tourists can damage delicate ecosystems, such as coral reefs, and generate a lot of pollution. But if conservation works with tourism, it can do a lot of good. Tourism, such as a vacation at a nature reserve in Africa (above), can bring money into a poor country to protect the environment.

Living-world facts

Life on Earth varies dramatically. The planet's thousands of millions of living things live in a very large range of different habitats and conditions, from the hottest deserts and rainforests to warm seas, cold oceans, and the frozen Antarctic.

LARGEST FORESTED AREAS

Russian Federation 2 billion acres
Brazil 1.2 billion acres
Canada 766 million acres
United States 749 million acres
China 487 million acres
Australia 405 million acres
Democratic Republic of the Congo 331 million acres

LARGEST DESERTS

Sahara, northern Africa 3,549,000 sq. mi. (9,100,000km^2)
Gobi, Mongolia/China 507,000 sq. mi. (1,300,000km^2)
Patagonian, Argentina 261,300 sq. mi. (670,000km^2)
Rub al Khali, Saudi Arabia/Yemen/Oman 253,500 sq. mi. (650,000km^2)
Great Sandy, Australia 152,295 sq. mi. (390,500km^2)
Great Victoria, Australia 152,180 sq. mi. (390,500km^2)
Chihuahuan, Mexico/U.S. 140,400 sq. mi. (360,000km^2)

WEATHER RECORDS

Driest place on Earth: Calama, Atacama Desert, Chile, with zero annual average rainfall
Wettest place on Earth: La Réunion, Indian Ocean, 712 in. (1,825mm) in 24 hours
Coldest recorded temperature: Vostok Station, Antarctica, –128°F (–89°C)
Hottest recorded temperature: Al Aziziyah, Libya, 136.4°F (58°C)
Strongest wind (not a tornado): Mount Washington, New Hampshire, 231 mph (372km/h)

LARGEST PROTECTED AREAS

Northeast Greenland 379,080 sq. mi. (972,000km^2)
Rub al Khali, Saudi Arabia 253,500 sq. mi. (650,000km^2)
Great Barrier Reef, Australia 134,316 sq. mi. (344,400km^2)
Papahanaumokuakea Marine National Monument, Hawaii 133,131 sq. mi. (341,362km^2)

Sand dunes of the Sahara Desert stretching to the horizon

USEFUL WEBSITES

www.mbgnet.net/ A good introduction to different biomes, plant life, and reproduction.
www.cotf.edu/ete/modules/msese/earthsys.html A colorful website about planet Earth.
http://ology.amnh.org/biodiversity/index.html Describes biodiversity and its effects.
www.nws.noaa.gov The National Weather Service, listing forecasts and weather warnings.

Animal Life

The range of animal life on our planet is amazing. There are animals big enough to crush us and others too tiny to see without a microscope. All animals need to eat, and many spend most of their time trying not to be eaten themselves. Human life is fairly new to this planet by comparison to the arrival of many animals. But the biggest threat to many animals today comes from human activity.

What is an animal?

Animals are living things that eat plants and other creatures and breathe oxygen. They can move and sense their surroundings.

Some animals spend most of their time alone, rarely seeing other creatures, except when it's time to breed. Others live in social groups that can be huge—both humans and ants build settlements with millions of inhabitants.

Animal makeup

Animals have a lot in common with each other. Almost all animals have brains, eyes, ears, and legs. Animals are the only living things with muscles and nerves for movement and sensation.

Where animals live

The area where an animal lives is called its habitat. Habitats range from the top of a mountain to the seabed. Some animals, known as parasites, live on or inside other animals—for example, there are more than 1,000 types of parasites that can live inside humans. Animals are very adaptable, and some can even survive being frozen solid or dried out.

Orangutans live in the rainforests on the islands of Borneo and Sumatra.

Warm-blooded animals

Animals that are mammals are warm-blooded. They warm up or cool down in order to keep a constant body temperature. They may have fur to keep them warm or big ears to flap themselves cool. They may sweat to cool down and shiver to warm up.

Cold-blooded animals

Reptiles, amphibians, and fish all control their temperature by moving between hot and cool places. They bask in the sun to warm up, for example, and are less active when it is cold. These animals are known as ectotherms because their heat comes from outside of their body. They all tend to move slowly until they begin to warm up.

Invertebrates

Today, 97 percent of all animals are invertebrates. Like this sea anemone, invertebrates have no backbone—and usually no bones at all! There are some, however, such as snails, that have a shell on the outside of their bodies, or an exoskeleton.

Vertebrates

These animals have a backbone, usually connecting to other bones to form an internal skeleton. Fish, amphibians, reptiles (below), birds, and mammals are all in this group.

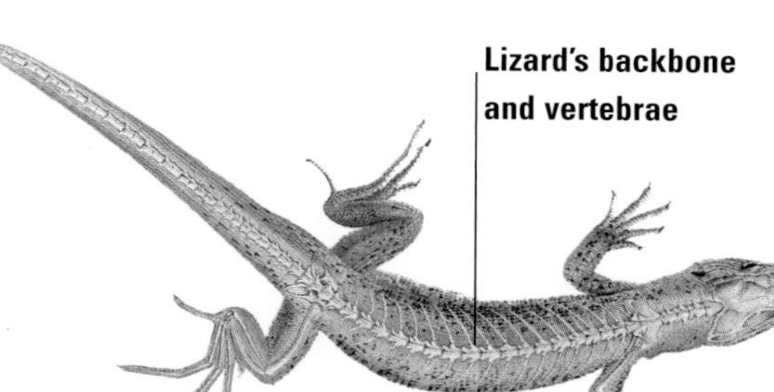

Lizard's backbone and vertebrae

AMAZING FACTS

PREDATOR AND PREY

Animals that hunt other creatures for food are called predators. Some run faster than their prey, whereas others sneak up, lie in wait, or make traps. They are equipped with weapons such as sharp teeth, claws, or poison to kill or stun. Defensive animals have a range of avoidance methods such as speed, color, spraying, hiding, or stingers. This ladybug (above) is advancing on its favorite food—a green aphid.

Evolution and extinction

Although around 30 million species are believed to live on Earth today, 4.5 billion have existed since life began. This means that almost all have become extinct.

CHANGING OVER TIME
Horses changed a lot over 55 million years, as they adapted to different habitats, climates, and roles.

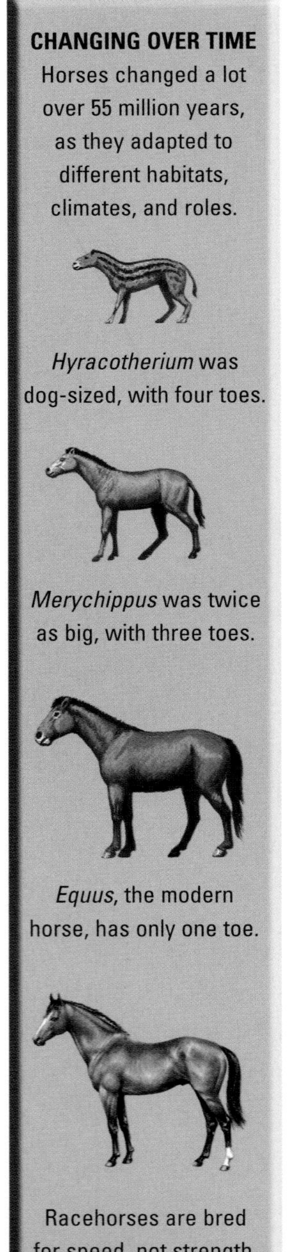

Hyracotherium was dog-sized, with four toes.

Merychippus was twice as big, with three toes.

Equus, the modern horse, has only one toe.

Racehorses are bred for speed, not strength.

Each generation of living things can be slightly different from the last one. Over a long period, these small changes become big differences. This is evolution—animals constantly adapting.

Adapt or die

Often animals must adapt or die out. Many extinctions were the result of changes in sea level, temperature, climate, or the gradual movement of landmasses.

The dodo was hunted to extinction in the 1600s.

Selective breeding

People have bred some animals to change their appearance, shape, and temperament. All dogs are descended from wolves, but some have been bred to hunt or to be sheepdogs or pets.

Natural selection

In his book *The Origin of Species* (1859), Charles Darwin showed how creatures have developed through "natural selection." Creatures compete for resources such as food, shelter, and mates. The weaker ones die, while the strong survivors slowly evolve over generations, as they adjust to any changes in their environment.

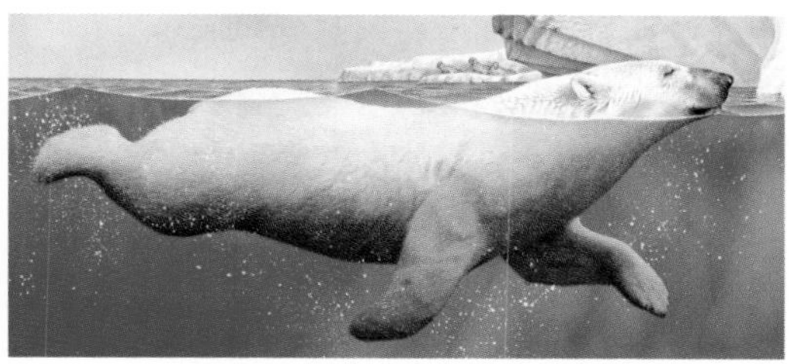

Suiting new environments

Animals adapt to new environments. The brown bears that moved to the colder north became better hunters and fighters. They developed more fat layers for warmth and paler fur for camouflage in the snow: they are now polar bears.

Fossil evidence

We know about animals from millions of years ago because of fossils—animal remains stored in rock. A sea animal, such as an ammonite, (1) sinks when it dies. Sediment covers it, (2) and it gradually hardens into rock (3). The fossilized shell can be preserved for millions of years (4).

Convergent evolution

This is when entirely different species develop similar features. For example, anteaters, armadillos, aardvarks, and echidnas all have sticky tongues for eating insects, but they are not closely related.

The anteater uses its long, sticky tongue to lick up termites from inside their mound.

EARTH EVIDENCE

END OF THE DINOSAURS

Dinosaurs died out 65 million years ago, having ruled Earth for 160 million years. No one knows exactly why, but it seems that the planet became much colder at this time. One idea is that a huge asteroid hit Earth, raising so much dust that it blocked out the Sun for months. This killed the plants that the herbivores fed on, which meant that the carnivores had nothing to eat. The "global winter" could also have been caused by volcanic eruptions.

CLASSIFYING NATURE

EVERYTHING THAT HAS EVER LIVED CAN BE GROUPED BY ITS CHARACTERISTICS, USING THE CLASSIFICATION SYSTEM DEVISED BY SWEDISH BOTANIST CAROLUS LINNAEUS IN THE 1700S. THIS SYSTEM USES LATIN SO THAT EVERYONE USES THE SAME TERMS.

THE FOUR ERAS

The Precambrian Era of life on Earth (purple) began 3.5 million years ago. The Paleozoic Era (blue) saw a huge rise in creatures and the beginning of plants. It was followed by the Mesozoic Era (green)—the age of reptiles. The Cenozoic Era (orange) is the age of mammals.

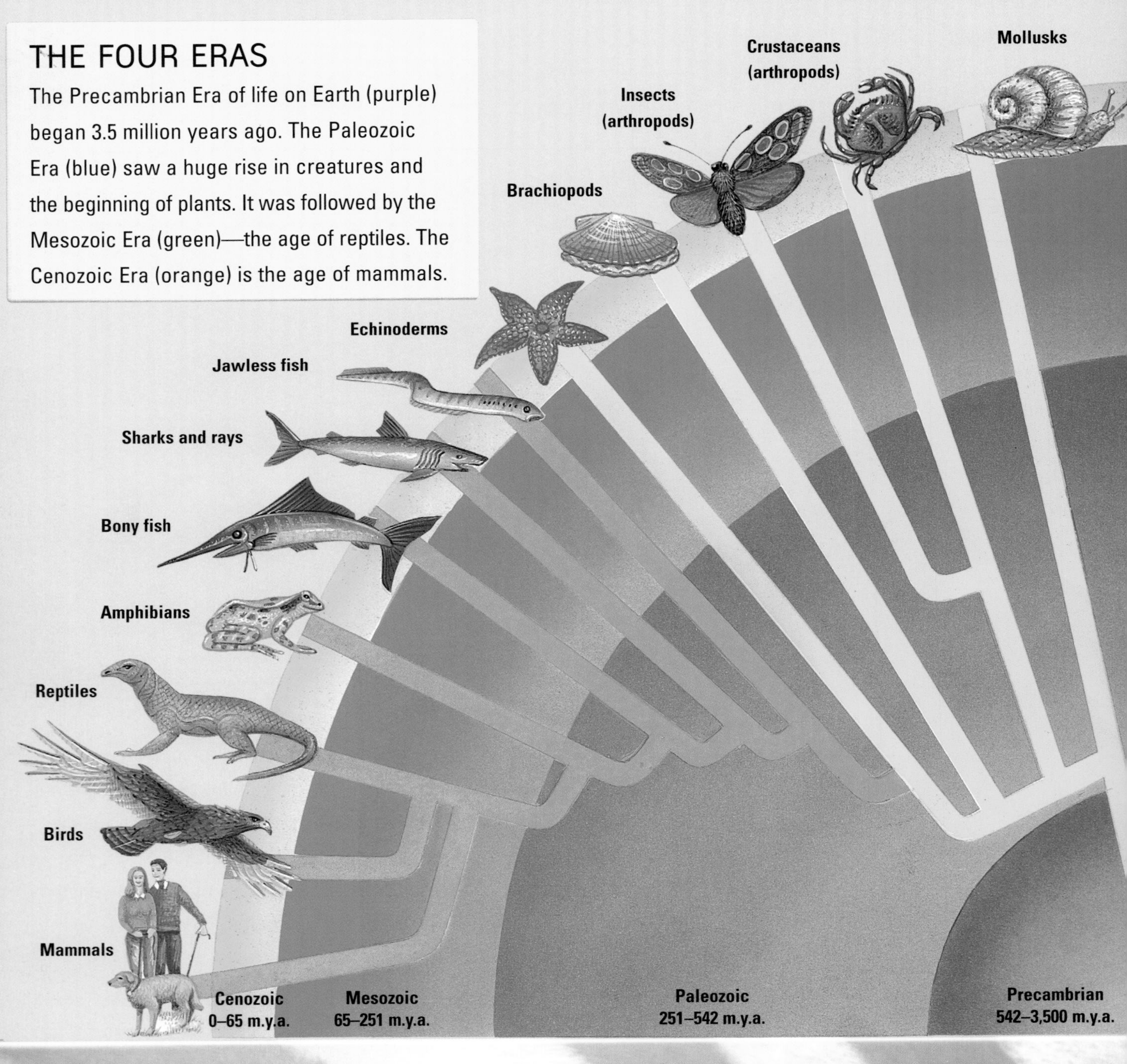

KINGDOMS

Living and once-living organisms are divided into groups called kingdoms—the largest of which are animals and plants. These are then divided into smaller groups, called phyla (*sing.* phylum). There are more than 20 phyla in the animal kingdom.

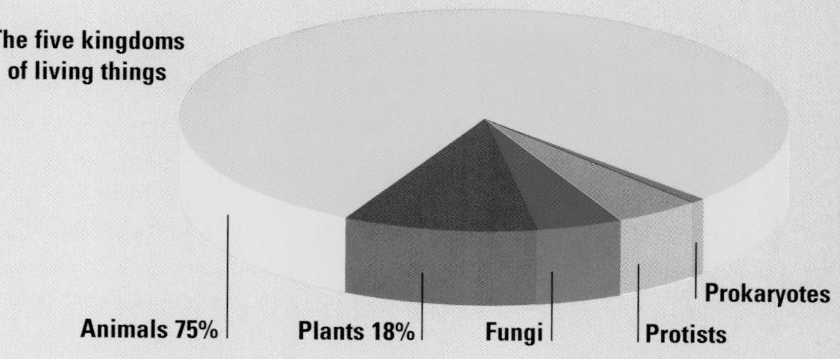

CLASS, FAMILY, AND SPECIES

Each phylum is divided by class, order, family, genus, and species. For example, humans are in the phylum Chordata (with backbones), class Mammalia (animals with hair that produce milk), order Primates (refined hands and feet and a large brain), family Hominidae (great apes), genus *Homo* (humans), and species *Sapiens* (thinking man).

Worms
Cnidarians
Single-celled organisms, sponges
Single-celled organisms
Bacteria
Fungi
Algae
Mosses
Ferns
Cycads
Conifers
Flowering plants

Precambrian 3,500–542 m.y.a.
Paleozoic 542–251 m.y.a.
Mesozoic 251–65 m.y.a.
Cenozoic 65–0 m.y.a.

How animal life developed

Life on Earth developed over billions of years and began as tiny, single-celled creatures. All these early animals were invertebrates, with no bones, and lived in the sea.

Scientists believe that life began 3.5 billion years ago, when chemicals containing carbon were mixed by chance. They combined to become living things.

Bacteria floating in seawater

First life

The first single-celled organisms were bacteria and amoebas. They floated in the warm, nutrient-rich sea, surviving either by eating tiny particles or by making their own food from sunlight. They still exist all over the world today.

Worms

The first worms were flat and small, and many of them lived inside other animals as parasites. Slowly, they developed thin, round bodies that were like a protective tube. The next stage of evolution was a segmented body that made burrowing into mud easier.

Worms are invertebrates.

Sponges collect food by pumping water through their bodies.

Multicelled creatures

Around one billion years ago, more complex, multicelled creatures evolved. Early ones, such as sponges, are groups of cells that can live separately or together, can become very large, but cannot move themselves around. Later ones, such as jellyfish and sea anemones, are much more complicated. For instance, they can hunt or protect themselves by stinging other creatures.

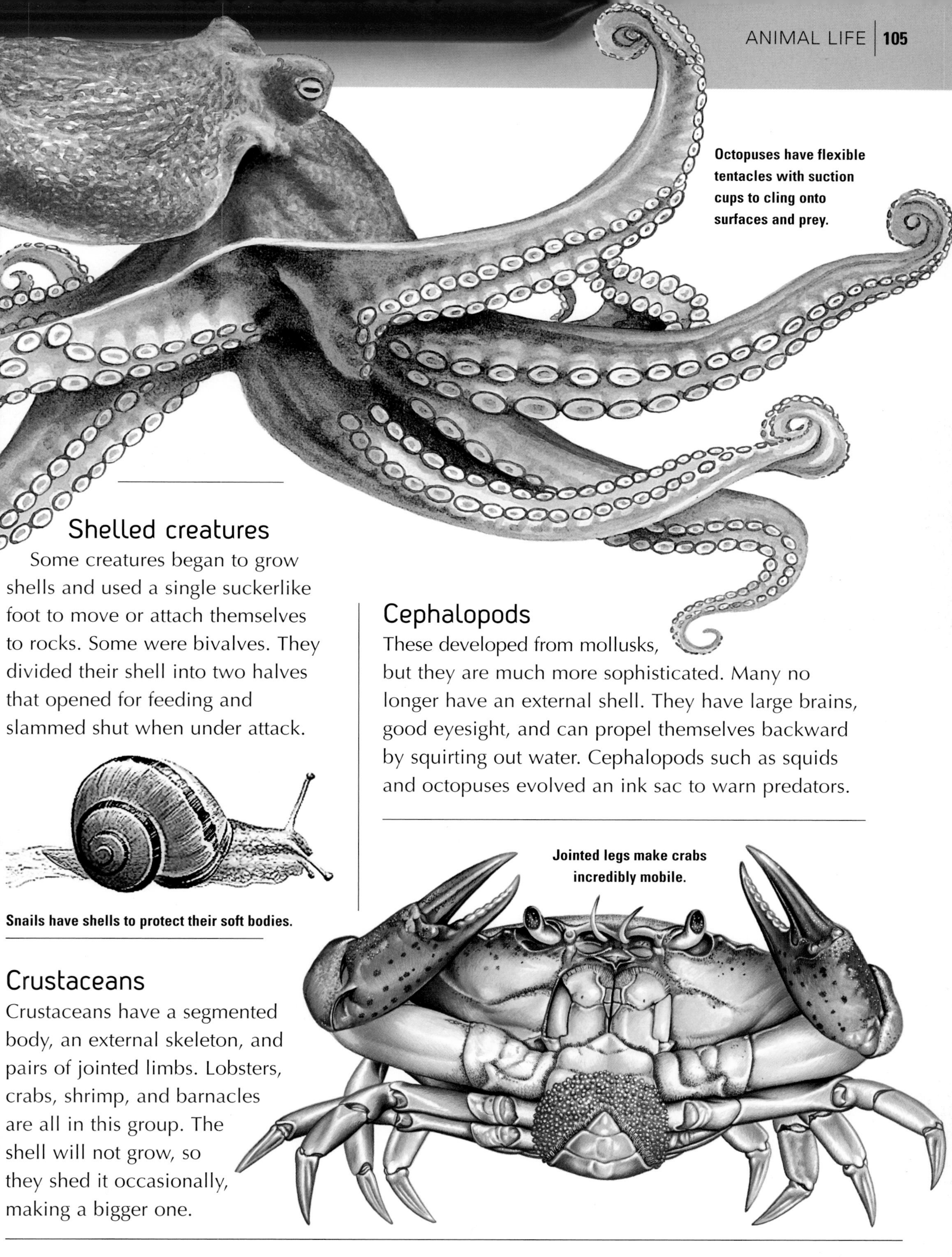

Octopuses have flexible tentacles with suction cups to cling onto surfaces and prey.

Shelled creatures

Some creatures began to grow shells and used a single suckerlike foot to move or attach themselves to rocks. Some were bivalves. They divided their shell into two halves that opened for feeding and slammed shut when under attack.

Snails have shells to protect their soft bodies.

Crustaceans

Crustaceans have a segmented body, an external skeleton, and pairs of jointed limbs. Lobsters, crabs, shrimp, and barnacles are all in this group. The shell will not grow, so they shed it occasionally, making a bigger one.

Cephalopods

These developed from mollusks, but they are much more sophisticated. Many no longer have an external shell. They have large brains, good eyesight, and can propel themselves backward by squirting out water. Cephalopods such as squids and octopuses evolved an ink sac to warn predators.

Jointed legs make crabs incredibly mobile.

Primates

The 180 species of primates have long limbs with flexible fingers and toes and forward-facing eyes. Most have nails instead of claws. The most advanced primates (including humans) are intelligent and live in social groups.

Most primates are suited to living in forests and survive mostly on fruit and vegetation, although some also eat meat. Many are under threat, either because they are being hunted or because their habitat is destroyed.

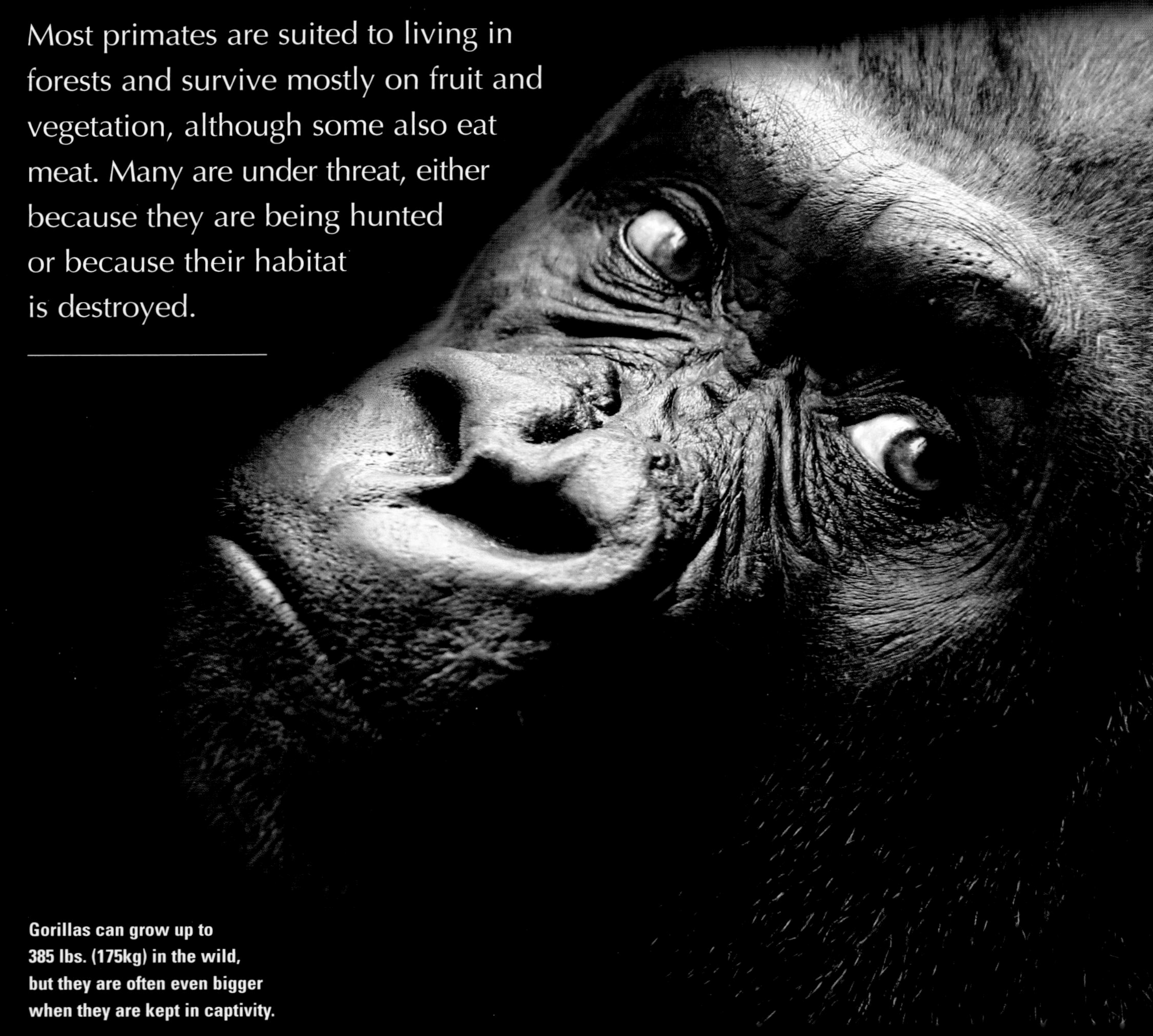

Gorillas can grow up to 385 lbs. (175kg) in the wild, but they are often even bigger when they are kept in captivity.

Monkeys

With their grasping hands and a long tail to help them balance, monkeys such as these howler monkeys are excellent at climbing, swinging, and running from tree to tree. They have tough pads to protect their bottoms when they sit and big stomachs to help them digest their main diet of leaves.

Humans

Like apes, humans have no external tail. Unlike apes, they do not have body hair all over, so they need clothes for warmth. Humans walk upright on two long, straight legs with large feet. They take a long time to grow, have the biggest and most complex brains on Earth, and are the only animals to use spoken and written languages.

Lemurs

Only found in Madagascar, off the coast of east Africa, lemurs have flourished because there are no rival primates. Ring-tailed lemurs have long, striped tails so that they can see each other as they forage for food on the ground.

pes

ılike monkeys, apes have no tail. e largest apes are gorillas. The most elligent apes are chimpanzees, which e sticks and stones as tools and pass s knowledge on to their young. Apes lk on all fours, supporting their weight their knuckles. They live socially in ge groups of up to 40.

Other mammals

Mammals replaced the ancient reptiles as the dominant animals
our planet. This is because mammals are able to adapt to so m
habitats on land and in the sea—there are even some that fly.

There are around 4,500 species of mammals. All have bones, teeth, some hair or fur, breathe through lungs, and give their young milk—even the dolphin, one of the few sea mammals.

Warm-blooded animals

All mammals, including humans, keep a constant body temperature of just under 98.6°F (37°C), unlike cold-blooded animals. This means that they can stay active all the time. In most mammals, hair, or fur helps keep heat in.

Flying mammals

Bats are the only flying mammals. Their wings are flaps of skin that connect their fingers together. Most bats have poor eyesight. Instead—like dolphins—they use echolocation. They send out bursts of high-pitched sounds to get an idea of their surroundings from how fast the sound bounces back.

MARSUPIAL GROWTH

Kangaroo and koalas give birth to live young that then grow in a body pouch.

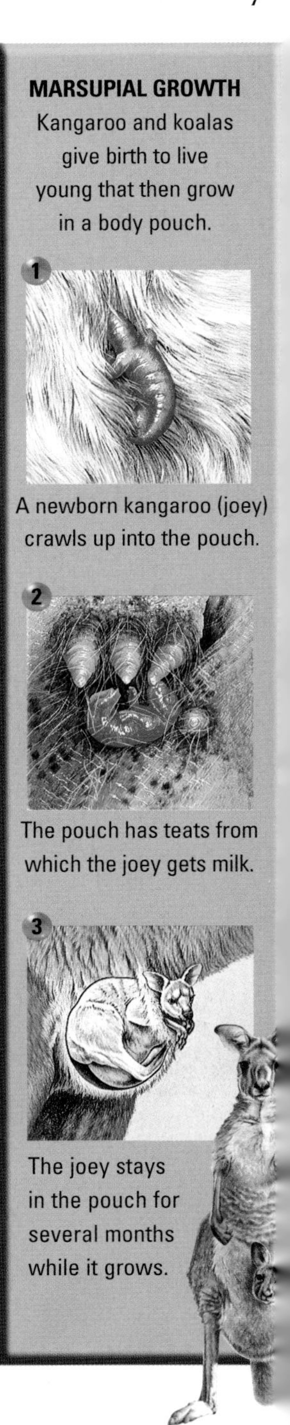

1 A newborn kangaroo (joey) crawls up into the pouch.

2 The pouch has teats from which the joey gets milk.

3 The joey stays in the pouch for several months while it grows.

Biggest mammal

The blue whale grows up to 108 ft. (33m) long and weighs up to 180 tons. Its heart is the size of a small car. It has no teeth, so in order to feed, it opens its massive mouth wide to take in water. It then filters out its food—tiny sea creatures called krill. The blue whale can swallow 3.6 tons of krill each day.

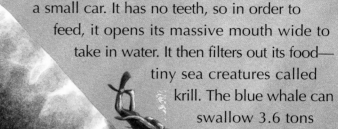

Monotremes

These are the only egg-laying mammals. These primitive animals include the platypus (below) and are found in Australia and New Guinea. The mother lays eggs but provides the young with milk.

Large cats

The lion is one of the five big cats—the others are the tiger, jaguar, leopard, and snow leopard. This male lion can rest out in the open because lions have no natural predators. He protects the pride, or group, while the females cooperate to hunt down their diet of fresh meat. Most other big cats hunt alone.

Smallest land mammal

An adult pygmy shrew weighs only 0.07 oz. (2g). It needs to eat all the time in order to stay alive, consuming its own weight in bugs and insects every day. Its heart beats 750 times per minute, but this almost doubles when it is frightened. It releases a foul-tasting liquid to deter predators.

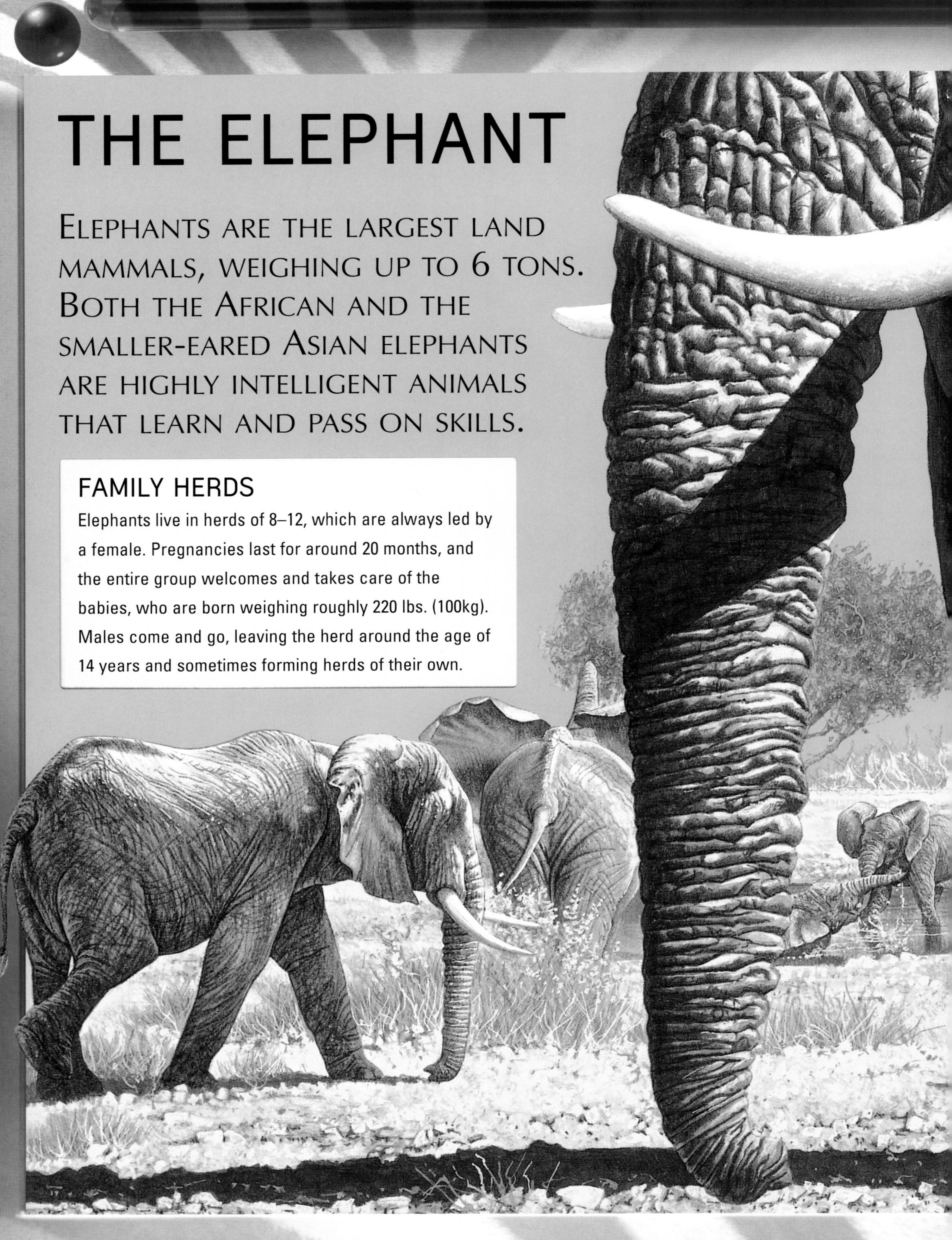

THE ELEPHANT

ELEPHANTS ARE THE LARGEST LAND MAMMALS, WEIGHING UP TO 6 TONS. BOTH THE AFRICAN AND THE SMALLER-EARED ASIAN ELEPHANTS ARE HIGHLY INTELLIGENT ANIMALS THAT LEARN AND PASS ON SKILLS.

FAMILY HERDS

Elephants live in herds of 8–12, which are always led by a female. Pregnancies last for around 20 months, and the entire group welcomes and takes care of the babies, who are born weighing roughly 220 lbs. (100kg). Males come and go, leaving the herd around the age of 14 years and sometimes forming herds of their own.

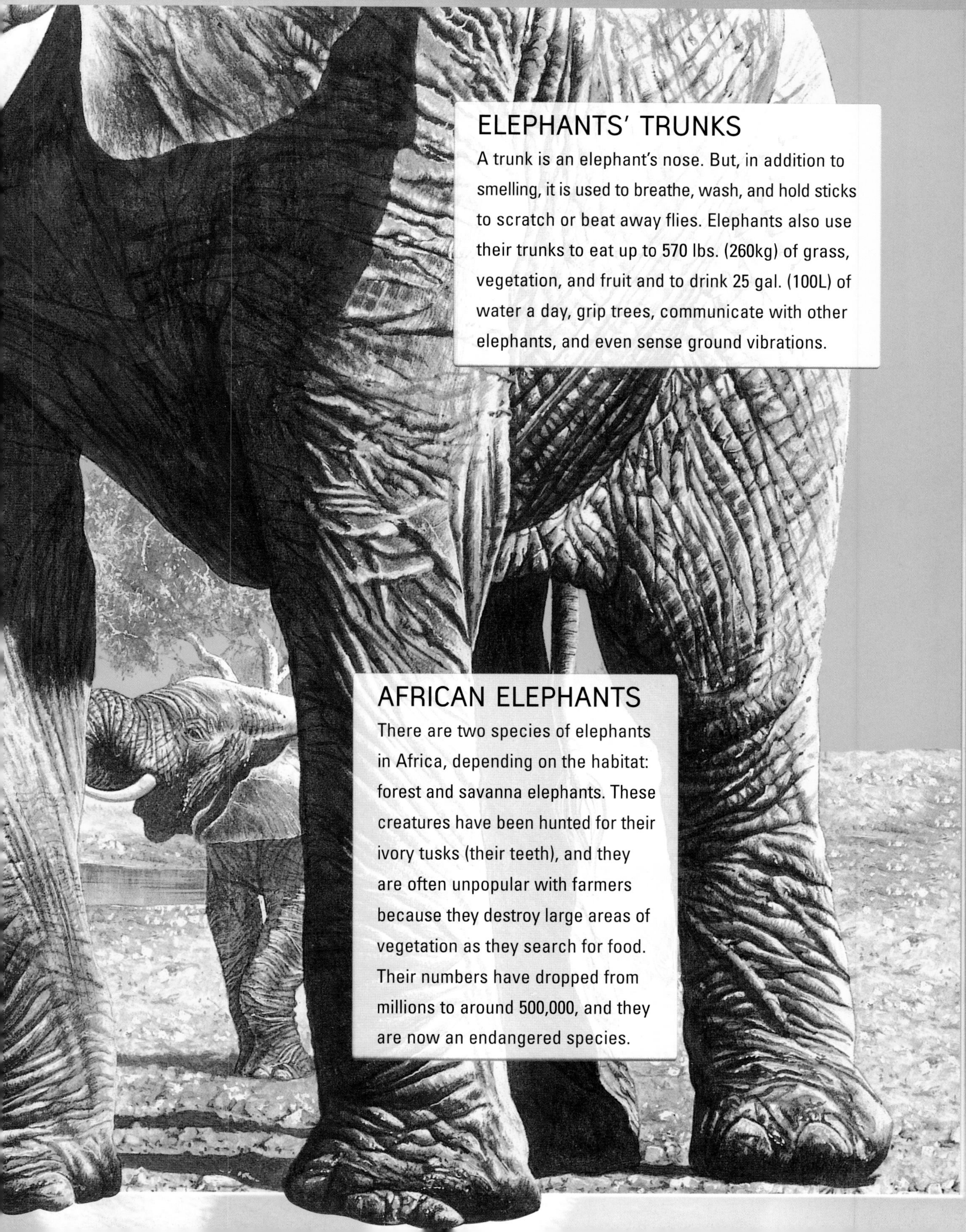

ELEPHANTS' TRUNKS

A trunk is an elephant's nose. But, in addition to smelling, it is used to breathe, wash, and hold sticks to scratch or beat away flies. Elephants also use their trunks to eat up to 570 lbs. (260kg) of grass, vegetation, and fruit and to drink 25 gal. (100L) of water a day, grip trees, communicate with other elephants, and even sense ground vibrations.

AFRICAN ELEPHANTS

There are two species of elephants in Africa, depending on the habitat: forest and savanna elephants. These creatures have been hunted for their ivory tusks (their teeth), and they are often unpopular with farmers because they destroy large areas of vegetation as they search for food. Their numbers have dropped from millions to around 500,000, and they are now an endangered species.

Birds

Birds fly by flapping their wings or by gliding. They are the only vertebrates that can do so. They are also the only animal with feathers.

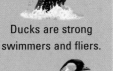

WATER BIRDS
Waterfowl, such as ducks and geese, are good swimmers, with webbed feet.

Ducks are strong swimmers and fliers.

Geese live together in large flocks

Herons are wading birds, with long, thin legs.

Swans are the largest of the waterfowl.

There are around 9,600 species of birds. Their flying ability allows them to live in places that other animals cannot easily reach such as cliffs and crags.

Sea birds

The sea and the shoreline are rich sources of food and attract many sea birds. Some only come to land in order to breed and raise their young. Black frigate birds (above) attack tropicbirds and steal their prey.

Birds of prey

These hunting birds only eat fresh meat. They can see four times better than humans can and spot prey from high above. They have sharp claws called talons for grabbing and hooked beaks for killing their prey.

Flightless birds

Some birds, such as rheas, emus, and cassowaries, are flightless. They are fast runners instead. Ostrich are the fastest, at 45 mph (72km/h). Others, such as the emperor penguins of Antarctica (below), are excellent swimmers.

Tropical birds

Exotic birds live in tropical rainforests and other warm habitats, where they live off the plentiful fruit. These birds include parrots (above)—the only bird that holds food with its feet—and are brightly colored to ward off predators.

Wading birds

These birds have long legs or bills to feed in the shallows and at the water's edge. Flamingos (above) use their bills to filter out the mud from the small plants and animals that they eat.

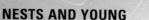

SCIENTIFIC INPUT

NESTS AND YOUNG

Birds lay eggs that then hatch into young. They often build nests in trees and other inaccessible places in order to protect them from predators. The females lay up to 20 eggs, depending on the species, and most sit on the eggs to keep them warm until they hatch. The chicks eat the food in the egg before pecking their way out through the shell. Often, both parents help feed the chicks until they can fend for themselves.

Snakes

Snakes are reptiles without legs, eyelids, or external ears. Their skin is covered with smooth, dry scales. They live anywhere that is warm.

Of the 2,700 species of snakes, around 700 are venomous. These have fangs through which they inject prey with poison that paralyzes, stuns, or kills.

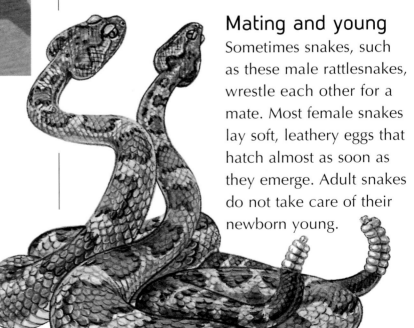

An anaconda prepares to swallow a capybara whole.

Diet and prey

Snakes are carnivorous, eating only meat or eggs. They either grab, stun, or constrict— squeeze and suffocate—their prey. The prey is always whole when the snake squeezes it past its elastic jaws.

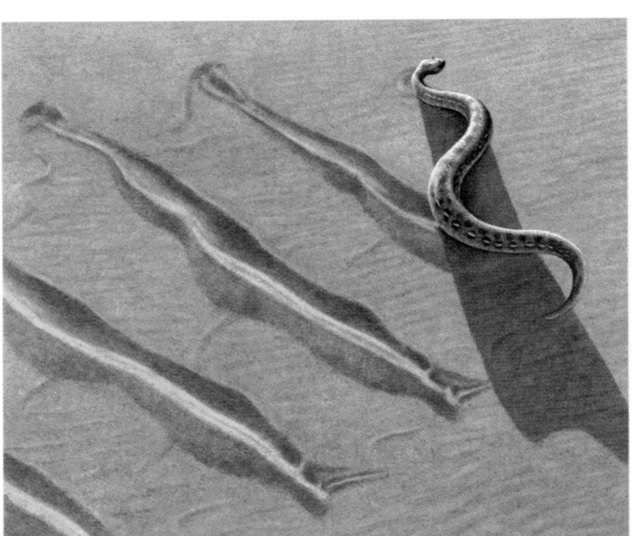

Movement

Snakes have different ways of moving. Some wiggle from side to side, some thrust the front of their body forward, while others raise and flatten the scales on their underside. The sidewinder (above) throws its body sideways across the sand. Some snakes can reach 12 mph (20km/h) in short bursts, which is fast enough to catch a running animal.

Mating and young

Sometimes snakes, such as these male rattlesnakes, wrestle each other for a mate. Most female snakes lay soft, leathery eggs that hatch almost as soon as they emerge. Adult snakes do not take care of their newborn young.

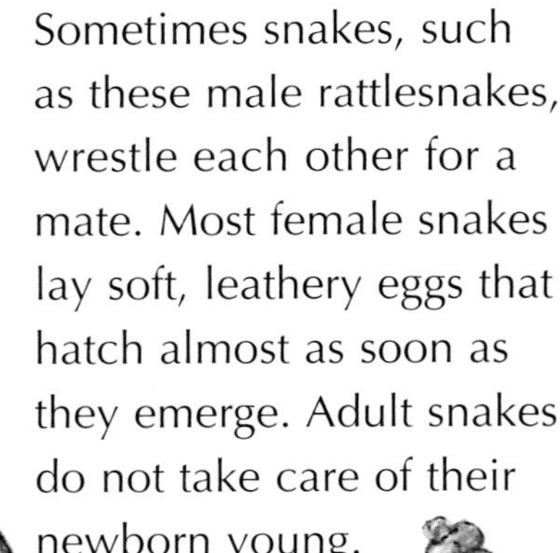

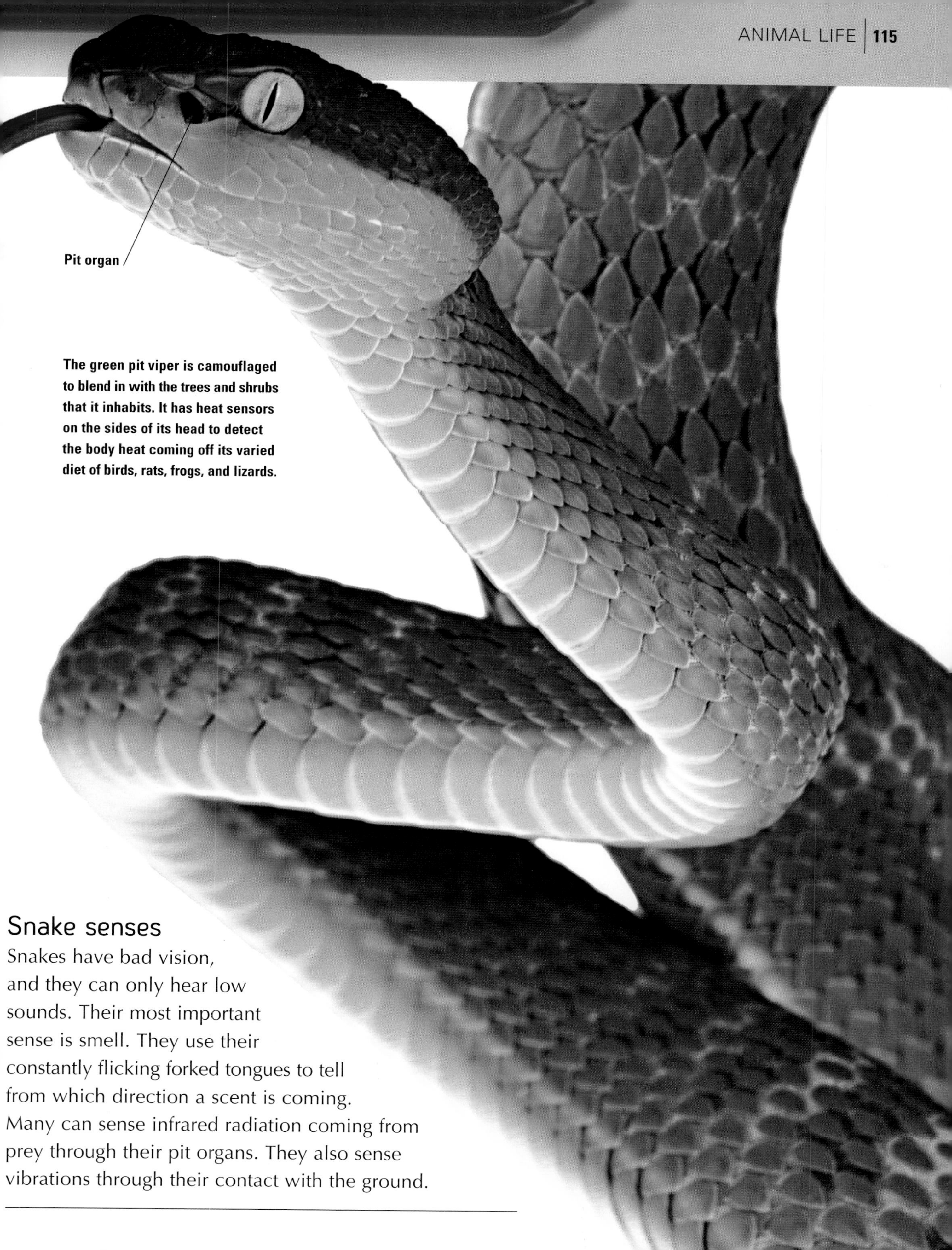

The green pit viper is camouflaged to blend in with the trees and shrubs that it inhabits. It has heat sensors on the sides of its head to detect the body heat coming off its varied diet of birds, rats, frogs, and lizards.

Snake senses

Snakes have bad vision, and they can only hear low sounds. Their most important sense is smell. They use their constantly flicking forked tongues to tell from which direction a scent is coming. Many can sense infrared radiation coming from prey through their pit organs. They also sense vibrations through their contact with the ground.

Other reptiles

Reptiles were the first animals with backbones that were able to survive on land. They now live on every continent except for Antarctica.

Reptile skin is tough because it is covered with scales made of tough keratin. It does not grow so it must be shed occasionally.

TURTLE BIRTH
Most reptiles lay eggs. Sea turtles return to land to lay eggs in the sand.

1 The female drags herself onto the beach.

2 She lays her eggs and returns to the sea.

3 The hatchlings use their snouts to break out.

4 They crawl toward the safety of the sea.

Tortoises and turtles

These are the only reptiles with hard shells, into which they can pull their heads, legs, and tails for protection. Turtles (left) live in water, while tortoises (above) stay on land.

Chameleons

These animals can change color to match their surroundings. They use this camouflage in order to hide in trees during the day, mostly coming out at night to catch their insect prey.

Lizards

Lizards usually have a long tail and four legs that stick out sideways, so they sway from side to side as they move. Many lizards can shed their tails to flee from predators. Most live on the ground, but some are good climbers.

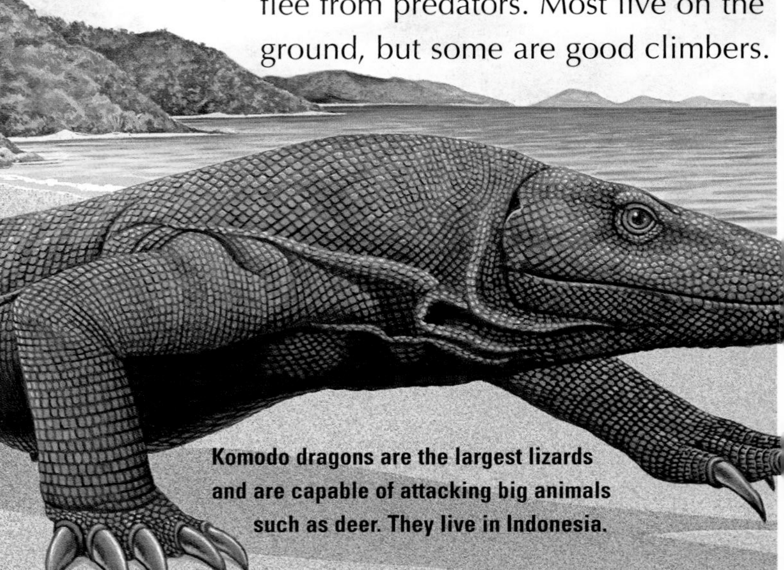

Komodo dragons are the largest lizards and are capable of attacking big animals such as deer. They live in Indonesia.

Lizard defense

When threatened, the frilled lizard makes itself look big and frightening by unfurling its yellow and red frill like an umbrella, showing its teeth, hissing, and waving its tail. If that fails, it scurries up the nearest tree.

Alligators live in the U.S.A. and China.

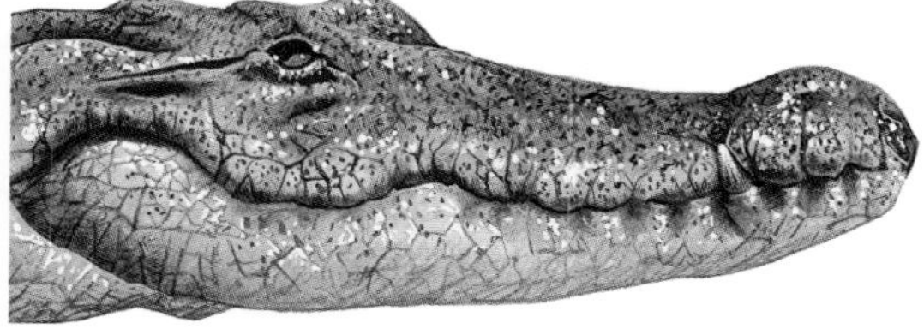

Crocodiles live in Africa, Asia, the Americas, and Australia.

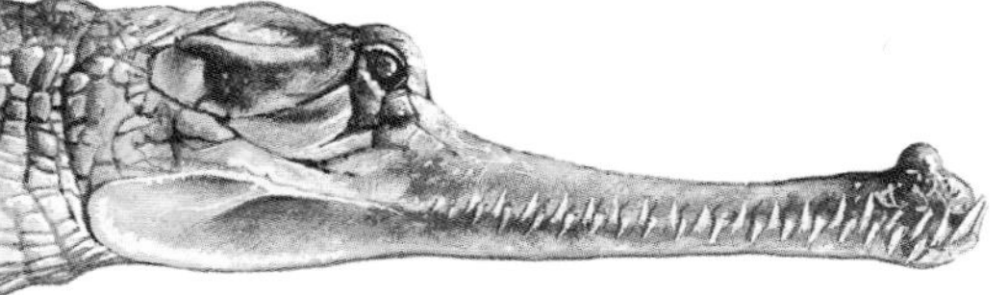

Gharials live in Asia.

Crocodiles and alligators

These reptiles lie low in the water with just their eyes and nostrils above the surface. Gharials have narrow snouts for catching fish. The crocodile's lower front teeth stick out when its mouth is closed.

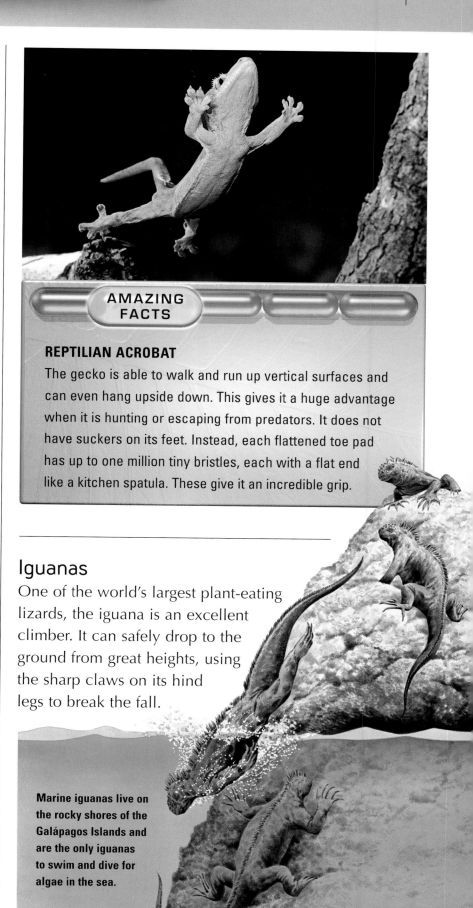

AMAZING FACTS

REPTILIAN ACROBAT

The gecko is able to walk and run up vertical surfaces and can even hang upside down. This gives it a huge advantage when it is hunting or escaping from predators. It does not have suckers on its feet. Instead, each flattened toe pad has up to one million tiny bristles, each with a flat end like a kitchen spatula. These give it an incredible grip.

Iguanas

One of the world's largest plant-eating lizards, the iguana is an excellent climber. It can safely drop to the ground from great heights, using the sharp claws on its hind legs to break the fall.

Marine iguanas live on the rocky shores of the Galápagos Islands and are the only iguanas to swim and dive for algae in the sea.

Amphibians

Amphibians can live both in and out of water. They thrive in many different habitats—deserts, mountains, rainforests—as long as there is fresh water. They are cold-blooded.

Toads have warty skin.

Amphibians breathe through gills (like fish) or lungs (like mammals) or sometimes both. Most adult amphibians can also breathe through their smooth, hairless skin.

Self-protection

Since they have no fur, feathers, or claws, amphibians are tempting snacks. They protect themselves with poison glands that irritate the mouth and eyes of attackers. Some have brightly colored skin to warn off predators.

Metamorphosis

The young of amphibians grow by metamorphosis—they change form as they develop. They start in a clump of eggs called spawn, become larvae or tadpoles with gills, and finally develop lungs and legs.

Frogs and toads

Both frogs and toads have bulging eyes, sticky-tipped tongues, and short, fat bodies with webbed feet. Frogs usually wait for their prey to pass by, while toads stalk their victims.

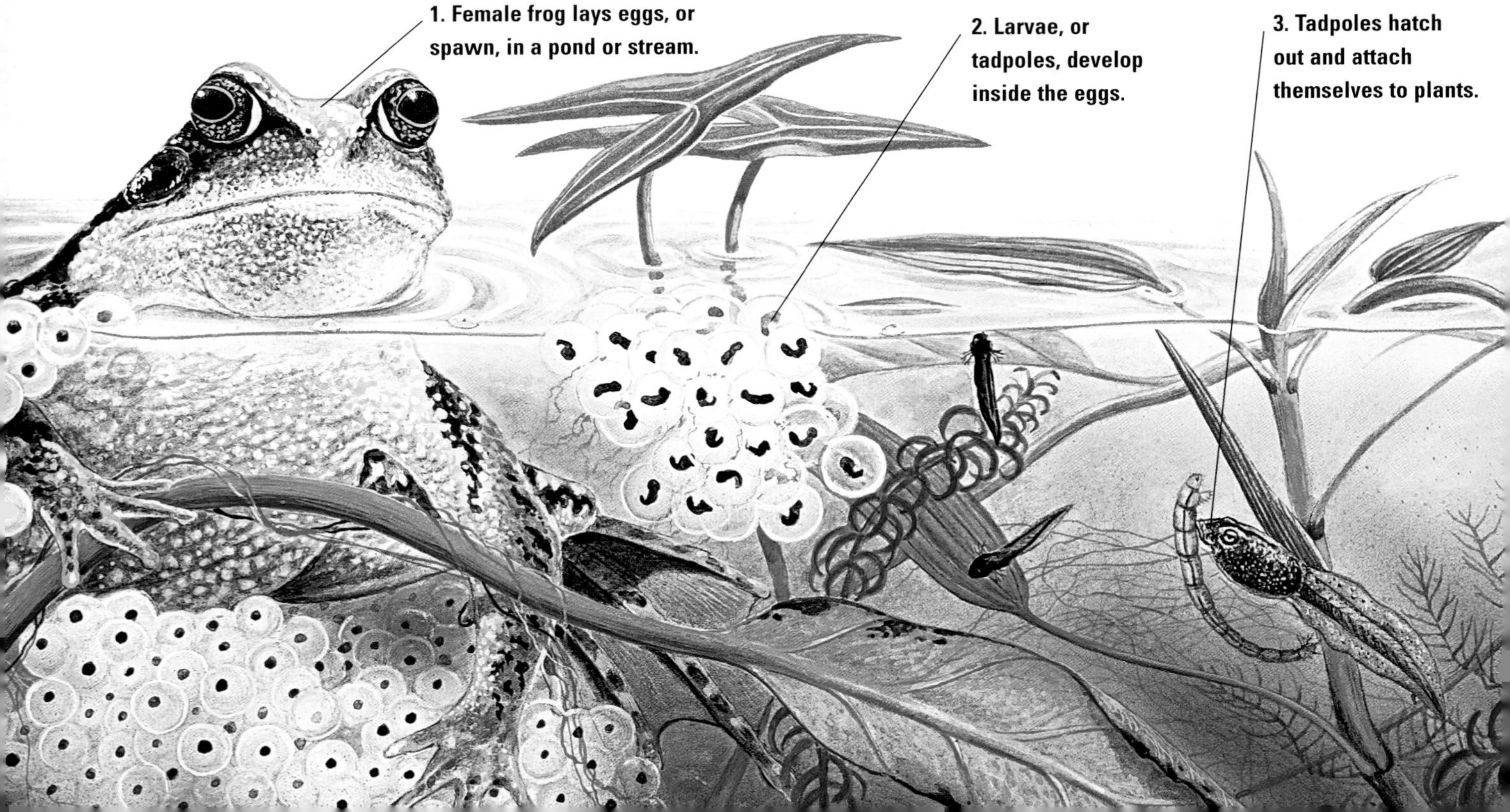

1. Female frog lays eggs, or spawn, in a pond or stream.

2. Larvae, or tadpoles, develop inside the eggs.

3. Tadpoles hatch out and attach themselves to plants.

Fire
salamander

Salamanders

These amphibians live close to or in water and have a long tail and short legs. They can grow these again if one is cut off. The fire salamander (above) has distinctive yellow and black markings and hunts prey at night.

Communication

Frogs and toads use sound to communicate. The loudest fill up pouches of stretchy skin in their throats with air, releasing it to make a distinctive croak.

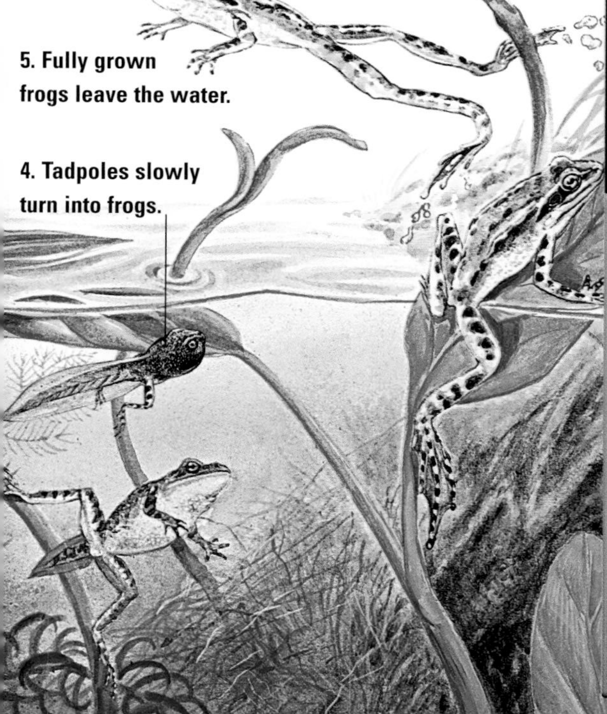
5. Fully grown frogs leave the water.
4. Tadpoles slowly turn into frogs.

Newts

This amphibian has no grooves on its body. Most newts are aquatic or semiaquatic, but some have adapted to life on land, returning to water only to breed. They swallow their fish and insect prey whole.

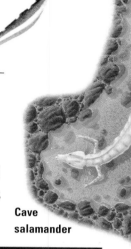

Crested newt

Cave dweller

Cave salamanders are thin enough to wiggle between rocks and cave walls as they hunt for insects and worms. The blind cave salamander (right) has scarlet gill tufts for breathing on both sides of its head.

Cave salamander

AMAZING FACTS

LIFE IN THE TREETOPS

Tree frogs have extra thick skin to help them survive their dry habitat in the treetops. They are small and lightweight, but they are exceptional climbers because they have sticky pads on the ends of their curled fingers and toes. These pads are filled with a gluelike mucus that allows them to rest on the most slippery leaf. Some tree frogs can leap through the air, spreading their toes like a parachute to glide safely onto a branch.

MIGRATION

SOME ANIMALS FOLLOW A PATTERN OF MOVEMENT DURING THE YEAR, TRAVELING GREAT DISTANCES TO FIND FOOD, TO ESCAPE THE COLD, OR TO BREED. SOME SEEM TO REMEMBER WHERE TO GO, WHEREAS OTHERS USE LANDMARKS OR EVEN NAVIGATE BY THE STARS. STRANGELY, BIRDS OFTEN FLY PAST SUITABLE HABITATS ON THEIR GLOBETROTTING JOURNEYS, POSSIBLY FOLLOWING ANCIENT INSTINCTS.

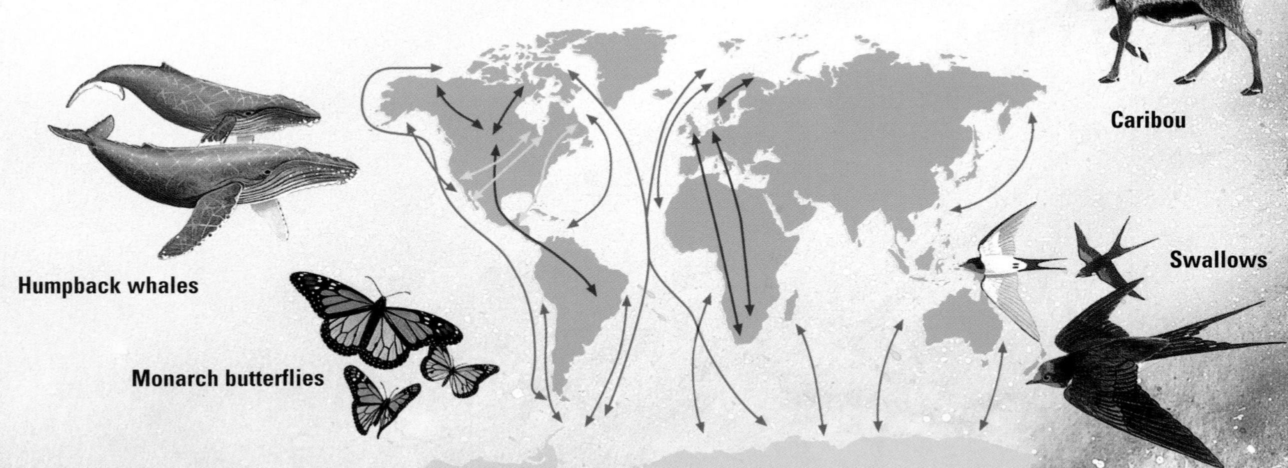

Swallow
Caribou
Monarch butterfly
Arctic tern
Humpback whale

Arctic tern

RECORD MIGRATIONS

Humpback whales feed in polar waters, but they breed in warmer seas close to the equator, traveling up to 15,500 mi. (25,000km) each year. Monarch butterflies flutter 1,980 mi. (3,200km) south from the Great Lakes of North America to Mexico. Caribou wander up to 1,240 mi. (2,000km) in huge herds across the arctic tundra. The longest migration is the tiny arctic tern's 21,700-mi. (35,000-km) round trip to the Antarctic, whereas some swallows fly 6,200 mi. (10,000km) in only six weeks, from Europe to South Africa.

A SALMON'S JOURNEY

Salmon are born in rivers, and they swim down to the sea in order to find food. After 1–4 years, they return to breed, traveling incredible distances across oceans. They do not eat during the journey and can lose half their body weight. They sometimes have to leap up out of the water to climb waterfalls, as here, and the long swim upstream against the current leaves them so exhausted that many die. Others make this epic journey several times.

Life in the water

Most of Earth is covered by water, where the main life form is fish. They breathe through gills, extracting (getting) oxygen from the water.

There are three types of fish: jawless, cartilaginous, and bony. Bony fish make up around 95 percent of all species of fish.

Freshwater fish

Some fish live in freshwater rivers and lakes. Some, such as trout, prefer fast-flowing streams, while others, such as carp, like slow-moving water.

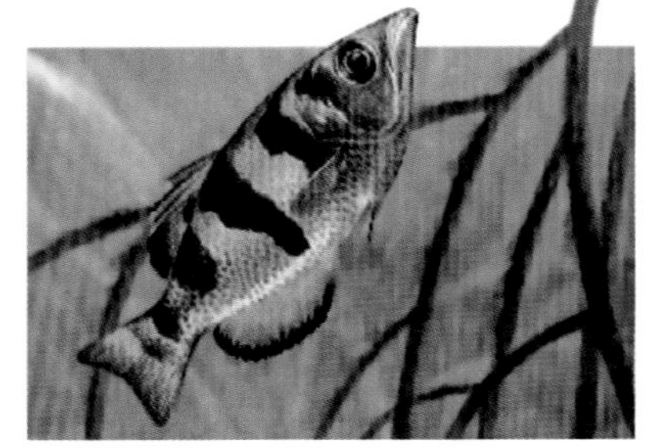

Archerfish spit water at their insect prey, toppling it into the water.

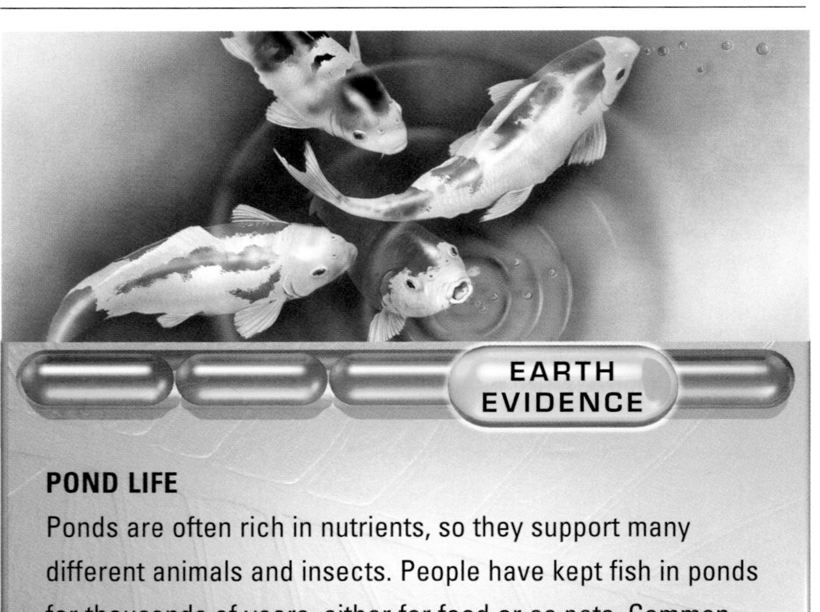

EARTH EVIDENCE

POND LIFE

Ponds are often rich in nutrients, so they support many different animals and insects. People have kept fish in ponds for thousands of years, either for food or as pets. Common pond fish include koi carp (above) and goldfish, which are often an easy target for predators such as the heron.

Jawless fish

These primitive creatures suck up food from the seabed or clamp themselves onto prey and tear at its flesh with their rough tongues. They were the first vertebrates. Only a few, such as this lamprey and the deep sea hagfish, have survived.

Deep-sea fish

Several hundred feet below the waves, the sea is dark and cold, with little food. Deep-sea fish tend to have big eyes or rely on long feelers to detect the prey there and to attract mates. They are slower and less agile than other fish.

The deep-sea anglerfish has a long spine like a fishing rod that it lights up to attract other fish for its food. Other deep-sea fish can also make light. This is called bioluminescence.

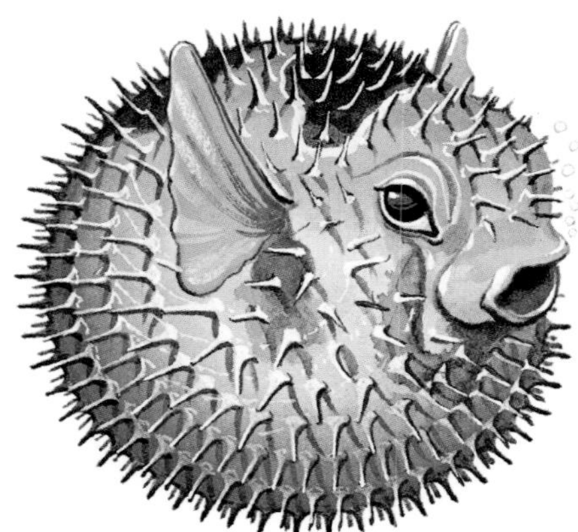

Self-defense

Some fish use bright colors or poison to deter predators. Some fish have much more dramatic means of protection. When it is threatened, the porcupine fish (above) swallows a lot of water. This causes it to swell up, and makes its spines stick out. It becomes impossible for predators to bite it.

Ocean predator

The shark is an extremely efficient killing machine, hunting its prey by smell. It has powerful jaws with an array of biting and crushing teeth that are continuously replaced by more rows of teeth that grow behind. Instead of bones, its skeleton is made of cartilage. Sharks have to keep swimming, otherwise they sink.

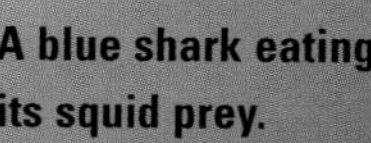

A blue shark eating its squid prey.

On the reef

Coral is alive. It is made up of millions of tiny animals called polyps that produce a protective shell, which, over a long period of time, creates a reef. This environment offers shelter and food to many animals, acting like a rainforest in the warm, clear water. Fish that are immune to polyp stings hide in the cracks and crevices of the coral, where octopuses, moray eels, starfish, clams, and other marine creatures also hunt and rest.

Camouflage

Some animals that need to hide from prey or predators use camouflage as a way of concealing their presence. The simple disguise is the worm's brown skin against brown dirt.

Camouflage is especially important for animals that are active during the day, when they can be seen easily . Some stay still so they do not give themselves away, while others mimic the call of fiercer creatures.

Color and camouflage

Color allows an animal to blend in with its surroundings. For example, shrimp match their background because they are transparent. The fur of the sloth (right) often has a green tinge. This is because it houses bacteria that reacts to the moist conditions of the South American rainforest in which the sloth lives, providing effective camouflage.

Imitation

Animals can also have shapes that mimic their environment. The stick insect's thin body and legs look like branches, and it is the same color as the wood. If it is disturbed, it drops to the ground like a dead twig, and if that does not work, it flies away. Other insects mimic the veins of leaves.

Distraction

Another camouflage technique is to distract with stripes, spots, or speckles that look like the animal's surroundings. The zebra's stripes look like tree shadows and also merge in the heat haze, making it hard for hunting lions to see individuals.

Insects and spiders

There are six insects for every other creature on Earth. Insects have been around for 500 million years and are found almost everywhere on the planet, except for in the sea.

Insects are the recyclers of the planet because they eat dead animals, fallen trees, and other garbage. However, some insects also transmit diseases. Others, such as bees, are vital to plant reproduction (*see pp. 78–79*).

Most winged insects have two pairs of wings.

Insect legs are jointed.

Insects use their antennae to "smell."

Insect anatomy

Insects have six legs and three body parts: the head, thorax (chest), and abdomen (stomach). Their bodies are held together by an outer shell called the exoskeleton. They do not have lungs and breathe through holes in their sides.

Winged insects

The rapid beating of an insect's wings creates a humming sound. Bees' or wasps' wings beat 200 times per second, while mosquitoes' wings reach up to 500 times per second, and syrphids', or hoverflies', reach twice that.

Grasshoppers rub or snap their wings together to make chirping sounds.

Ants

There are many types of ants, all living in colonies where each one has a job to do. These leafcutter ants bite off leaves and carry them to their nest. The leaves are used to grow fungus, which is the ants' food.

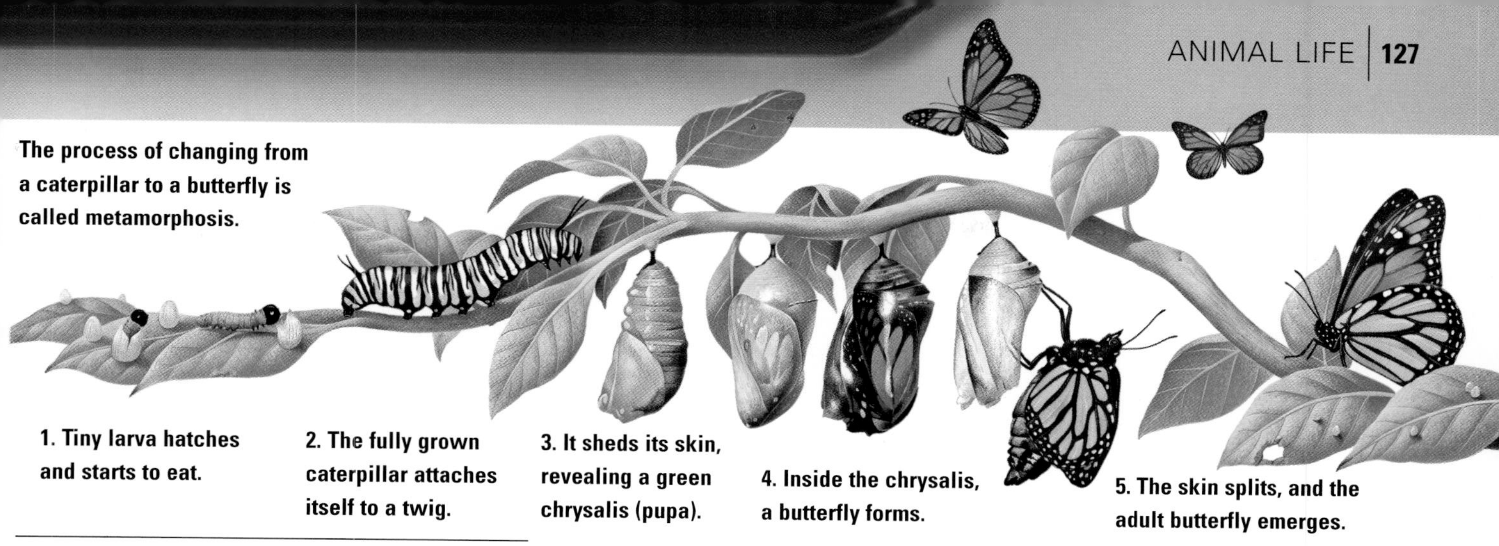

The process of changing from a caterpillar to a butterfly is called metamorphosis.
1. Tiny larva hatches and starts to eat.
2. The fully grown caterpillar attaches itself to a twig.
3. It sheds its skin, revealing a green chrysalis (pupa).
4. Inside the chrysalis, a butterfly forms.
5. The skin splits, and the adult butterfly emerges.

Stag beetles fighting

Beetles

Beetles make up the largest group of insects and are the most heavily armored because of their thick shells. Many beetles are pests and eat crops or trees, but some, such as ladybugs, feed on plant-eating creatures.

Dragonflies

The dragonfly has two pairs of wings, which work separately. This means that it can change direction instantly when it spots danger or food with its massive eyes. The dragonfly is one of the fastest of all flying insects.

Insect life cycle

Some insects, such as butterflies, grow in four stages. From the egg hatches a caterpillar larva or grub that eats leaves. Later, it sheds its skin and creates a hard shell called a pupa, or chrysalis. It emerges from the chrysalis as an adult. Other insects, such as grasshoppers, have only a three-stage cycle, progressing from an egg to a wingless nymph to an adult.

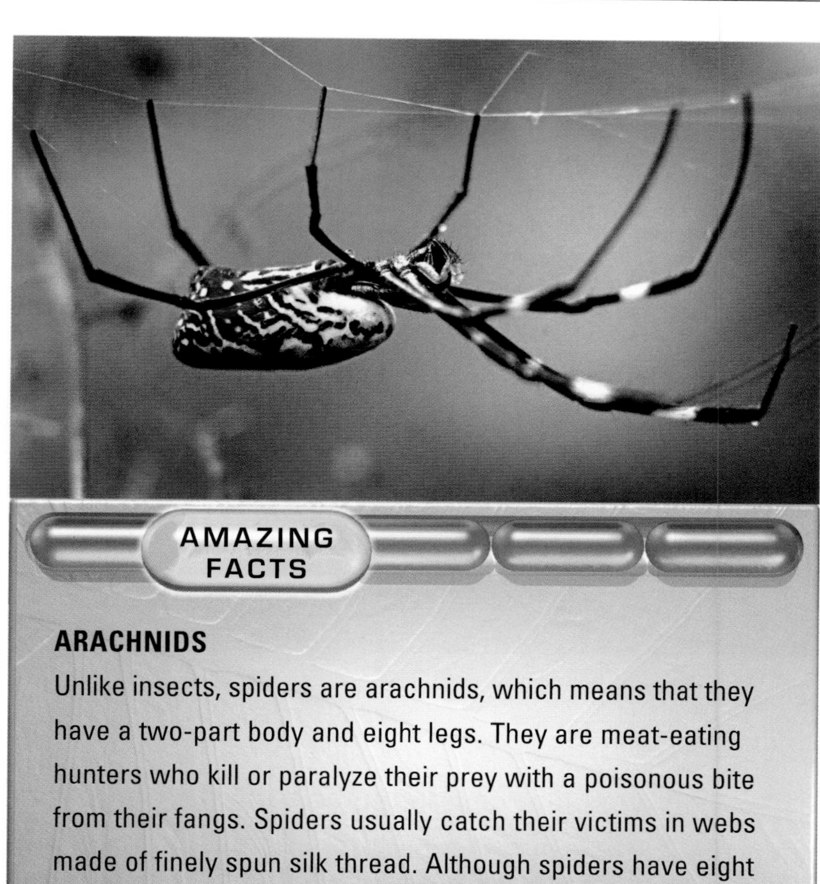

AMAZING FACTS

ARACHNIDS

Unlike insects, spiders are arachnids, which means that they have a two-part body and eight legs. They are meat-eating hunters who kill or paralyze their prey with a poisonous bite from their fangs. Spiders usually catch their victims in webs made of finely spun silk thread. Although spiders have eight simple eyes, they hunt by feeling vibrations with their legs.

Animal facts

Humans are in the minority. For every person on Earth, there are around 200 million insects, one million of which are ants. We are not only outnumbered by bugs. There are two dolphins and—probably—one rat for every human on Earth.

AVERAGE LIFE SPANS

Dragonfly 24 hours
Mouse 2–3 years
Rabbit 5 years
Kangaroo 9 years
Chicken 15 years
Lion 25 years
Hippopotamus 40 years
Dolphin 65 years
Elephant 70 years
Rhinoceros 70 years
Parrot 80 years
Tortoise 100 years
Deep-sea tubeworm 170–250 years
The longest-living animal recorded is an ocean quahog clam 405 years

FASTEST . . .

In the air: peregrine falcon 200 mph (322km/h)
Attacking: the jaws of the trap-jaw ant snapping shut 145 mph (233km/h)
On land: cheetah 69 mph (112km/h)
In the water: sailfish 68 mph (109km/h)
Racehorse 50 mph (80km/h)
Racing dog: greyhound 45 mph (72km/h)
Over long distances: pronghorn antelope 45 mph (72km/h)
Nonflying bird: ostrich 43 mph (69km/h)
Insect: dragonfly 36 mph (58km/h)
Whales: killer whale 35 mph (56km/h)
Human 28 mph (45km/h)
Reptile: spiny-tailed iguana 21 mph (34km/h)

PREGNANCY, AVERAGE LENGTH

Hamster 16 days
House mouse 19 days
Rabbit 32 days
Cat 62 days
Dog 65 days
Lion 108 days
Sheep 148 days
Chimpanzee 237 days
Human 260–290 days
Dolphin 276 days
Whale 365 days
Giraffe 395–425 days
Camel 406 days
Rhinoceros 560 days
Indian elephant 624 days

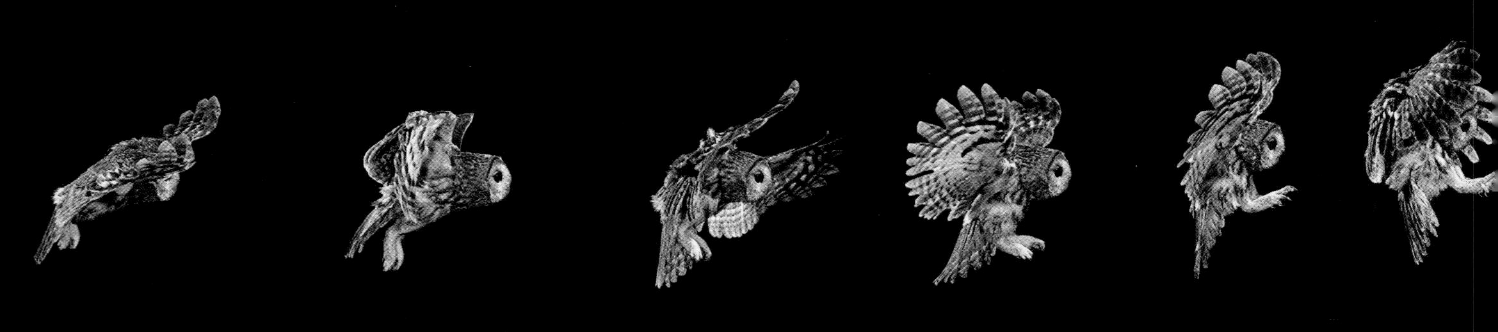

A tawny owl preparing to land

USEFUL WEBSITES

www.amnh.org Information on the natural world from the American Museum of Natural History.

www.g-kexoticfarms.com/funanimalfacts.html A wealth of animal facts and statistics.

www.kidscom.com/games/animal/animal.html Animal facts and games.

http://kids.nationalgeographic.com/Animals/CreatureFeature/ Fact files on animals.

Body Science

Humans dominate other animal species through intelligence, not physical strength. Our bodies have mouths that can speak and hands that can build. Unlike other animals, the human body needs the protection of clothes, health care, and prepared foods. However, it is highly adaptable and outlasts the bodies of most other animals.

Bones and skeletons

The skeleton is the body's support structure. The muscles attached to the skeleton allow us to move.

From the six tiny bones inside the ears to the six long bones in the legs, every part of the skeleton is constantly renewing itself.

Teeth are made of enamel, the hardest material in the body.

The ribs protect the soft organs of the body such as the heart.

Bones keep the amount of calcium in the bloodstream in balance, absorbing and releasing it as required.

The femur is a long bone and is adapted to withstand stress.

Bone structure

Every bone is coated with a thin membrane that covers a hard, dense outer layer. There is lighter, spongelike material underneath this layer. In the core of each bone is a fatty substance called marrow. Bones also contain networks of nerves and blood vessels.

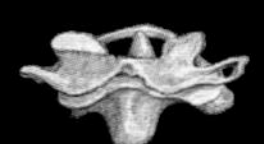

Pivot—first vertebra of backbone rotates around second

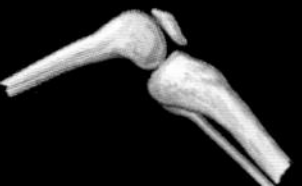

Hinge—one knee bone fits into curved end of another

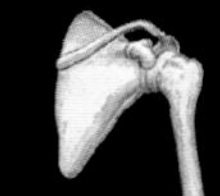

Ball-and-socket—at shoulder, ball shape fits into cup shape

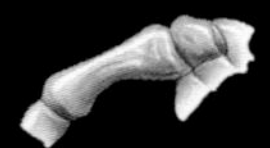

Saddle—base of thumb bone fits into U-shape of wrist bone

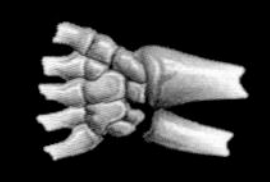

Ellipsoidal—egg shape of arm bone fits in cup of wrist

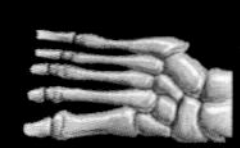

Plane—gliding joint between heel bones in each foot

Joints

A joint is the meeting point of two or more bones, and most joints allow free motion in one or more directions. Ligaments encase joints to protect them. Only a few joints are not mobile

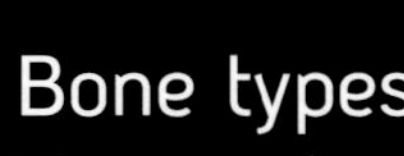

Bone types

There are five main types of bones: long bones, such as the main bones in the limbs; short bones, such as the heel; flat bones, such as those in the dome of the skull; sesamoids, such as the kneecaps, which are small and round; and irregular bones, such as the vertebrae of the spine

Cartilage

This strong but flexible material is connected to some bones. It has a smooth surface that allows joints to move easily, and it lets our ears and noses be flexible while still keeping their shape.

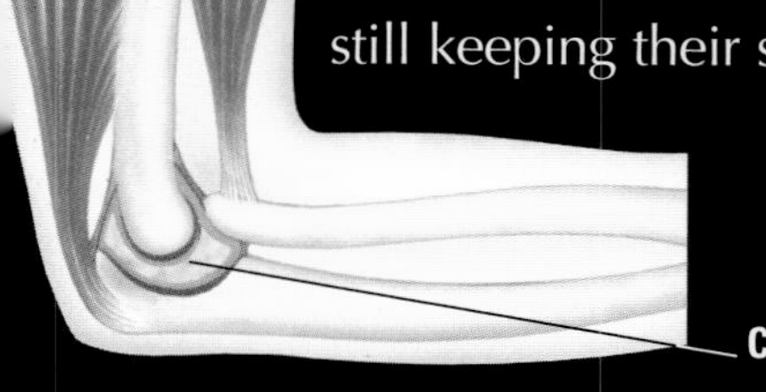

Parts of the skeleton

The skeleton is made up of 206 bones. These allow motion and give shape to the body, as well as giving protection to internal organs. Most blood cells are made inside bones.

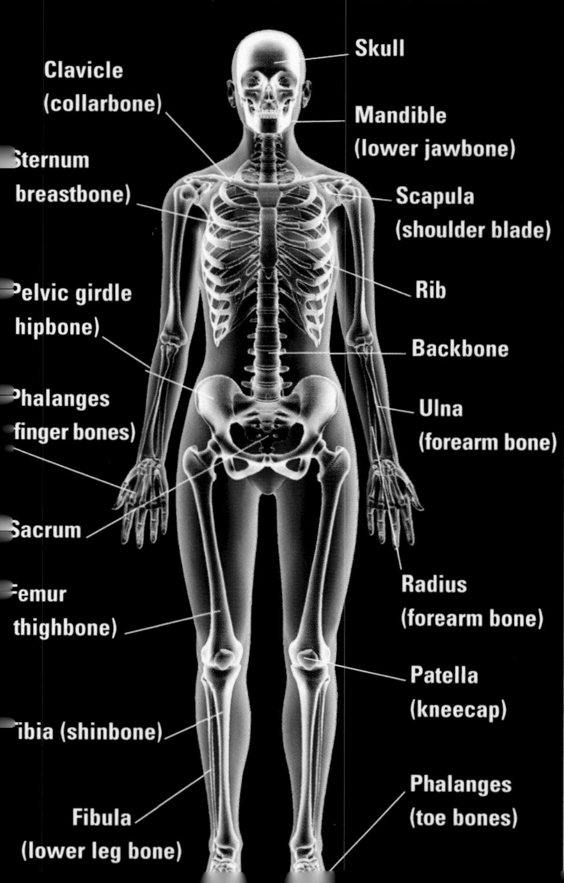

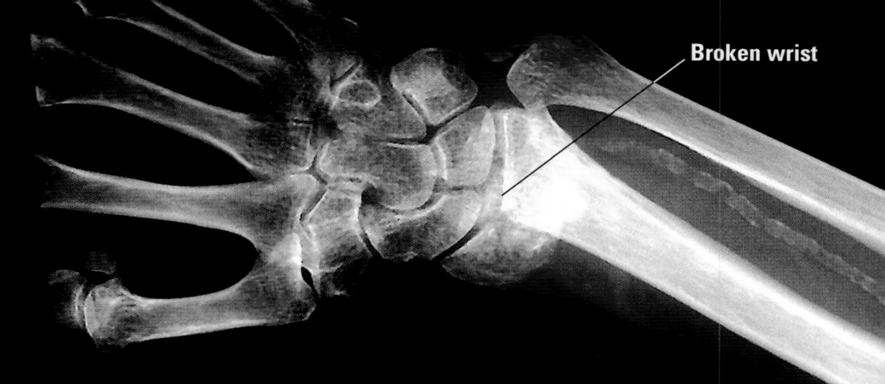

Breaking and repairing

When a bone is broken, it usually repairs itself, as long as the ends are held together. This can be done by the surrounding tissues, as with broken ribs, or by plaster casts, as with broken limbs. First, a blood clot forms to stop bleeding. Fibers grow across the break, and soft bone forms on them. Gradually, hard bone replaces soft bone.

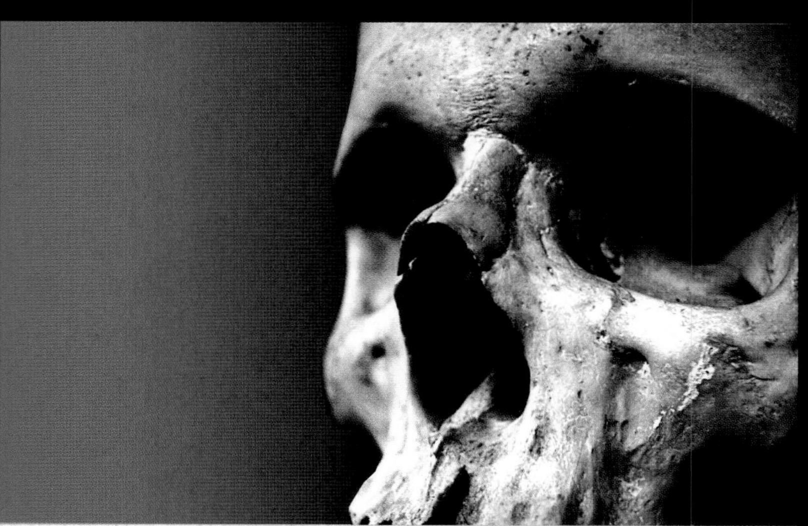

AMAZING FACTS

THE SKULL

The skull protects the brain, as well as protecting the eyes and nasal passages. The bones that form the skulls of babies and children have some flexibility to allow for growth. Adults' skulls are locked solidly together, except for the jawbone. Inside the skull, six tiny bones in the ears magnify vibrations of the eardrum so that these can be heard as sounds.

Muscles and movement

Muscles allow us to move, hold us upright, and keep many of our internal organs working.

TYPES OF MUSCLES

The structures of the three muscle types have evolved for different types of functions.

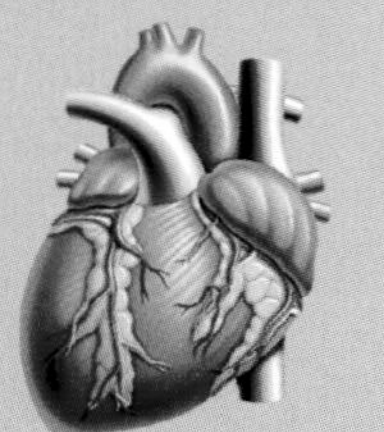

The heart is made of a unique type of muscle that contracts and relaxes in a rhythm.

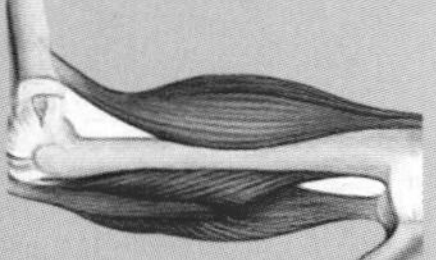

Skeletal muscle allows the body to move and can be consciously controlled.

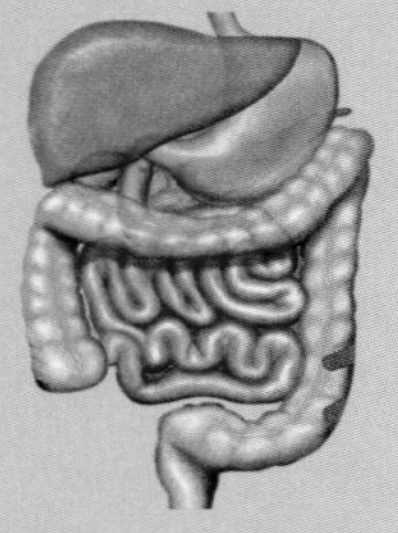

Smooth muscle is used for unconscious actions such as digestion.

Muscles make up around one half of the weight of an average person. They become stronger or weaker depending on how much they are used.

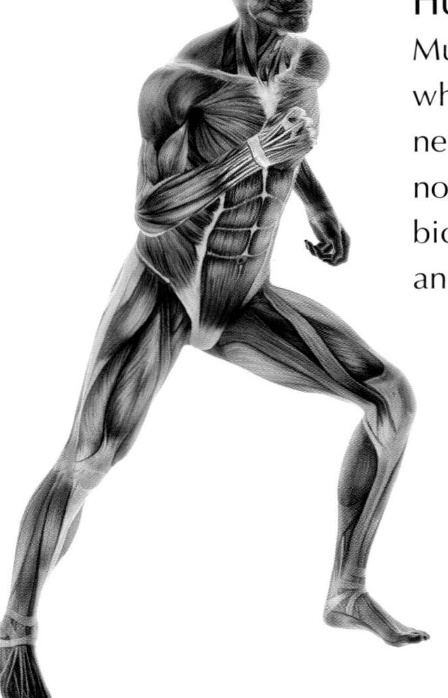

How muscles work

Muscles are made of fibers that shorten when they receive a signal from the nerves. Because muscles can only pull, not push, they often work in pairs. The biceps, for example, bends the arm, and the triceps straightens it again.

Tendons and ligaments

The ends of a skeletal muscle (see left) are usually attached to the bones that they move by cords of very strong tissue called tendons. Where tendons move across bones—such as in the hands and feet—they are often covered in a lubricating layer, called a synovial sheath, to reduce friction.

Tendon from muscle straightens fingers

Band that holds tendons in place

Using muscles

The more muscles are used, the stronger they become. By exercising muscles, you increase the strength and size of the individual muscle fibers. The process also "teaches" muscles how to work effectively by ensuring that fibers contract together. Muscles usually need oxygen to contract but can work without it.

Muscle fibers

Every skeletal muscle is made of two types of fibers, in roughly equal numbers. Fast-twitch fibers contract quickly and powerfully but tire rapidly. They allow people to sprint and to lift heavy weights. Slow-twitch fibers contract more slowly but can work for longer. They are used for cycling and long-distance running.

Some very athletic soccer players are able to use their muscles to execute extraordinary maneuvers in order to reach the ball.

BLOOD AND CIRCULATION

BLOOD CARRIES BOTH NUTRIENTS AND OXYGEN AROUND THE BODY. THE OXYGEN BREAKS DOWN THE NUTRIENTS SO THAT THE ENERGY THAT THEY CARRY CAN BE USED.

CIRCULATION

The heart continuously pumps blood through the lungs to receive oxygen from them, which turns it bright red. This fresh blood is then pumped throughout the body. The oxygen is used up and replaced by the waste gas carbon dioxide, which darkens the blood. This blood then flows back through the heart to the lungs, where the carbon dioxide is removed and exhaled.

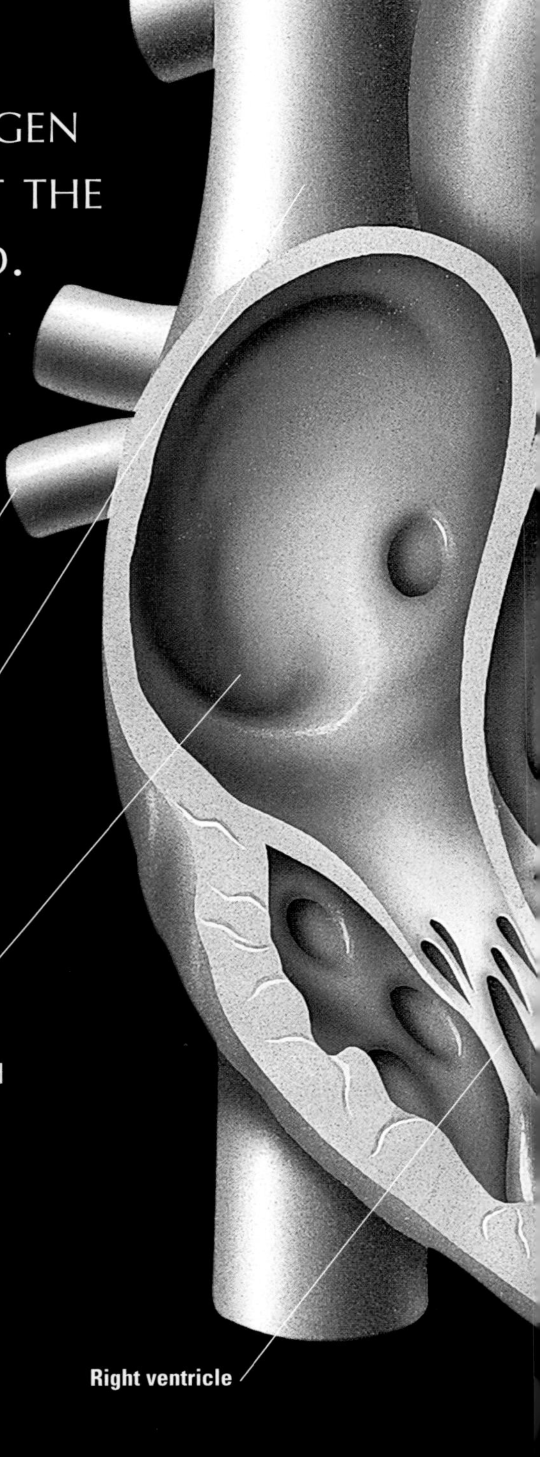

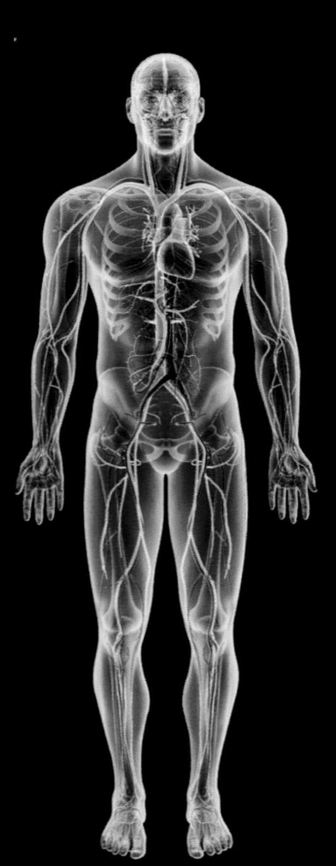

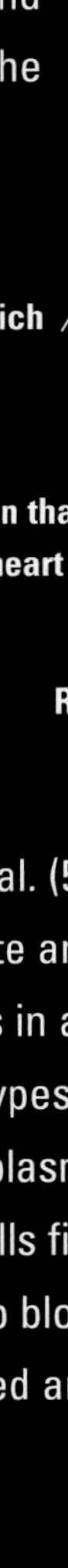

BLOOD

The heart pumps around 1 gal. (5L) of blood around the body every minute and beats more than three billion times in a lifetime. Blood consists of different types of cells suspended in a fluid called plasma. Red cells carry oxygen, white cells fight infections, and platelets help blood clot so that wounds can be closed and healed.

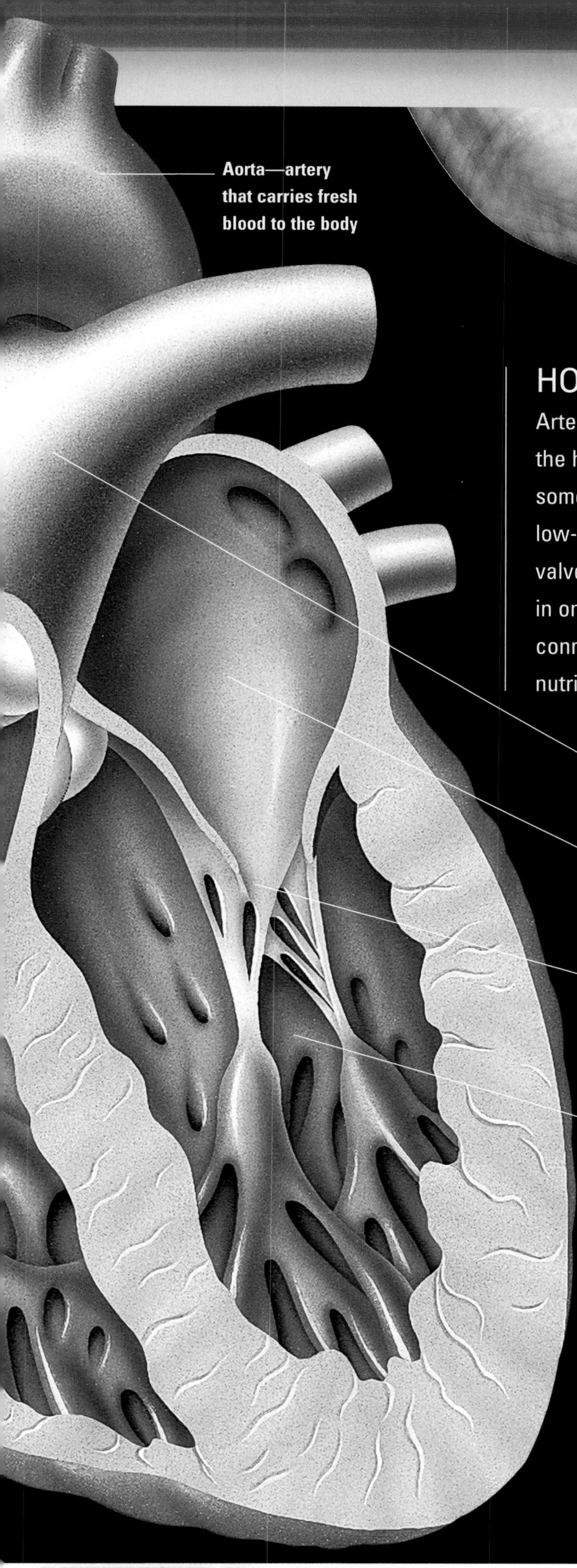

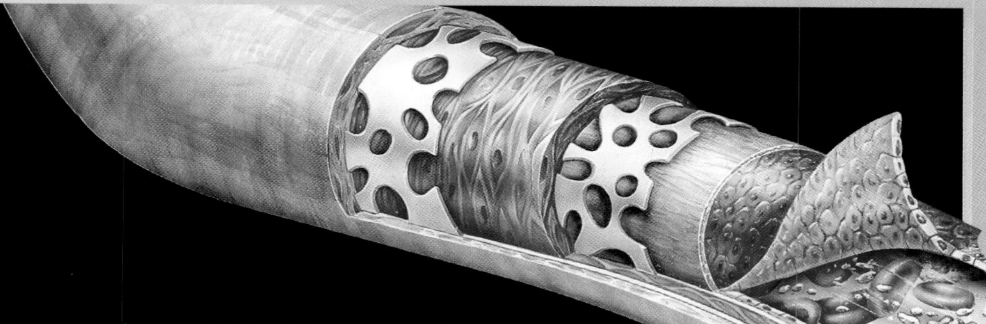

HOW ARTERIES WORK

Arteries carry high-pressure blood away from the heart via the lungs. They have muscular walls, some of which help pump blood. Veins carry low-pressure blood back to the heart. Some have valves to ensure that blood only flows along them in one direction. A network of narrow capillaries connects veins and arteries, with thin walls so that nutrients and waste can leave and enter them.

THE HEART

The heart beats automatically, with no need for instructions from the brain. It speeds up during exercise in order to supply cells with the extra nutrients and oxygen that they need. The *lub-dub* sound of the heart's beat is made by the valves inside it closing.

Brain and nerves

All of your thoughts, ideas, and emotions—and your sense of who you are—exist in your brain. But exactly how the mind is linked to the brain is a mystery.

The brain sends a constant stream of control signals to the body. However, we are conscious of only a few of them.

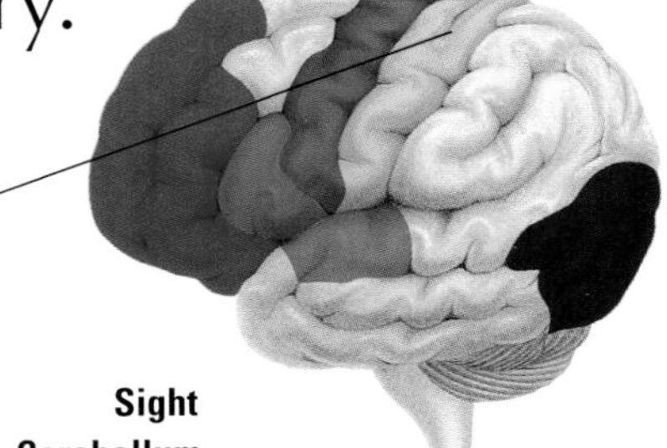

The nervous system

The brain and spinal cord make up the central nervous system, which controls the body. The peripheral nervous system is a complex network of nerves throughout the body. It carries messages to and from the central nervous system.

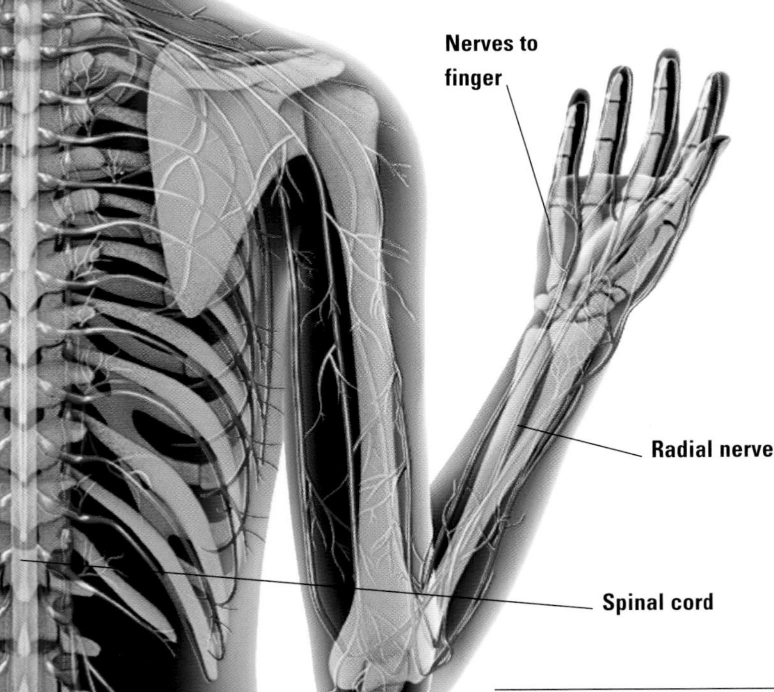

The brain

The brain is composed of three main parts: the cerebrum, where thought occurs, the cerebellum, which coordinates the muscles, and the brain stem, which controls breathing and heart rate. Different areas of the brain control different body functions.

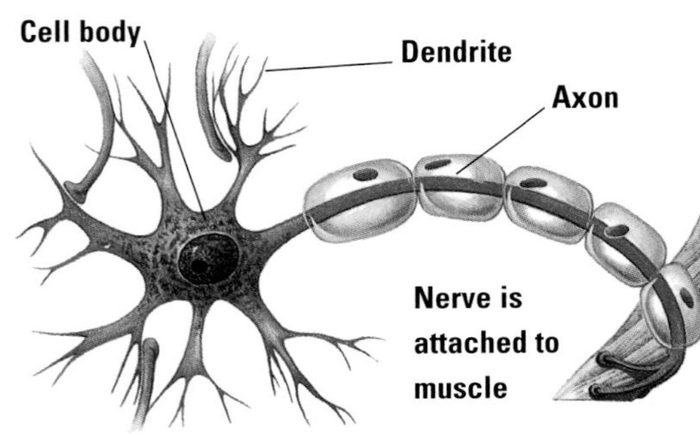

How nerves work

Electrical nerve signals travel along nerve cells (neurons, above). Chemical messengers, neurotransmitters, control the way the signals travel across the gaps (synapses) between neurons.

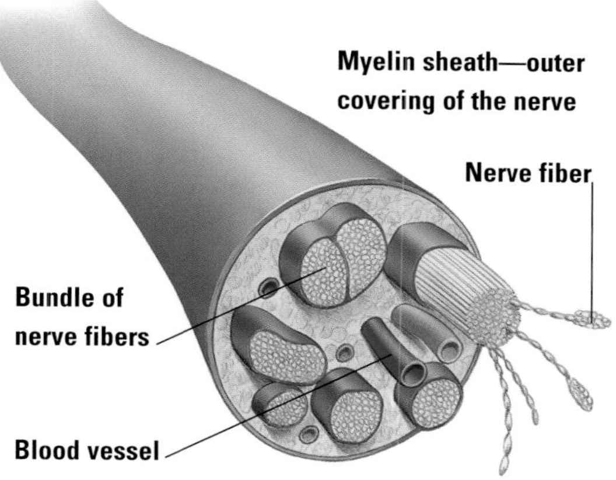

Sensory and motor nerves

Sensory nerves send signals from receptor cells (such as those in the skin that detect heat, cold, pressure, and pain) to the brain. Motor cells transmit signals from the brain to the muscles, which contract in response.

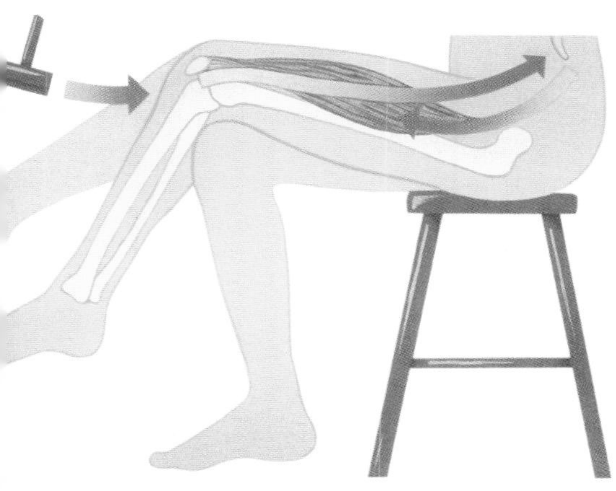

Reflexes

The brain is not involved in responding to every nerve signal. When a knee is tapped with a hammer, the spinal cord reacts to the signals from the skin receptors. It sends a signal along a motor nerve to contract the muscles, causing the leg to kick out in a reflex action.

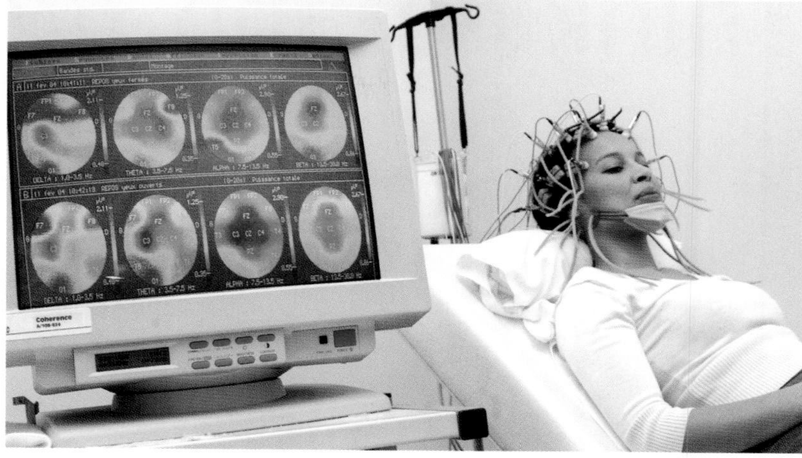

Brain waves

The many tiny electrical signals in the brain change depending on what we see and hear. Some can be measured on the scalp and displayed on the screen of an electroencephalograph (above). The pattern of activity also shows whether we are awake, asleep, or dreaming.

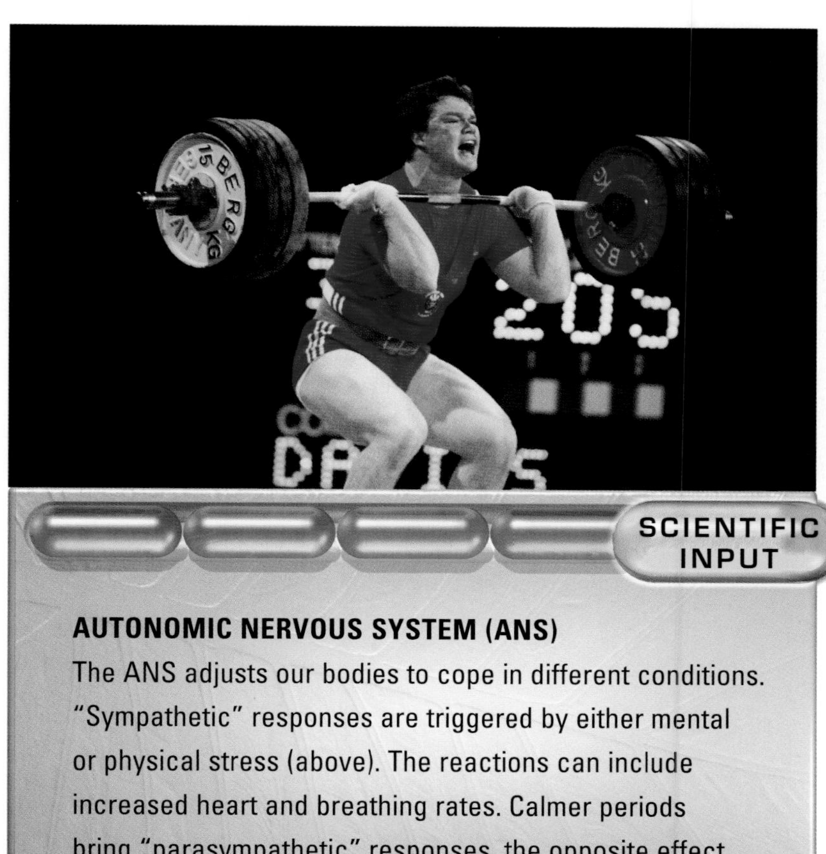

SCIENTIFIC INPUT

AUTONOMIC NERVOUS SYSTEM (ANS)

The ANS adjusts our bodies to cope in different conditions. "Sympathetic" responses are triggered by either mental or physical stress (above). The reactions can include increased heart and breathing rates. Calmer periods bring "parasympathetic" responses, the opposite effect.

Thinking and dreaming

No one knows exactly how emotions or memories work nor how we make mental "models" of the world around us, but these are important features of being human.

We have little idea about how the mind can create new ideas nor how it can be aware of itself. These two abilities seem to be unique to human beings.

Memory

There are three levels of memory. For around one second we remember all we see and hear in our sensory memory. Anything we focus on is stored for several seconds in our short-term memory. And if we think about something repeatedly, it becomes part of our long-term memory.

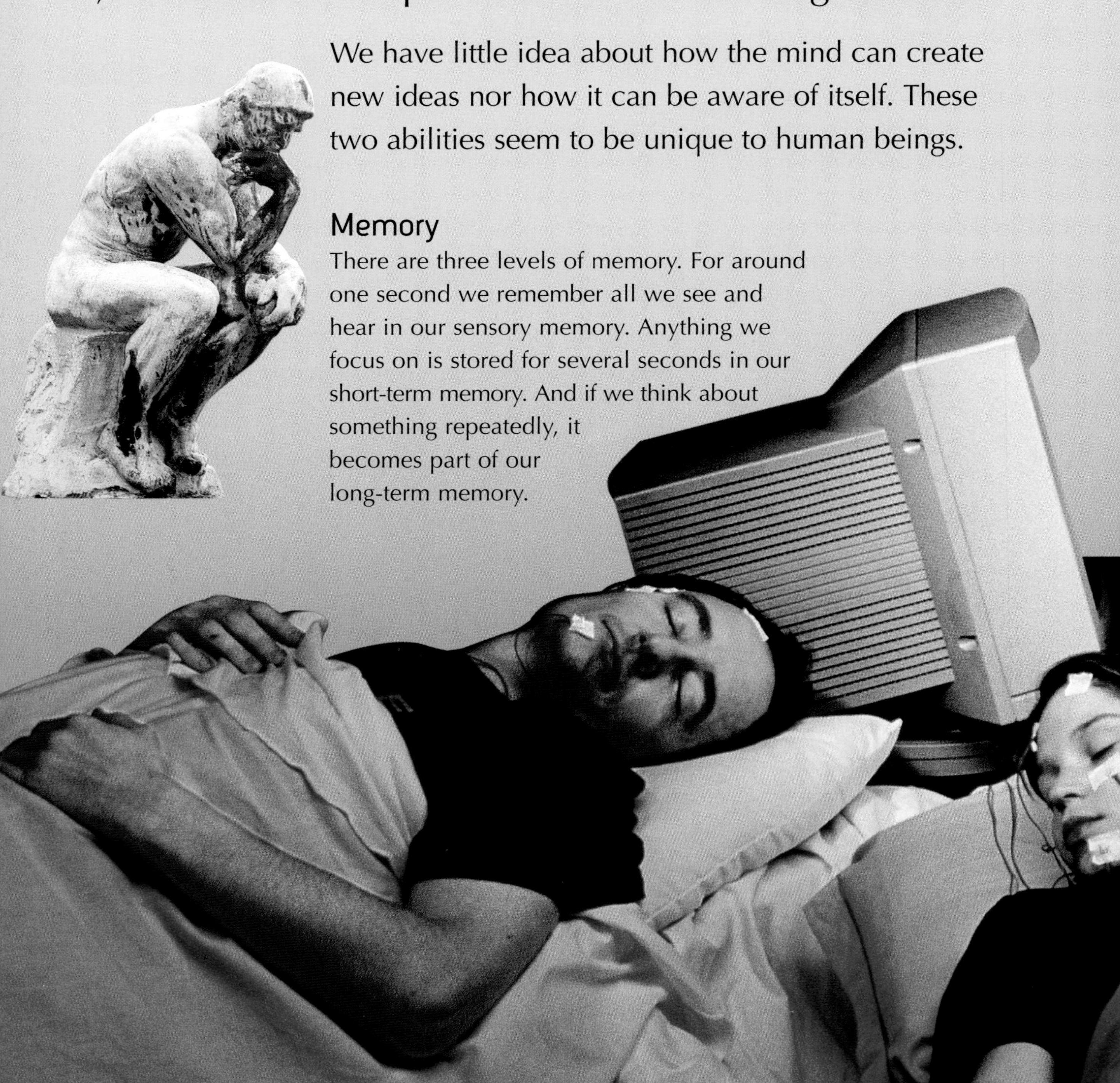

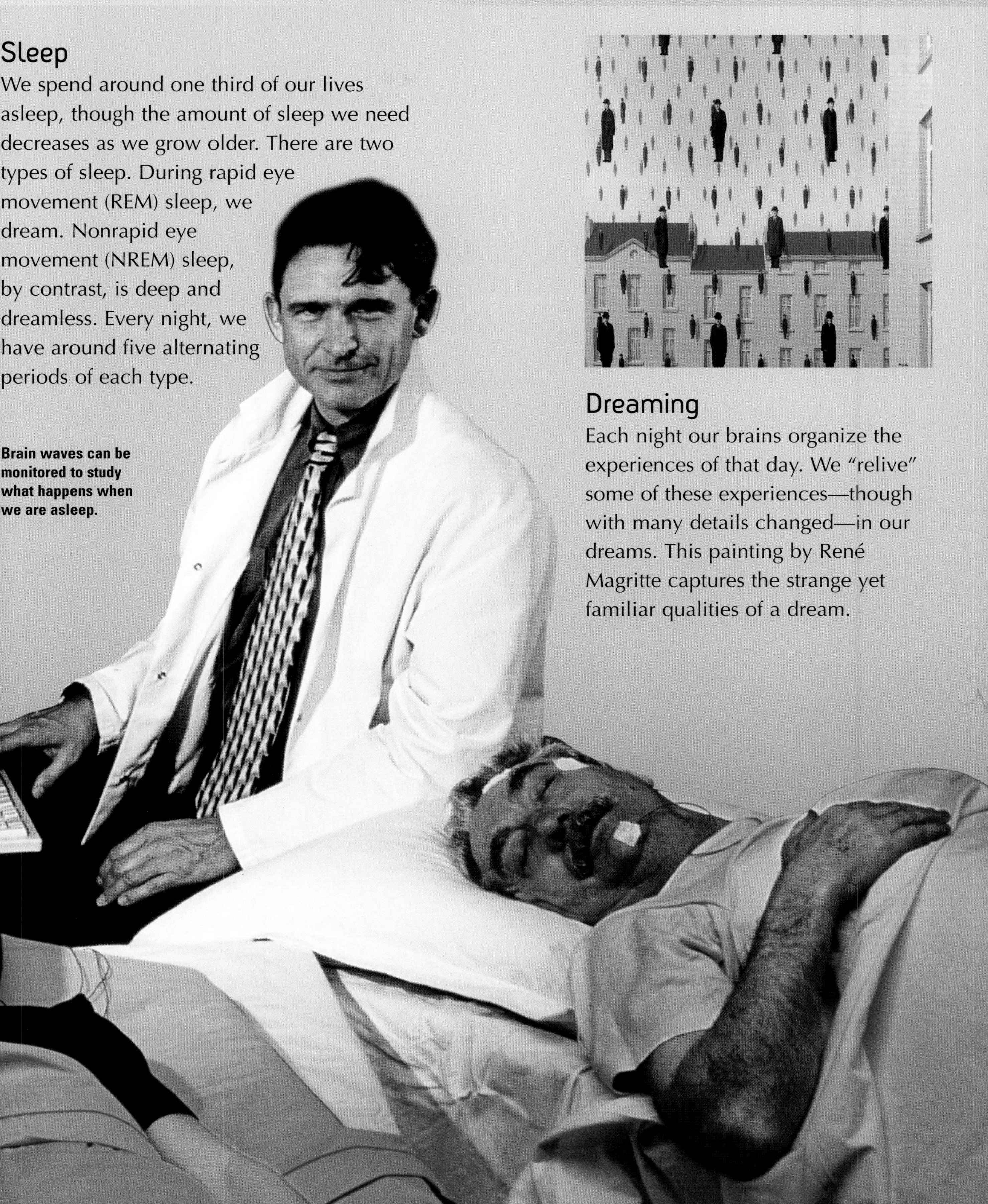

Sleep

We spend around one third of our lives asleep, though the amount of sleep we need decreases as we grow older. There are two types of sleep. During rapid eye movement (REM) sleep, we dream. Nonrapid eye movement (NREM) sleep, by contrast, is deep and dreamless. Every night, we have around five alternating periods of each type.

Brain waves can be monitored to study what happens when we are asleep.

Dreaming

Each night our brains organize the experiences of that day. We "relive" some of these experiences—though with many details changed—in our dreams. This painting by René Magritte captures the strange yet familiar qualities of a dream.

Senses

All the information about our world comes through our five senses. These are sight, hearing, touch, smell, and taste.

The brain organizes the signals that it receives from our sense organs. It uses them to create a mental "model" of the world.

Touch

Touch tells us about the temperature, weight, texture, and shape of objects. Touch receptors are concentrated where they are needed, so there are more in the skin on our fingers than in the same size area on our backs.

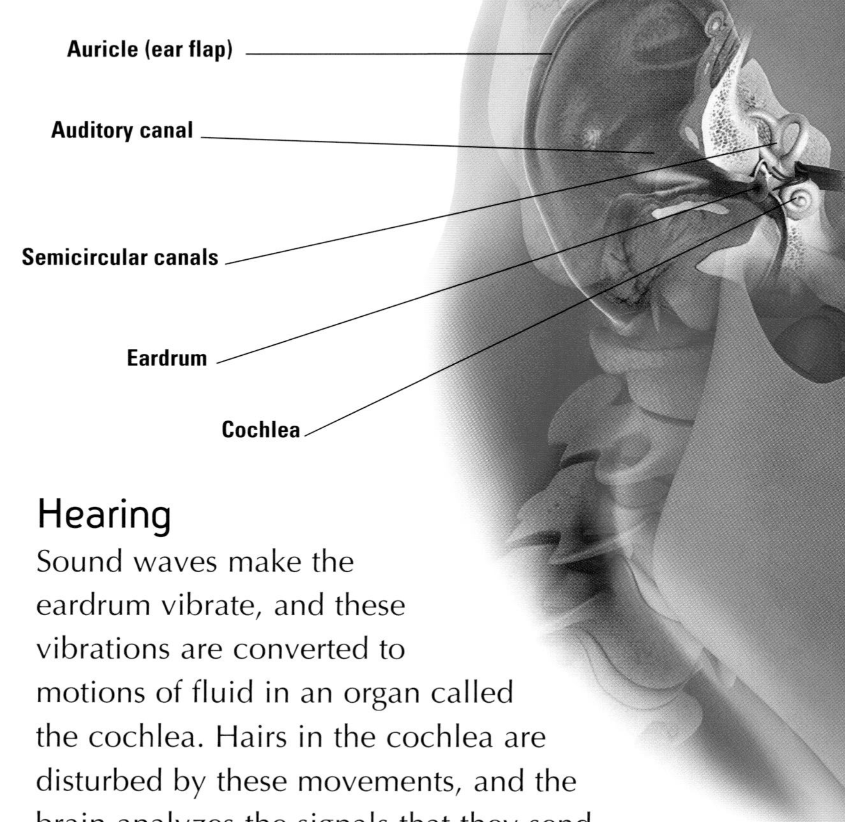

Hearing

Sound waves make the eardrum vibrate, and these vibrations are converted to motions of fluid in an organ called the cochlea. Hairs in the cochlea are disturbed by these movements, and the brain analyzes the signals that they send.

Taste

Chemical receptors called taste buds tell us how salty, sweet, sour, or bitter things are, but we need to use our sense of smell to identify different foods. It is difficult to distinguish chocolate, tea, and coffee with the sense of taste alone.

Balance

Our inner ears enable us to stand and walk without falling over. They also allow us to hear. In each ear there are three fluid-filled tubes called semicircular canals. The motion of the fluid sends signals to the brain so that it can stabilize our movements.

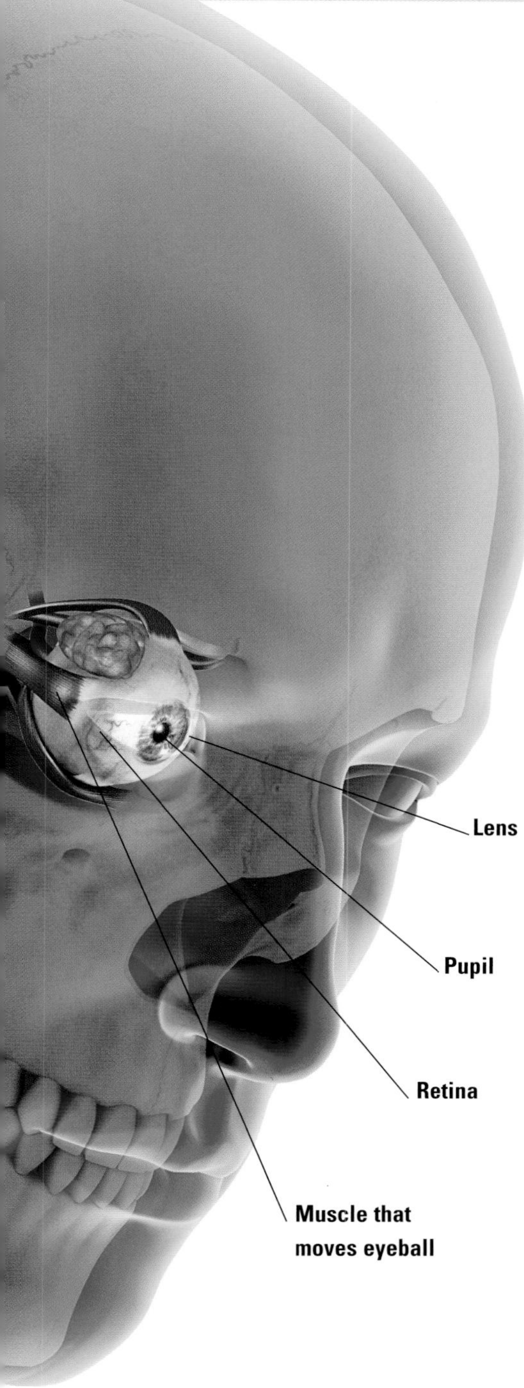

Sight

Light entering the eyes is focused by flexible lenses onto the light-sensitive retinas. There, different colors and brightnesses are changed into electrical signals and sent to the brain. The brain adds extra information to the signals, generating a complete picture.

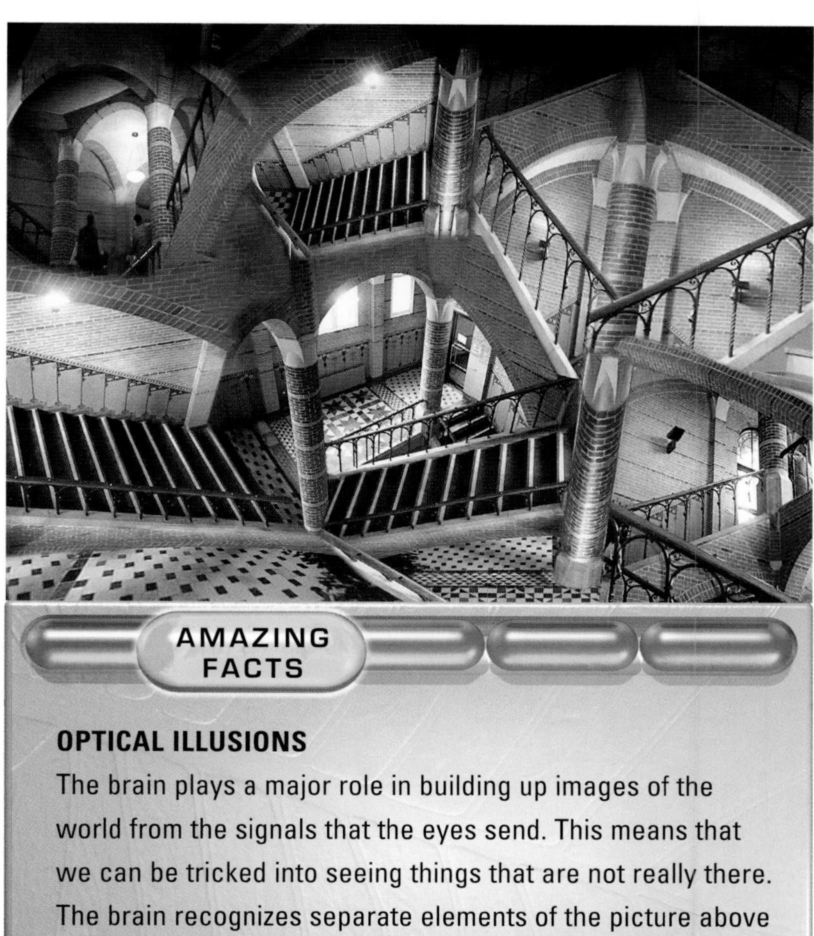

AMAZING FACTS

OPTICAL ILLUSIONS

The brain plays a major role in building up images of the world from the signals that the eyes send. This means that we can be tricked into seeing things that are not really there. The brain recognizes separate elements of the picture above such as the descending staircases. It then assembles them all together so that the whole image seems to make sense—even though it is impossible!

Smell

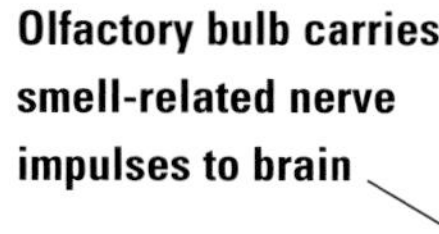

We have hundreds of different smell receptors, each able to identify a different airborne chemical. By combining the responses from groups of these receptors, we can identify thousands of different smells. Taste and smell are linked senses. Together they allow us to enjoy many different flavors.

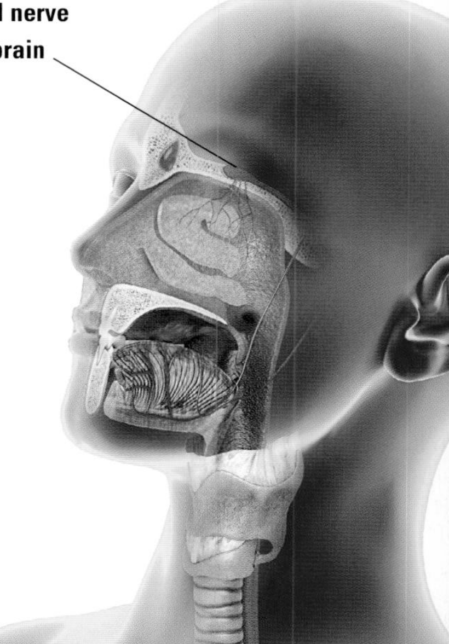

Skin, hair, and teeth

Except for the eyes, every part of a person that you can see is dead! The outer layers of skin, nails, hair, and teeth are made up completely of dead cells. They form a protective barrier against the environment.

Throughout our lives, these layers wear away and are replaced. The teeth are replaced only once, but skin, hair, and nails grow continuously to renew themselves.

Girl with the longest hair in the world

Hair

Hair on our head protects it from the hot sun and cold air. Eyebrows and eyelashes keep sweat and grit out of our eyes. Our distant ancestors had thick body hair that stood up in the cold, providing a warm layer. We still get goose bumps, but we no longer have enough body hair to keep us warm.

Skin

The skin protects us in many ways. It is a barrier against diseases and rough surfaces, and it senses damaging heat or cold. The amount of blood flowing through it varies in order to regulate the amount of heat that we lose, preventing us from overheating or freezing.

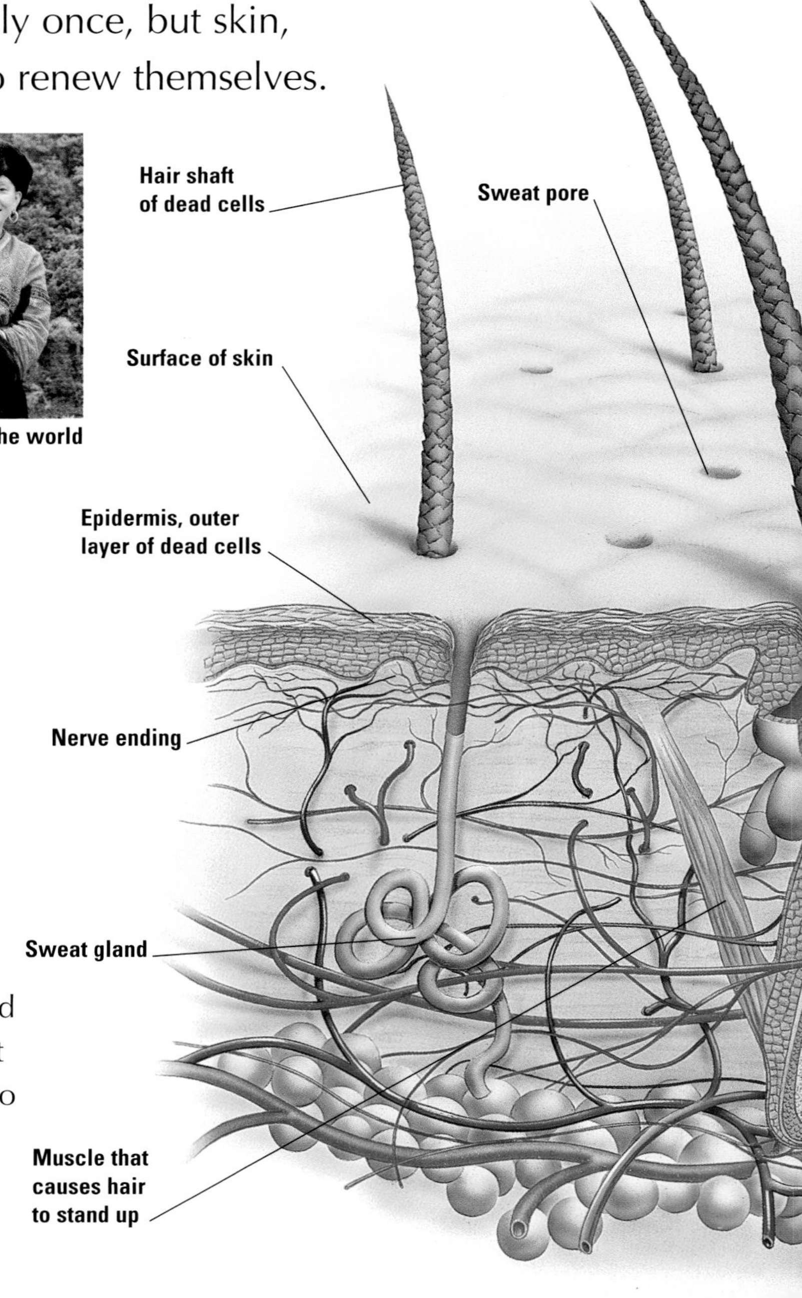

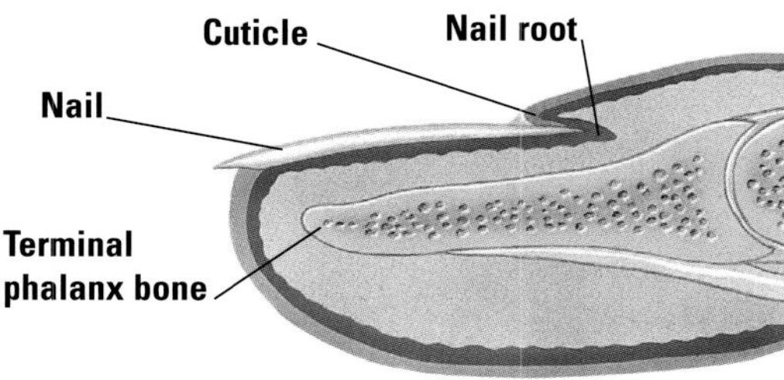

Nails

Our fingertips come into contact with hard and rough surfaces throughout the day, but the skin on them has to be quite thin to allow us to feel things. Nails have evolved to enable the fingers and toes to be both tough and sensitive.

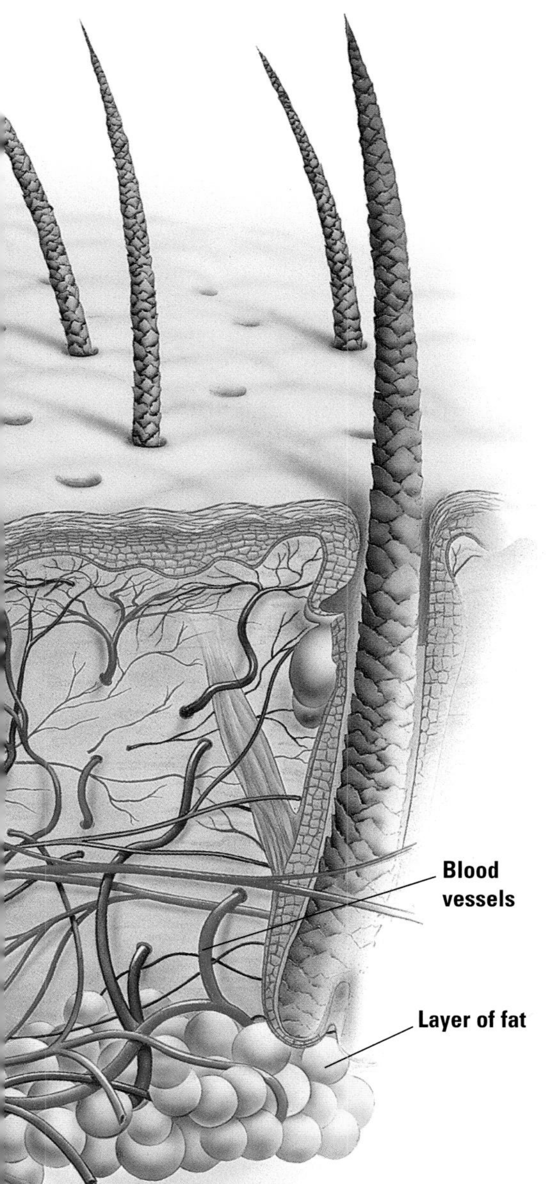

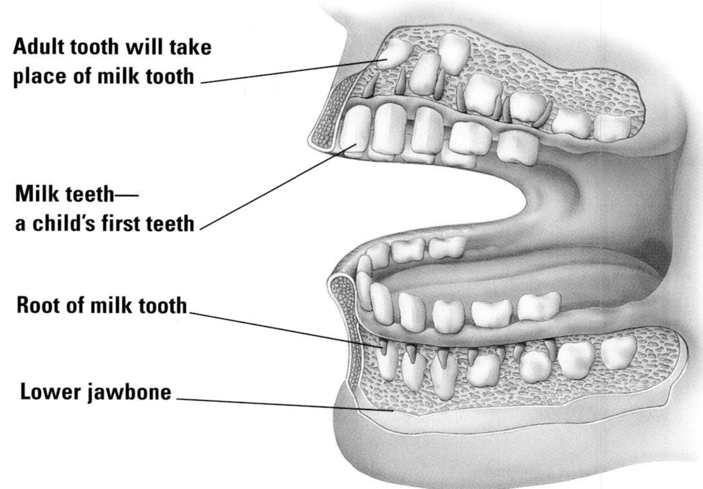

Teeth

The shapes of teeth have evolved for different functions. The incisors cut off pieces of food, canines are for tearing, and premolars and molars are used for grinding. Teeth are covered in a layer of protective enamel, which is the hardest substance in the human body.

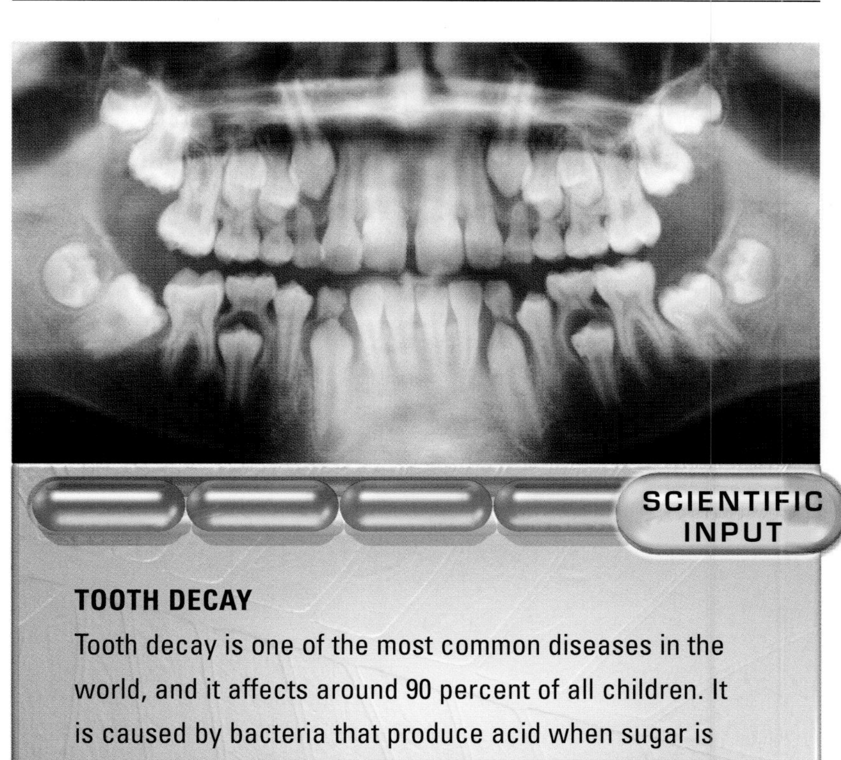

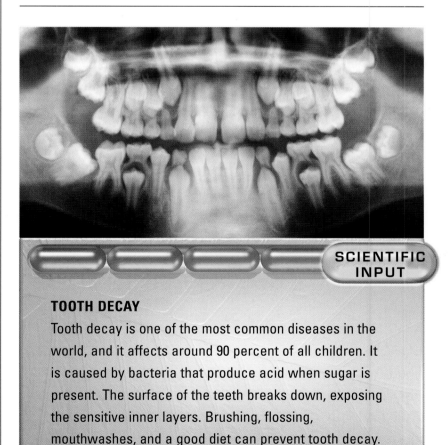

SCIENTIFIC INPUT

TOOTH DECAY

Tooth decay is one of the most common diseases in the world, and it affects around 90 percent of all children. It is caused by bacteria that produce acid when sugar is present. The surface of the teeth breaks down, exposing the sensitive inner layers. Brushing, flossing, mouthwashes, and a good diet can prevent tooth decay.

Lungs and breathing

Every minute, around 1 gal. (5L) of air passes into and out of the lungs. The air drawn into the lungs is around one fifth oxygen, and some of this oxygen is absorbed by the blood.

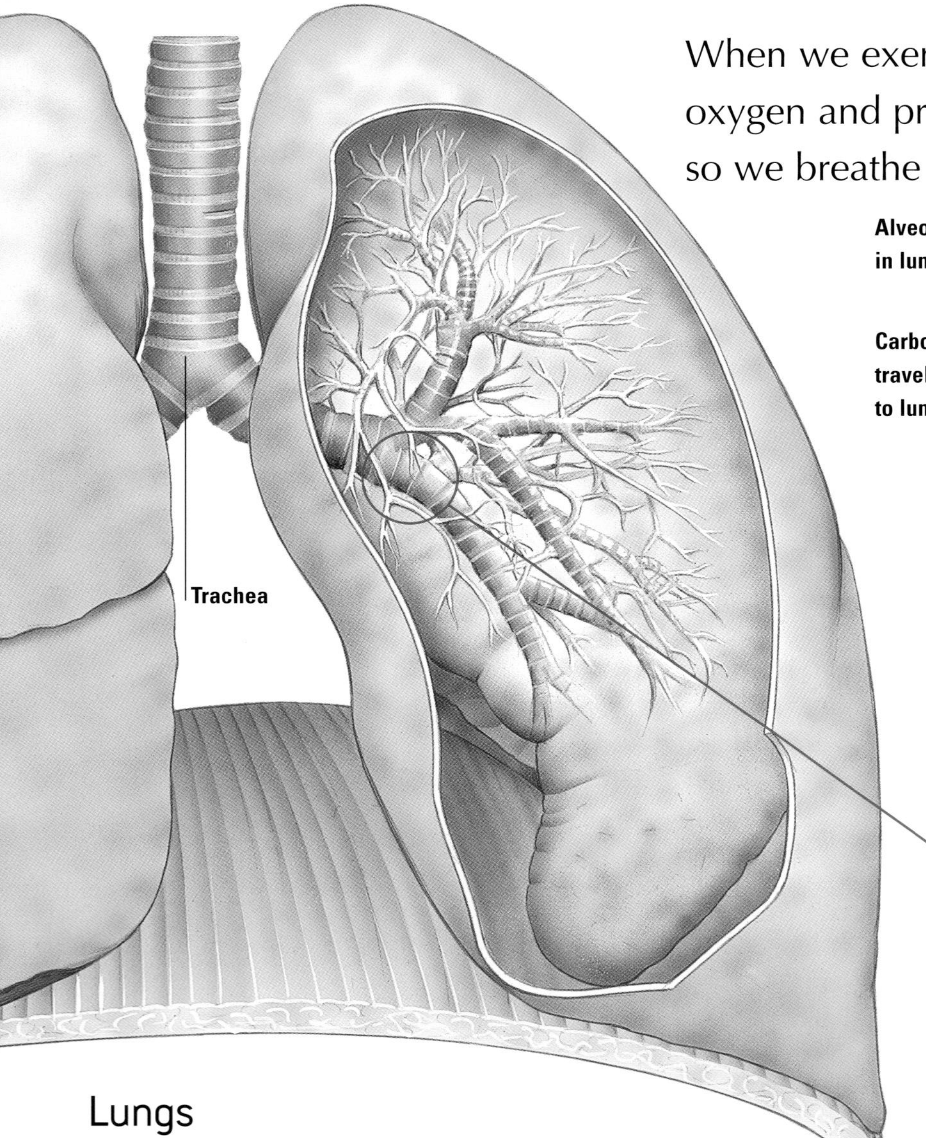

When we exercise, the body needs more oxygen and produces more carbon dioxide, so we breathe faster and more deeply.

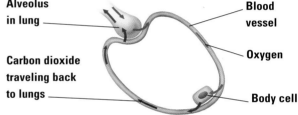

Alveolus in lung
Blood vessel
Oxygen
Carbon dioxide traveling back to lungs
Body cell

Gas exchange

The heart pumps the oxygen-rich blood around the body, where it is transferred through the capillary walls to the cells. Carbon dioxide is transported by the blood from the cells to the lungs to be exhaled.

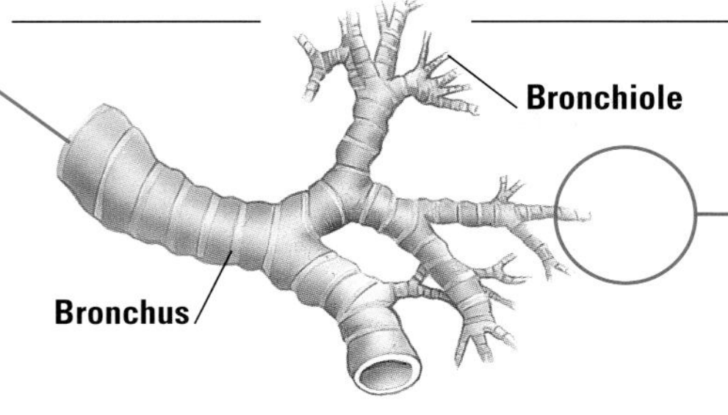

Lungs

The lungs are delicate but are protected by the ribs and a lubricating membrane called the pleura. The windpipe, or trachea, connects the throat to the lungs. A flap of skin called the epiglottis stops food and liquids from entering the lungs.

Bronchi and bronchioles

The trachea divides into two bronchi, each one going to a lung, where it is further divided into bronchioles. The bronchioles change diameter to control the flow of air into the lungs.

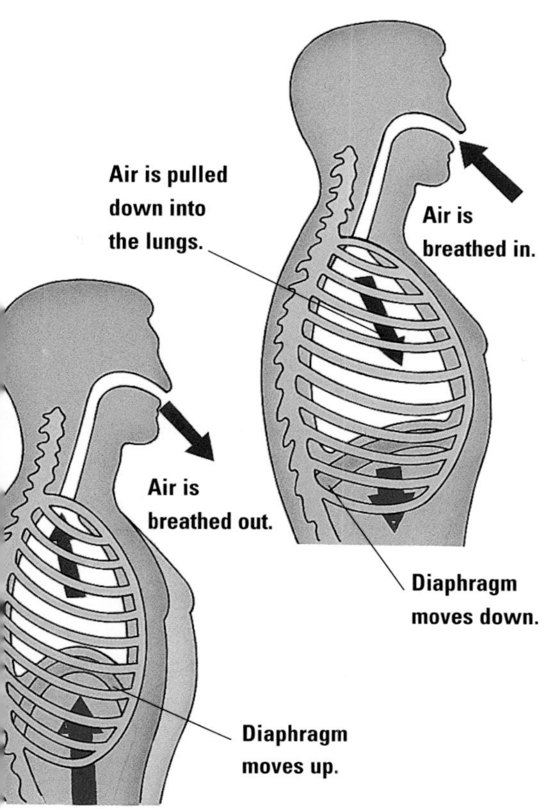
Air is pulled
down into
the lungs.
Air is
breathed in.
Air is
breathed out.
Diaphragm
moves down.
Diaphragm
moves up.

Breathing

When we breathe, many muscles work together to take in air. The diaphragm under the lungs flattens, and the intercostal muscles spread the ribs. The lungs expand, drawing in air. To exhale, the muscles relax again.

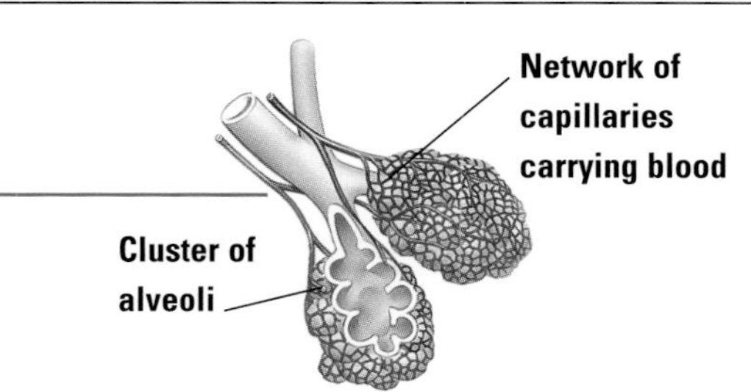
Network of
capillaries
carrying blood
Cluster of
alveoli

Alveoli

The bronchioles end in bunches of tiny, round alveoli. The lining of each alveolus is damp and very thin, allowing gases to pass easily into and out of the blood.

Vocal cords

Humans are unique in our ability to speak—even advanced animals, such as chimpanzees, can produce only a few simple sounds. When we speak, two folds of tissue in the throat called vocal cords are pulled close together. They vibrate as air from the lungs passes between them. The tongue, teeth, lips, nose, and "roof" of the mouth all modify the vibrations to form word sounds.

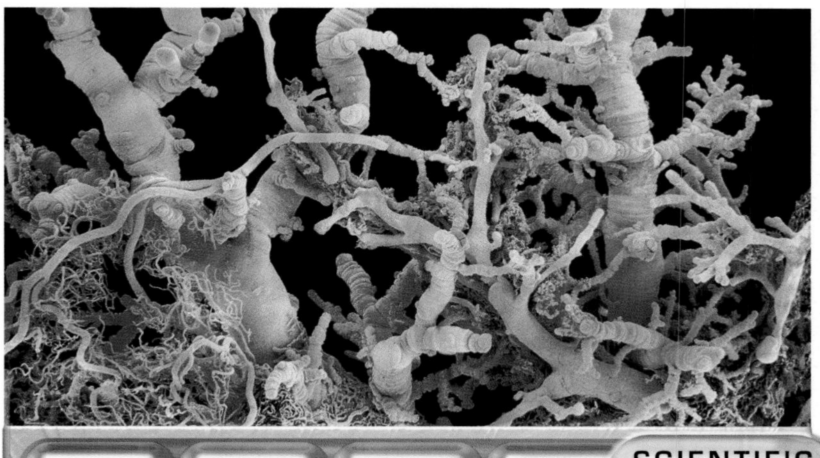

SCIENTIFIC INPUT

GAS TRANSPORTATION

Oxygen travels through the thin capillary walls of the lungs. It is captured in the blood's red cells by a chemical called hemoglobin. Carbon dioxide from the cells is then dissolved in the plasma of the bloodstream before being passed out through the capillary walls. This model shows capillaries in a lung and has been magnified many times.

EATING AND DIGESTION

LIKE ANY MACHINE, THE BODY HAS TO HAVE FUEL TO SUPPLY IT WITH THE ENERGY THAT IT NEEDS. BECAUSE THE BODY CONSTANTLY RENEWS ITSELF, CHEMICALS FROM FOOD ARE ALSO NEEDED TO BUILD CELLS.

Cakes and candies contain a lot of sugar and unhealthy types of fat and should be eaten sparingly.

FOOD FOR LIFE

Carbohydrates supply us with readily available energy, fats provide stored energy for later use, and proteins give us bulk-building material. Small amounts of vitamins and minerals are needed in order for the body to function. Water makes up 70 percent of the body and needs to be replaced constantly. It is important to eat the right amount of each of the food groups (right) to be healthy.

Milk, cheese, and yogurt supply calcium and protein, but some contain unhealthy types of fats.

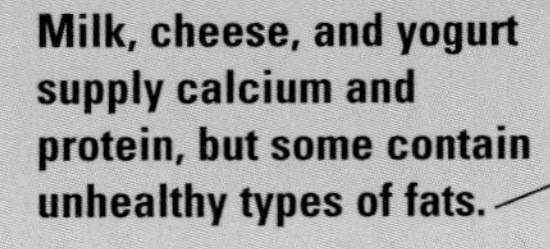

Vegetables contain vitamins, minerals, and fiber, which help in the process of digestion.

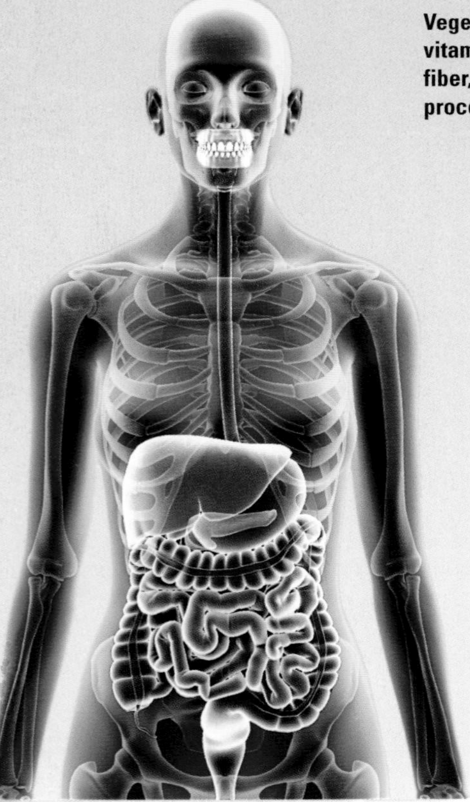

DIGESTION

Once swallowed, food is mixed with acids in the stomach and then moves on to the intestines. There, the chemicals that the body needs are absorbed into the body. The chemicals used to break down food are produced in the pancreas and liver, as well as in the walls of the intestines.

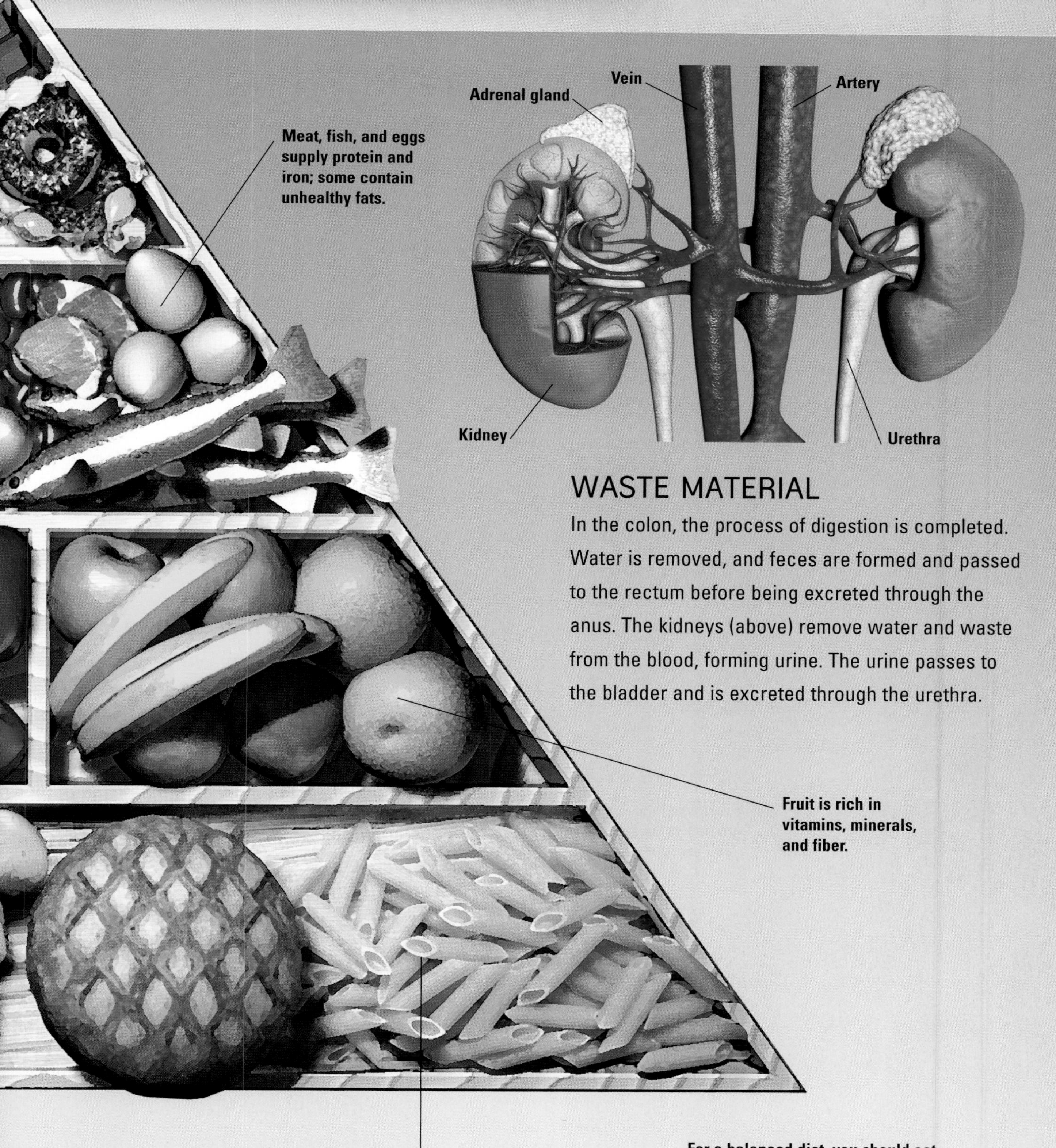

Meat, fish, and eggs supply protein and iron; some contain unhealthy fats.

WASTE MATERIAL

In the colon, the process of digestion is completed. Water is removed, and feces are formed and passed to the rectum before being excreted through the anus. The kidneys (above) remove water and waste from the blood, forming urine. The urine passes to the bladder and is excreted through the urethra.

Fruit is rich in vitamins, minerals, and fiber.

Bread, pasta, and rice are the main sources of carbohydrates.

For a balanced diet, you should eat some of all of the food groups in the pyramid. However, the higher up the pyramid a food is located, the less you should eat of it.

Hormones and metabolism

The body is not only controlled by electrical signals sent through the nervous system. It also uses chemicals called hormones to regulate the processes of life.

Hormones are produced in organs called glands and released into the bloodstream to be transported to the areas that they control.

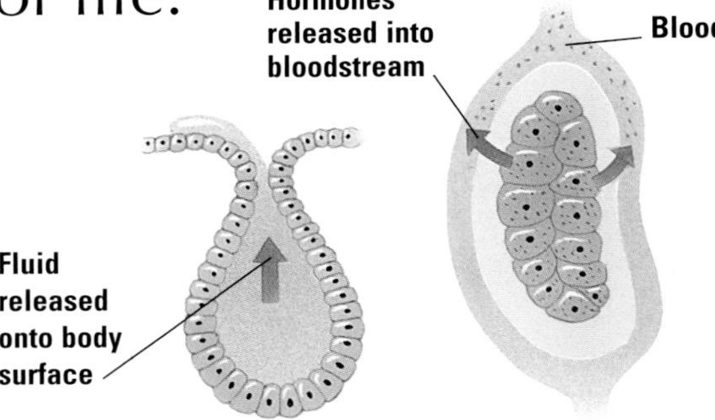

The endocrine system

Not all glands produce hormones. Those that do make up the endocrine system. This system controls growth and metabolism and affects feelings and emotions.

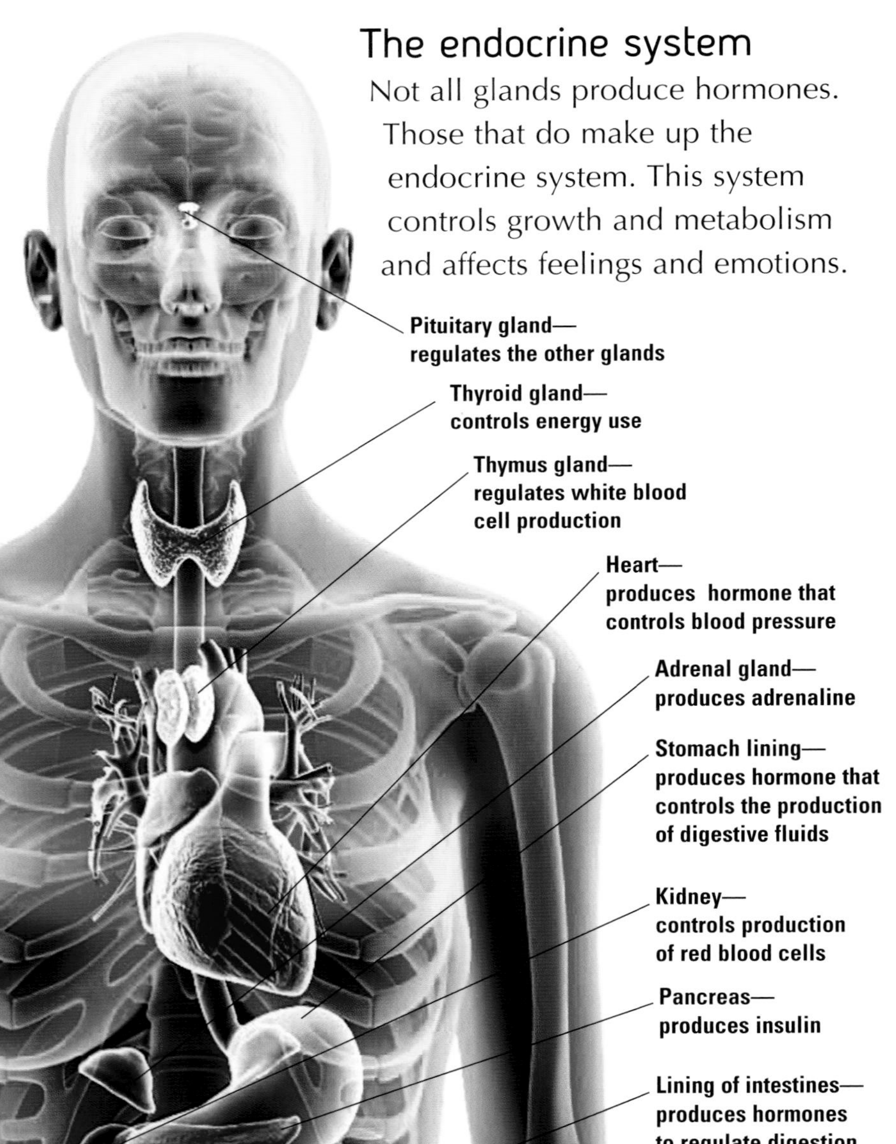

Glands

Glands that produce fluids—such as milk, tears, saliva, mucus, or sweat—secrete them through tubes called ducts. Endocrine glands do not have ducts. The hormones they produce are secreted from their surfaces.

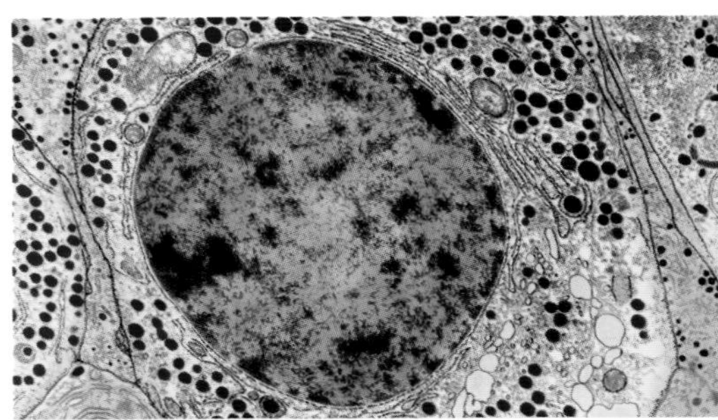

Pituitary gland

This controls all other glands. It also produces hormones that control growth and trigger the production of eggs in women each month. This is a hormone-producing cell (pink, above) inside the pituitary gland.

Daily rhythms

The levels of some hormones vary throughout the day, and our behavior changes as a result. Most people are most alert in the mornings, are physically strongest in the afternoon, feel tired in the late evening, and are most deeply asleep at around 2:00 A.M. Blood pressure and temperature are lowest in the early morning and highest in the early evening.

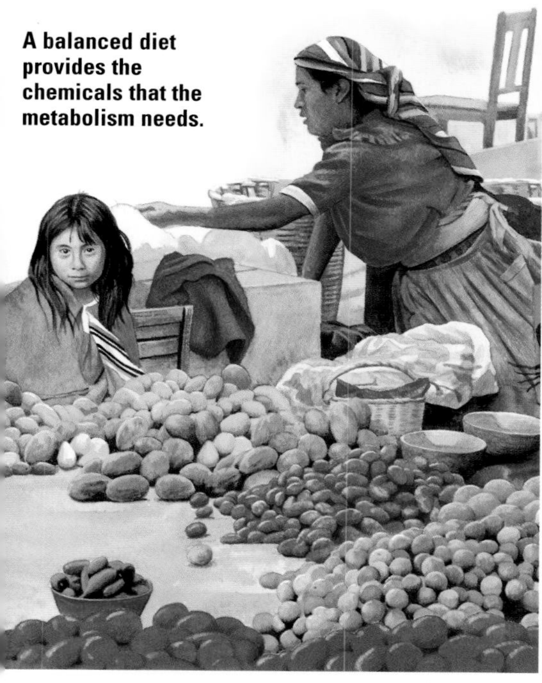

A balanced diet provides the chemicals that the metabolism needs.

Metabolism

The many chemical reactions that take place in the body all make up the metabolism. Metabolism does two things. First, metabolic reactions build up chemicals to make tissues. Second, they break them down, often to release energy.

Epinephrine

When we are frightened or startled, a hormone called epinephrine, or adrenaline, is released that prepares our bodies to fight or run away. Extra blood flows to the muscles and less flows to the digestive system and skin, our pupils widen, and the heart speeds up. The amount of energy-producing glucose in the blood increases.

SCIENTIFIC INPUT

INSULIN AND THE PANCREAS

The pancreas produces a number of hormones. These include insulin, crystals of which are shown above. Insulin controls the way in which a type of sugar called glucose is transferred from the blood to the tissues, where it is used to produce energy. A disease called diabetes reduces insulin production, resulting in too much glucose in the blood.

Genes and chromosomes

Our bodies are made up of organs, organs are made of tissues, and tissues are made of cells. Inside each cell are complex chemicals that control the body's shape and functions.

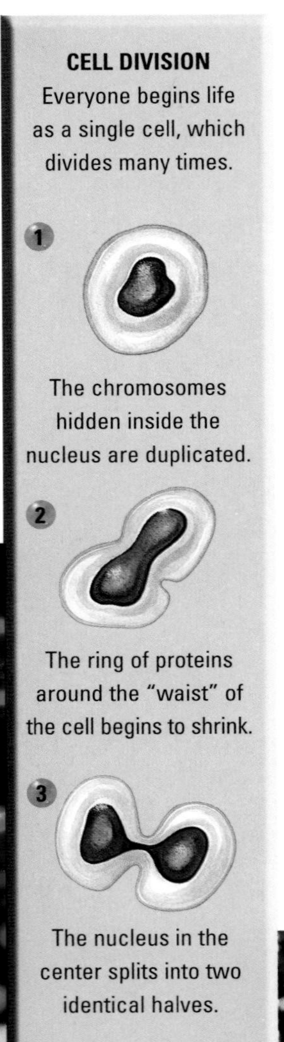

CELL DIVISION
Everyone begins life as a single cell, which divides many times.

1 The chromosomes hidden inside the nucleus are duplicated.

2 The ring of proteins around the "waist" of the cell begins to shrink.

3 The nucleus in the center splits into two identical halves.

4 The two "daughter" cells separate from each other.

The structures of these chemicals are passed down through the generations, which is why we may look similar to our parents. But they merge and change in the process, which is why we are not identical to them.

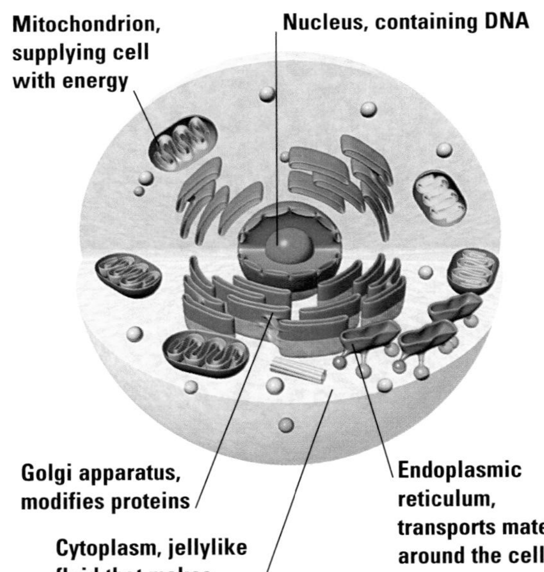

Cells and nuclei

Every part of the body is made up of cells, each too small to see. Bones, nerves, muscles, and other tissues are each built from cells of a particular type. Except for red blood cells, every cell is controlled by a central nucleus.

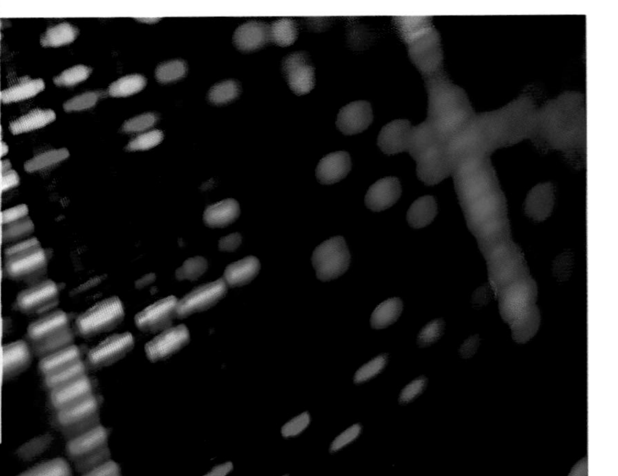

Genes

Cell nuclei contain a set of chemical instructions called genes, which tell the ce how to grow. Characteristics—such as eye color—are passed on from parents to children through genes. The image on the left is a computer representation of th genome—the human genetic code.

DNA and chromosomes

A gene is made up of a sequence of structures, each of which looks like the rungs of a twisted ladder. The ladder is a molecule of a chemical called deoxyribonucleic acid (DNA). The DNA molecules are coiled up tightly to form chromosomes (far right).

The DNA strands wind around each other to form a double helix.

Each "rung" of the DNA ladder is a pair of chemical units called bases.

Strips made of sugar and other molecules hold the DNA together.

Mutations

When cells divide, the DNA is not copied perfectly. It can also be altered by chemicals or by radiation. These changes in DNA are called mutations. They can result in offspring who look very different from their parents.

Inheritance

When an egg is fertilized by a sperm cell, the chromosomes (above) from one parent exchange some DNA with the chromosomes of the other. A new set of chromosomes forms with the mixed DNA. These chromosomes are those of the child that grows from the egg. So the child will inherit some of the characteristics of each parent.

Evolution

Over many generations, through the process of evolution, animal species develop to suit where they live. When resources are limited, animals fight. Those with differences that give them an advantage survive to continue breeding and passing on their DNA. For example, these finches (above) have evolved beaks that are best suited to the types of food available in their different habitats.

Sex and reproduction

Human beings are able to have children because of their reproductive systems. A man's and woman's genes combine, producing a child who has the characteristics of both parents.

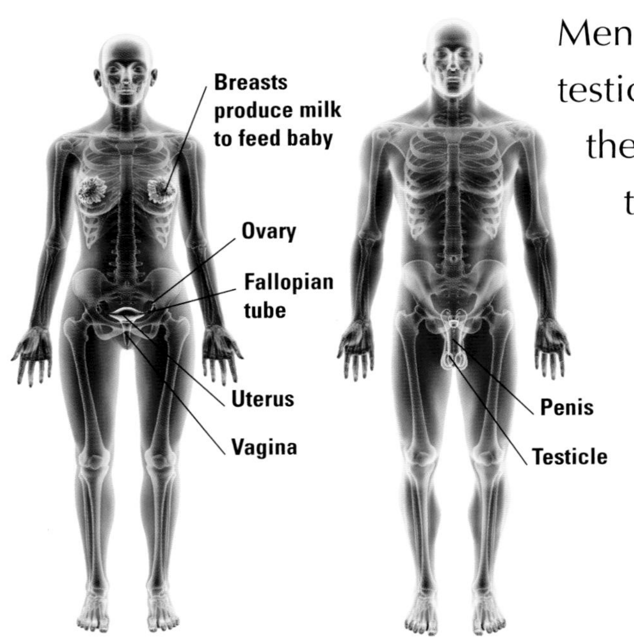

Men produce moving cells called sperm in their testicles, and women produce cells called eggs in their ovaries. A sperm can fertilize an egg, which then develops into a new human being.

Male and female

The type of chromosomes (genetic material) carried by the sperm determine whether a person is male or female. From puberty until menopause, women produce eggs during a monthly cycle called a period. Men produce sperm from puberty until old age.

Conception

To conceive a child, a man inserts his penis into a woman's vagina. He releases a fluid called semen, which contains millions of sperm. The sperm swim through the woman's uterus. On the way, one of them might fertilize an egg in one of the two fallopian tubes.

Early stages of life

The instant a sperm has penetrated the egg, no othe sperm may enter. The fertilized egg travels down the fallopian tube to the uterus. The egg cell divides man times, developing into an embryo and then a fetus. Within three months, the fetus has a face and a beating heart.

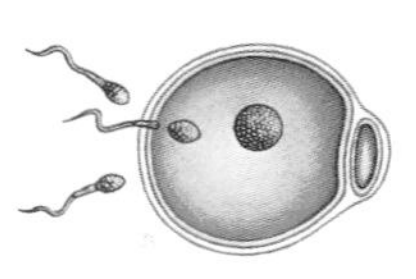

Fertilized egg cell

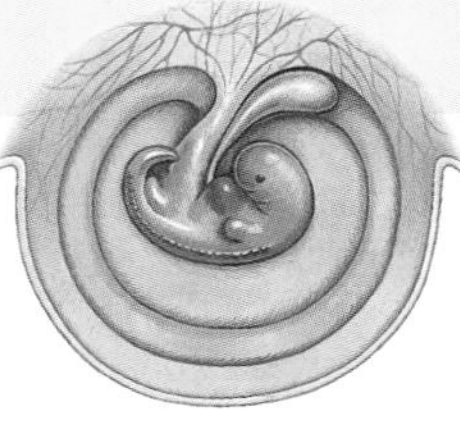

4 weeks

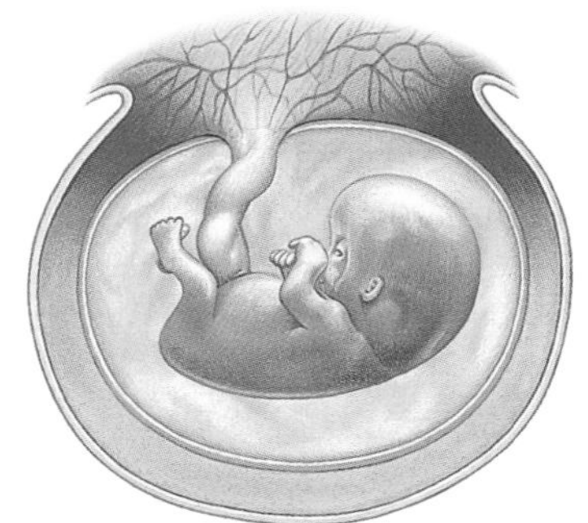

8 weeks

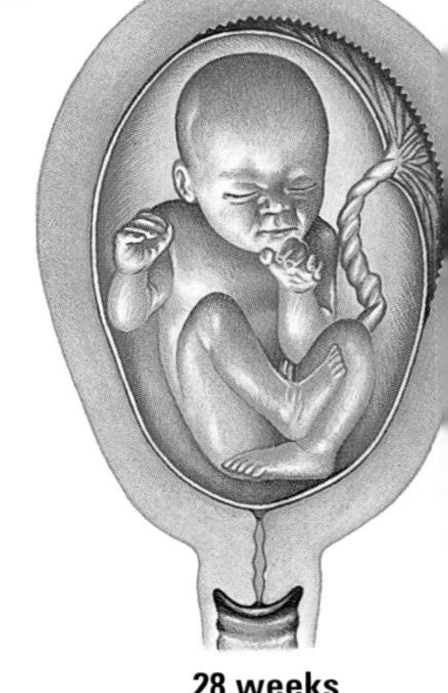

28 weeks

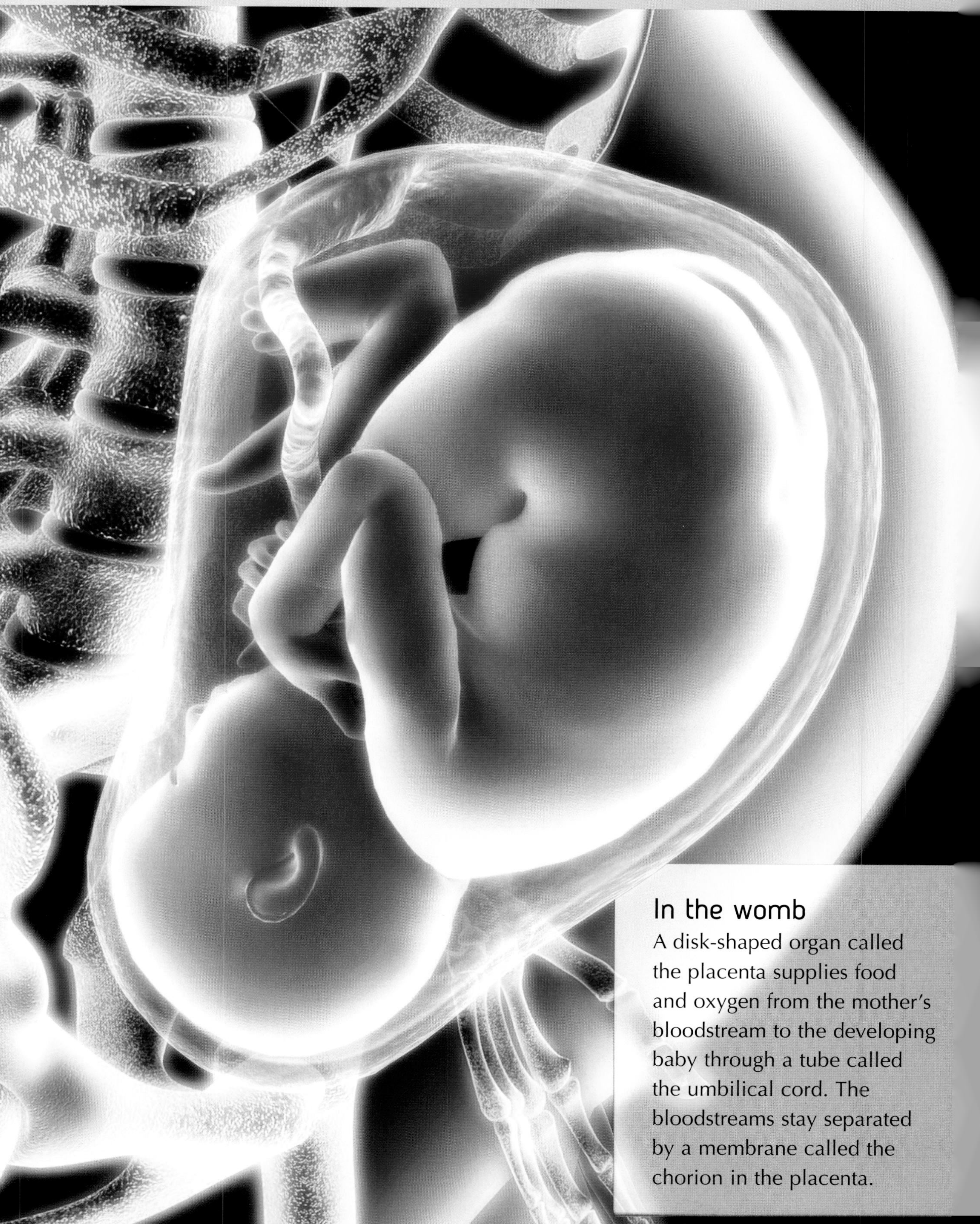

In the womb

A disk-shaped organ called the placenta supplies food and oxygen from the mother's bloodstream to the developing baby through a tube called the umbilical cord. The bloodstreams stay separated by a membrane called the chorion in the placenta.

Growth and aging

Human beings take around 20 years to complete their physical growth and become adults. The processes of physical decline and aging begin soon afterward.

Alongside the physical changes throughout life, there are emotional changes, too, especially during puberty. The development of the brain and intelligence can be continuous throughout a person's life.

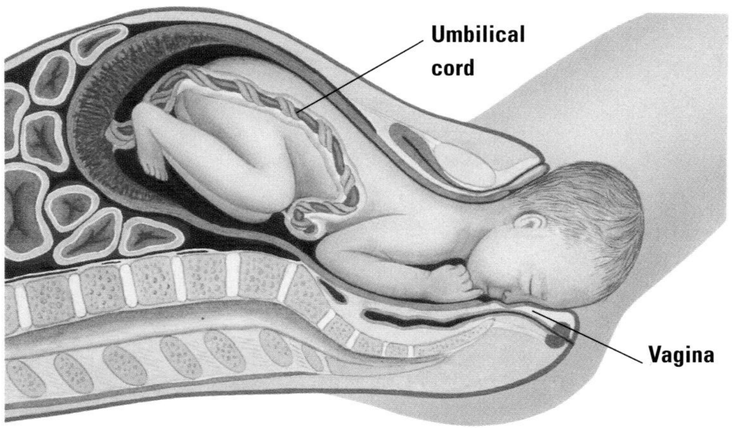

Giving birth

Around nine months after conception, the uterus begins to contract powerfully and rhythmically. It pushes the baby out of the uterus through the vagina—usually headfirst. After the baby has emerged, the umbilical cord is cut.

Early years

Compared to many other animals, newborn babies are vulnerable—to begin with, they cannot even control their body temperature. But development is very rapid, and within three years most children can walk, talk, and have well-developed personalities.

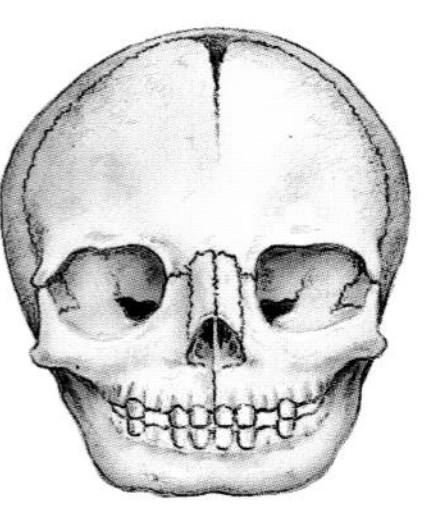
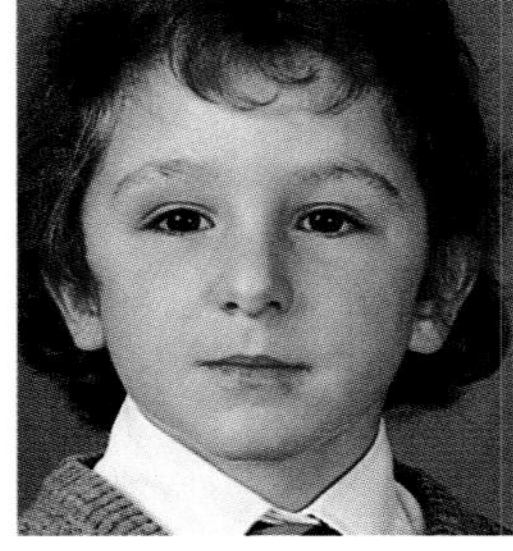

When young, children's skulls are rounded.

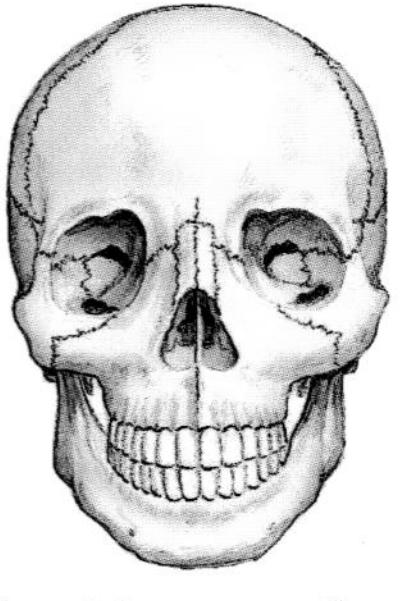

In adolescence, the face becomes longer.

Bone development

Bones develop at different rates, which means that the shapes of the body and face change. At around ages 12–14, both boys and girls experience a "spurt" in height, due to an increase in the growth rate of their long bones. Bones become less flexible and more brittle with age.

Puberty

Puberty usually takes place between the ages of around 9–14 for girls, and 10–17 for boys. It is when the hormones estrogen (in girls) and testosterone (in boys) cause many changes. The production of eggs (girls) and sperm (boys) begins, body hair appears, and voices get lower.

Aging

When someone ages, their muscles get weaker, their sight and hearing deteriorate, and some of their mental skills, such as memory, decline. Egg production ceases in women around the age of 50 during menopause.

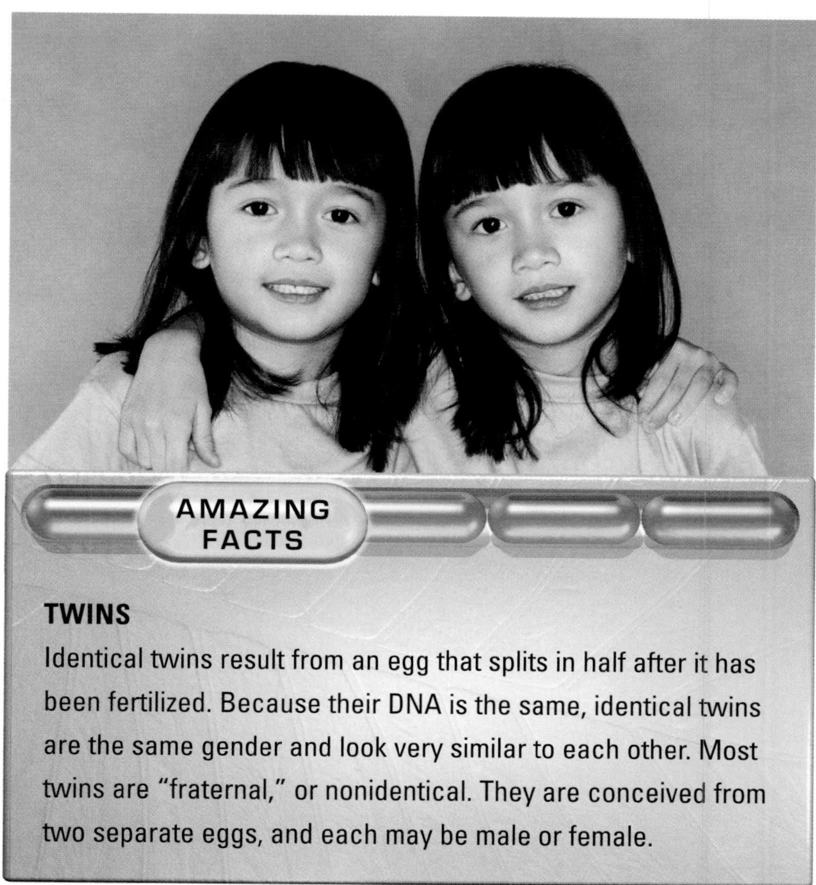

AMAZING FACTS

TWINS

Identical twins result from an egg that splits in half after it has been fertilized. Because their DNA is the same, identical twins are the same gender and look very similar to each other. Most twins are "fraternal," or nonidentical. They are conceived from two separate eggs, and each may be male or female.

The family unit

Humans are social, preferring to live in groups. Often the most important group is the family. Families often protect and support both their children and their older members. The roles and sizes of families vary greatly in different countries and cultures.

DEFENSE SYSTEMS

THE BODY FACES MANY DANGERS, FROM PHYSICAL DAMAGE, EXTREME ENVIRONMENTS, AND INFECTIOUS DISEASES. IN ORDER TO DEFEND ITSELF, THE BODY HAS MANY DIFFERENT SYSTEMS AND BARRIERS.

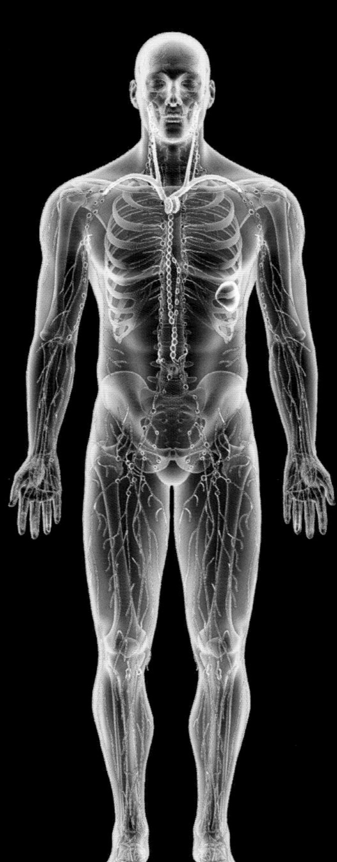

A RANGE OF DEFENSES

Shivering and sweating defend against cold and heat, and the skin tans as a protection against sunburn. A network of vessels called the lymphatic system extends throughout the body (left). Lymph fluid moves between blood, tissues, and lymph vessels. Lymph nodes in the groin, armpits, and neck filter out and destroy harmful organisms.

THE IMMUNE SYSTEM

The immune system consists of the lymphatic system and white blood cells. It produces special proteins called antibodies in order to destroy bacteria. The system can "remember" many of the organisms that infect it so that it can respond very rapidly and effectively if it meets them a second time.

***Bacillus anthracis* (orange) are the rod-shaped bacteria that cause the disease anthrax.**

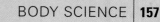

SURFACE DEFENSES

The skin and mucous membranes, such as those in the nose and lungs, act as barriers to infections. They have disease-fighting bacteria and fungi living on them. If the lungs are punctured, their damaged tissues produce chemicals that attract white blood cells to them. The walls of blood vessels in the area also change to allow white cells to pass through them easily.

A neutrophil white blood cell engulfs *Bacillus anthracis* bacteria to protect the body.

WHITE CELL DEFENSES

There are five types of white cells. Basophils release chemicals that trigger tissue defenses. Eosinophils help fight viruses. Lymphocytes attack cancer cells and viruses. And monocytes and neutrophils physically engulf dangerous microorganisms. White cells live in both the bloodstream and the lymphatic system and are manufactured in the marrow of the larger bones.

Health and fitness

Staying in shape and healthy can add years to a person's life and make it more enjoyable. Public services, such as clean water and vaccinations, are vital for this, too.

Health and fitness depend on getting enough sleep, exercising, and having regular checkups.

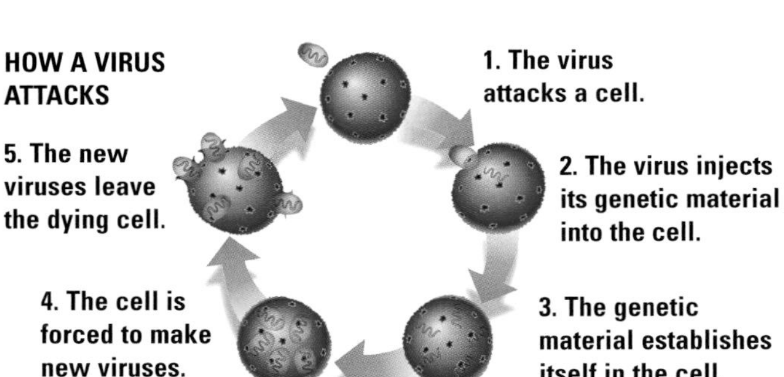

HOW A VIRUS ATTACKS
1. The virus attacks a cell.
2. The virus injects its genetic material into the cell.
3. The genetic material establishes itself in the cell.
4. The cell is forced to make new viruses.
5. The new viruses leave the dying cell.

Body-defense systems

The body can defend itself from infections, but if it responds too slowly, it might not survive. Vaccination involves injecting a weakened version of a virus such as measles. This triggers the immune system to develop a defense against the full-strength virus.

Daily portions of fruit and vegetables are essential for good health.

A balanced diet

A balanced diet includes plenty of fresh fruit and vegetables and whole-wheat bread or healthy cereals, which all provide dietary fiber. It also includes a lot of water and only small amounts of sweet or fatty foods. Eating either too much or too little leads quickly to poor health.

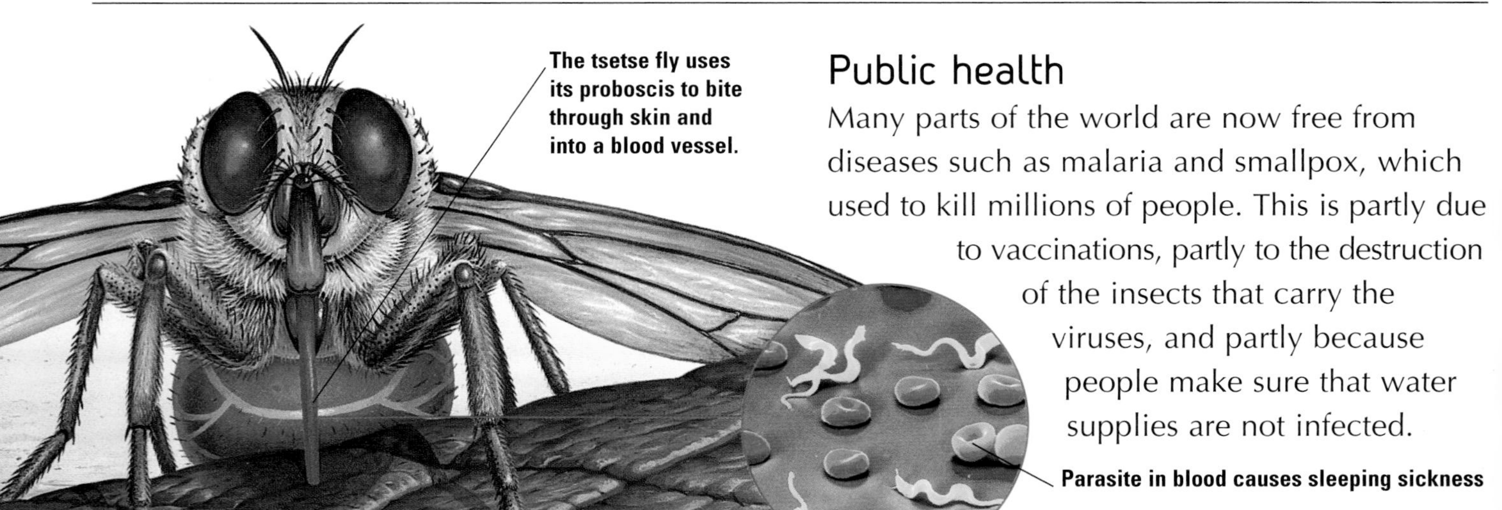

The tsetse fly uses its proboscis to bite through skin and into a blood vessel.

Parasite in blood causes sleeping sickness

Public health

Many parts of the world are now free from diseases such as malaria and smallpox, which used to kill millions of people. This is partly due to vaccinations, partly to the destruction of the insects that carry the viruses, and partly because people make sure that water supplies are not infected.

Staying in shape

The best way to stay in shape is to spend at least 30 minutes each day doing activities that will raise your heart rate. This can include running or swimming or taking part in sports such as soccer, volleyball, tennis, or basketball. It may involve visiting a gym or simply walking briskly. Being fit extends the life span of a person, increases their resistance to diseases, and is also very enjoyable.

Training

The body adapts to cope with the way that it is used. Muscles strengthen and grow if they are exercised. Speed, coordination, and stamina also improve with regular training. The right clothes—including footwear—are important for reducing the risk of injuries, allowing free movement, and avoiding overheating or getting too cold.

Stretching

If an exercise session is started or stopped too quickly, especially in cold conditions, strained ("pulled") muscles and other problems may result. Stretching before and after exercising helps avoid these problems. Regular stretching also helps reduce the stiffness that affects the joints of older people.

Body facts

All the body systems must support one another in order to survive, and they need the right materials to do this. As well as large amounts of water, proteins, fats, carbohydrates, and fibers, small quantities of many other chemicals are essential.

BODY SYSTEMS

Circulatory: transports nutrients and oxygen to the cells and waste (including carbon dioxide) away from them.

Digestive: breaks down food into nutrients.

Endocrine: controls the body through hormones.

Immune: defends against diseases (the lymphatic system is part of the immune system).

Integumentary (skin, hair, and nails): provides a protective barrier.

Muscular: provides movement and structure.

Nervous: allows thinking, control, and sensation.

Respiratory: supplies the blood with oxygen and returns carbon dioxide to the air.

Reproductive: produces children.

Skeletal: gives shape and protection and is moved by the muscular system.

Urinary: removes waste.

VITAL VITAMINS AND MINERALS

Vitamins

A: Retinol
B1: Thiamine
B2: Riboflavin
B3: Niacin
B5: Pantothenic acid
B6: Pyridoxine
B7: Biotin
B9: Folic acid
B12: Cyanocobalamin
C: Ascorbic acid
D: Ergocalciferol and Cholecalciferol
E: Tocopherol
K: Naphthoquinone

Minerals

Calcium
Chlorine
Chromium
Cobalt
Copper
Fluorine
Iodine
Iron
Magnesium
Manganese
Molybdenum
Phosphorus
Potassium
Selenium
Sodium
Sulfur
Zinc

Skateboarders have balance, agility, and muscular strength.

USEFUL WEBSITES

www.innerbody.com/htm/body.html A comprehensive tour of the body's systems.

www.apples4theteacher.com/elibrary/bodybook.html Interactive website about the body.

www.kidskonnect.com/content/view/337/27/ Fast facts for kids on the human body.

www.bbc.co.uk/science/humanbody/ Information about the human body and mind.

The Story of the Past

Throughout history, there have been many changes, from the early farmers who grew crops rather than roaming for food to the growth of cities with very large populations. These constant shifts can create conflicts as people try to preserve their ways of life or impose them on others. Many empires have developed before disappearing forever, and this cycle continues in today's world.

Early civilizations

Humans evolved over thousands of years. They were always on the move, searching for food and hunting wild creatures. Later they learned how to grow crops and breed animals.

They built permanent settlements and organized societies. This was the beginning of civilization.

Australopithecus "southern man"

Homo habilis "handy man"

Homo erectus "upright man"

Homo sapiens "thinking man"

Development of humans

Almost five million years ago, humans evolved from hominids (great apes). They were bipedal, which means walking on two legs. Scientists have called them Homo sapiens, which is Latin for "thinking man."

Prehistory

The word "prehistory" describes the many thousands of years when modern humans lived but before written records began. People hunted animals and gathered foods such as nuts, seeds, fruit, and roots. Some illustrated their everyday lives in cave paintings.

The stone ages

The stone ages lasted from around 700,000 to 3000 B.C. During this period, humans began to use sophisticated tools such as axes, spears, and grindstones to hunt, cut, and process food.

From around 8000 B.C., great centers, such as the Neolithic settlement of Catal Huyuk in Turkey (below), were built. There, several mud houses were crammed together and entered via ladders and holes in the roofs.

The Bronze Age

Metals came into use during the Bronze Age. The hardest was bronze, an alloy of tin and copper that could be cast into any shape. Bronze was in use all across Europe and into India by 1500 B.C. The Assyrians used bronze to make weapons but later tipped their arrows with iron.

Development of writing

The earliest examples of writing were at the beginning of the Bronze Age. The cuneiform writing of Sumer (modern-day Iraq) used wedge-shaped marks cut into soft clay tablets (right). The Egyptians used hieroglyphs.

The Iron Age

The first people to heat iron ore, hammer out its impurities, and dip it in cold water to set it were the northern Asian Hittites in the 1300s B.C. Iron tools encouraged the spread of farming, and the material was also used to make items such as weapons, cooking pots, and statues.

AMAZING FACTS

INVENTION OF THE WHEEL

Early wheels were simple solid wooden disks with a hole for the axle, possibly inspired by the use of turntables to make pottery. The first wheels used for transportation were made by the Sumerians sometime before 3000 B.C., the date that they first appear in drawings. The invention of the wheel allowed people to move heavy loads over long distances, and this had a huge influence on farming, trade, and war.

The ancient Egyptians

The Egyptians created a highly organized civilization that lasted from around 3100 to 30 B.C. Their powerful country had a rich culture based around a belief in an afterlife.

EGYPTIAN SOCIETY
Everyone had a rank in society, which was usually decided by their father's occupation.

Pharaohs had absolute power, linking the people and the gods.

Scribes and priests were very powerful in the pharaoh's court.

The skills of masons, carpenters, and goldsmiths were valued.

Farmers worked in the fields and also helped build the pyramids.

The kingdom developed from desert peoples who settled along the banks of the Nile River in northeastern Africa.

Farming

Every summer, the Nile River flooded and washed fertile mud onto the land. Canals and ditches were dug in order to irrigate the fields. Typical crops were wheat and barley, which were used to make bread and beer, and flax that was needed to produce linen cloth.

Cheops, or Khufu 2558–32 B.C.

Hatshepsut 1473–1458 B.C.

Rameses II 1279–1213 B.C.

Cleopatra 51–30 B.C.

Godlike rulers

In total, more than 300 pharaohs ruled Egypt. They were almost all men, who passed on power from father to son. Pharaohs were both political and religious leaders for their people. A pharaoh made laws and decided when to go to war. He or she also represented the gods on Earth.

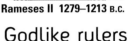

The Great Pyramid

The largest ancient Egyptian structure was the Great Pyramid in Giza. The tomb of King Cheops, or Khufu, it took 20 years to build and was completed in 2528 B.C. At 480.5 ft. (146.5m) high, it is the largest of three pyramids in Giza.

Hieroglyphs

Egyptian writing was based on an alphabet of 700 picture symbols called hieroglyphs. Scribes either wrote on paper made from the dried reeds of papyrus that grew by the Nile River, or the writing was carved into the stone of temples and tombs. It took years to learn how to write it.

Egyptian gods

The Egyptians had many gods, each one with specific roles. Everything about the gods was symbolic. Osiris (right), as the god of the dead, wears mummy bandages. He has a green face and holds a farmer's crook and flail to show that he is also the god of new life.

Building a pyramid

Huge blocks of stone were floated along the Nile River and placed tightly together by thousands of workers. The completed structure was then covered in creamy white limestone and capped with gold so that it glistened across the red desert. Later pharaohs were buried in hidden tombs in an attempt to stop tomb raiding.

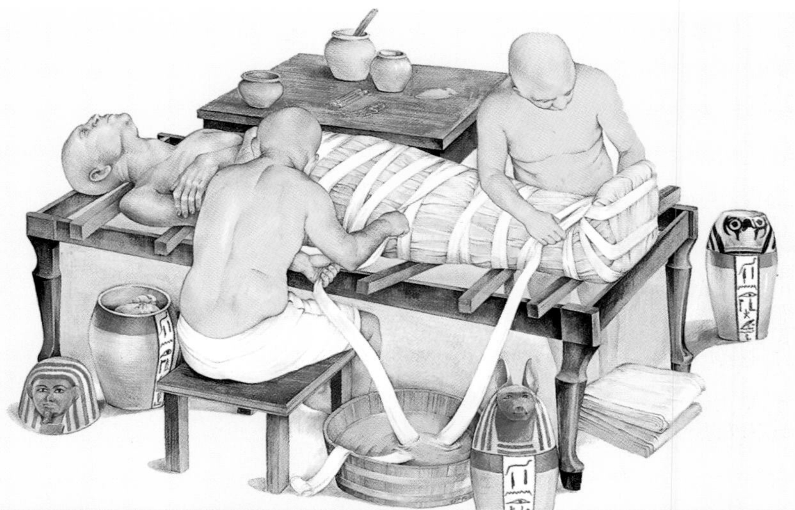

CULTURAL NOTE

MUMMIFICATION

In order to preserve a pharaoh for the afterlife, the dead body was mummified. Priests removed the vital organs and stored all of them, except for the brain (which was considered worthless), in canopic jars. The corpse was dried out using natron salt and then stuffed, wrapped in bandages, and placed in a set of richly decorated coffins. The body was buried with ushabtis, or shabtis—slave statues that would serve their master.

THE QIN DYNASTY

THIS CHINESE DYNASTY, LED BY THE RUTHLESS QIN SHI HUANGDI (LEFT), UNIFIED CHINA FROM 221 B.C. HE STANDARDIZED THE WRITTEN LANGUAGE, THE CURRENCY, AND WEIGHTS AND MEASURES.

The first wall was built of rammed earth. During the Ming dynasty of the A.D. 1400s, large parts of the wall were rebuilt using bricks and stone.

THE GREAT WALL

At this time, the fortifications that protected northern China against attacking tribes were improved with the building of large sections of a Great Wall. It was up to 30 ft. (9m) high and wide enough for five galloping horses. Thousands of Chinese people died while building it. Rebuilt many times since, at 3,970 mi. (6,400km) long , it is the longest and largest construction in the world.

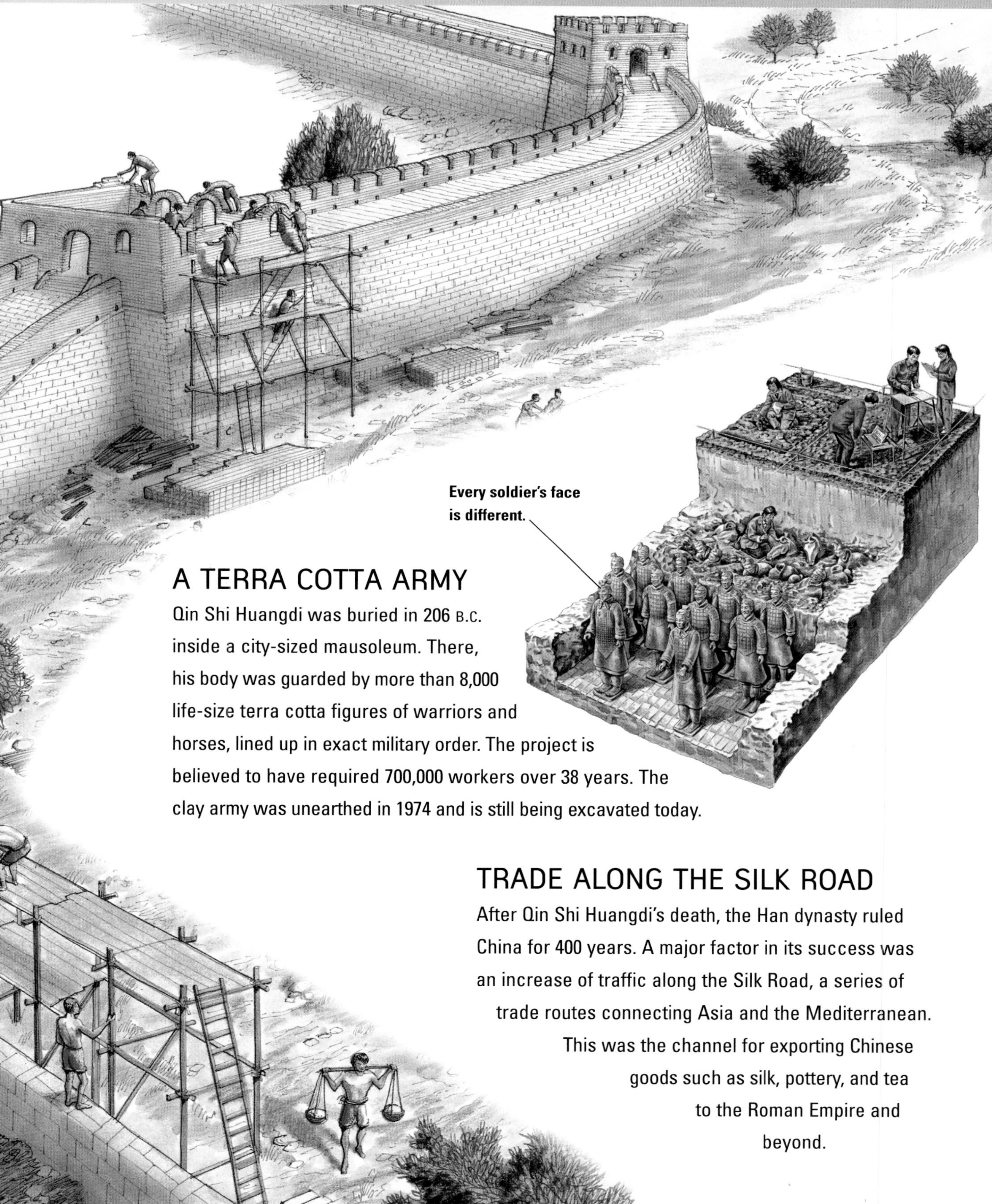
Every soldier's face is different.

A TERRA COTTA ARMY

Qin Shi Huangdi was buried in 206 B.C. inside a city-sized mausoleum. There, his body was guarded by more than 8,000 life-size terra cotta figures of warriors and horses, lined up in exact military order. The project is believed to have required 700,000 workers over 38 years. The clay army was unearthed in 1974 and is still being excavated today.

TRADE ALONG THE SILK ROAD

After Qin Shi Huangdi's death, the Han dynasty ruled China for 400 years. A major factor in its success was an increase of traffic along the Silk Road, a series of trade routes connecting Asia and the Mediterranean. This was the channel for exporting Chinese goods such as silk, pottery, and tea to the Roman Empire and beyond.

The ancient Greeks

The sophisticated ancient Greek civilization left lasting legacies in politics, medicine, science, the arts, and architecture.

The Greek Empire was a loosely linked set of city-states on the mainland and islands close to Athens. The period from 500 to 350 B.C. is known as the Greek Classical Age.

Greek warfare

Wars were common between Greek city-states as well as with neighboring countries. In sea battles, the Greeks sailed triremes (ships with three rows of oars) at full speed to ram into enemy boats. They were also well organized on land. For example, soldiers from Sparta fought in close formation, overlapping their shields for protection.

A painted "all-seeing eye" to help and guide the Greeks at sea.

The Olympics

The first Olympic Games were held in 776 B.C. and then at four-year intervals after that. They grew out of military training and included discus and javelin throwing, the long jump, wrestling, and sprinting.

City-states

The Greek Empire was made up of around 300 city-states, some of which were tiny. Greece was frequently torn by rivalry, especially between Athens and Sparta. Athens introduced democracy, while Sparta was run like a military camp. Most city-states were prosperous and relied on slaves to do a lot of the hard work.

Doctors and scholars

The Greeks valued education, using observation and reasoning to learn about the world around them. Doctors such as Hippocrates studied the body and illnesses. Scholars such as the mathematician Archimedes and the philosopher Aristotle laid the groundwork for modern science.

Greek architecture

The Greeks loved public buildings and left an incredible legacy of architectural ideas. Best known is the Parthenon, a beautifully proportioned temple located on the sacred hill of the Acropolis in Athens. Completed in the 400s B.C., it is still standing. Other major buildings included huge open-air theaters that could seat audiences of 10,000.

Alexander the Great

In 336 B.C., aged just 20, Alexander became the king of Macedonia. This well-educated and accomplished soldier took over the Greek Empire before ruthlessly conquering huge areas from Greece to northern India.

CULTURAL NOTE

THE GODS OF ANCIENT GREECE

The ancient Greeks believed that their gods lived on Mount Olympus. There were many gods, and they used their powers to help or hinder ordinary people. The head god was Zeus (3), with his wife Hera (4) by his side. His brother Hades (6) ruled the underworld, Demeter (5) was the goddess of Earth, and Aphrodite (2) was the goddess of beauty. Hermes (1) was the gods' messenger.

The Roman Empire

At its peak, the Roman Empire covered most of Europe and reached into Africa and Asia.

The Romans had a sophisticated way of life, with planned cities and organized government, but their society relied on slavery.

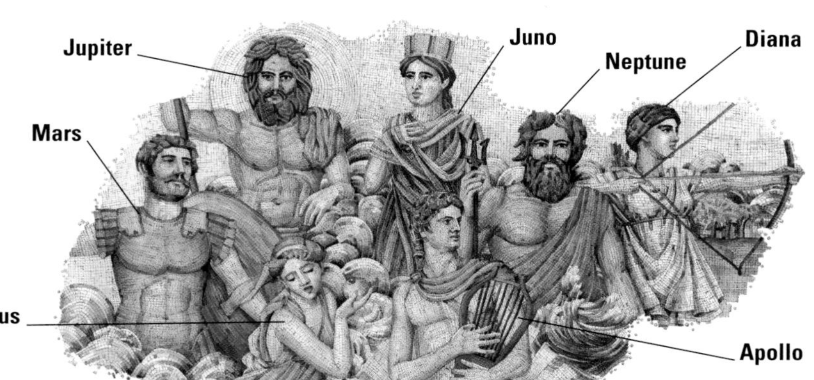

CULTURAL NOTE

GODS OF ANCIENT ROME

Many Roman gods were borrowed from the Greeks but given different names. For example, the main Roman god was Jupiter, not Zeus. Every home had a shrine or room dedicated to a god, and there were public temples across the empire—the largest of which was the domed Pantheon in Rome.

Efficient army

The army was organized into groups called legions, cohorts, and centuries. Most fighting was done on foot, and the well equipped soldiers could link their shields together into an impenetrable barrier called the tortoise formation.

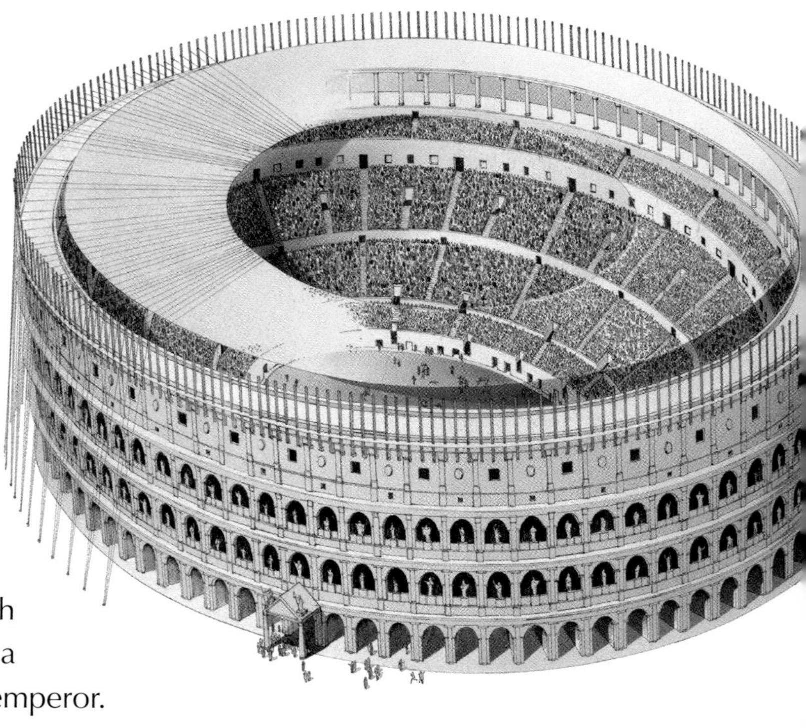

Roman games

Amphitheaters, where bloodthirsty games and fights, sea battles, and animal hunts were held, were very popular. Rome's Colosseum (right), opened in 80 B.C. and could seat 50,000 spectators on three levels to cheer on the gladiators fighting to the death in the arena. Losers were spared or killed on a thumbs-up or thumbs-down signal from the emperor.

The Roman baths

Every major Roman town had public baths, heated by an underfloor hot-air system called a hypocaust. All baths had a cold room, a warmer area where dirt could be scraped from the skin, and a pool for a refreshing dip.

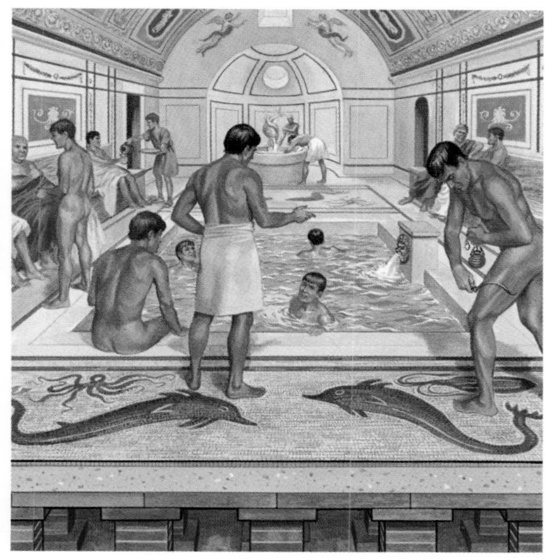

Emperors and the empire

Rome became an empire when Augustus was appointed to be the emperor in 27 B.C. Known as "First Citizen," an emperor was all-powerful and his word was law. Many of the Roman emperors were plotted against, and several, including Julius Caesar, were assassinated.

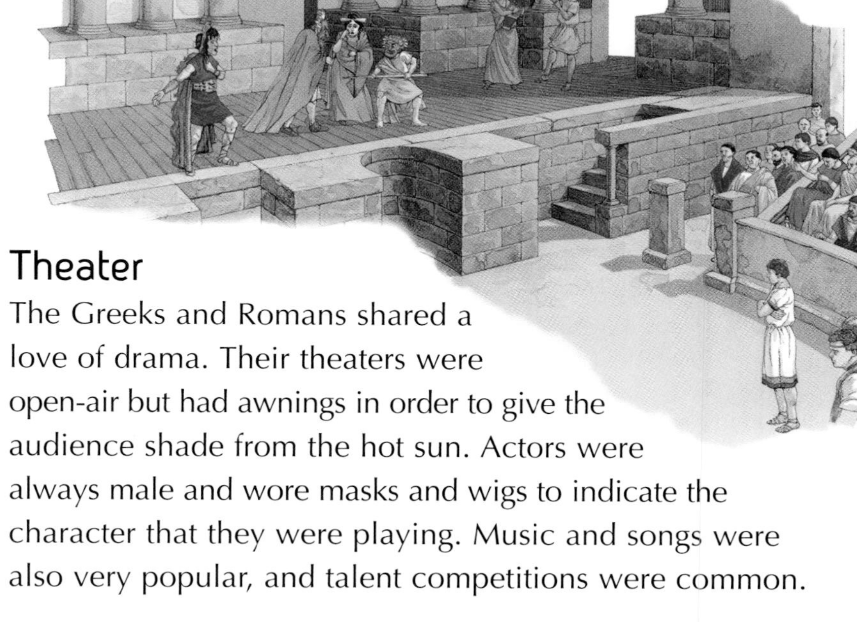

Theater

The Greeks and Romans shared a love of drama. Their theaters were open-air but had awnings in order to give the audience shade from the hot sun. Actors were always male and wore masks and wigs to indicate the character that they were playing. Music and songs were also very popular, and talent competitions were common.

Feats of engineering

The Romans were great builders and engineers. Cities were planned on a grid pattern, and public fountains got their supply of fresh water through a system of aqueducts. The channels and pipes of the aqueducts would usually travel underground, but they were built on high arches in order to cross valleys.

THE MAYA

THE MAYAN CIVILIZATION WAS AT ITS PEAK BETWEEN A.D. 250–900, BUT THEN IT MYSTERIOUSLY WENT INTO DECLINE.

TEMPLES AND RELIGION

The Maya were skillful builders, erecting pyramid-shaped temples without the use of metal tools. They painted these temples red, the color of life and power, and decorated them with green jade stone. They worshiped gods of the Sun, Moon, Earth, rain, and their most important crop, corn. They made human sacrifices to please the gods.

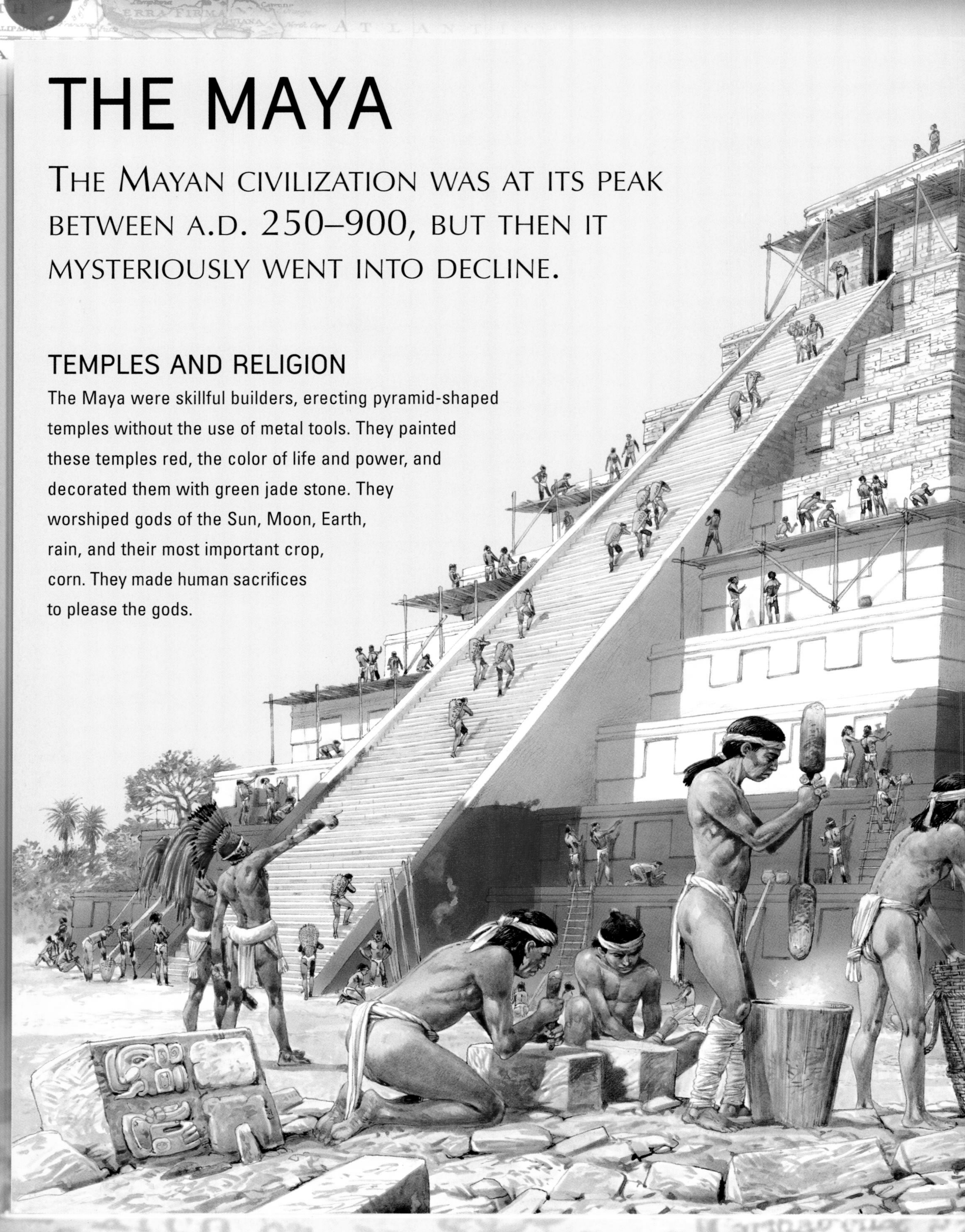

CITIES AND VILLAGES

The Mayan civilization was made up of several city-states, each one ruled by a king who claimed to have descended from the gods. Although most Maya lived in farming villages, they built huge cities with vast populations such as Copán, which was 8 mi. (13km) long and 2 mi. (3km) wide and featured temples, palaces, and squares. Many of its monuments were carved with images of astronomy and astrology.

The Castillo, the main pyramid in the city of Chichén Itzá, was built around A.D. 800. Its base is 592 sq. ft. (55m²).

The four staircases each had 91 steps, and there was a platform on top, making a total of 365—the number of days in the Mayan year.

MAKING WAR

Mayan kingdoms often fought each other for trade and power and to capture prisoners for religious sacrifices. Soldiers wielded short spears and wooden axes with stone blades, as well as throwing weapons such as sticks and javelins. For armor, they wore cotton jackets that were stuffed with salt as padding.

Medieval Europe

The medieval period, or Middle Ages, lasted from the 500s to the 1400s. It was a time of hardship, with many wars, famines, and plagues.

Religion was more important than countries. Great cathedrals were built in order to praise God, and the Church influenced everyday and political life.

Castles and fortifications

Built to protect the land and survive the frequent wars, castles became gradually more fortified. Narrow slit windows meant that arrows could be fired at attackers from a safe place. Most castles could withstand sieges.

WEAPONS OF WAR

Methods of war changed when the stirrup made horseback riding easier, and knights on horseback became an essential part of armies.

Archers fired a barrage of deadly arrows—and the longbow was greatly feared.

Crossbows shot a bolt with great power. They were easier to use than bows, so less practice was needed.

Knights carried shields and wore chain mail—small, linked iron rings that protected them against most weapons.

The crusades

A series of crusades were made between 1096 and 1291. Christian armies from Europe tried, and failed, to drive the Muslim Turks from the Holy Lands of the Bible. Knights took part to win lands and fortune.

Joan of Arc was captured and burned at the stake by the English in 1431.

The Hundred Years' War

From 1337 to 1453, there was a series of conflicts between England and France, mostly over English claims on French land. Despite setbacks, the French won due to the leadership of Joan of Arc and their superior resources.

Feudal life

For most of this period, the social order was unchanged. The king, at the top, offered land in return for support from the nobles. They, in turn, allowed peasants to farm the land in exchange for goods or their service when required.

The Black Death

In the 1300s, this plague killed 25 million people, around one third of the people of Europe. The Black Death was carried by fleas traveling on rats. It quickly spread throughout countries that had been weakened by famine. No treatment was possible, and villages and towns were left deserted as the inhabitants died or fled.

AMAZING FACTS

THE VIKINGS

These fighters sailed their fast, strong boats across the sea from Scandinavia and up rivers to raid rich settlements such as monasteries. They were good traders, fierce warriors, and eventually settlers, giving their name to the Normans (Norsemen) of France and the English city of York (Jorvic).

Tournaments

These were a popular way of practicing fighting skills and providing entertainment. Knights fought each other on foot, or sometimes in a joust on horseback, toppling opponents with long lances. Those who were defeated paid a ransom of money or equipment.

Explorers

From the 1400s onward, European explorers sought new lands, gold, silver, and precious spices. Some of them also wanted to spread the Christian faith.

Improved navigation and mapmaking, as well as the manufacture of caravels (small, fast ships that could sail against the wind), made longer journeys possible.

Henry the Navigator discusses the building of a new ship.

Henry the Navigator

Between 1424 and 1434, Prince Henry, the son of the king of Portugal, paid sailors to explore the coast of Africa. This opened up new trading routes along the east coast of Africa. Henry had ships built and even founded a school of navigation in Portugal to train future explorers. Later Portuguese sailors reached India and the Far East.

Conquering the Aztecs

The Aztec civilization of Mexico was among the first casualties of European exploration. It was destroyed by a mix of Western diseases and Spanish firepower. The Aztecs had a strong religious culture based around sacrifice.

The New World

Between 1492 and 1502, the Italian sailor Christopher Columbus sailed his fleet west from Spain four times. He hoped to find a new route to Asia. However, he did not realize that the islands and mainland where he landed were part of a new world, the then unknown continent of North America.

Eastern trade route

In 1497–1498, the Portuguese explorer Vasco da Gama led the first European expedition to sail around Africa and straight to India. This new route allowed Portugal to be the first to take over lands and colonize parts of east Africa. It increased opportunities for Europeans to trade in valuable Indian spices and jewels.

Around the world

Between 1519–1522, Ferdinand Magellan sailed around the tip of South America, across the Pacific Ocean, and back around Africa to Spain—the first around-the-world journey. He died on the way, as did most of his crew of 270—only 18 survived.

Magellan was killed in Mactan, in the Philippines.

AMAZING FACTS

INCA GOLD

The Inca civilization of around 12 million people, based in and around the Andes Mountains in South America, was known by the Spanish to have a lot of gold. In 1532, the adventurer Francisco Pizarro held the Inca king for a ransom of a room filled with 11 tons of the precious metal. Then he killed the king anyway.

Cook and Australia

It took hundreds of years for European explorers to reach the southern Pacific. It was not until 1768–1779 that James Cook mapped many of its islands. He found some communities that had been established by local seafarers 1,500 years before.

THE AGE OF REVOLUTION

ACROSS EUROPE AND NORTH AMERICA, A PERIOD OF REVOLUTION HELPED SHAPE THE MODERN AGE. IN MANY COUNTRIES, DEMOCRATIC GOVERNMENTS REPLACED THE RULE OF KINGS AND QUEENS.

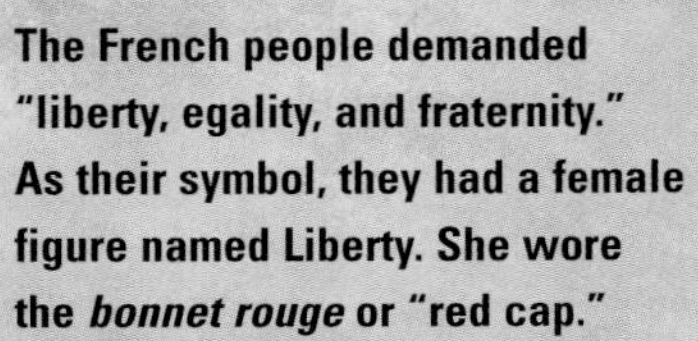

The French people demanded "liberty, egality, and fraternity." As their symbol, they had a female figure named Liberty. She wore the *bonnet rouge* or "red cap."

FRENCH REVOLUTION

From 1789, bad government and a huge gulf between the rich and the poor fueled a revolution in France. This marked the end for the unpopular king, Louis XVI, and his wife Marie Antoinette. She was one of at least 18,000 nobles and their allies who were sent to the guillotine during the Reign of Terror, from 1793–1794. It was also the start of a ten-year upheaval as a new republic was established.

During the French Revolution, on July 14, 1789, the Bastille prison in Paris, France, was stormed by the revolutionaries. The prison was a symbol of royal power and a place where ammunition and weapons were stored.

THE RISE OF NAPOLEON

An excellent general named Napoleon used his position as a war hero to become the military dictator of France, electing himself emperor from 1804. He reformed the way that France was governed. Banished to the Italian island of Elba, he briefly regained power but was finally defeated in the Battle of Waterloo in 1815. In 1821, he died in exile on the island of Saint Helena.

THE AMERICAN REVOLUTION

The 13 colonies of North America resented the taxes and laws that were imposed on them by Great Britain. Partially funded by France, and fueled by ideas of independence, they fought against the British from 1775. The British could not sustain the distant conflict. The war was won by 1781, and American sovereignty was recognized from 1783.

The industrial revolution

During the 1700s, the introduction of new technology and new sources of power led to the beginning of mass production.

TEXTILE REVOLUTION
Machines that allowed one person to do the work of many transformed the economy.

The spinning jenny spun yarn by turning a handle.

Arkwright's water frame made thread quickly.

The cotton gin separated cotton fibers and seeds.

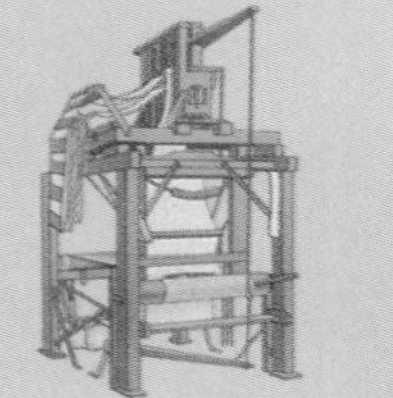

The jacquard loom used punch cards to make cloth.

There was social change all the way across Europe. People who had typically farmed and lived in small villages moved to work in factories or offices in smoky towns.

Water wheels

Waterpower began to take the place of horsepower. The energy taken from moving water powered the new machines, which were grouped together to create the first factories.

Factory towns

Larger and larger factories and mills were built—many of them providing houses for the workers. New towns sprang up around these new industries.

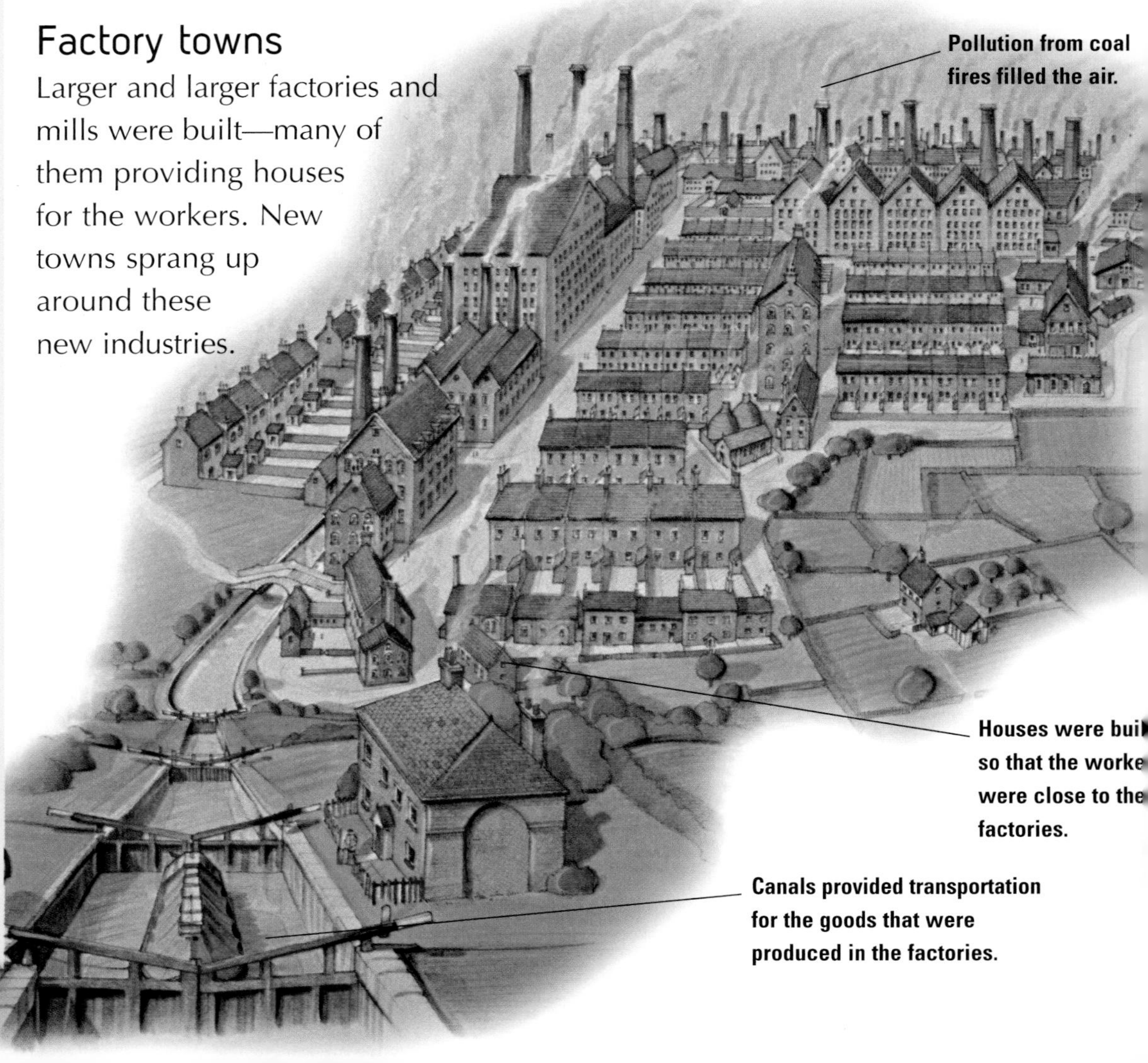

Pollution from coal fires filled the air.

Houses were buil so that the worke were close to the factories.

Canals provided transportation for the goods that were produced in the factories.

Iron construction

A new, cheap material called cast iron allowed engineers to develop new techniques for building large structures such as bridges. This is the first iron bridge (right), built in England in 1779. From 1784, the even stronger wrought iron was also available.

Child labor

Factories and coal mines needed cheap labor, and children were the solution. They were small enough to crawl along tunnels and under machinery, and they were forced to work long hours in return for low pay.

Steam power

Steam began to replace water and wind as a means of power. The need for rapid transportation prompted the development of steam locomotives and railroad systems.

HISTORICAL DATA

SLAVERY

The industrial revolution increased the use of slavery as a source of labor. Crowded slave ships carried chained-up human cargo from Africa to America in terrible conditions. The slaves were then made to work on plantations to produce cotton, sugar, and tobacco. In 1780, Pennsylvania was the first U.S. state to abolish slavery, and other states and countries gradually followed.

The Saint Pierre, or Number 33, built in France in 1844

Migration

From 1800, Western countries created huge empires in Africa and Asia. Powerful navies protected the ships that ferried slaves and raw materials around the globe.

North America and Australia attracted many migrants from Europe. The first settlers were sometimes exiled criminals, but many people followed in search of work and then stayed on and sent money back home.

The Irish potato famine

Food shortages and economic problems were major causes of migration. One example is the Great Irish Famine of 1845–1851, when the failure of the potato crop starved one million people and led at least half that number to board ships traveling to the U.S.A.

Gold rushes

The discovery of gold deposits started gold rushes in the U.S.A, Canada, New Zealand, and Australia during the 1800s. People traveled across the world to mine and pan for the precious nuggets, and many new settlements were established.

Miners pan for gold in California.

Migration to the U.S.A

For many years, packed boats full of immigrants arrived in the U.S.A. This led to the creation of an entry point on Ellis Island, in New York Harbor. Between 1892 and 1954, more than 20 million immigrants arrived there for registration and medical checks before scattering all over the country.

WORLD WAR I

THE GREAT WAR WAS THE WORST CONFLICT THE WORLD HAD EVER SEEN. AN ENTIRE GENERATION OF YOUNG MEN DIED: 8.5 MILLION SOLDIERS AND MORE THAN TWICE THAT MANY CIVILIANS.

THE START OF THE WAR

On June 28, 1914, Archduke Franz Ferdinand of Austria was assassinated by an enemy Serb. Allies of both Austria and Serbia were drawn in, and Europe was at war within six weeks. This was the first "total war," fought on a scale never known before.

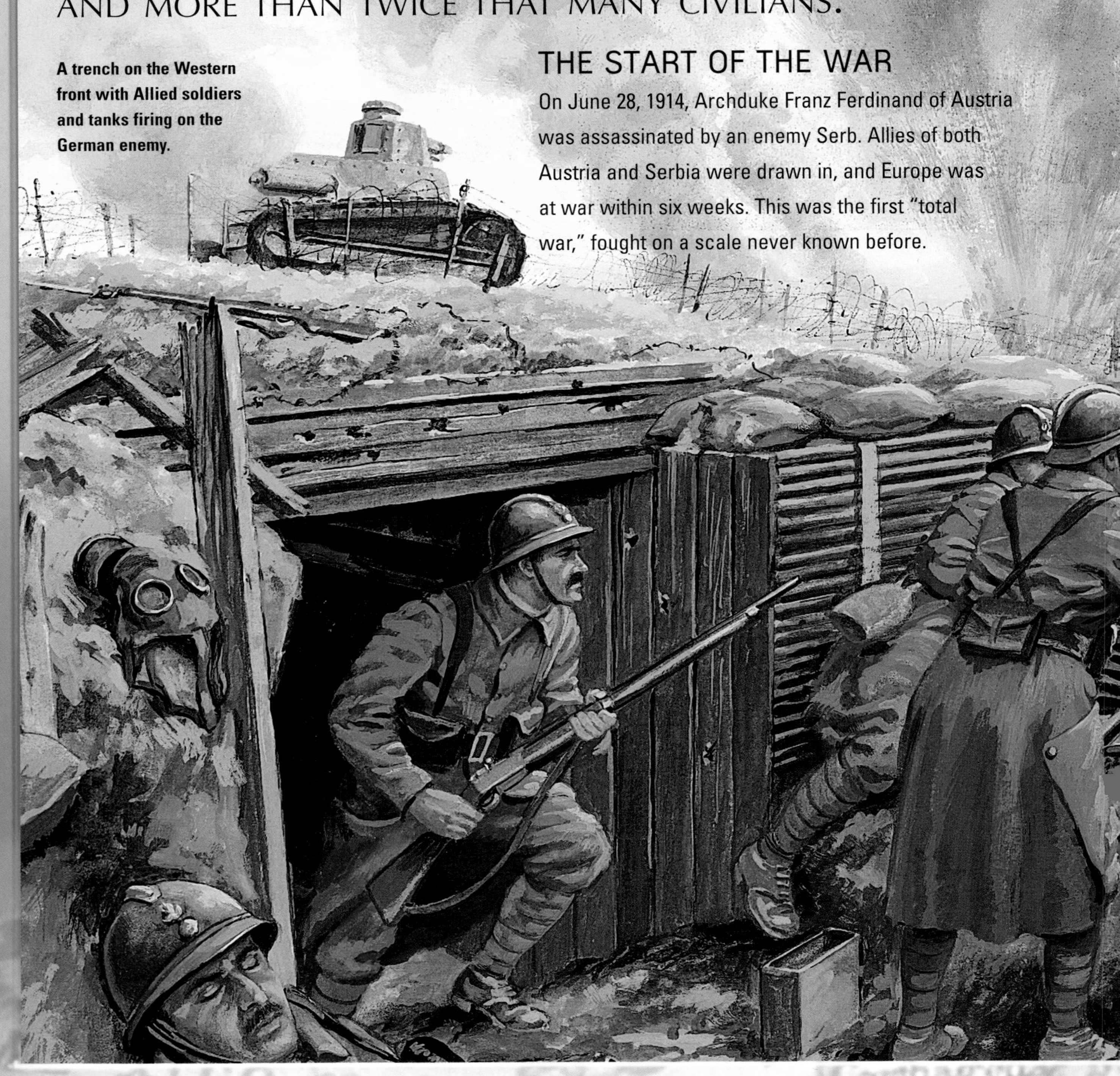

A trench on the Western front with Allied soldiers and tanks firing on the German enemy.

TRENCH WARFARE

The "Western front" of trenches and fortifications stretched for more than 370 mi. (600km), from the French coast to Switzerland. A similar "Eastern front" separated Austria and Russia. The trenches were cramped, waterlogged, and rife with rats and diseases. Lines of troops were ordered "over the top," often to be mowed down by machine guns.

German soldiers defended their position on the Western front with machine guns and poison gas.

AFTER THE SLAUGHTER

The turning point in the war came when the U.S.A. entered the conflict in April 1917, following the sinking of some of their merchant ships. American supplies and reinforcements, combined with a naval blockade to starve Germany, brought an end to the war on November 11, 1918.

World War II

This war was fought on land, at sea, and in the air around the glo
Some people estimated the total dead to have been as high as
million, either directly from fighting or from famine and disease

WEAPONS OF WAR
Key weapons were battleships and submarines at sea, fighters in the air, and tanks on land.

The Spitfire fighter was a single-seater plane used by the British and their allies.

Tiger 1 was the common name given to the German heavy tanks.

The USS *Gearing DD710* was the ultimate World War II destroyer.

German U-boats enforced naval blockades against Allied shipping.

The war set Great Britain, the U.S.A., and the Soviet Union against Germany, Italy, and Japan. It was fought across Europe, Asia, and Africa and in the Pacific Ocean. A major turning point was the German failure to conquer the Soviet Union in 1943.

Adolf Hitler

Adolf Hitler gained power in Germany in 1933. He occupied neighboring territories without opposition until the invasion of Poland prompted Great Britain and France to declare war.

War in the air

With Germany in control of most of Europe, it needed to win the war in the air in order to be able to invade Great Britain. But the British were developing new, faster planes, and these won the Battle of Britain in the summer of 1940.

Beginning of the end

On April 30, 1945, realizing that he had lost the war, Adolf Hitler killed himself in a bunker in Berlin, Germany. On May 7, 1945, the German high command signed unconditional surrender documents (below)—the war was over in Europe and Africa.

Pearl Harbor

In December 1941, the Japanese attacked the U.S. fleet in Pearl Harbor in Hawaii. Expecting the Americans to join the war anyway, they hoped to destroy their navy first. This led to years of sea battles in the Pacific Ocean.

Hiroshima and Nagasaki

The Japanese refused to surrender, so in August 1945, the U.S.A. dropped atom bombs on two Japanese cities. Around 150,000 people died instantly, and World War II was finally over.

HISTORICAL DATA

THE HOLOCAUST

Hitler blamed many of Germany's problems on the Jews and began to persecute them soon after he came to power. During the war, around six million Jews died. Many were taken by train to concentration camps where they were killed by poison gas or were worked or starved to death. Tens of thousands of Romany gypsy people, the mentally ill, the physically disabled, and homosexuals were killed in the same way.

Independence

Many former Asian and African colonies gained their independence after the war. These included India in 1947 after a long campaign led by Mohandas Gandhi (above). One of the first acts of the United Nations was to divide Palestine into two, creating the new state of Israel.

The cold war

This was a period of international tension that lasted from 1945 until the 1990s. It was between two great superpowers, the U.S.A. and the Soviet Union, supported by their own allies.

This was a clash of beliefs. The U.S.A. believed in capitalism—an economic system of free trade and private profit. The Soviet Union championed communism—state-controlled, common ownership.

The Soviet leader Nikita Khrushchev (left) and the U.S. president John F. Kennedy (right) in a cartoon about the 1962 Cuban Missile Crisis.

Superpower struggle

The U.S.A. and the Soviet Union each tried to get the upper hand by using technology and spies. They also sent troops or aid to opposite sides in wars fought in Korea, Vietnam, and Afghanistan. In 1962, disagreement over the location of nuclear missiles in Cuba threatened to cause a third world war.

Space race

There was also a lot of competition between the superpowers in the area of space exploration. The Soviet Union was the first into orbit, launching the *Sputnik* satellite in 1957. The U.S.A. landed the first astronauts on the Moon in 1969 with the *Apollo 11* mission.

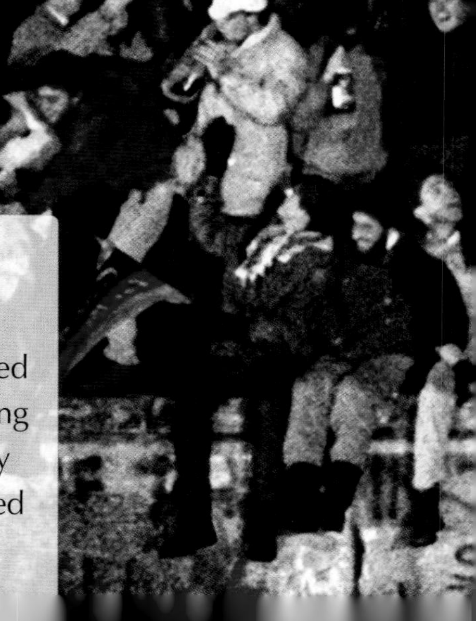

The fall of the Berlin Wall

On August 13, 1961, the Soviet Union began to build a large wall in Germany to separate West Berlin from East Berlin. The wall symbolized the division of Europe and over the years, many people were killed trying to cross from east to west. Here, young people are celebrating shortly before the wall was pulled down in 1989. Germany was formally unified in 1990. The Soviet Union collapsed into a set of republics in 1991.

Chairman Mao

From 1949–1976, communist China was led by the strong military and political leader Mao Zedong. He isolated China from the rest of the world by controlling everything. Everyone had to work on collective farms, and the people were made to read his political ideas in the Little Red Book (left). Many opponents were executed.

The modern world

The late 1900s and the beginning of this century ha seen the growth of Asian economies, climate change, and an increase in terrorist activities

One of the biggest developments has been the growth of international trade and communication. Brands and technologies have become global. It is now possible to buy identical goods in many different countries around the world.

End of apartheid

In South Africa, the apartheid system separated people by their color or race. It ended in 1990, when the activist Nelson Mandela was released from 28 years in jail and then elected president.

Middle East unrest

Israeli–Palestinian conflict over Gaza and the West Bank (above) has led to unrest. Iraq has suffered badly since the 2003 fall of Saddam Hussein during the Iraq War. There is also tension between Iran and the West over the development of nuclear technology.

Peacekeeping forces

In troubled parts of the world, the blue-helmeted soldiers of the United Nations peacekeeping force try to maintain order. They enforce the rule of law and help with economic development. The force received the Nobel Prize for Peace in 1988.

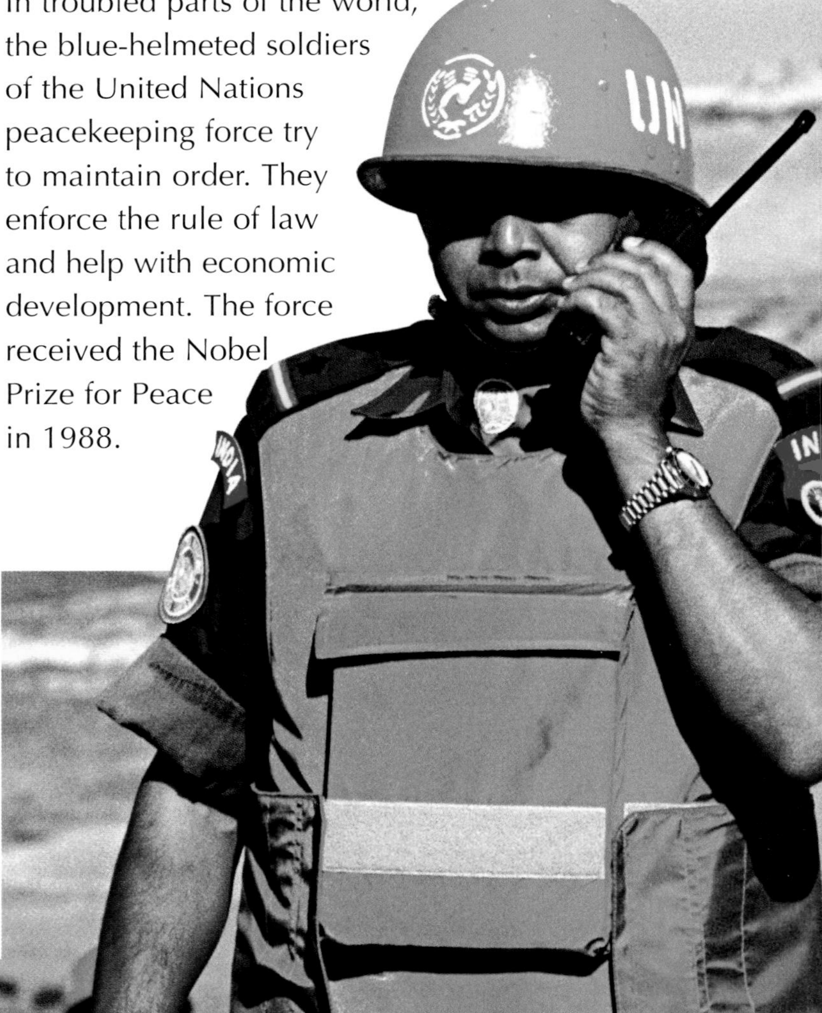

Living in space

Since 2000, astronauts from several countries have visited the International Space Station (ISS), orbiting 210 mi. (340km) above Earth. The ISS is used for research, but it has also welcomed five paying tourists. Space has now become a vacation destination!

Financial markets

Around the world, people buy and sell goods, stocks, and bonds in huge amounts. For example, a decision made in a stock exchange in Chicago, Illinois (above), could have results in Hong Kong or Zurich. This "globalization" is changing the world in which we live.

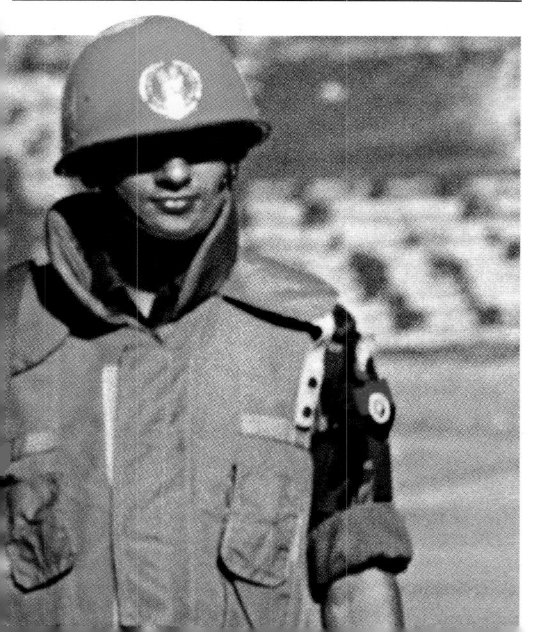

Terrorism

The 9/11 terrorist attack on the World Trade Center in New York City in 2001 showed that global terrorism had arrived. Extremists are prepared to kill themselves in order to publicize their views.

EARTH EVIDENCE

GLOBAL WARMING

Average temperatures on Earth are rising because of the gases that are released by factories, cars, and planes, among other things. This is changing the climate, making both floods and droughts more likely. Entire environments are affected—arctic ice is melting, and mountains have less snow. In Switzerland (above), twice as much ice melted in Alpine glaciers between 1991 and 2004 than during the previous 30 years.

Historical facts

The world has a population of around 6.6 billion, living in around 200 countries. It is estimated that, in total, more than 100 billion people have lived on Earth. Life spans were short at first—only 20–35 years. Now they average 67 years.

WORLD POPULATION

25000 B.C.	3 million
10000 B.C.	4 million
1 B.C.	200 million
1000	275 million
1500	450 million
1650	500 million
1750	700 million
1850	1.2 billion
1900	1.6 billion
1950	2.55 billion
1975	4 billion
1990	5.3 billion
2000	6.1 billion
2010	6.8 billion predicted
2020	7.6 billion predicted
2050	9.2 billion predicted

SEVEN ANCIENT WONDERS

Great Pyramid of Giza
Hanging Gardens of Babylon
Temple of Artemis, Ephesus
Statue of Zeus, Olympia
Mausoleum at Halicarnassus
Colossus of Rhodes
Pharos (Lighthouse) of Alexandria

SEVEN MODERN WONDERS

Empire State Building, New York, NY
Itaipú Dam, Brazil/Paraguay
CN Tower, Toronto, Canada
Panama Canal, Panama
Channel Tunnel, France/U.K.
Delta Works, the Netherlands
Golden Gate Bridge, San Francisco, CA

PEOPLE KILLED IN WARS (mi. = million)

Second Congo War, 1998–2007 5.4 mi.
Vietnam War, 1959–1973 2.1 mi.
Korean War, 1950–1953 2.5–3.5 mi.
World War II, 1939–1945 60–72 mi.
Second Sino-Japanese War, 1931–1945 20 mi.
Russian Civil War, 1917–1921 5–9 mi.
World War I, 1914–1918 20 mi.
Taiping Rebellion, China, 1851–1864 20 mi.
Napoleonic Wars, 1804–1815 3.5–6 mi.
Thirty Years' War, 1618–1648 3–11.5 mi.
Manchu conquest of Ming China, 1616–1662 25 mi.
Conquests of Tamerlane, 1360–1405 7–20 mi.
Mongol conquests, 1200s 30–60 mi.

Oil fields on fire, Kuwait, Persian Gulf War, 1990

USEFUL WEBSITES

www.bbc.co.uk/history/ A wide range of historical facts, fun, and games for kids.

www.channel4.com/history/ Many different topics, including children in history.

www.historyforkids.org/ Comprehensive information on many aspects of world history.

www.un.org/Pubs/CyberSchoolBus/ Covers current global issues.

People and Society

People are social creatures. They live and work in groups in order to solve major tasks that they cannot perform on their own. Over many years, people have occupied lands that have become countries with their own leaders and laws. They often have a similar culture founded on shared beliefs. Food, language, customs, clothing, art, and music are all part of their society.

The human population

The first human beings probably lived in Africa. Today, there are more than six billion people living on Earth.

No two people are completely alike in looks, beliefs, and personality. They belong to different cultural or religious groups and vary in the way that they live and behave.

Population and growth

The world population passed three billion for the first time in 1960. By 2000, it had doubled. Many of these people live in large cities. As its population boomed, Tokyo, Japan (below), began to form a large urban area with the city of Yokohama. Together, these cities are home to more than 34 million people.

Family

The family is the basic social unit of most people on the planet. A family that is made up of parents and their children is called a nuclear family. Extended families are where grandparents and other relatives live under the same roof.

Living in a community

Some groups of families live closely together. The Yanomami tribes (above) live in South America's rainforests in giant communal houses called a *shabono* or *yano*.

Life expectancies

Advances in health and medicine mean that people live longer lives than in the past. In wealthy nations, people have a life expectancy of more than 80 years, but it is less than 50 years in the poorest countries.

Ethnic groups

The common ties of language, history, culture, and religion link people in ethnic groups. In a busy city, there are dozens of different ethnic groups, and this can sometimes cause problems when the different cultures clash.

Growing up

Many cultures have some form of coming-of-age ceremony to signal a child's passage into adulthood. Boys from the Shan people of Myanmar (Burma) and northern Thailand take part in the Poy Sang Long ceremony. This is a three-day event in which boys dressed as princes are carried to a monastery, where they become novice monks for a period of time.

CULTURAL NOTE

WEDDINGS

Marriage is a decision made by two people to join together, usually to build and care for a family. Marriages often begin with a joyful ceremony called a wedding where the two pledge themselves to each other. Sometimes there are very large weddings. Here, 25,000 couples take part in a mass wedding held by the Unification church in 1995.

HOMES AND SETTLEMENTS

SHELTER IS ONE OF THE MOST BASIC HUMAN NEEDS. PEOPLE FIRST TOOK SHELTER IN TREES AND CAVES. OVER TIME, THEY BEGAN TO BUILD PERMANENT HOMES THAT WERE GROUPED TOGETHER IN SETTLEMENTS.

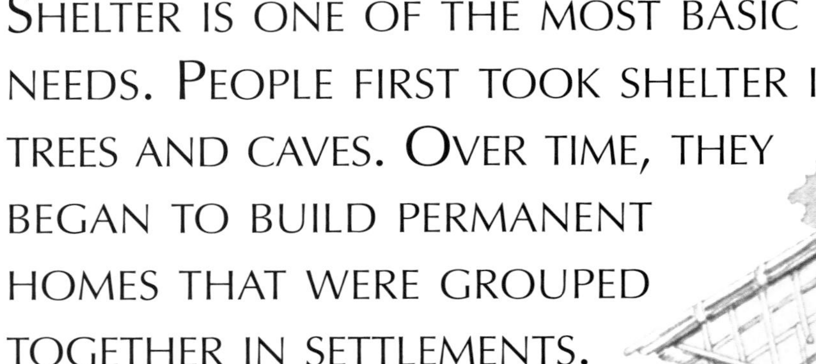

CITY LIFE

Cities contain thousands, sometimes millions, of people who live very closely together. Many have homes in tall apartment buildings. Sometimes very poor people are forced to live in homemade shacks and shelters in shantytowns that develop around the edges of a city such as São Paulo, Brazil (above).

BUILT TO SUIT

Homes are built using whatever materials are available and to suit the local environment. This longhouse in Borneo, Indonesia, is built on giant stilts to avoid the area's regular flooding and to let cool air circulate underneath. People live in private spaces on one side of the building, while there is a large public shared area on the other side.

The longhouse has ladders into each of the private dwellings. The space underneath can be used to prepare crops or shelter livestock.

TEMPORARY HOMES

In some parts of the world, people do not live in one place. They move around to find food for themselves or for their herds of animals. These people are known as nomads and often live in tents. Other people are forced to live in temporary homes because of natural disasters, a lack of food, or war.

Health and education

Public services work to improve the health of people and to provide a system of education for everyone.

In some countries, education is poor and hospitals are few and far between. Sometimes charity organizations provide aid.

Disease

Some diseases, such as typhoid fever (see salmonella bacteria, right), are caused by eating rotten food. Others are carried by insects or passed between people. Medicines fight many diseases.

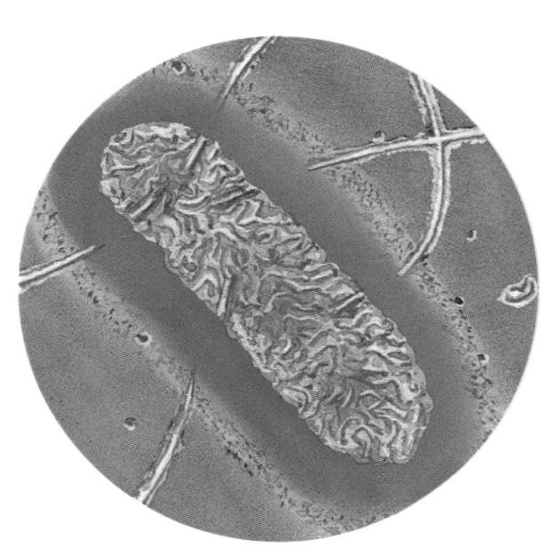

Literacy

Literacy is the ability to read and write. In wealthy countries, most children learn these skills at a young age, and there are plenty of books, schools, and teachers. In poorer countries, there are not as many resources.

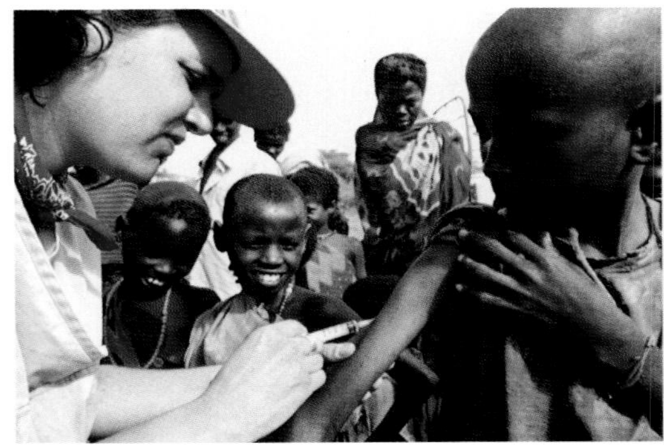

Health organizations

These organizations help improve health by showing people safer ways of behaving such as keeping wounds clean. They also help fight disease. Here, a medic gives a young child a vaccination that will protect him.

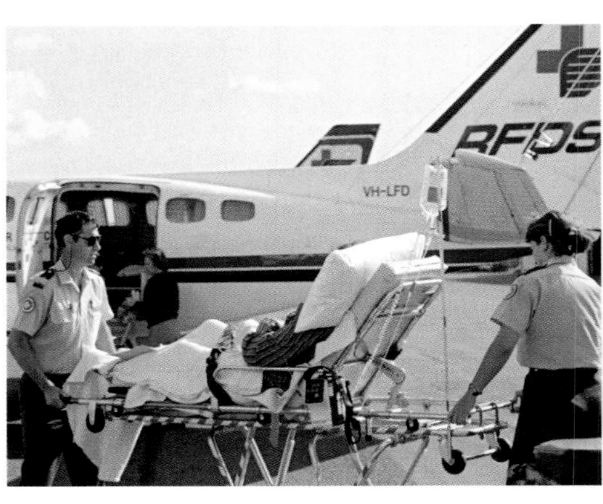

Flying doctors

In places such as Australia, there are many people who live far away from towns. They rely on education by radio. When they are seriously ill, they call on a flying doctor (above) to bring medical help to them or, if necessary, airlift them to a hospital.

Finding water

People in wealthy nations use around ten times more water per day than those in poor countries who have no water pipes and supplies. These women near Sukhna Lake in India are carrying their family's daily supply of drinking water in jars.

Education

Education involves gathering information about the world. Most education is carried out in schools—these schoolchildren are being taught how to measure the weather. Education is not only for children. Many adults take courses at home or at colleges and universities.

SCIENTIFIC INPUT

LIFESTRAW

For millions of people, stale, dirty rivers and lakes are the only sources of water. Every day more than 6,000 people in the world's poorest regions die because they have drunk water that is contaminated with dangerous diseases. The Lifestraw is an ingenious tube that contains filters and chemicals. Water sucked up through the Lifestraw is made safe to drink.

CELEBRATIONS

AROUND THE WORLD, PEOPLE CELEBRATE DIFFERENT EVENTS ACCORDING TO THEIR LOCAL TRADITIONS. MANY CUSTOMS AND CELEBRATIONS DEVELOPED OUT OF RELIGIOUS BELIEFS.

CARNIVALS

Carnivals are holiday or festive events that may last anywhere from a few days to several months. Most developed out of Christian religious festivals, and they are popular in many parts of Europe, the Caribbean, and South and Central America. The Rio Carnival in Brazil is the largest and most spectacular. There are giant parades of floats, powerful samba music, dancing, and firework displays.

ANNUAL EVENTS

Every country has important holidays or annual events. Some, such as Halloween, honor the spirits of the dead. In Mexico, for the Day of the Dead, families dress in costumes and leave food and other gifts called *ofrendas* for the spirits. Models of skeletons (left) and skulls are made from papier-mâché and items of food.

During Chinese New Year, giant paper dragons weave and dance their way through the streets.

CHINESE NEW YEAR

The arrival of the new year based on the Chinese calendar is China's most important holiday. It is celebrated with lanterns, spectacular parades, special foods, and events. Families exchange gifts, blessings, and good wishes.

LOCAL CUSTOMS

The tradition of giving gifts to celebrate Saint Nicholas, a Greek bishop who lived more than 1,600 years ago, is known as Sinterklaas in the Netherlands (above). From this came the image of Santa Claus in the U.S. during the 1800s.

Religions of the world

A religion is a belief in a higher power—for example, spirits or gods. Millions of people around the world are devoted followers of a particular religion. Atheists do not believe in any religion.

FIVE RELIGIONS

Most religions make use of art to create important symbols of their faith.

The cross, or crucifix, is the symbol of Christianity.

The crescent and star are symbols of Islam.

The six-pointed Star of David is a symbol of Judaism.

The god Shiva dancing in a halo of flames is a symbol of Hinduism.

The Dharmacakra, or Dharma wheel, is a symbol of Buddhism.

There are many different religions. Most have holy writings or scriptures that provide followers of the religion with ways to lead good lives.

Buddhism

Buddha founded Buddhism in India. Buddhists believe that they are reincarnated (born again) as another creature or human being. Their monks are often brought offerings of food.

Islam

Islam was begun in the A.D. 600s by the prophet Muhammad. Followers of Islam are called Muslims. They pray five times each day to one god called Allah and follow the teachings contained in the Koran.

Christianity

Christians follow the teachings of Jesus Christ, who they believe is the son of God. There are different forms of Christianity. The most popular is the Roman Catholic church, which is led by the pope.

Hinduism

Hinduism is the oldest of the world's major religions, beginning 4,000 years ago. Hindus worship many different gods, including Vishnu, Shiva, and the elephant god, Ganesh (above). Hinduism's most important holy writings are called Vedas, which means "books of knowledge."

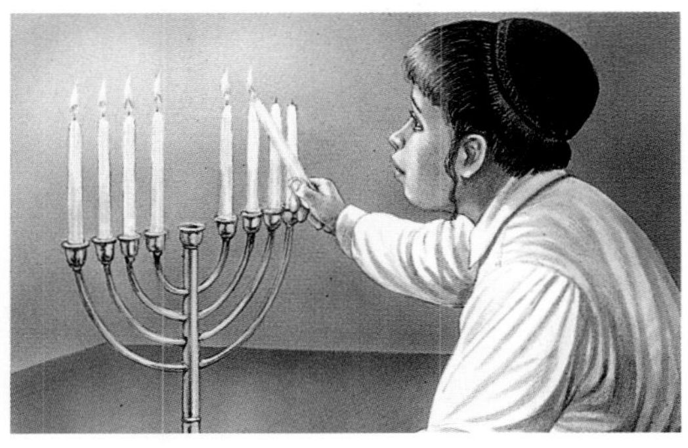

Judaism

Followers of Judaism are called Jews. They believe that they have been chosen by God. Here, a Jewish boy lights a nine-branched candlestick called a menorah during one of the important Jewish holidays, Hanukkah.

Shintoism

Unlike many other religions, Shintoism does not have a single major god. Instead, its followers believe that eternal truth is called kami and that kami can be found everywhere in nature, from rivers to forests. People go to Shinto shrines, mostly in Japan but also in other countries, when they want to pray and give thanks.

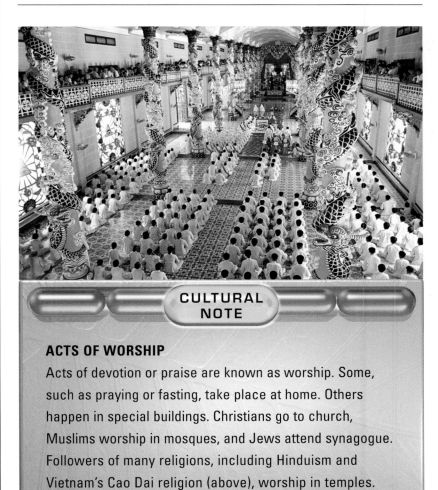

CULTURAL NOTE

ACTS OF WORSHIP

Acts of devotion or praise are known as worship. Some, such as praying or fasting, take place at home. Others happen in special buildings. Christians go to church, Muslims worship in mosques, and Jews attend synagogue. Followers of many religions, including Hinduism and Vietnam's Cao Dai religion (above), worship in temples.

Religious ceremonies

All religions have a variety of rituals and ceremonies performed by their followers. These may be about birth, becoming an adult, or death.

Some ceremonies celebrate a god or prophet's birthday such as Christmas for Christians or Buddha's birthday. Other ceremonies are designed to honor ancestors or give thanks to gods or spirits.

Bar mitzvah and bat mitzvah

These are coming-of-age rituals for Jewish boys (bar) and girls (bat) when they reach their 13th birthdays. They read from the Torah, the sacred scroll containing the first five books of the Hebrew Bible. From this point on, the child is expected to follow all the laws of Judaism.

The haj

Islam calls on all Muslims to pray regularly, give charity to their community, and fast during the month of Ramadan. Muslims also have a duty to make a pilgrimage to the most holy place in Islam, the city of Mecca in Saudi Arabia. This journey is called a haj, and thousands of pilgrims visit the holy shrine of the Kaaba there

Ganga Aarti ceremony

Some religious rituals are held once each year, while others are held every day. The Ganga Aarti is an important daily ritual in Hinduism. It takes place beside the Ganges River in the Indian town of Varanasi. Lamps or dishes containing ghee (clarified butter) and incense are set on fire by young priests. They are then swung in circular movements to ward off evil spirits.

Sports

Most people take part in sports to get or stay in shape, for the challenge, and also for fun and enjoyment.

Most people are amateurs—they play sports without getting paid. Some people are paid to play and are called professionals.

The origins of sports

Many sports developed from skills needed for hunting and fighting. The ancient Egyptians played several sports, including forms of hockey, fencing, and tug of war, and the ancient Sumerians held wrestling contests more than 4,500 years ago.

Sumo wrestling

Influenced by wrestling in China and Korea, sumo wrestling developed in Japan between 300 and 200 B.C. The wrestlers attempt to push each other out of a circle, the *dohyÿ*.

Sailing

Sailing is a sport that ranges from single-person boats, like this dinghy, to larger oceangoing yachts that compete in around-the-world events.

Basketball

Invented in 1891 by Dr. James Naismith, basketball is a fast five-on-five team sport. Players pass and dribble the ball around a court. They score points by shooting the ball through an 18.-in (46-cm)-wide hoop attached to a backboard that is 10 ft. (3.05m) off the ground.

Tennis

Tennis pits individuals—singles—or pairs of players—doubles—against one another. The players use rackets to send a tennis ball around a court, trying to hit winning shots. They play on grass (above) or on hard courts.

Rowing

Rowing races are held for a range of different-size craft. In a sculls event, individuals pull two oars each. The largest boats are rowing eights (above), which are around 62 ft. (19m) long. They contain eight rowers, each pulling a single oar. A ninth person, the coxswain or cox, steers and helps the rowers keep their rhythm.

HISTORICAL DATA

SOCCER

The most popular team sport in the world, soccer developed out of various ancient ball sports and got its first set of rules in the 1800s. Two teams of 11 players each contest a game held over two halves of 45 minutes each, trying to score goals. The FIFA World Cup, held every four years, is the pinnacle of the sport, attracting hundreds of millions of TV viewers.

THE OLYMPICS

THE FIRST MODERN OLYMPICS WAS HELD IN 1896 IN ATHENS, GREECE, AND ATTENDED BY JUST OVER 250 COMPETITORS. TODAY, IT IS THE SINGLE BIGGEST SPORTING EVENT ON EARTH.

A gold medal is given to the winner of an Olympic event. Second place receives silver and third place receives bronze.

SWIMMING

Swimming is one of the most popular sports. The races take place over a range of distances, from 50-m (164-ft.) sprints to the 10-km (6.2-mi.) marathon, which first appeared at the 2008 Beijing Games. At the 1972 Olympics, American Mark Spitz won an astonishing seven swimming gold medals.

TRACK AND FIELD

Track-and-field events are mostly divided into throwing and jumping competitions called field events and races run on a 400-m (1,312-ft.)-long oval track. Track events include sprints of 100m (328 ft.) and 200m (656 ft.), hurdles races, and relays such as the 4x400m (1,312 ft.), which in 2004 was won by the U.S. team (right). The U.S. has dominated track-and-field events, winning 306 gold medals between 1896 and 2004.

WINTER OLYMPICS

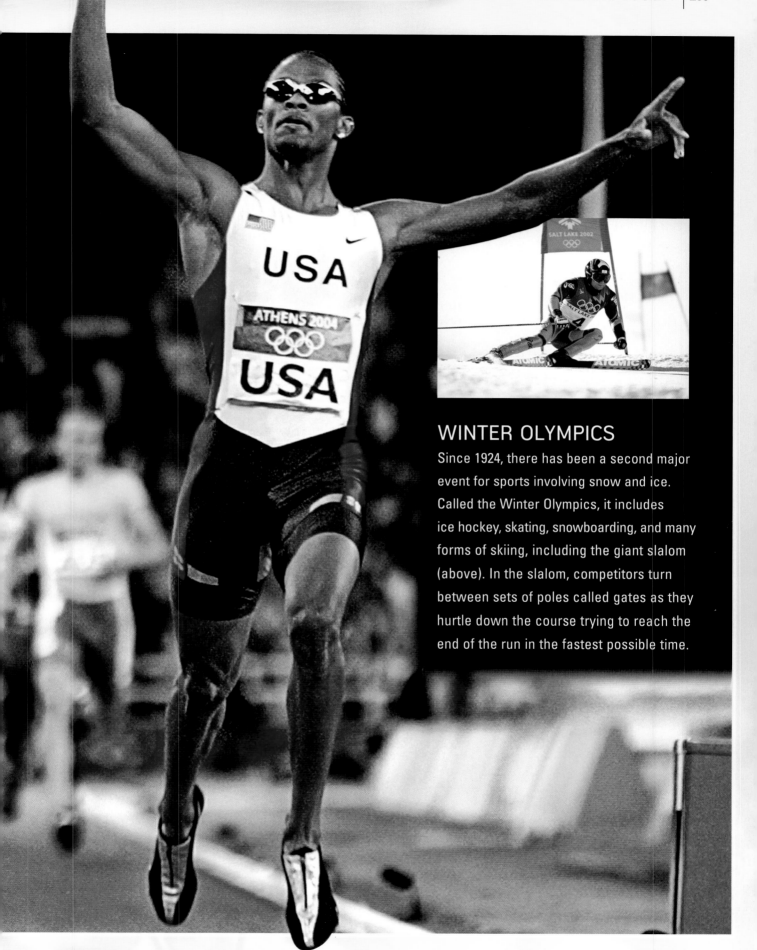

Since 1924, there has been a second major event for sports involving snow and ice. Called the Winter Olympics, it includes ice hockey, skating, snowboarding, and many forms of skiing, including the giant slalom (above). In the slalom, competitors turn between sets of poles called gates as they hurtle down the course trying to reach the end of the run in the fastest possible time.

Countries and nations

A country is an area of land run by a single government. There are more than 190 countries in the world. China has the most people, with a population of more than 1.3 billion.

The land of a country does not have to be connected. For example, Alaska and the islands of Hawaii are not joined to the mainland United States but are still part of that country.

Colonies

Some parts of the world are controlled from a distance by another country. These are often known as colonies or dependencies. Many countries today were colonies or dependencies in the past. Australia (above) was a British colony from 1788 until 1901, when it became an independent country.

National borders

A national border is the point at which two countries' territories meets. Countries protect their borders with officials or soldiers who check travelers entering their countries. The longest single border is between Canada and the U.S. (above) and is 5,512 mi. (8,891km) long.

National anthems

Countries often have a particular piece of music, a national anthem, that represents their nation. It is played to honor a leader of that country or for an important event, like this rugby game between South Africa (below) and Argentina.

Royal families

In the past, many countries were ruled by a king or a queen. Their powers were often passed down to their sons or daughters. Today, there are still royal families, but they are often figureheads with little or no say in running the countries.

Independence

Independence happens when a colony or region of another country gets the freedom to make all of its own decisions and be counted as a nation. Many nations only became independent during the 1900s. In 1991, for example, the Soviet Union split up, creating Russia and 14 other independent countries, including Ukraine and Belarus. In 2008, Kosovo (above) declared independence from Serbia.

Flags

Every country has a different national flag. They are flown from government buildings and sometimes from schools and private homes. These 15 children are each holding his or her country's rectangular flag. Only Switzerland and Vatican City have square flags, while Nepal has a flag made of two triangles.

Government

Governments make laws, provide public services, and control trade and defense. The work is mostly funded by taxes paid by the governed people.

Most countries have a national government and then one or more levels of local government. In some countries, local governments have the power to make some laws and to collect their own taxes.

Dictatorships

A dictatorship occurs when one or a few people have total control. Dictators do not usually hold elections and often rule until they die or are overthrown. Cuban leader Fidel Castro (left) took power in 1959 and was the longest-serving dictator in the world. In 2008, his brother, Raúl (right), took over.

Political parties

People with similar views band together in political parties. They campaign on issues and try to get members of their parties elected. Pressure groups have strong views on one or a small number of issues. Pressure groups rarely seek to get elected. Instead, they try to influence public opinion and politicians.

Legislatures and lawmaking

A legislature, or parliament, is a meeting of people to discuss and make a country's laws. Many legislatures, such as the Australian Parliament in Canberra (above), have two separate chambers with different duties.

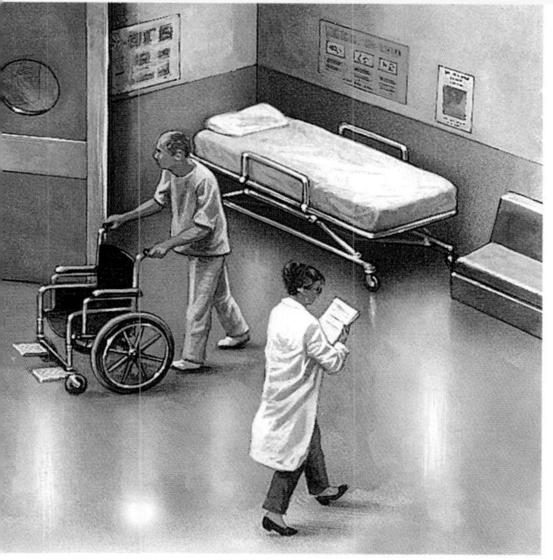

Public services

Modern governments spend enormous amounts of money on defense and on a wide range of public services, from road and bridge building to education and health care (above). Many countries also spend large portions of their budgets on social-security programs for the sick, the elderly, the unemployed, and the poor.

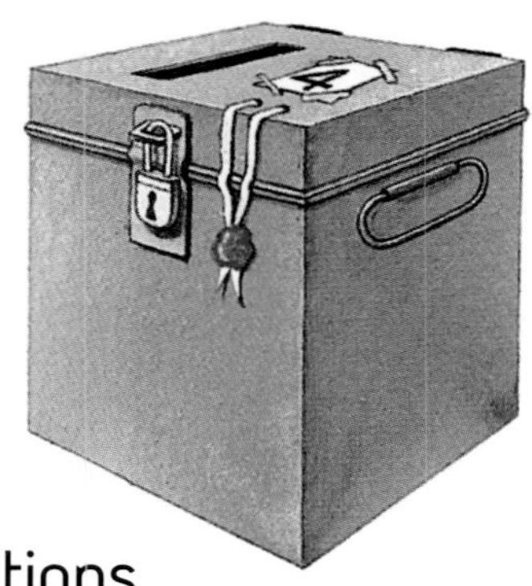

Elections

Elections give people a chance to choose a new government or leader. In many elections, people have to make their choices by selecting from a list of candidates on a ballot paper. Ballot papers are then placed in a sealed ballot box to be counted.

Power bases

There are three main branches of government; the judicial enforces laws, the legislative branch makes laws, and the executive carries out the daily running of the country. In the U.S, these branches are completely separate. The legislative branch is the U.S. Congress (above), and the executive branch is led by the U.S. president.

HISTORICAL DATA

WINNING THE RIGHT TO VOTE

In South Africa, the policy of apartheid allowed the small white population of the country to control black South Africans and deny them many rights, including the right to vote. In 1994, the first election was held in which all South Africans, regardless of color, could vote. More than 19.7 million people lined up to vote in an election that saw Nelson Mandela become South Africa's first black president.

Law and human rights

In order for a society to run smoothly and in peace, it needs laws that everyone follows. These laws vary from country to country.

Most countries have criminal laws against acts such as murder and theft. Civil law deals with disagreements between people—for example, whether or not a marriage ends in a divorce.

Law and order

Most people obey the laws of their country at all times. But the police, armed forces, and other officials, such as customs officers, are needed to enforce the laws, keep the peace, and protect the public. Police try to solve crimes and bring criminals to justice in a court, where their guilt or innocence is decided.

Crime and punishment

A person found guilty of a crime faces punishment. They may be forced to pay a fine, be banned from doing something such as driving, or sentenced to serve time in prison. In some countries, the punishments are physical. For example, criminals may be whipped in public (corporal punishment) or even lose their lives (capital punishment).

In court

In court, one set of lawyers acts for the defendant, and another set, the prosecution, argues the opposing case. The trial often takes place in front of a jury and a judge. The jury is made up of ordinary adult members of the public, and they decide whether the defendant is guilty. If he or she is guilty, the judge decides on the exact sentence.

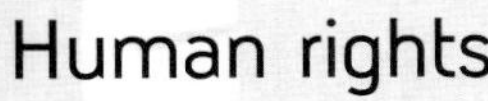

Human rights

Human rights are certain basic rights such as the right to observe a chosen religion and the right to be free from slavery. In many countries, people find their basic human rights abused because they are critical of the government or are members of a different religious or racial group. Some are forced to flee their country and travel to places of safety by whatever means they can find (above).

Money

Money is a form of payment or method of exchange that is widely used to pay for goods people sell or work that they do.

DIFFERENT MONIES
Many different items have been used as forms of money.

Cowrie shells were used in ancient China, Africa, and Arabia.

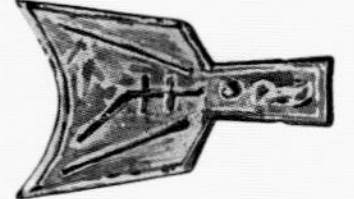

The Ancient Chinese used bronze cast into a spade shape.

Strings of shells were used as money by Native Americans.

Gold formed into large bars is another way to store wealth.

In ancient times, people bartered or swapped goods, but then money was introduced and today is still used in most places. Money is also a way for wealth to be stored or saved for future needs.

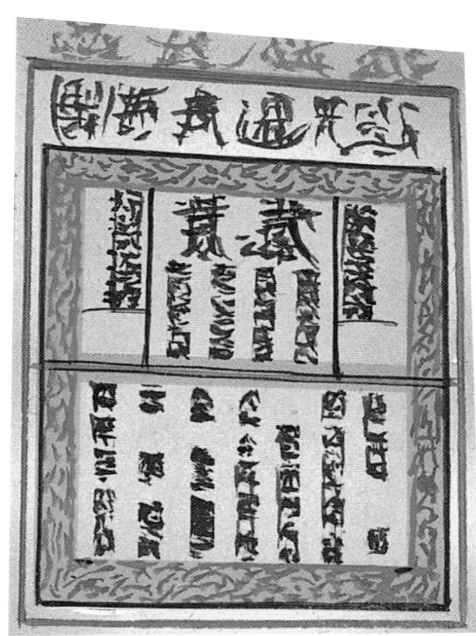

The first bank notes

Shortages of metals and the sheer weight of large amounts of coins led to the invention of paper bank notes. These were first produced in China in the A.D. 600s. They are not valuable in themselves, but they are a promise to pay a sum of real money.

Currency

Currency is a form of money that people can use easily. Bank notes and metal coins are the most common types today. Every country has its own currency system. The exchange rate is the cost of selling or buying a currency.

Rich and poor

Money is not shared equally among people or countries. Some are much richer or poorer than average. Around 1.2 billion people—many in Africa, Asia, and Latin America—live on less than $1 each day. They cannot afford even basic items.

Electronic currency

Today, people use plastic cards to access money. Each card contains a microchip or magnetic strip that carries information about the user's identity and bank account. Automated teller machines (ATMs) allow people to deposit or withdraw money by using the card and typing in their personal code, which is called a PIN (personal identification number).

Hyperinflation

Inflation is when the prices of goods and services rise over time. Hyperinflation is when the prices rise by more than 50 percent every month. In Germany in 1923, prices doubled every two days, making printed money worthless.

Financial institutions

There are many different institutions connected with money. Coins are made in a factory called a mint. Most countries have a central bank that controls the amount of coins and bank notes in circulation. Banks hold people's money for safekeeping in accounts and make loans of money to individuals and businesses.

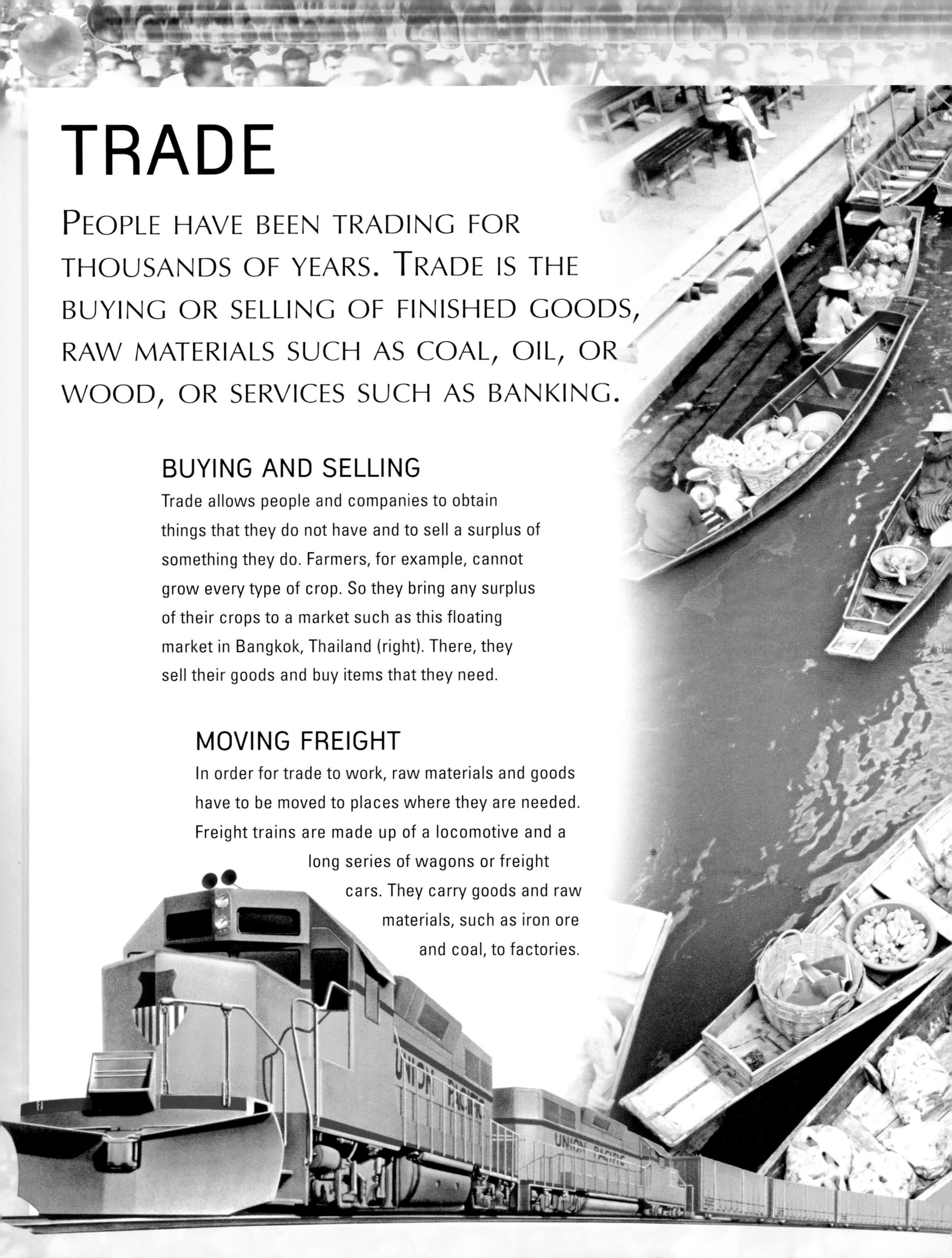

TRADE

PEOPLE HAVE BEEN TRADING FOR THOUSANDS OF YEARS. TRADE IS THE BUYING OR SELLING OF FINISHED GOODS, RAW MATERIALS SUCH AS COAL, OIL, OR WOOD, OR SERVICES SUCH AS BANKING.

BUYING AND SELLING

Trade allows people and companies to obtain things that they do not have and to sell a surplus of something they do. Farmers, for example, cannot grow every type of crop. So they bring any surplus of their crops to a market such as this floating market in Bangkok, Thailand (right). There, they sell their goods and buy items that they need.

MOVING FREIGHT

In order for trade to work, raw materials and goods have to be moved to places where they are needed. Freight trains are made up of a locomotive and a long series of wagons or freight cars. They carry goods and raw materials, such as iron ore and coal, to factories.

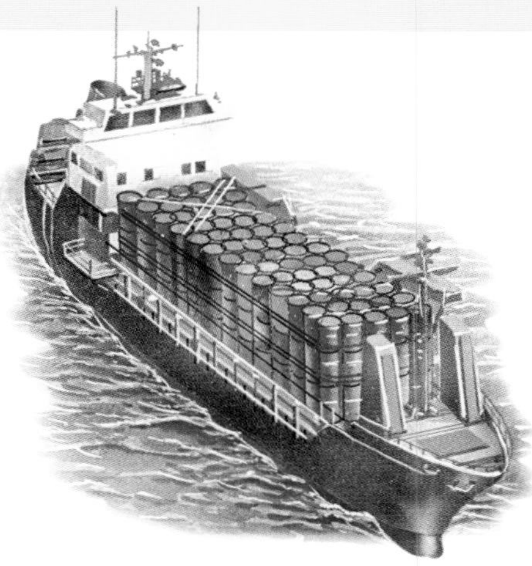

INTERNATIONAL TRADE

Goods sold to foreign customers are called exports, and imports are goods or services bought from another country. Giant container ships and planes transport millions of tons of imports and exports around the world.

FINANCIAL MARKETS

Financial markets are places where shares in a company or large quantities of commodities (goods), such as gold, oil, wheat, and sugar, are bought and sold. The prices of the shares and commodities go up and down. These traders at the London Stock Exchange in the U.K. (above) are trying to buy goods or shares at a lower price than they will eventually sell at, thus making a profit.

Warfare

People go to war to win territory, to capture riches or hostages, or to defend their borders and the population.

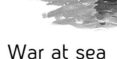

Many wars are short or confined to a local area. Some wars occur in distant places and last many years. A war continues until one side surrenders or both sides sign a peace treaty.

Guerrilla warfare

In this type of fighting, small groups carry out hit-and-run attacks and sabotage enemy equipment and buildings. Many rebel groups, such as these soldiers in Guatemala, resort to using guerrilla-warfare tactics.

War at sea

A navy consists of many different craft, from submarines to giant aircraft carriers (above), the decks of which serve as mobile runways for dozens of jet aircraft. A navy protects a country's coastline and ships and transports troops, equipment, and supplies.

Motorized military

In the past, wars and battles were fought mostly by infantry on foot and cavalry on horseback. The invention of motor vehicles and, from 1915 onward, heavily armored tanks changed military tactics completely. Today, tanks and lighter, faster armored vehicles, such as these U.S. Army Humvees serving in Iraq, often lead an army's forces in battles and invasions.

War in the air

Air forces sometimes attack targets on the ground using bombs and missiles or fight enemy aircraft in the air. They also patrol the skies, act as transporters, and drop supplies and troops into battle areas.

Civil war

Many wars are caused by one nation invading its neighbors to extend its territory. However, conflicts can also take place inside a country. During these civil wars, people who share the same culture or politics fight against one another for political power.

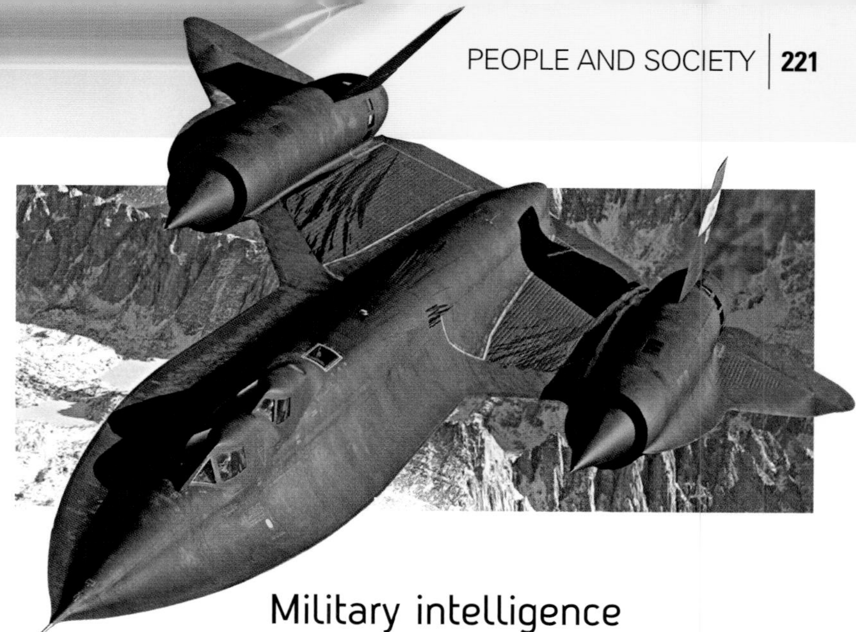

Military intelligence

Intelligence is information that is thought of as vital to a country's security. Spies on the ground seek out top-secret intelligence. Spy planes, such as this SR-71 Blackbird, operate at very high altitudes, using powerful zoom cameras to photograph the ground below.

AMAZING FACTS

HIGH-TECH WARFARE

Military machines no longer need drivers to risk death or injuries in risky situations. In the air, pilotless drones and unmanned aerial vehicles (UAVs) can be controlled from hundreds of miles away. On the ground, mobile crawler robots, such as the PackBot (above), can be sent ahead of troops to scout out dangers such as unexploded mines.

International organizations

International organizations have been formed to allow countries to discuss ideas and share information on global issues.

Some international organizations exist to tackle a specific problem. These include WADA (World Anti-Doping Agency), which fights drugs in sports, and Interpol, which helps police forces from different countries work together.

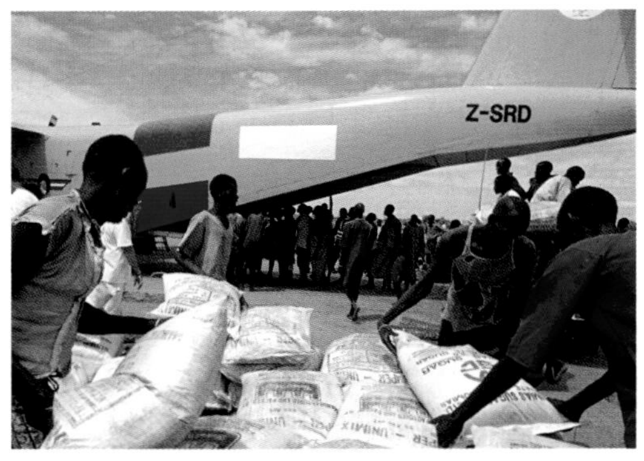

Worldwide charities

Major charities, such as the Red Cross, collect money and goods. They use these to improve the lives of people in poor countries hit by famine, war, and disease.

Peacekeepers

These soldiers, police officers, and other officials work with peacekeepers from other countries to restore calm to war-torn areas. These men (right) are blue-helmeted United Nations peacekeepers.

NATO

Countries sometimes group together in military alliances. The North Atlantic Treaty Organization (NATO) was formed in 1949 by the U.S. and 11 other countries. Today, NATO has representatives of 26 countries in its headquarters in Brussels, Belgium.

United Nations

The United Nations (UN) was formed in 1945 after the end of World War II. Its goal is to maintain peace in the world and to improve people's lives. The UN General Assembly in New York City (pictured) provides every member country (almost 200) with a chance to air its views. Each nation gets one vote on all decisions.

Society facts

The different countries of the world vary in many ways, including size. The smallest country, Vatican City, the home of the pope, has an area of only 0.17 sq. mi. (0.44km^2), while the largest, Russia, covers a massive 6,659,328 sq. mi. (17,075,200km^2).

LARGEST URBAN POPULATIONS

Tokyo/Yokohama, Japan	34,450,000
New York City, NY	20,420,000
Seoul/Incheon, South Korea	20,090,000
Mumbai, India	19,380,000
Jakarta, Indonesia	19,300,000
Delhi, India	18,560,000
Mexico City/Toluca, Mexico	18,410,000
São Paulo, Brazil	18,130,000
Manila, Philippines	17,320,000
Osaka/Kobe/Kyoto, Japan	17,280,000
Cairo, Egypt	16,000,000
Los Angeles, CA	15,350,000
Kolkata (Calcutta), India	14,580,000
Shanghai, China	14,530,000
Moscow, Russia	14,100,000

AVERAGE LIFE EXPECTANCY (HIGHEST AND LOWEST)

1	Japan	82.6 years
2	Hong Kong	82.2 years
3	Iceland	81.8 years
4	Switzerland	81.7 years
5	Australia	81.2 years
6	Spain	80.9 years
7	Sweden	80. 9 years
188	Afghanistan	43.8 years
189	Zimbabwe	43.5 years
190	Angola	42.7 years
191	Lesotho	42.6 years
192	Sierra Leone	42.6 years
193	Zambia	42.4 years
194	Mozambique	42.1 years
195	Swaziland	39.6 years

LARGEST ORGANIZED RELIGIONS

Christianity	2.1 billion
Islam	1.3 billion
Hinduism	851 million
Buddhism	375 million
Sikhism	25 million
Judaism	15 million
Baha'ism	7.5 million
Confucianism	6.4 million
Jainism	4.5 million
Shintoism	2.8 million

MOST POPULOUS COUNTRIES

China	1,322,570,000
India	1,129,291,310
U.S.	303,475,518
Indonesia	231,627,000

Portland in Oregon, U.S., at twilight

USEFUL WEBSITES

http://cyberschoolbus.un.org/ Facts about every country, the UN, and world issues.

www.timeforkids.com/TFK/hh/goplaces Information about 35 countries and language tips.

www.globalgang.org.uk/ A look at different lives and cultures around the world.

www.bbc.co.uk/religion/religions/ A detailed guide to many religious beliefs and ceremonies.

Arts and Entertainment

People have always wanted to be entertained, to express themselves, and to find out what others have to say. They do this in many ways—through art, design, music, dance, and acting. Many of the arts bring these elements together—for example, a theatrical show might include acting, dance, and music, all performed in front of painted scenery.

Architecture

Architecture is the process of designing buildings and other structures. Architects choose the materials and styles that allow us to live, work, and play in comfort and safety.

There are many different architectural styles, from basic "box" houses to curved, glass-walled skyscrapers.

Built for a purpose

Every building has a purpose, but some look interesting, too. The Sydney Opera House in Australia (above) has a roof made of concrete panels that look like shells or sails, to fit in with Sydney Harbor.

Bridge design

Bridges are structures that have been created by architects and engineers to cross an open space or gap such as a valley. One of the most amazing is the 980-ft. (300-m)-high Millau Bridge, in France, with its web of steel cables stretching from tall masts.

Taller and taller

Skyscrapers began to dominate city views from the 1890s onward. The invention of safe elevators made it possible for people to reach the high stories without running out of breath.

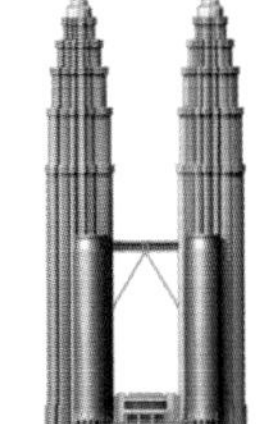

Eiffel Tower, France

Empire State Building, U.S.A.

Petronas Twin Towers, Malaysia

Taipei 101, Taiwan

CN Tower, Canada

Burj al Dubai U.A.E

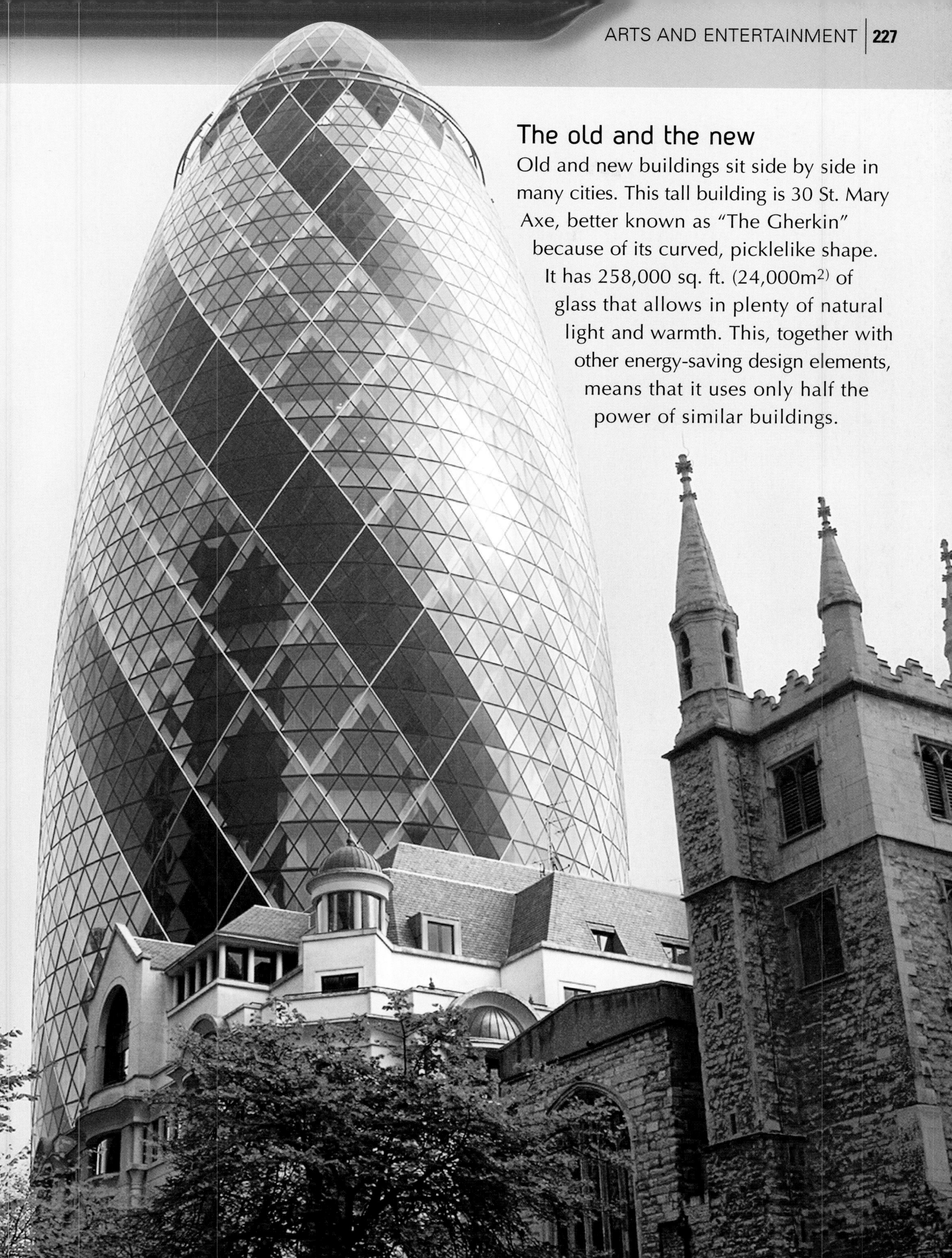

The old and the new

Old and new buildings sit side by side in many cities. This tall building is 30 St. Mary Axe, better known as "The Gherkin" because of its curved, picklelike shape. It has 258,000 sq. ft. (24,000m^2) of glass that allows in plenty of natural light and warmth. This, together with other energy-saving design elements, means that it uses only half the power of similar buildings.

Dance

Dance is movement that is used to express feelings and ideas. It is full of rhythm and often accompanied by music. Most people dance from the time that they learn to walk.

Ancient carvings and drawings show that dance has been a part of human rituals and ceremonies for thousands of years. Dance is a truly international art form because it does not need any words.

Folk dance

Groups of people sometimes develop their own style of dance. They wear costumes and use movement and music to tell stories about their culture.

Flamenco

This dramatic style of dance comes from Andalusia in Spain. Dancers respond to the powerful rhythms of flamenco guitar music. They perform intricate toe- and heel-clicking steps (mostly the men) and graceful body and hand movements (mostly the women).

Ballet

This classical style of dance began hundreds of years ago and is often set to orchestral music. It needs precise movements, and dancers need to train for years to learn the technique. They wear special shoes with wooden blocks in the toe to help them stand tall *en pointe*. Ballet usually has solo dancers backed by a "chorus" of other dancers.

Tap

Tap dancing started in the U.S. and gets its name from the clicking sound that is made by metal plates on the dancers' shoes as they strike the ground. Many types of dance make use of the sounds made by the feet.

Telling a story

Many classical Indian dances tell stories, usually either religious or epic. The story can be told through mime or by set gestures, with the hands occasionally used for a type of sign language to add extra expression. Costumes are often very elaborate and brightly colored.

Jazz dance

In modern jazz dance, performers make a wide range of movements, which are set to lively music. There are standard jazz moves, but the dancers use these to create their own personal style. Jazz dance is faster and freer than ballet, and it is often performed in groups.

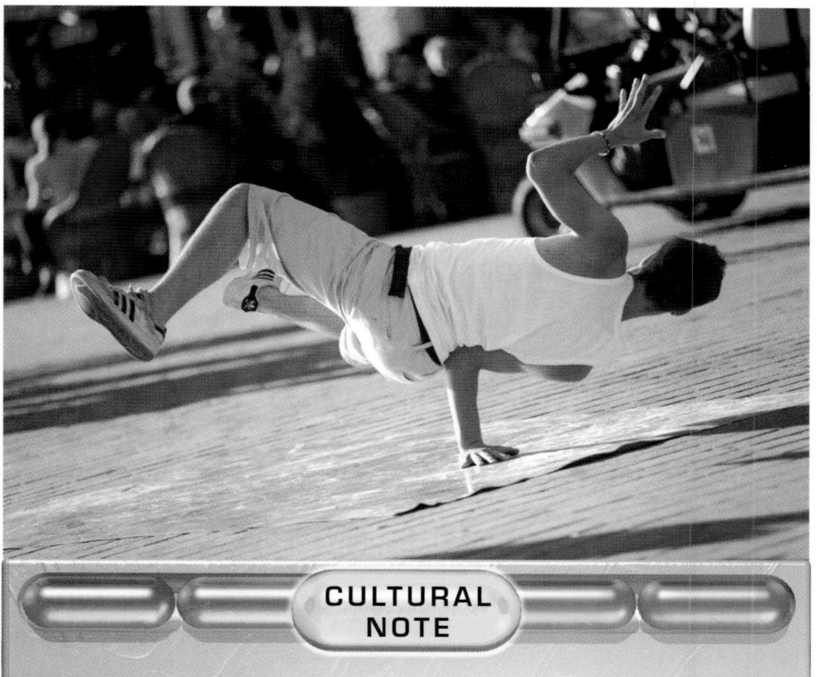

CULTURAL NOTE

STREET DANCE

This modern dance style is performed to music such as rap, hip-hop, and funk. It often involves break dancing, in which dancers improvise a series of movements to show off their skill and flexibility. They might start with some standing steps (toprock) before performing moves with hands and feet on the floor (downrock). Another element is the freeze, when the dancer holds a stylish pose before continuing a movement.

Decorative arts

Some artists make attractive objects out of ceramics, wood, glass, metal, or textiles. The finished work, such as a vase, may be useful or simply made to be beautiful.

GLASS BLOWING
In this ancient craft, the raw materials are mixed together and melted at high temperatures.

1
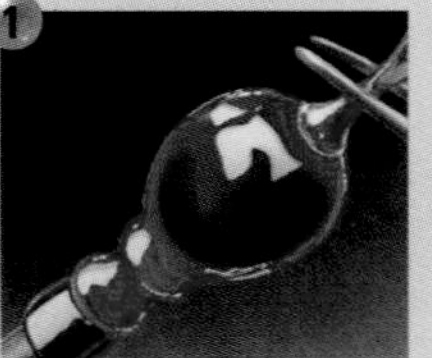
The artist blows in air to form a bubble.

2
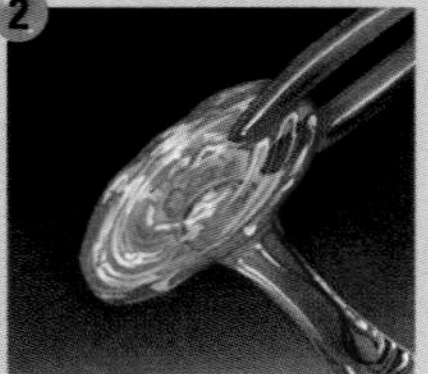
The molten glass is pulled into shape.

3

Unwanted glass is then cut away.

4
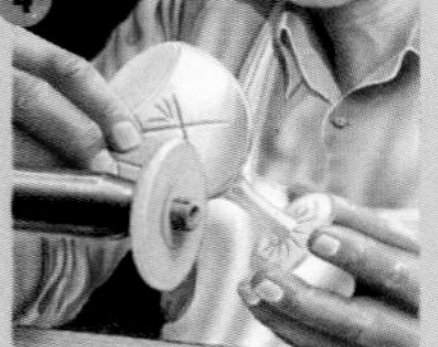
The glass is decorated using a cutter.

Some people make decorative art as a job, but others enjoy making attractive objects as a hobby. The materials can be cheap, but often great skill is needed to produce the object.

Ceramics

Ceramics, or pottery, involves shaping clay, for example to make a pot. The shape is "fired" (or heated) in a kiln to make it solid. Here, a pot is being shaped on a revolving stand called a potter's wheel. The finished object can be decorated or left its natural color.

The potter sits at a potter's wheel, which she turns as she shapes the object.

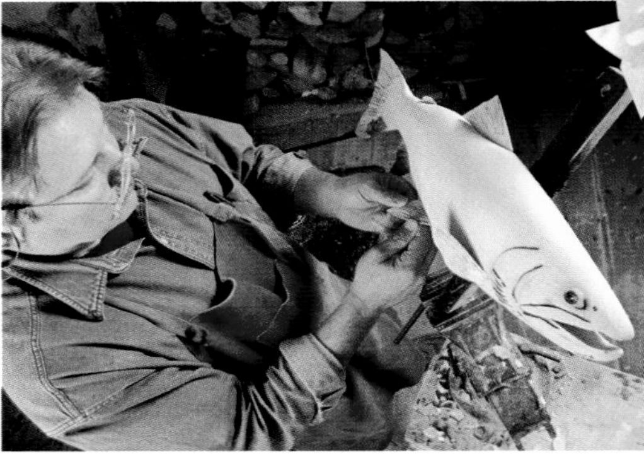

Woodcarving

People have been carving wood since the introduction of sharp tools thousands of years ago. The wood could be made into pieces for a chess set or a fish (above). Turning the wood while cutting it creates rounded shapes such as lamp stands.

Decorative art can use fresh materials such as flowers, here (right) combined with gold and silk to create an elaborate headdress for this Indonesian dancer.

Weaving

Weavers use wooden looms to turn thread or yarn into cloth. The fabric can be plain or patterned and will become a rug (below), tapestry, or an item of clothing.

Cross-stitch

This is one of the oldest forms of embroidery. It creates pictures using X-shaped stitches of thread. For hundreds of years, people have used this method to sew samplers showing the alphabet or phrases such as "Home sweet home."

Jewelry

Simple jewelry might just involve stringing beads along a thread to make a necklace or bracelet. More complicated jewelry combines precious metals such as gold or silver with gemstones. The end product could be a wedding ring, an intricate brooch, a royal tiara, or a child's first pair of earrings.

GAMES

GAMES HAVE LONG BEEN PART OF HUMAN CULTURE BECAUSE THEY ENTERTAIN AND ARE A GOOD WORKOUT FOR THE BRAIN. SOME GAMES ARE THOUSANDS OF YEARS OLD—DICE CARVED FROM BONES HAVE BEEN FOUND AT MANY ANCIENT SITES.

The players in this 19th-century Japanese print are taking their game of go very seriously!

BOARD GAMES

Simple games such as chutes and ladders rely on luck to win, but more complicated games need a good strategy. Many board games are based around our everyday lives—for example, the property-dealing game Monopoly or Scrabble, where players create words. Some, such as chess (below) were based on warfare. The pieces are moved to get an advantage and capture the most important piece, the king. Online versions of board games allow you to play against anyone in the world at anytime.

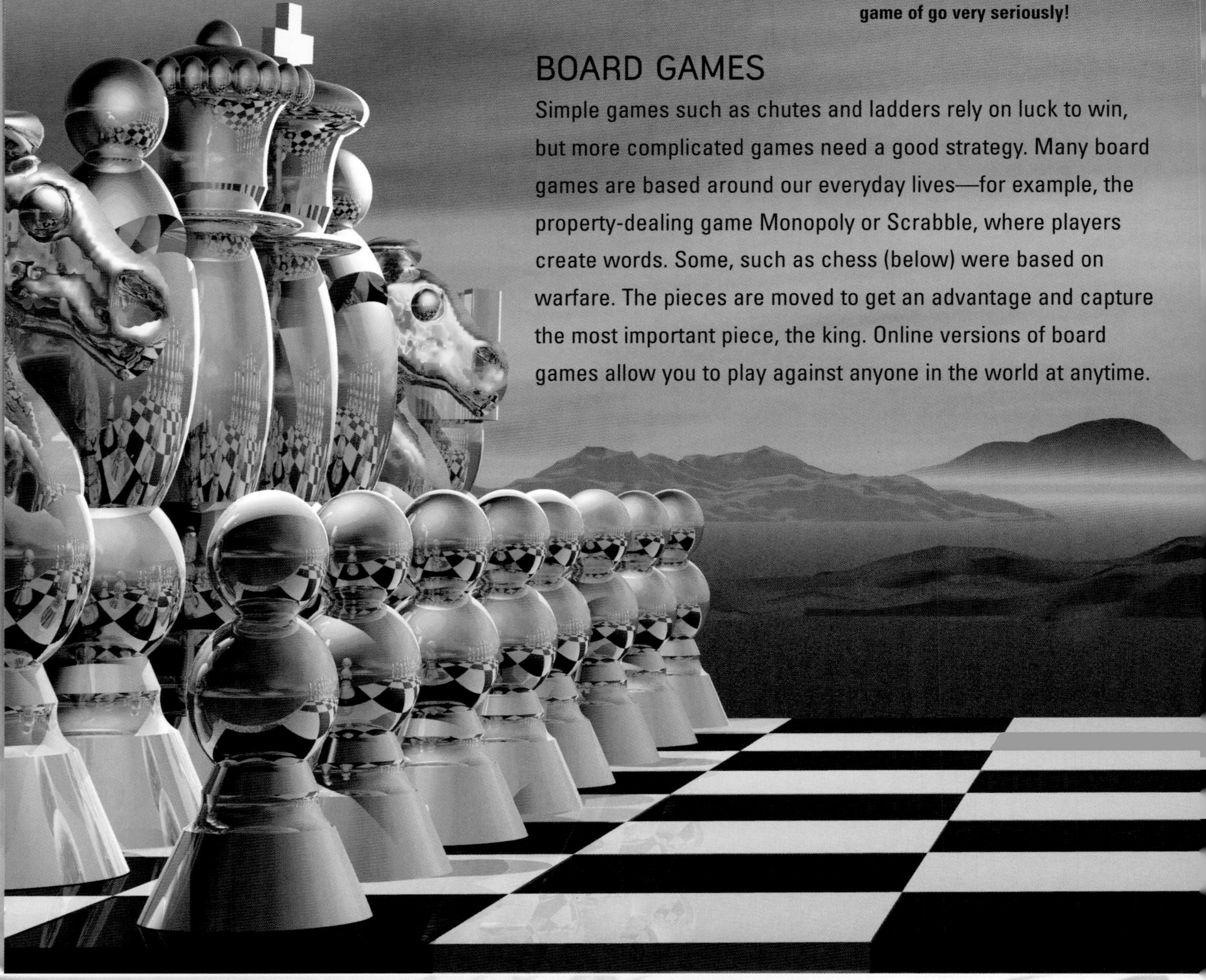

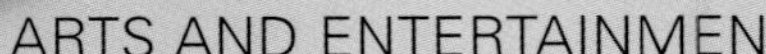

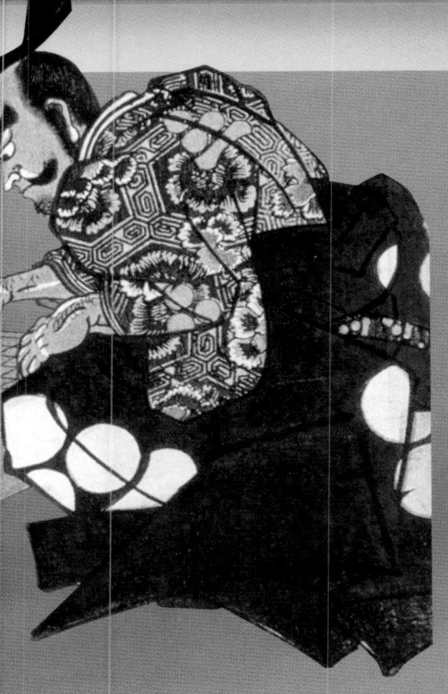

This "hand" is part of the standard "deck," which consists of 52 cards in four suits (the pattern on the card such as hearts, diamonds, spades, or clubs).

CARD GAMES

Card games began in China around 2,000 years ago using paper money. There are thousands of card games, ranging from those for a solo player to games for large groups. Some games, such as Uno, have their own special sets of cards.

EARLY BOARD GAMES

The first board games probably involved moving pebbles around in the dirt. Then dried beans or clay tablets were used for counters, and boards were introduced. A 4,000-year-old papyrus board was once used by the ancient Egyptians to play senet, which resembles the modern game of backgammon.

Chess as we know it today is around 2,000 years old, when it developed from an earlier Indian game. Some chess sets are beautifully carved.

Movies

Movies use moving pictures to tell stories. Movie cameras take 24 pictures per second. When the images are shown at that speed in a movie theater or on television, it looks as if they are moving.

The first "motion pictures" were made in Hollywood, California, where the natural light was ideal for filming. Today, top movie stars earn millions of dollars.

Making a movie

Filming can take place in studios, where massive sets are built to look like real places. It also happens "on location"—on real city streets or in the countryside. A huge crew is needed to make a movie, with different teams responsible for pictures, sound, lighting, and acting.

Silent movies

Until the 1920s, movies were silent because there was no way to record sound. Musicians would play along to them in the movie theater. They were also shot in black-and-white until color filming became possible in the 1930s.

Animation

In animated movies, each frame is photographed, either as a drawn picture or as a figure that is moved slightly and photographed again, like Wallace and Gromit (right). It takes a very long time to make an animated movie.

Series

Some movies are made as part of a series, using the same characters who have different adventures. Examples are space sagas, such as *Star Trek* (above) or *Star Wars*, and the James Bond action movies.

Bollywood

The massive Indian movie industry produces around 1,000 films every year, and they are bursting with colorful costumes, singing, and dancing. Bollywood movie plots are always romances with some comedy and thrills.

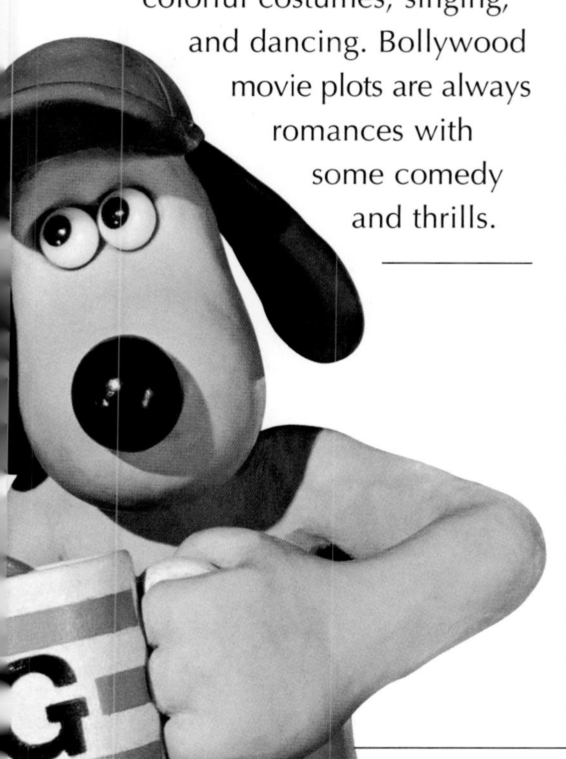

Movies at home

Most movies are made to be shown in a movie theater, but after a short time they are then available as DVDs to be watched at home. Later, they may be broadcast on television. Some less popular movies never make it to movie theaters and are known as "straight to DVD" movies.

AMAZING FACTS

THE OSCARS

Since 1929, the movie industry has given annual awards at a special ceremony. The Academy Awards—better known as the Oscars, after the small golden statuettes presented as trophies—are given for categories such as Best Actor, Best Actress, Best Film, and Best Director. A winning movie is likely to attract a much larger audience and earn more money.

Special effects

Special effects are tricks that convince the audience that something is happening. They range from special stunts to the blending of images to make people "fly."

During live-action filming, scenery effects can transform the set, while mechanical effects create illusions, for example, that a dinosaur is attacking.

Bluescreen technique

Also known as a traveling mat, this is a technique in which actors are filmed against a blue or green backdrop (above left). The color is later replaced with scenery to make it appear that the action is taking place at sea, in space, or in some other location.

Models in action

If something is too complicated to film, or does not exist, it can be created as a model. It can then be moved around like a giant puppet—this is called animatronics. Or it might be filmed in stop motion as an animation (*see p. 234*). Models are usually created on a small scale and made to move in front of a miniature or computerized backdrop.

Out of a fireball!

There are several ways to make a plane appear to fly through an explosion (above). One is to actually do it—although often an optical illusion is created, and the plane is really at a distance from the flames. Another is to film the plane and fire separately and then fit the images together. Alternatively, a model plane could be used, or the entire event could be created on a computer!

Classical music

Classical music is usually played by orchestral instruments or sung. Most of the music that was written in the past is still played today because it is good at expressing ideas and feelings.

TYPES OF INSTRUMENTS
A symphony orchestra has four sections.

Percussion instruments are hit to make sounds and include the piano.

Most string instruments are played with a bow and include the violin.

Brass instruments such as trumpets are made of metal and are blown.

Woodwind instruments include the clarinet, oboe, and flute (above).

Music developed through performances in churches and at royal courts. It changed as new instruments were invented, and it is still developing. Some modern pieces use electronics.

Solo performers

Classical musicians train for years to become good performers. Some may have the chance to perform solos, for example in a concerto, when single instruments are accompanied by the orchestra.

Early music

In the several hundred years before music could be recorded, it had to be played live. Musicians such as Johann Sebastian Bach (below) made their living by performing in churches and composing new music.

Famous composers

Some composers, such as Wolfgang Amadeus Mozart, became big stars. The young pianist Ludwig van Beethoven traveled to Vienna, Austria, in 1787 to try to meet him (left). Beethoven went on to achieve great fame himself.

Chamber music

Not all classical music is played by orchestras or solo instruments. Small groups of between 2 and 40 people play chamber music. For example, a string quartet of two violins, a viola, and a cello is known as a quartet. With no conductor, chamber groups have to listen carefully to each other.

The orchestra

A symphony orchestra can have around 100 players in sections. The music is usually very complex, and melodies and rhythms move between the instruments. The conductor stands at the front, moving his or her body and arms to show how they want the musicians to play.

Opera

Opera began in Italy in the 1500s. It tells a dramatic story with singing that is set to music played by the orchestra. The players sit low down in front of the stage in an area called the "pit." Opera singers act out the story and use their powerful voices to fill the theater, expressing the emotions of their characters. All the characters' conversations are sung. Modern musical shows are a type of opera.

Modern music

There are several types of modern music, from relaxing ambient to exotic world music, and they often influence each other. Many of them are used to accompany dance.

MUSIC FORMATS
The way we listen to music has changed greatly over the years.

Vinyl records were large and fragile but had good sound quality.

Cassette tapes could be played on the move but wore out easily.

Digitally recorded CDs took music into the computer age.

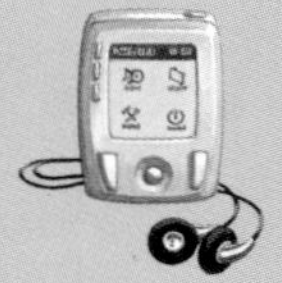

MP3 players and computers allow you to store and play music.

Today, music can be sent electronically to a computer or cell phone.

Much of modern popular music developed from the rock and roll music that began in the U.S. in the 1950s. The basic equipment for modern music is guitar, bass, keyboard, and drums.

Rock

Rock music can be songs or longer pieces, usually with a heavy beat and featuring energetic electric guitar solos. Really loud, insistent rock is called "heavy metal," while the quieter, more melodic type is called "soft rock." There are many other types.

Pop

Pop is short for "popular" and aims to appeal to the largest possible number of listeners, who are mostly young. It is generally written to be good to dance to and comes in the form of short, fairly simple songs that have a memorable tune.

Hip-hop

Hip-hop is rap music in which rhyming lyrics, mostly about city life, are rhythmically spoken or chanted. The backing is in many styles, usually electronic, and has a very strong beat.

Reggae

This began in Jamaica in the 1960s and has a distinctive, chopped-up beat that is often strummed on an electric guitar. The most famous and popular reggae star was Bob Marley (above).

Jazz

Jazz has its origins in New Orleans, Louisiana, early in the 1900s. It can be very complicated, sophisticated music in which the players make up, or improvise, some of what they play.

World music

This is traditional music made by people anywhere in the world. For example, Indonesian gamelan music (above) is played on drums, gongs, xylophones, and chimes and is part of the country's culture. Its magical, rhythmic, tinkling sound can now be heard all the way around the globe.

HISTORICAL DATA

BLUES

Developed in the U.S. early in the 1900s, blues music influenced many other types of music, especially rock. The lyrics are about the bad things that can happen in life, and the singer is often simply accompanied by a guitar or harmonica. Bessie Smith (above) was a major blues star in the 1920s and 1930s and sang about poverty and sadness.

Painting

Painting is putting colors onto a surface such as paper or canvas. Some of the earliest paintings are illustrations of hunting on the walls of caves.

Some painters have been successful in their lifetime. However, many of the artists that we enjoy today struggled to make a living and would be amazed to see people lining up to see their work in art galleries.

Subject matter

Early paintings were often religious, but then artists began to paint landscapes, still lifes, and portraits. The portraits could be of important people such as a king, or perhaps of the artist themselves (right).

Perspective

Early paintings had no perspective and so they look flat, with no depth. During the Renaissance (from the 1400s), painters learned to use angled lines to create depth (below).

Paints and painting

The main painting materials used by artists are oil, acrylic, and watercolor (above), although others, including chalk, oil pastels, and inks, are also used. Oil paints can be very thick, and some artists paint it in layers on the canvas to add texture to their work. Oil paints also dry slowly, allowing colors to be mixed on the canvas. This technique is also used with watercolors.

Abstract art

Abstract art does not try to show actual objects. Instead, it expresses ideas or explores new processes. Jackson Pollock created some of his works (left) by pouring paint onto a canvas on the floor in an "action painting."

Different techniques

This woodcut, or woodblock, image was created by cutting shapes into a block of wood. The wood was then inked and used to print an image. This technique is very popular in China and Japan.

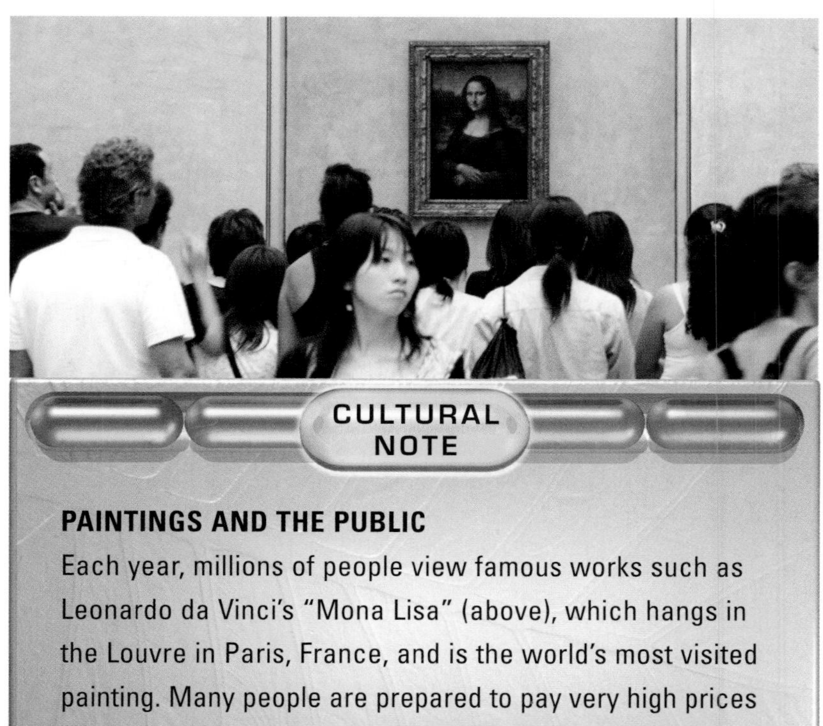

CULTURAL NOTE

PAINTINGS AND THE PUBLIC

Each year, millions of people view famous works such as Leonardo da Vinci's "Mona Lisa" (above), which hangs in the Louvre in Paris, France, and is the world's most visited painting. Many people are prepared to pay very high prices in order to own works of art. In 1987, one of Van Gogh's paintings of sunflowers was sold for an amazing $49 million.

Other art forms

Not all painters use an easel and paintbrushes. There is digital art, where images are drawn or photographic images are changed using a computer. In video art, moving images are put together to create a "piece" that is usually viewed as a picture, not a movie.

Sculpture

Sculpture is 3-D art that we can look at, move around, and sometimes touch.

Sculptures are made out of materials such as stone, metal, wood, plastic, and glass. Some sculptures are carved out of the material. In other cases, the material is melted before being molded or cast.

Sculpting in stone

On Easter Island in the south Pacific, there are 3,000-year-old stone statues. They represent ancestors who were believed to be gods. Some are 30 ft. (10m) tall.

Sculpting in metal

Metal sculptures are cast from a mold. The technique has been used for hundreds of years, but this bronze bull, with its head lowered and ready to charge, is a modern sculpture in New York City. It weighs 7,000 lbs. (3,200kg).

Art and contrast

Old and new sculptures sit side by side in Trafalgar Square in London, England. On the right is the traditionally styled 160-ft. (50-m)-high stone column and statue of Admiral Nelson, dating from 1843. On the left is a modern sculpture in colored glass, called "Model for a Hotel," by Thomas Schutte. Its 21 stories rise up 16 ft. (5m) from a stone plinth and are designed to catch and reflect the changing lights of the area.

Photography

Photography is the recording of still images with a camera. It is used for many businesses, especially advertising and newspapers, as well as in art and to take vacation snaps.

Camera technology

A camera is simply a box with a hole that lets in light. Today, black-and-white and color film is being replaced by digital technology that uses an electronic sensor instead. We can even take moving pictures on many cellular phones.

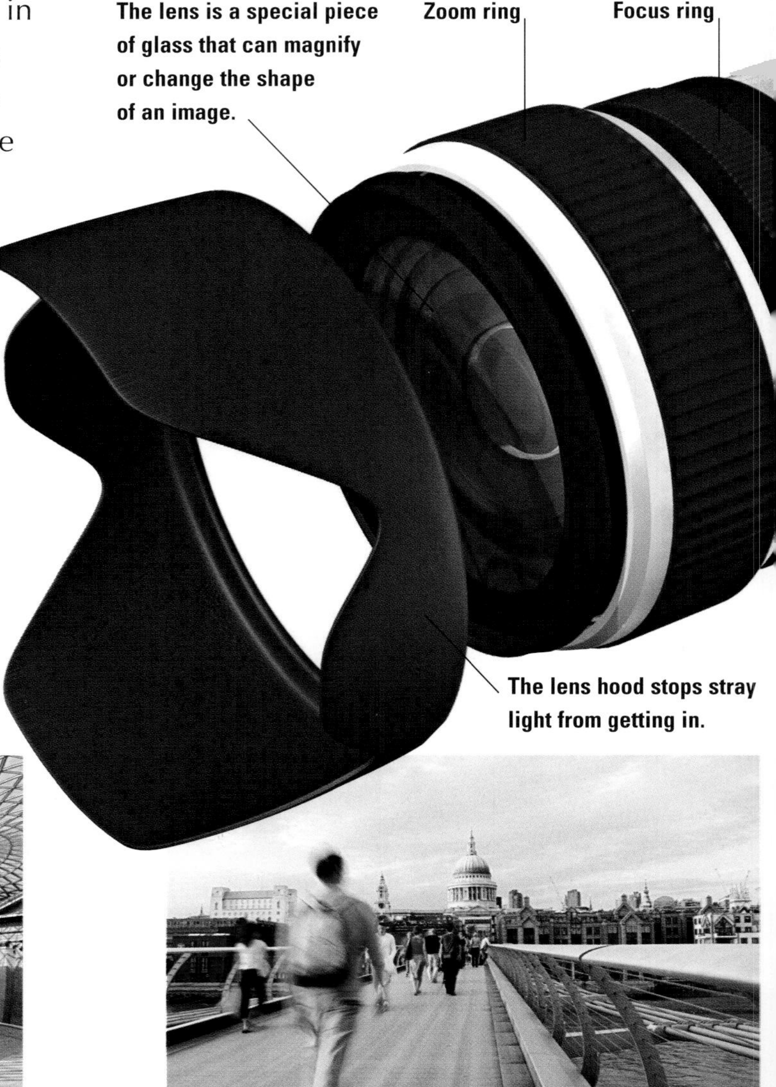

The lens is a special piece of glass that can magnify or change the shape of an image.
Zoom ring
Focus ring
The lens hood stops stray light from getting in.

Wide angle: a wide-angle lens shows more than the eye can see, capturing everything over a large area, even things that are almost out of sight; it is great for shots of big buildings.

Fish eye: this special lens gives a special effect by bending the image so that the foreground is pushed toward the viewer and the background is forced away.

Zoom: a zoom lens on a camera acts as a powerful magnifier that allows the photographer to zero in on objects that are far away.

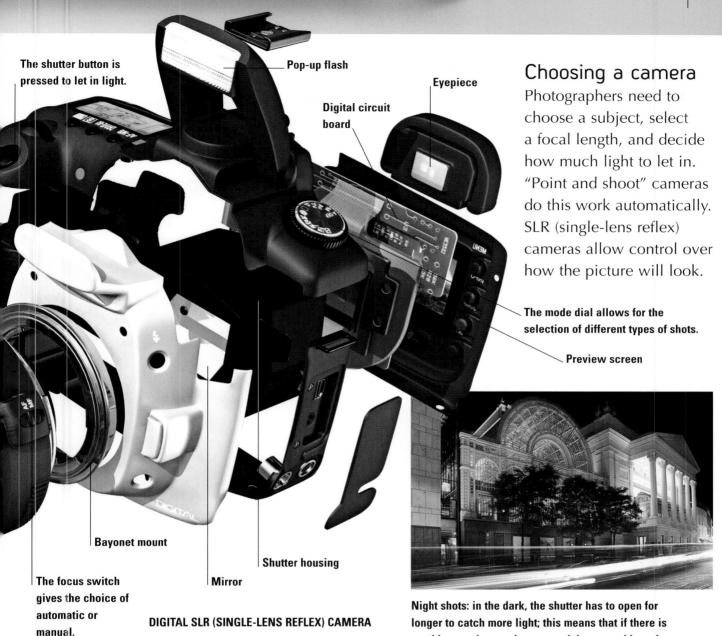

The shutter button is pressed to let in light.

Pop-up flash

Eyepiece

Digital circuit board

The mode dial allows for the selection of different types of shots.

Preview screen

Bayonet mount

Shutter housing

The focus switch gives the choice of automatic or manual.

Mirror

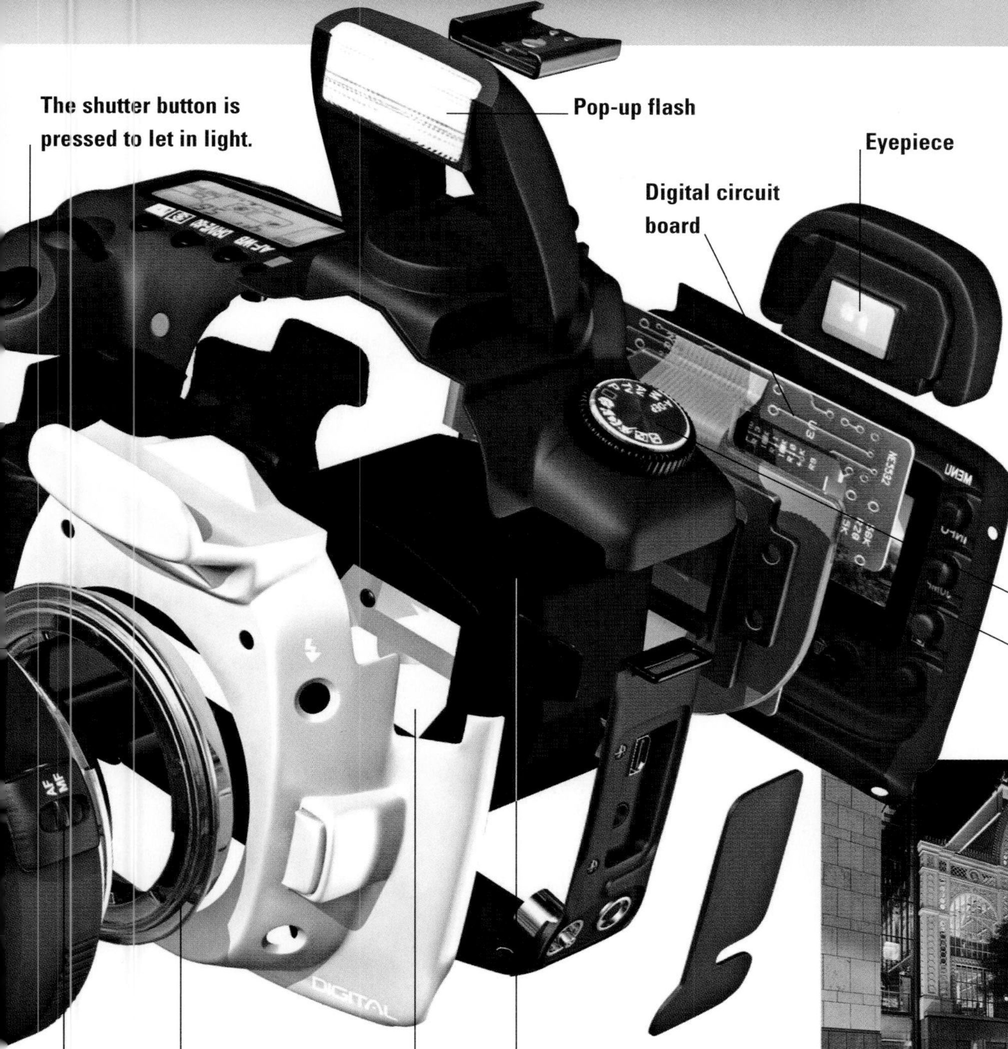

DIGITAL SLR (SINGLE-LENS REFLEX) CAMERA

Choosing a camera

Photographers need to choose a subject, select a focal length, and decide how much light to let in. "Point and shoot" cameras do this work automatically. SLR (single-lens reflex) cameras allow control over how the picture will look.

Night shots: in the dark, the shutter has to open for longer to catch more light; this means that if there is anything moving, such as a car, it becomes blurred.

Portrait: pictures of people are called portraits and are often deliberately posed for the camera.

Landscape: these pictures are often very dramatic, portraying an environment such as a park in a city (above) or fields and mountains in the countryside.

Macrophotography: these close-up shots often reveal details that cannot be seen with the naked eye.

Print

Printing is the process of putting words and images onto paper. For the last 500 years, printing has been the most effective way of communicating ideas to a wide audience.

The Chinese were the first people to print material, in the A.D. 600s, by rubbing impressions from a block of wood. The method was being used in Europe to decorate cloth by the year A.D. 1300.

Storytelling

Before printed books, a popular method of communication was storytelling. The role of the storyteller was often passed down from generation to generation.

Early writing

Early writing was done by scratching symbols onto clay tablets. Later, scrolls (rolls of papyrus or parchment) were used. The writing was done by hand, so there were no standard books. Texts such as the Bible were copied out by hand by monks, so each one was different from the others.

Printing revolution

Mechanical printing began in Germany in the 1450s after Johann Gutenberg developed the printing press out of a machine for crushing grapes to make wine. He employed his knowledge of metals to create movable type that could be used over and over, allowing the cheap, fast production of good quality books. By 1500, there were 9 million books in circulation.

Modern printing

Today's books and newspapers are made with offset lithography, in which the ink image is transferred from a rolling plate onto the final surface. This process is fast and practical for large quantities of print.

Newspapers and magazines

The first daily newspapers appeared in the 1600s. Today's papers are printed on cheap, off-white paper known as newsprint, which is often partially made up of recycled paper. Magazines are general- or special-interest publications that are circulated regularly, usually every week or month.

Fiction and nonfiction

Printed books are either fiction (stories and poetry) or nonfiction (information books, like this one). Fiction publishers are offered many more stories than they can sell, so it can be very hard to get new work into print. The best-selling single book in the world is the Bible.

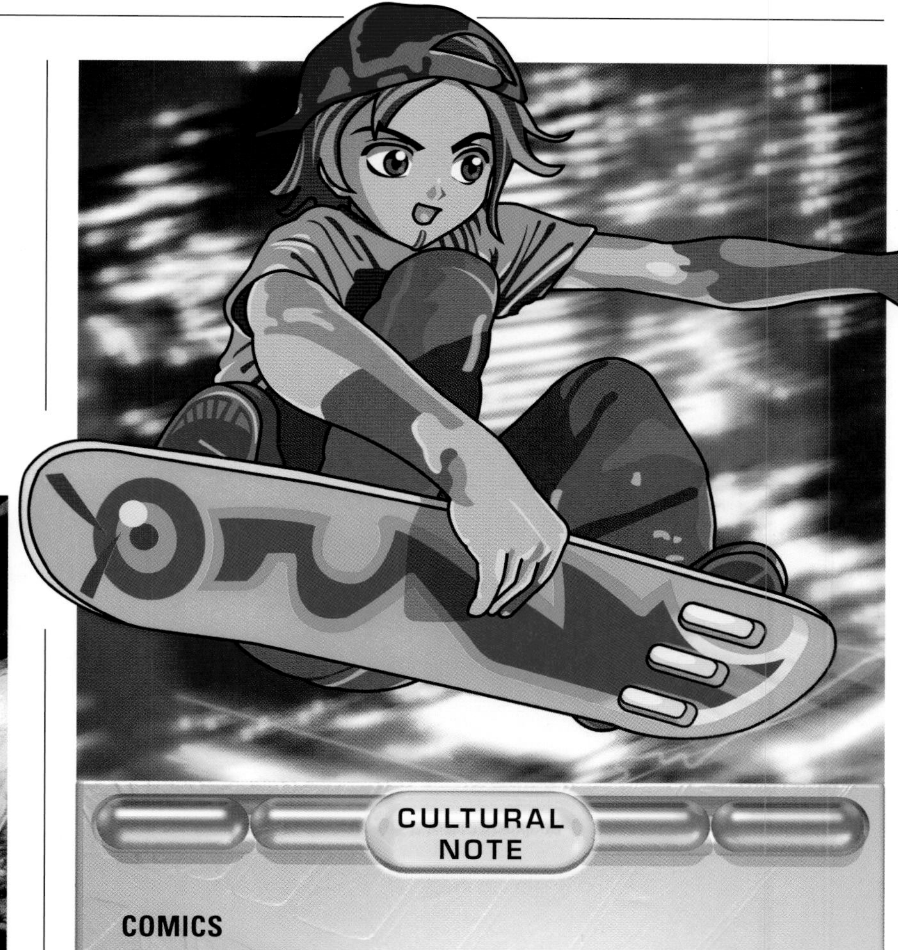

CULTURAL NOTE

COMICS

Comics combine words and cartoon-style illustrations to tell stories. There are many types of comics, including those telling tales of superheroes such as Batman and Superman. Comics use speech bubbles and text in panels to convey extra information, but the most important element is the drawings. Japanese comics known as "manga" (above) are colorful, and their stories often become TV shows or movies.

Theater

Theater is the performing of plays by actors, usually done in a special building, sometimes in parks, or on the street. The stories can be about feelings or ideas.

The action usually takes place on the stage, with the audience sitting in front. Some plays are performed by one actor; others need a large cast and complicated scenery.

The Greek masks represent tragedy and comedy.

Early theaters

The Greeks invented theater thousands of years ago, building open-air arenas where thousands of people watched plays. The actors wore masks (above) to show their characters, and very little scenery was used. A "chorus" group at the side also told part of the story.

Kabuki plays are about historical events and people.

Japanese theater

Kabuki is a traditional Japanese theater style that dates back to the 1500s. All the actors are men. They wear elaborate makeup and costumes and perform stories by singing, dancing, and speaking. A Kabuki show lasts an entire day and is very popular.

Puppets

Plays can be performed by puppets. People who live on the island of Java in Indonesia use shadow puppets. The figures are moved behind white screens that are lit from behind.

Mime

Mime is performing without speaking. Instead, mime artists tell a story using gestures and facial expressions. Mime has a very long history, but the most famous silent performer was Frenchman Marcel Marceau, with his painted white face.

Musicals

Musicals, such as *Starlight Express* (above), combine songs, dance, and dialogue to tell a story in a lively and entertaining way. Some musicals need a huge cast and many special effects. Some are turned into movies.

Pantomime

This is a type of theater that is usually performed around Christmastime. The stories are generally traditional such as Cinderella or Jack and the Beanstalk. The main male character is played by an actress, while a man portrays the older woman—the dame (right). Pantomimes have lots of silly jokes and singing.

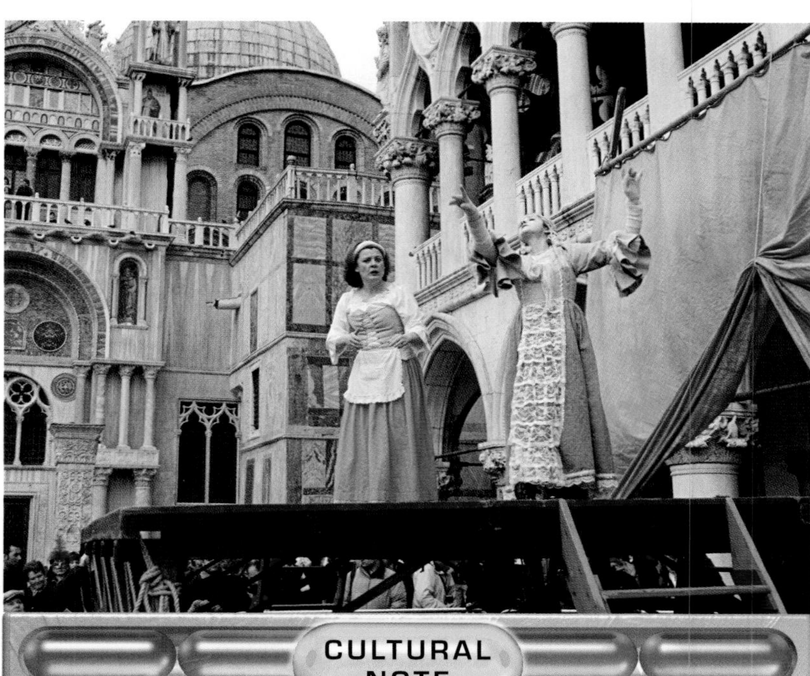

CULTURAL NOTE

STREET THEATER

These performances take place in an outdoor space such as a park or town square. Sometimes street theater is part of a festival. There is little or no scenery, and the actors do not usually have microphones. They have to project their voices farther than usual, and they need to use big gestures that can be seen across a crowded area.

THE GLOBE THEATER

THE GLOBE THEATER WAS BUILT IN 1599 BUT WAS DESTROYED BY A FIRE IN 1613. IT WAS ONE OF LONDON, ENGLAND'S FIRST PUBLIC THEATERS. THERE, EVERYONE, NOT JUST THE RICH, COULD SEE PLAYS BY WRITERS SUCH AS SHAKESPEARE.

THE PEOPLE'S THEATER

People could pay a penny to stand in the "pit" in front of the stage. Known as "groundlings," they were sometimes a noisy and difficult crowd. They bought nuts and oranges from passing sellers to eat—or throw at the stage if the actors were not thought to be good enough.

It cost two pennies for a seat higher up in the galleries under the roof, and the richest people paid four pennies to sit behind the stage.

SHAKESPEARE THE BARD

William Shakespeare (1564–1616) is one of the world's greatest playwrights. He began as an actor and became part owner of the Globe. He is most famous for his 38 plays, which included histories, comedies, and tragedies. His works, including *Romeo and Juliet* and *Macbeth*, are full of intelligent wordplay and are still performed today.

The Globe was a three-story building that could hold up to 3,000 people.

Women's roles were played by young boys who wore wigs and heavy makeup.
The stage stuck out into the pit. There was a trapdoor so that actors could enter from below.
Flagpole
The first Globe Theater burned down when sparks from a cannon set fire to the wooden beams and thatched roof.
Stairs to the upper galleries
There was not much scenery and no special lighting, but the costumes were very bright and colorful and there was plenty of music and sound effects.
Entrance

THE NEW GLOBE

In 1997, a reconstruction of the Globe opened by the Thames River in London, around 650 ft. (200m) from its original site. Historic drawings were studied to make the theater as authentic as possible. Plays are performed there from May to October each year.

Out and about

People want to enjoy themselves and are willing to travel in order to find new experiences. Devising and operating places of entertainment is now a massive industry around the world.

WORLD CULTURE
In some of the most famous buildings, you can view collections of art and antiquities.

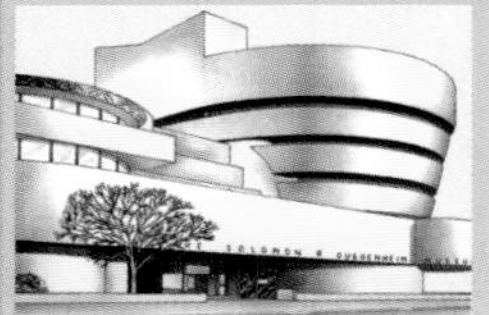

The Guggenheim in New York City is a famous modern art gallery.

The Louvre in Paris, France, houses one of the finest art collections.

The Altes ("old") Museum in Berlin, Germany, is built in the classical style.

The Hermitage in St. Petersburg, Russia, has three million works of art.

While there have never been more home entertainment choices—television, DVDs and videos, radio, computer and online games—there are also many places that are fun to visit.

Theme parks

Theme parks, or amusement parks, developed from fairgrounds and offer many rides and other fun events. Top attractions are "thrill rides," where people travel very fast—and sometimes upside down—for example, on a rollercoaster (below) or on water.

Art galleries

These are buildings with exhibitions of art, sometimes by one artist or by artists who belong to one particular art movement. More often, there are many types of art from throughout the ages. In addition to paintings, there might be sculptures and photographs, as well as other media such as textiles.

Circuses

A group of traveling performers set up a "big top" (tent) and perform shows. The ringmaster introduces popular acts such as acrobats, clowns, jugglers, and trained animals.

Zoos and safari parks

Before movies and television, zoos were often the only place where people could safely see animals from around the world. Wild animal parks (above), or safari parks, are toured by car.

Arcades

People battle on coin-operated machines in street arcades. Typical arcade games include racing or fighting video games, pinball, and slot machines.

Museums

Museums contain different collections based around themes such as science, history, or transportation. They show us how our world developed. Museums employ experts to study a subject and buy in new exhibits. Many museums are interactive, letting visitors experience objects in action.

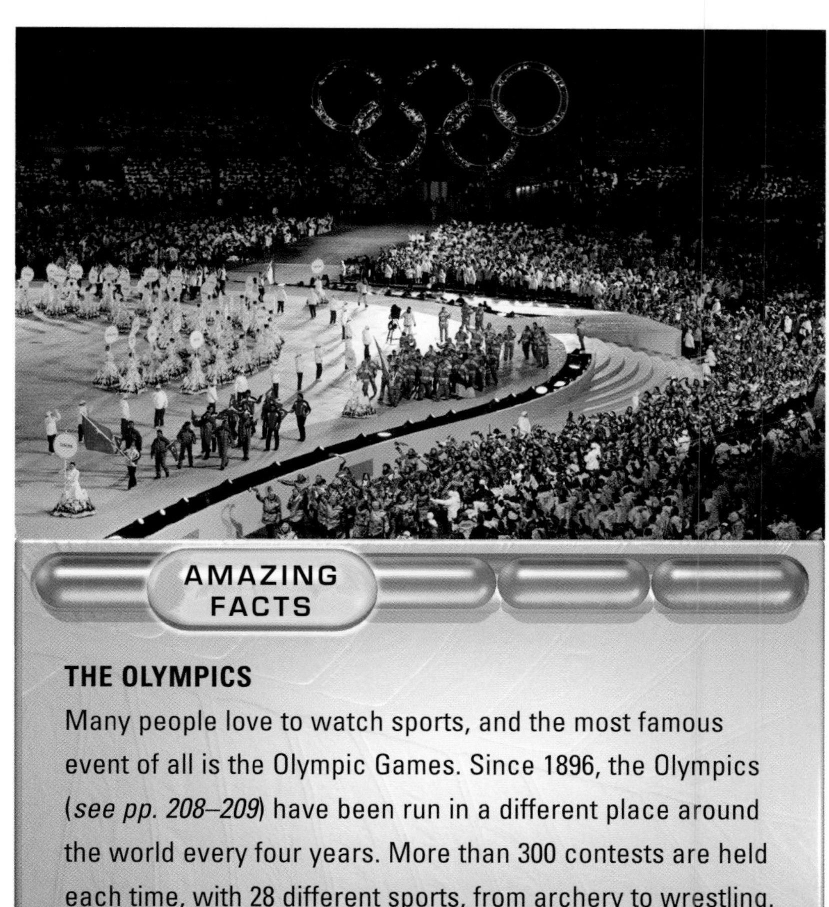

AMAZING FACTS

THE OLYMPICS

Many people love to watch sports, and the most famous event of all is the Olympic Games. Since 1896, the Olympics (*see pp. 208–209*) have been run in a different place around the world every four years. More than 300 contests are held each time, with 28 different sports, from archery to wrestling.

Arts-and-entertainment facts

Many countries are recognized for their enthusiasm for particular art forms. Italy is famous as the home of opera. Russian ballet dancers are known throughout the world. And Chinese and Indian art and sculpture have flourished for years.

MOST-SEEN MOVIES (mi. = million)

Gone with the Wind (1940) 35 mi.
The Sound of Music (1965) 30 mi.
Snow White and the Seven Dwarfs (1938) 28 mi.
Star Wars (1977) 20.76 mi.
Spring in Park Lane (1948) 20.5 mi.
The Best Years of Our Lives (1947) 20.4 mi.
The Jungle Book (1968) 19.8 mi.
Titanic (1998) 18.9 mi.
The Wicked Lady (1946) 18.4 mi.
The Seventh Veil (1945) 17.9 mi.

BIGGEST-SELLING SINGLES

Candle In The Wind (Princess Diana Tribute) Elton John 37 mi.
White Christmas Bing Crosby 30 mi.
Rock around the Clock Bill Haley and His Comets 17 mi.
I Want to Hold Your Hand The Beatles 12 mi.
Hey Jude The Beatles 10 mi.
It's Now or Never Elvis Presley 10 mi.
I Will Always Love You Whitney Houston 10 mi.
Hound Dog Elvis Presley 9 mi.
Diana Paul Anka 9 mi.
(Everything I Do) I Do It For You Bryan Adams 8 mi.
I'm a Believer The Monkees 8 mi.

BEST-SELLING BOOKS SERIES

Perry Rhodan (German science fiction), began 1961 1 billion
Star Wars, began 1977 750 mi.
Harry Potter, began 1997 535 mi.
The New Park Street Pulpit and the Metropolitan Tabernacle Pulpit, began 1854 300 mi.
Goosebumps, began 1992 300 mi.
Choose Your Own Adventure, began 1979 250 mi.
Nancy Drew, began 1930 200 mi.
Peter Rabbit, began 1902 150 mi.
Dirk Pitt, began 1973 120 mi.

MOST POPULAR BOARD GAMES

1 Monopoly
2 Risk
3 Mahjong
4 Scrabble
5 Beyblade
6 Backgammon

Onstage in the musical *A Chorus Line*

USEFUL WEBSITES

www.shakespeares-globe.org The Globe Theater and links to theaters worldwide.
www.nga.gov/kids/zone/zone.htm Interactive site where kids can create pictures.
www.creatingmusic.com/ Interactive site where kids can compose and hear their own music.
www.rudimentsofwisdom.com/ Full of cartoons that relate to arts and entertainment.

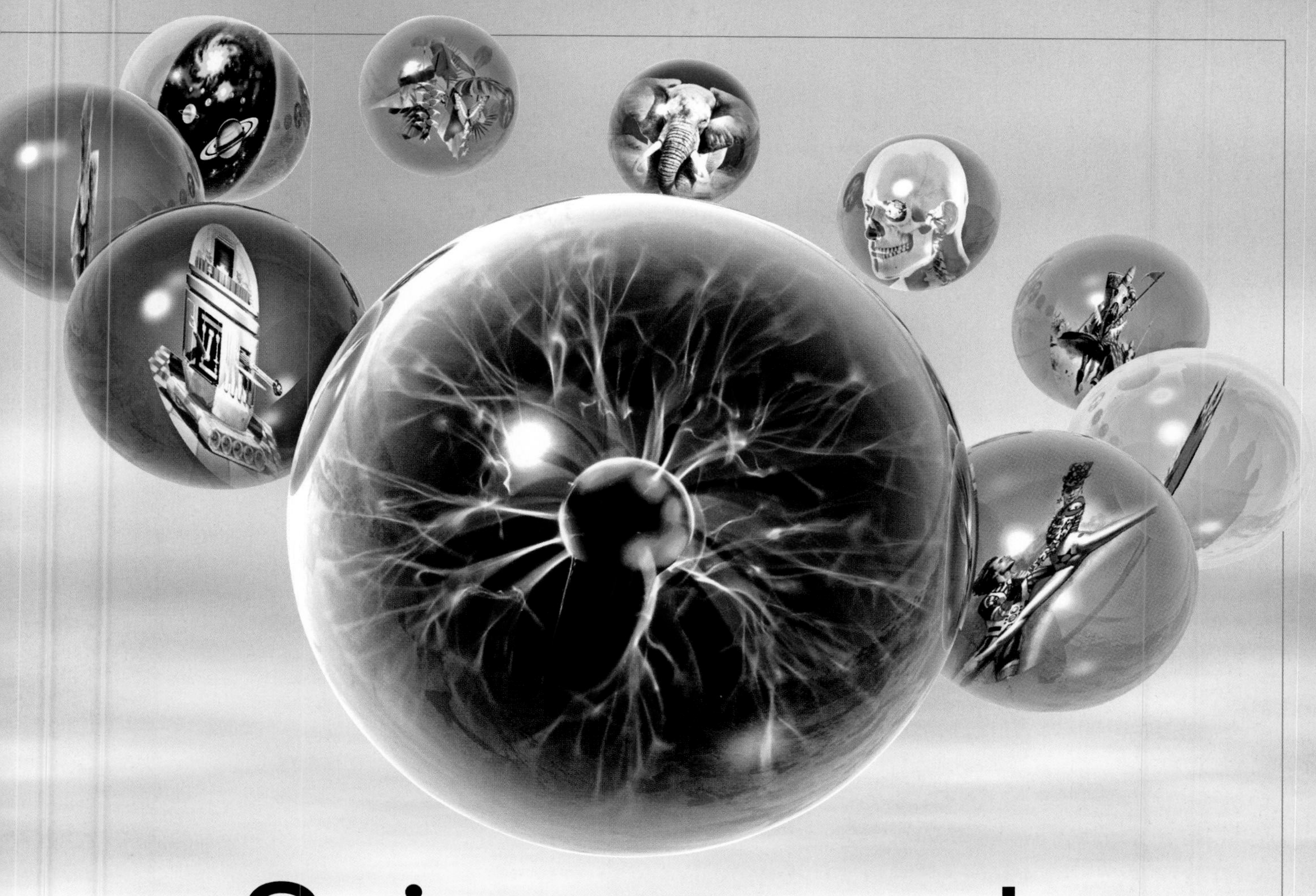

Science and Technology

Science is a powerful tool for understanding how and why things happen. Through technology, this understanding has given people enormous power and changed the whole world. Although science is a vast and complex subject, it is based on a small number of laws that took years of study to discover. However, there are still many mysteries to explain.

What is science?

Science is a way of finding out about the universe and using that knowledge to control the world around us.

GREAT SCIENTISTS
In the past, individuals developed new areas of knowledge. Today, science relies on teams

Galileo Galilei
(1564–1642)
First to figure out the mathematics of motion

Isaac Newton
(1642–1727)
Formulated the laws of motion and gravity

Charles Darwin
(1809–1882)
Discovered how species evolve

Albert Einstein
(1879–1955)
Linked gravity, time, and space

Areas of science include mathematics (the science of numbers), physics (the study of matter, energy, time, and space), chemistry (the study of different substances and their interaction), biology (the science of living things), and astronomy (the investigation of the universe).

Ancient science

Science has its roots in Greece. More than 2,000 years ago, Greek philosophers debated the nature of the universe and developed many different theories about it. But they did not experiment to test their ideas, so they could not be sure who was correct.

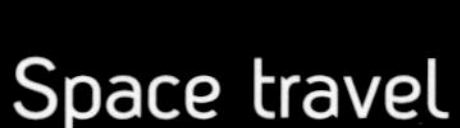

Space travel

The exploration of space is one of the great achievements of science. Isaac Newton's laws are used to figure out the motion of planets and spaceships. Advanced technology is used to build and control spacecraft.

Mathematics and computers

Mathematics is used to figure out the details of theories and to make predictions that can be tested. Usually, computers are needed to carry out the complex calculations.

Physics and machines

Physical laws are applied to build the machines that people use, from TVs, bikes, and phones to power plants, robots, and space stations. Physicists also rely on machines such as computers and lasers to do their work. Lasers can also be used for entertainment (right).

Chemistry and industry

The production of industrial materials relies on an understanding of the laws of chemistry. These materials include hard-wearing fabrics, strong, lightweight building materials, cheap fertilizers, and low-pollution fuels. All of these are scientifically designed and manufactured

Biology and medicine

Without medicine, many of us would not survive our first few months of existence. Death in childhood was common until a few decades ago. Today, biologists understand more about how our bodies function, what causes illnesses, and how to improve people's health.

How science works

Science starts with thinking of explanations for the way things happen. To test these ideas, scientists make predictions that they can check.

Gradually, the explanations that scientists have thought of are developed into theories that are both complete and accurate.

Radio waves can be measured very accurately inside this special chamber.

The scientific method

Scientists apply a logical approach in which ideas are tested and developed into theories and laws. For example, it was once believed that heavy objects fall faster than light objects. But after observing hailstones falling, Galileo questioned this belief. He experimented with falling objects to discover the mathematical law of falling.

Measurement

We can see light, hear sound, taste and smell some chemicals, and feel heat, force, and electricity. But without machines, we would neither be able to make the accurate measurements needed to test theories nor detect things such as radio waves and x-rays.

Observing phenomena

Scientists begin by observing as wide a range of phenomena as possible and trying to explain them. Microscopes, spectroscopes, and telescopes allow us to observe things that cannot otherwise be sensed.

Science in action

Some things, such as the motions of planets, can be predicted years ahead. "Chaotic" systems, such as weather, can be predicted only roughly. In a chaotic system, any one of many small changes may lead to big effects such as a hurricane.

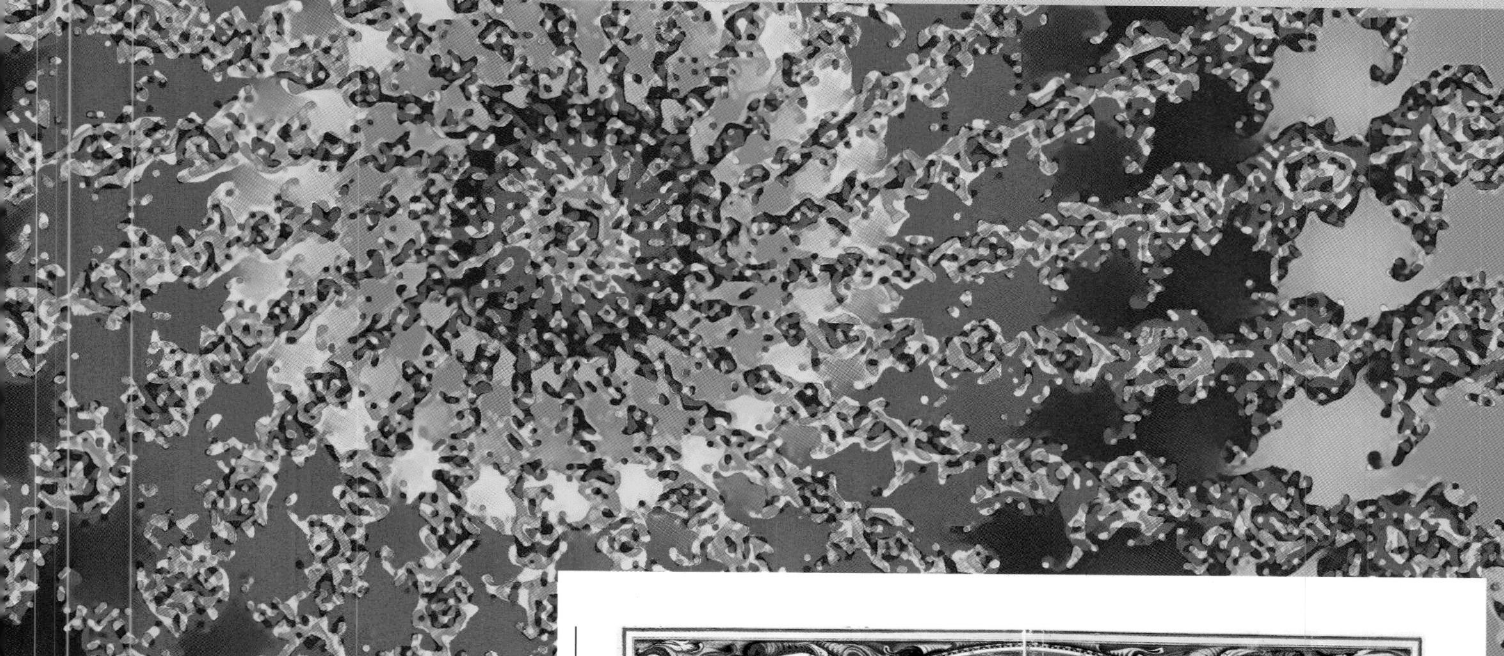

This computer-generated picture is of a fractal, an endless mathematical pattern that occurs in nature.

Mathematical models

Using powerful computers, scientists can make mathematical models of things such as stars, germs, or transportation systems. These models are used by them to predict what will happen in different situations.

Big science

Modern science is expensive, whether it is a planet or the inside of an atom that is being studied. This huge underground laboratory in Switzerland is called CERN. It uses powerful blasts of energy to break apart atomic particles.

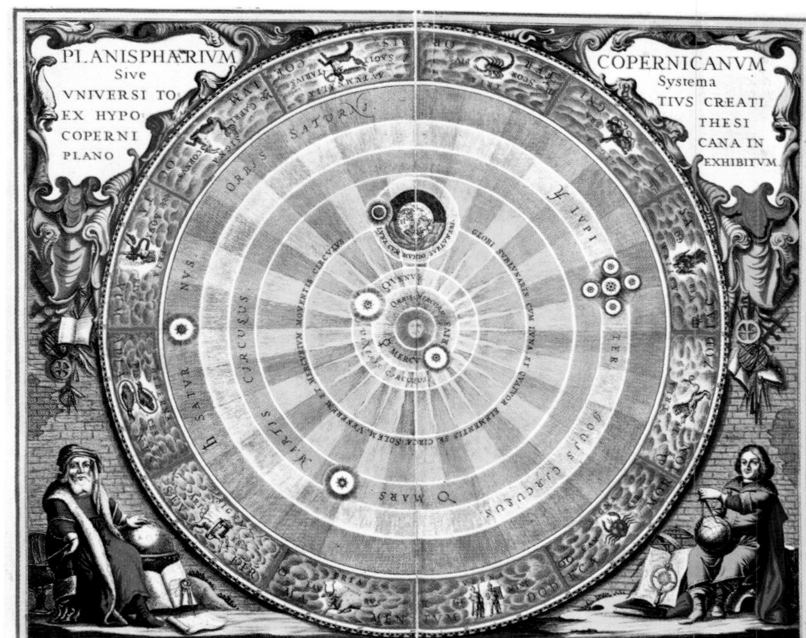

HISTORICAL DATA

REVOLUTIONS IN SCIENCE

Science does not move forward steadily. Successful theories explain most things for a while, and then new evidence builds up until a new and more powerful theory replaces the old ones. For years, it was believed that the Sun moved around Earth—until Copernicus's theory, that Earth moved around the Sun (above), replaced it. Similarly, in the 1900s, Albert Einstein's powerful new theories replaced those of Isaac Newton.

A sundial

The world's time system is based on the moment at which the Sun is at its highest when seen from the prime meridian.

It is 4:00 A.M. in California and time to sleep.

It is 11:00 A.M. in western Africa, and this class is hard at work.

TIME

WE ALL KNOW WHAT TIME IS, BUT TRY PUTTING IT INTO WORDS! TIME IS CLOSELY LINKED TO SPACE—NEITHER CAN EXIST WITHOUT THE OTHER. BUT WHILE WE CAN MOVE AS WE WANT THROUGH SPACE, WE CAN MOVE ONLY IN ONE DIRECTION THROUGH TIME.

Most time zones are one hour later than the neighboring zone to the west.

TIME ZONES

Earth is divided up into time zones. Within each zone, the clocks are set to the same time. The edges of the zones often follow the borders of different countries.

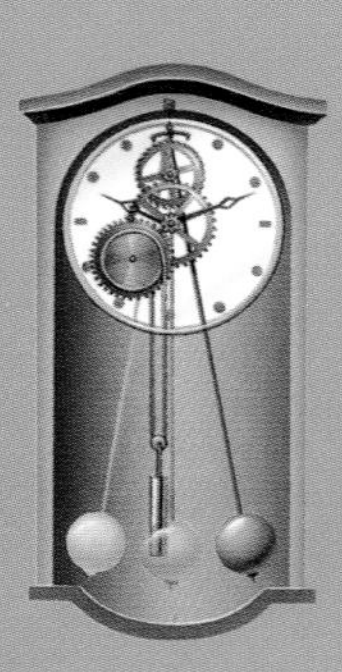

A mechanical pendulum clock

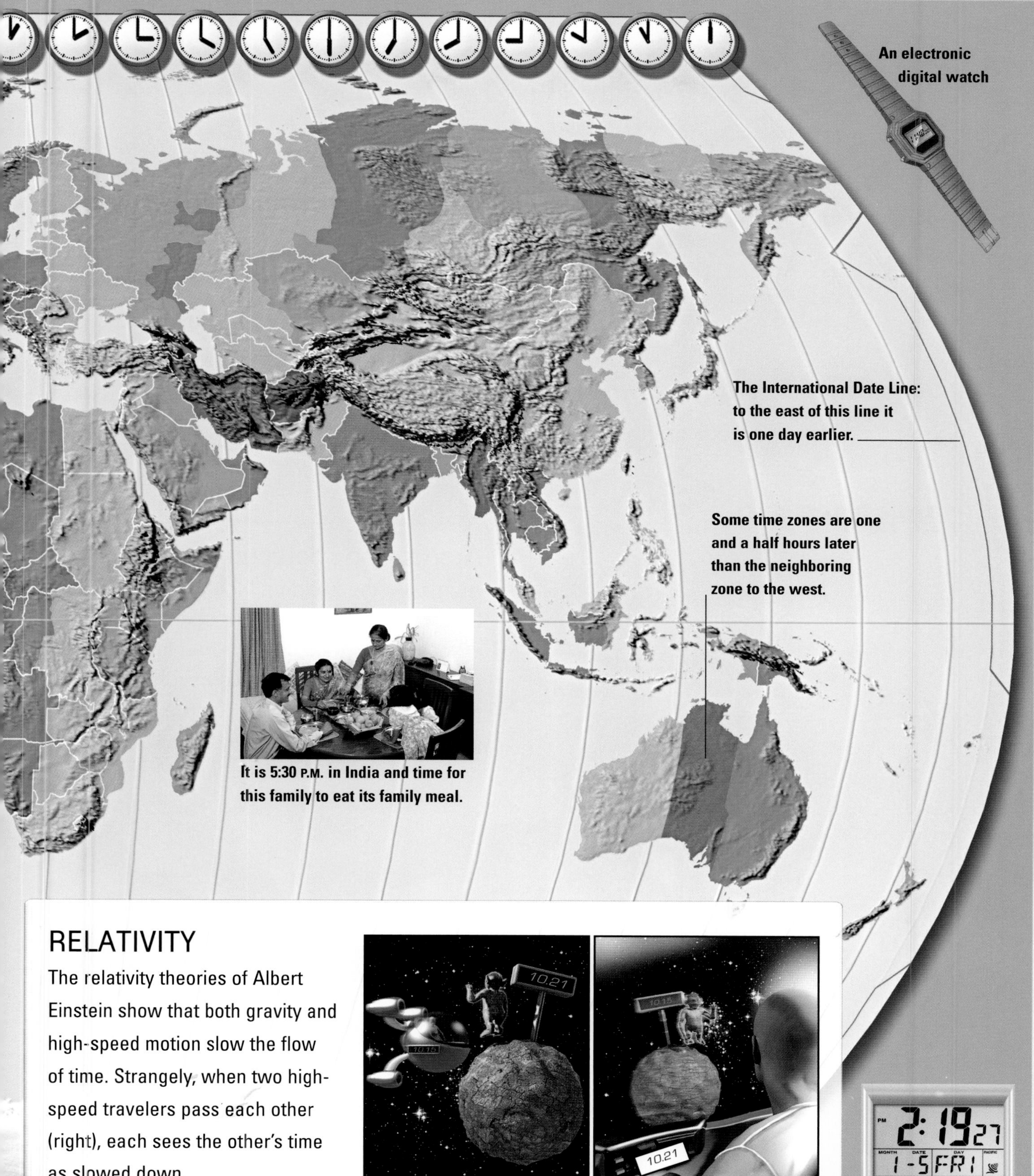

An electronic digital watch

The International Date Line: to the east of this line it is one day earlier.

Some time zones are one and a half hours later than the neighboring zone to the west.

It is 5:30 P.M. in India and time for this family to eat its family meal.

RELATIVITY

The relativity theories of Albert Einstein show that both gravity and high-speed motion slow the flow of time. Strangely, when two high-speed travelers pass each other (right), each sees the other's time as slowed down.

A digital clock and calendar

Matter and atoms

Everything, including you, is made of matter. All matter is made of atoms that are less than one millionth of a millimeter wide.

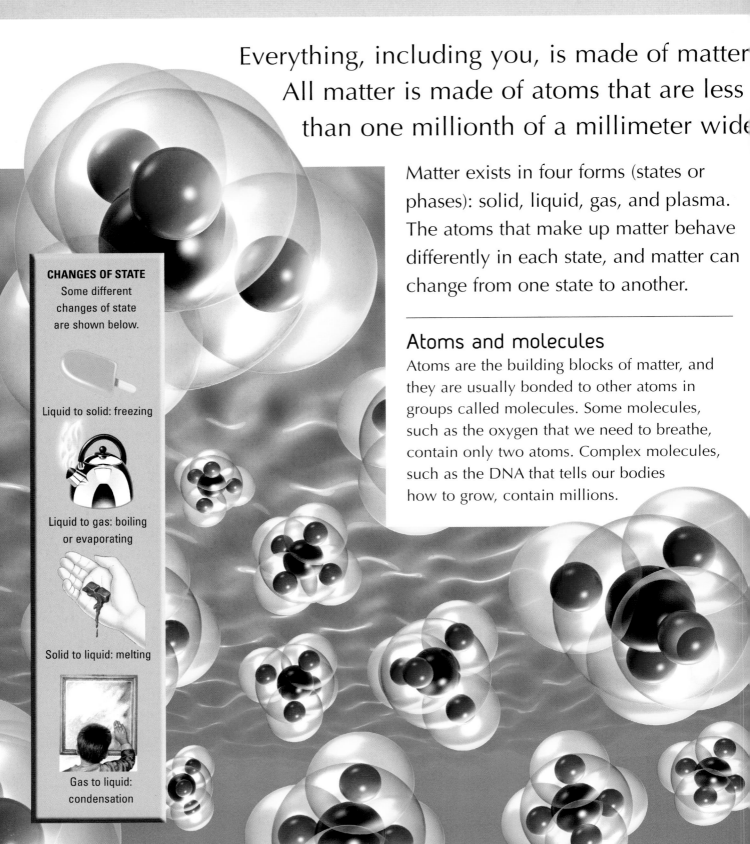

Matter exists in four forms (states or phases): solid, liquid, gas, and plasma. The atoms that make up matter behave differently in each state, and matter can change from one state to another.

CHANGES OF STATE
Some different changes of state are shown below.

Liquid to solid: freezing

Liquid to gas: boiling or evaporating

Solid to liquid: melting

Gas to liquid: condensation

Atoms and molecules

Atoms are the building blocks of matter, and they are usually bonded to other atoms in groups called molecules. Some molecules, such as the oxygen that we need to breathe, contain only two atoms. Complex molecules, such as the DNA that tells our bodies how to grow, contain millions.

Solids, liquids, and gases

In solids, the molecules are held together and cannot move easily. In liquids, they can move past one another but still remain close. In gases, the molecules can move freely, and in plasmas, they are broken down into atomic nuclei and electrons.

Atomic nuclei

Atoms are mostly empty space, with a tiny, dense core called the nucleus in the center. Nuclei are made of particles called neutrons and protons. Nuclei have diameters 100,000 times smaller than an atom's.

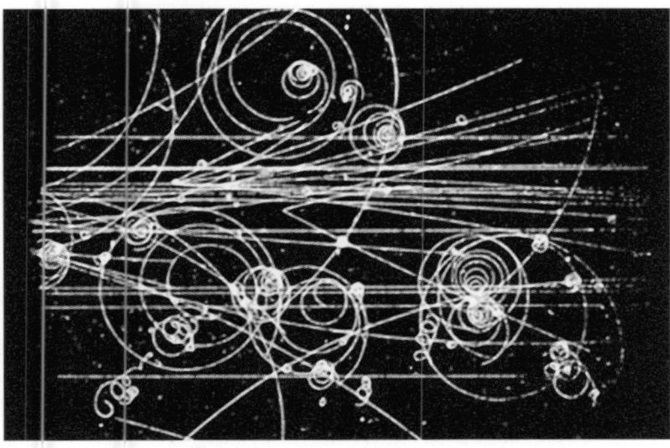

Subatomic particles

Protons and neutrons are made of even smaller particles called quarks. These are held together by particles called gluons. To study nuclei, quarks are smashed into pieces in particle accelerators and special instruments show how they move (above). Their masses, electric charges, and other properties can be figured out from these images.

Electrons and ions

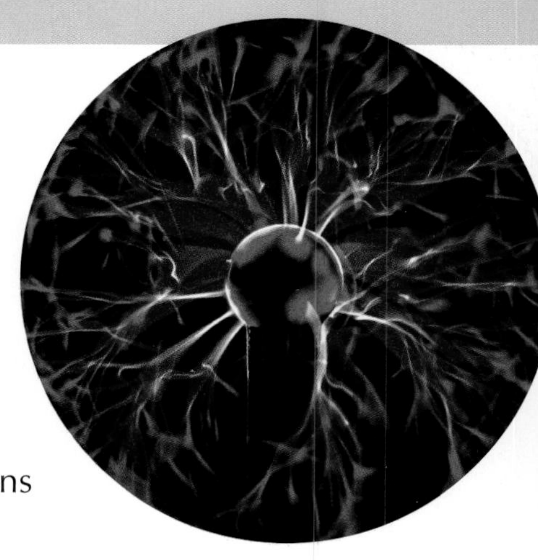

Atomic nuclei are surrounded by particles called electrons. Electrons have a negative electric charge that usually balances the positive charge of the protons. An atom with an unequal number of electrons and protons is called an ion.

Isotopes

The atoms of a chemical element all have the same number of protons but not always the same number of neutrons. Atoms of the same element with different numbers of neutrons are called isotopes.

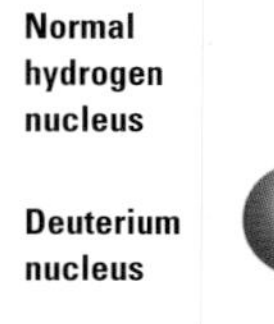

Isotopes of hydrogen used in nuclear reactors

AMAZING FACTS

QUANTUM PHYSICS

Tiny things, such as electrons, do not behave like the larger objects that we are used to in our everyday lives. Electrons do not have exact speeds and positions. In the group of atoms above, the electrons can be defined only as being somewhere in the red and yellow areas. And they behave like light waves as well as particles. The study of these strange properties is called quantum physics.

Elements and compounds

An element is a substance made up of atoms, each of which has the same number of protons. Everything in the universe is composed of around 100 different elements.

The atoms of different elements can join together. The resulting substance is called a compound and usually has very different properties to the original elements.

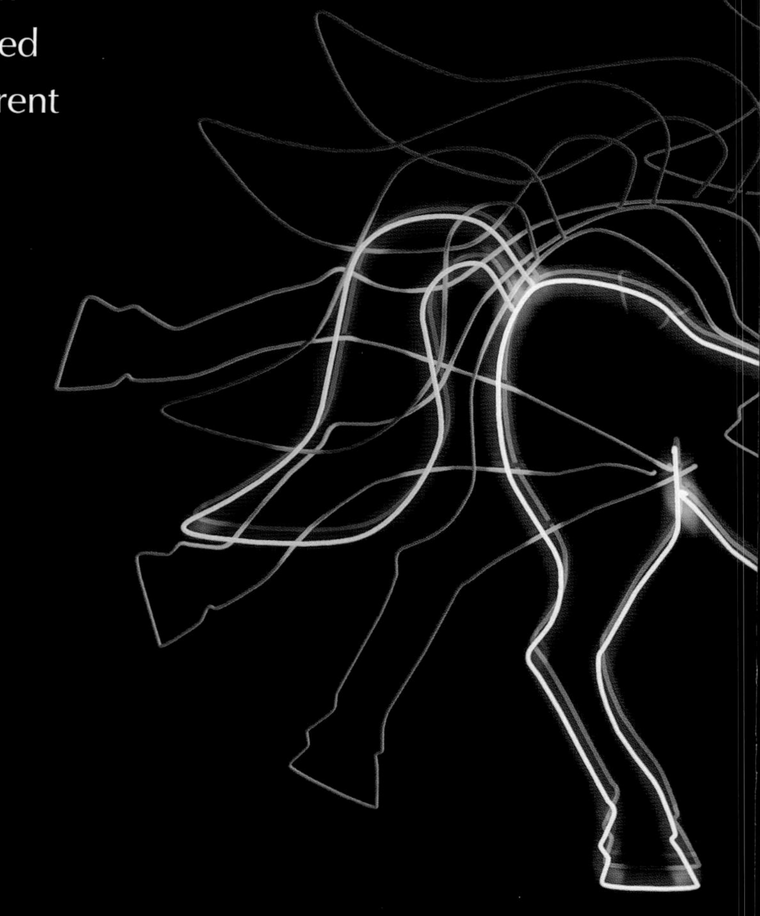

Elements and atoms

The properties of an element depend on the properties of its atoms. So hydrogen and helium, which are made of very small atoms, are both very light gases. Lead, which is very heavy, is made of much larger atoms.

Metals

Metals are a very useful group of elements, partly because they conduct electricity and heat. Metal atoms all share their outer electrons. This makes it easy for electrical or thermal energy to move between them. Some metals react easily with oxygen to form oxides. Rust, for example, is iron oxide.

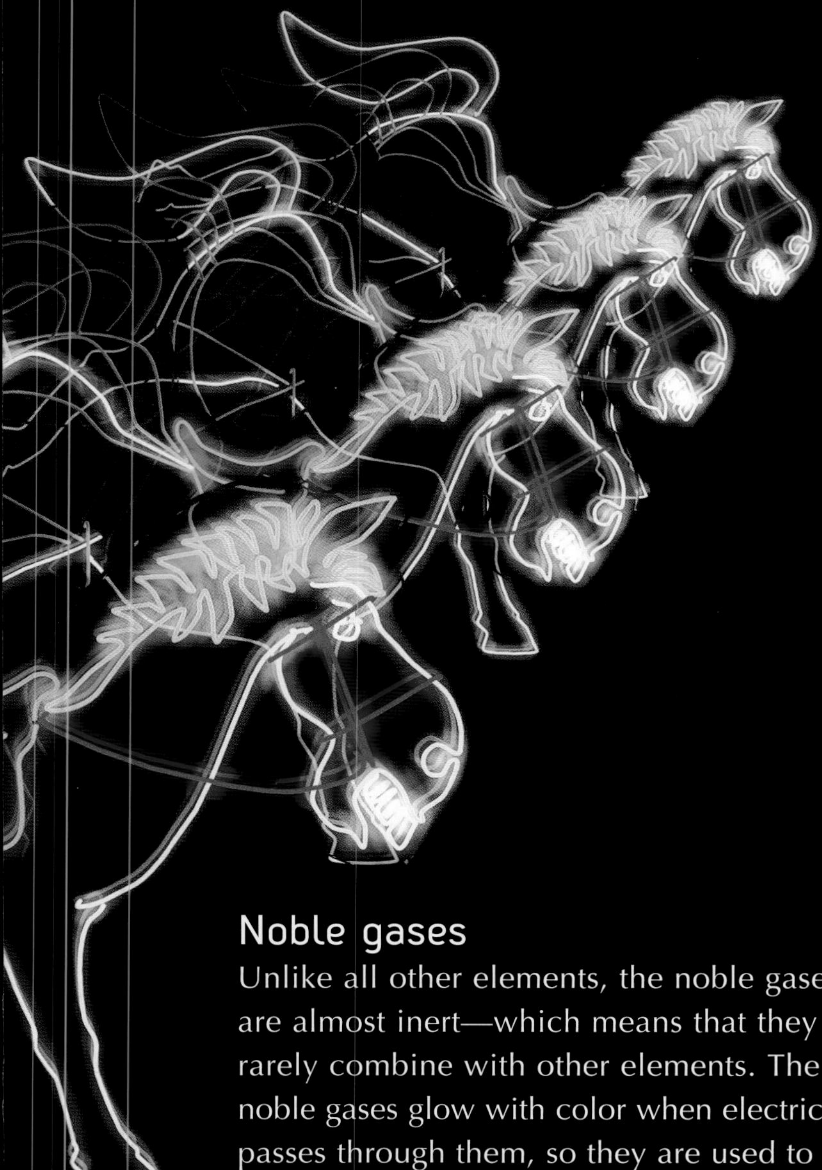

Noble gases

Unlike all other elements, the noble gases are almost inert—which means that they rarely combine with other elements. The noble gases glow with color when electricity passes through them, so they are used to make lights and signs (above).

Radioactive elements

The atoms that make up some heavy elements, such as uranium, are unstable. They break apart unpredictably and release energy in the form of intense radiation (gamma rays) and particles (alpha and beta particles). Radioactive elements can both cause and cure some forms of cancer and are used in nuclear weapons and power plants.

Reactive elements

Elements whose atoms have a single outer electron are all highly reactive, combining easily with other elements. A small amount of potassium reacts violently with water (above), releasing hydrogen and forming a compound called a hydroxide.

Compounds

Often, heating will cause elements to combine into compounds. When the elements hydrogen and oxygen are mixed and heated, they produce water. The symbol of water is H_2O, because its molecules contain two hydrogen atoms and one of oxygen.

Materials

Some of the materials we use are natural such as wool, wood, and stone. But most things are made from artificial (synthetic) materials such as concrete, glass, and plastic.

OIL PRODUCTS
Oil from Earth can be made into many useful everyday items.

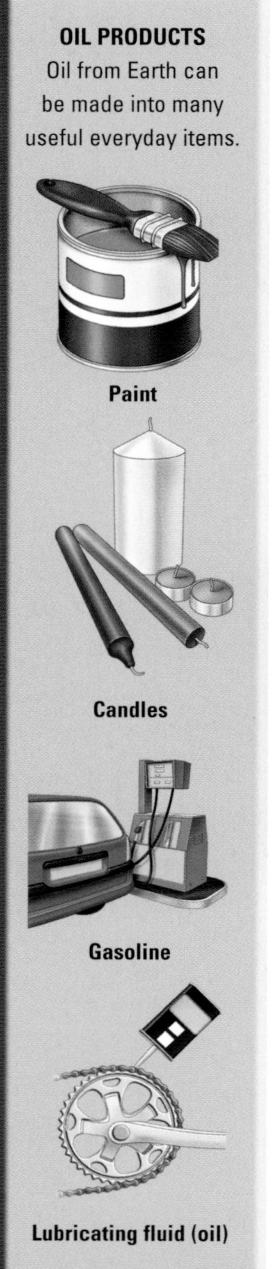

Paint

Candles

Gasoline

Lubricating fluid (oil)

Today, people design materials with the properties they need such as building materials that are strong and lightweight.

Wood

Wood is used all over the world for building and for making paper and furniture, too. Different types have different properties—balsa is light, oak is strong, and teak is hard.

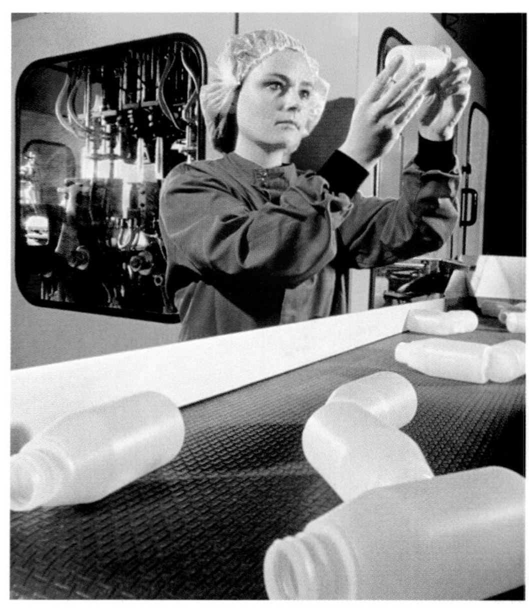

Plastics

Most plastics are made from oil-based chemicals, and they are easy to mold, shape, and color. They can be flexible and transparent for food packaging or hard and tough for vehicles.

Metals

Metals have many useful properties. They can be shaped when heated, and many are tough and hard wearing. Alloys are mixtures of metals and sometimes other materials. The most useful alloy is steel, which is iron with carbon added to harden it.

Glass

Glass is made from sand and can be shaped by blowing, molding, or rolling it. Although naturally brittle, it can be toughened to resist heat or impact. Metallic chemicals are used to color it.

Adhesives

Adhesives are substances that stick objects together. Some are made from natural materials. The strongest and longest-lasting adhesives are artificial.

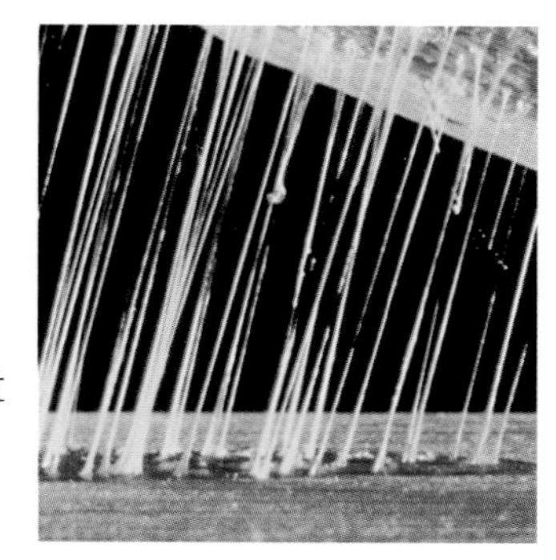

Smart materials

It is possible to change the properties of some artificial materials by applying heat, electricity, or magnetism to them; these "smart" materials can change shape or turn into a liquid at the press of a button. Objects made of shape memory alloys (SMAs) spring back to their original shapes when heated.

ENERGY

ENERGY IS THE ABILITY TO DO WORK. WITHOUT IT, NOTHING COULD HAPPEN. ENERGY CANNOT BE DESTROYED, AND IT EXISTS IN MANY FORMS, INCLUDING MASS.

Inside the Sun, hydrogen nuclei are crushed together to form helium nuclei. This process releases enormous amounts of energy and is called nuclear fusion. We see this energy as sunlight.

TYPES OF ENERGY

The many forms of energy can be converted into one another. Sunlight is converted to chemical energy by plants and to electrical energy by solar cells. Televisions convert electrical energy to sound and light. Animals convert the chemical energy in food into kinetic energy when they move. All of these energy changes also produce heat (thermal energy).

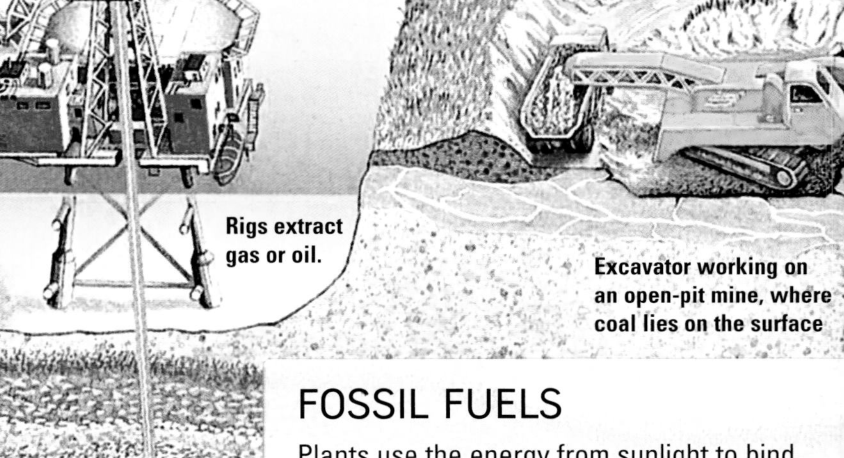

Surplus natural gas is burned as a flare.

Rigs extract gas or oil.

Excavator working on an open-pit mine, where coal lies on the surface

Gas and oil

NUCLEAR ENERGY

Some large atoms are unstable and disintegrate naturally, releasing energy (nuclear fission). In a nuclear power plant, these disintegrations are kept under control and used to produce electrical energy.

FOSSIL FUELS

Plants use the energy from sunlight to bind together water and carbon dioxide in order to make their leaves and other structures. The remains of entire forests of plants that lived more than 200 million years ago, crushed deep underground, change gradually to coal, oil, and gas. When these fossil fuels are burned, the energy of ancient sunlight is released again.

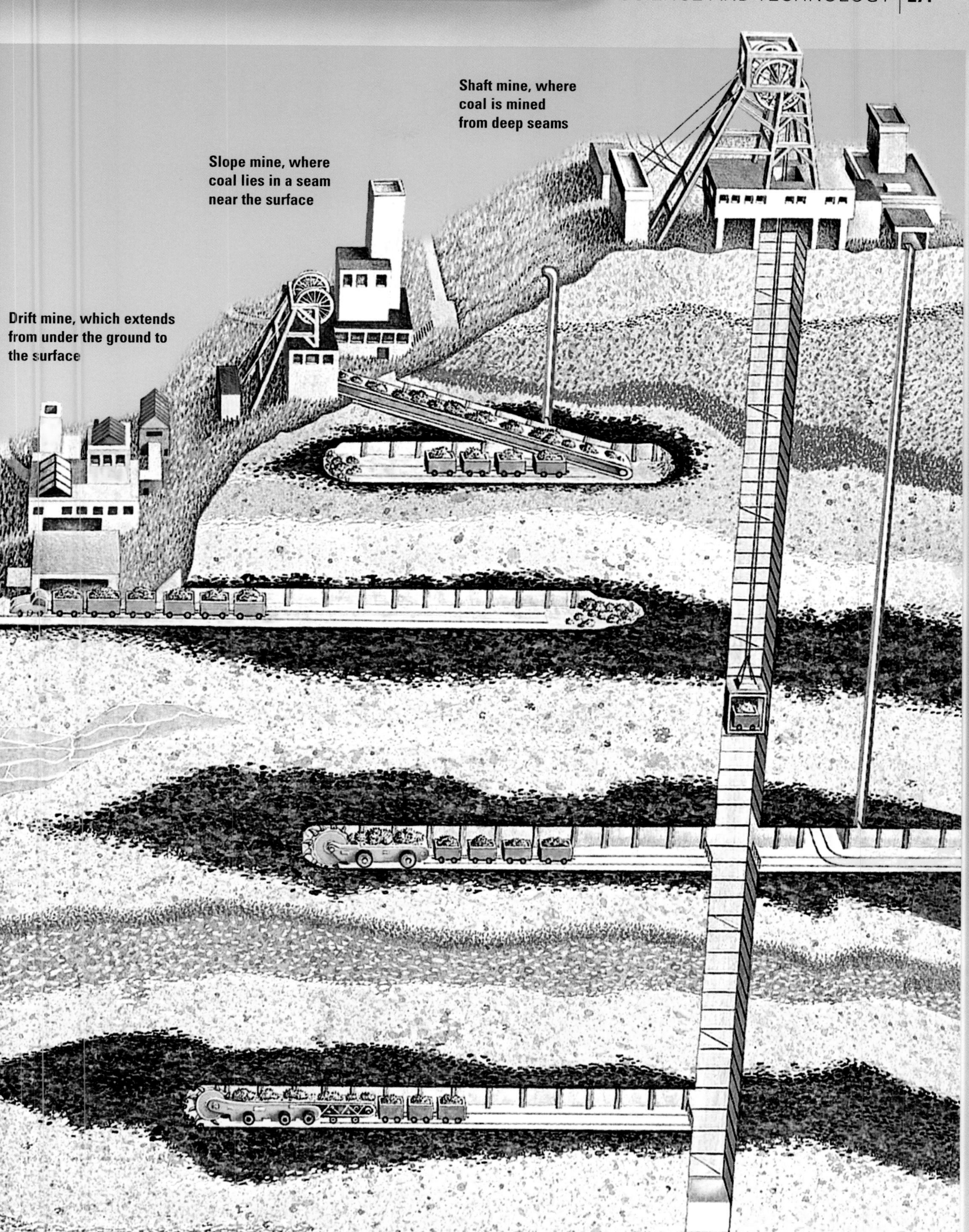
Shaft mine, where coal is mined from deep seams
Slope mine, where coal lies in a seam near the surface
Drift mine, which extends from under the ground to the surface

Sound, light, and color

Most of our information about the world comes to us as sound or light. Both are forms of energy that travel in waves.

ELECTROMAGNETIC SPECTRUM
The wavelength of an electromagnetic wave determines its properties.

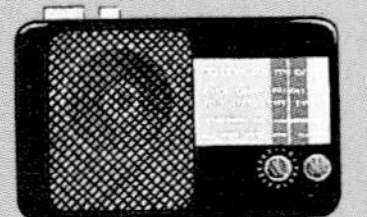

Radio waves
longer than 4 in. (10cm)

Infrared
0.7 micrometers to 1mm

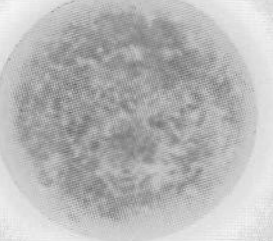

Light
0.4 to 0.7 micrometers

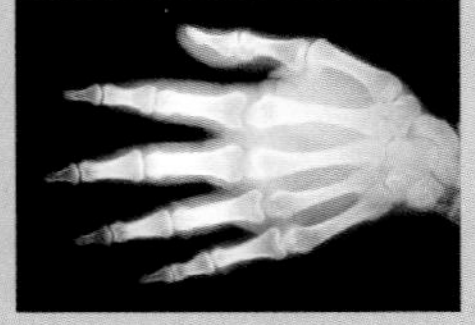

X-ray
0.01 to 10 nanometers

There are sound waves we cannot hear and light waves we cannot see. Infrasound and infrared frequencies are too low for us, and ultrasound and ultraviolet are too high.

Sound

Sound usually starts as a vibration in an object. It travels through air, water, or solids as longitudinal (backward and forward) waves of pressure. Sound travels much faster in solids and liquids than in air.

Noise

Noise is unwanted sound, whether it comes from cars, planes, or radios. Even quiet noise can be annoying, and high levels can damage hearing.

Pitch and frequency

Frequency is the number of backward and forward motions of a sound wave per second. Sounds of a higher frequency are higher pitched. Most of the sounds we hear are a mixture of many frequencies.

Light

Light travels at 983,571,056 ft. (299,792,458m) per second through empty space but slightly slower in liquids and solids. Light, like radio signals and x-rays, travels as a rapidly changing electromagnetic field.

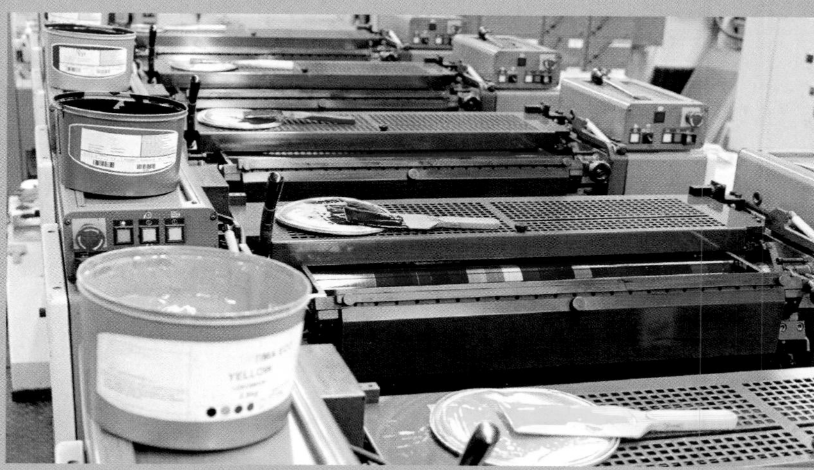

Color

We see different light frequencies as different colors, from low-frequency red, through the colors of the rainbow, to high-frequency violet. Mixtures of different frequencies can be seen as further colors such as pink. When light of all colors is mixed, we see white.

Fiber-optic cables inside a telephone wire

Optics

Optics is the science of light. Geometrical optics describes how light bounces and scatters. Physical optics studies the nature of the photons of which light is composed. The photons behave as both particles and waves.

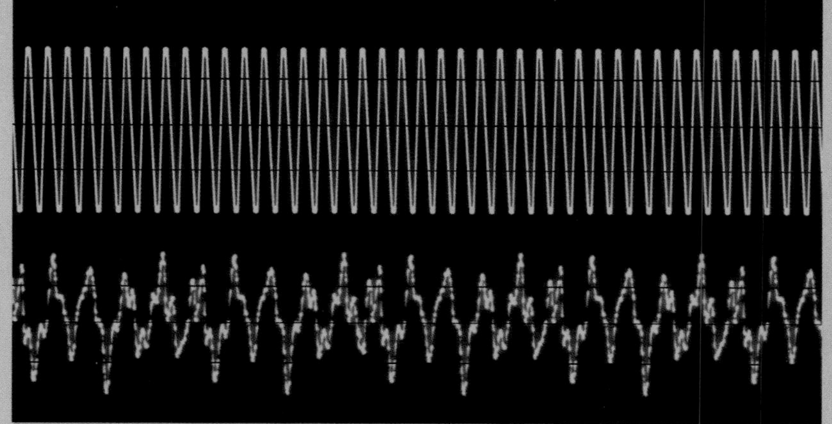

SCIENTIFIC INPUT

SOUND WAVES AND LIGHT WAVES

Sound and light are very different. Light travels around one million times faster than sound. Even the shortest sound waves that we can hear are many thousands of times longer than light waves. Sound needs a medium (air, for example) to travel in; light does not. Machines called oscilloscopes (above) can display the rapidly changing pressures of sound waves as rising and falling lines of light.

Heat

Heat is a form of energy created by the random motion of particles. Every process in the universe generates heat—even a running refrigerator heats the air around it.

KINETIC ENERGY

As the temperature rises, the energy of molecules increases until they break free, causing changes of state.

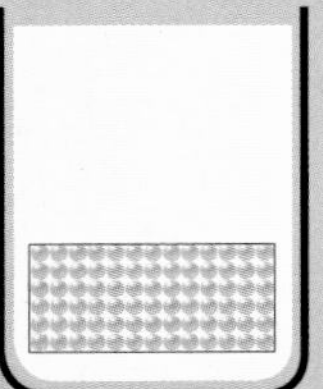

In a solid, molecules are locked together.

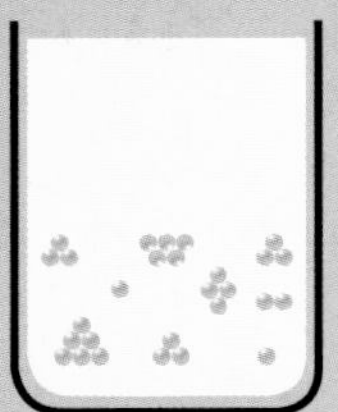

A solid melts when the molecules have enough energy to break their bonds.

A liquid boils when the molecules can move freely, filling their container.

The melting and then boiling of substances as they are heated happens because the increasing energy of molecules allows them to break their bonds. They then escape from one another. Even more heat breaks down the molecules themselves.

Heat and temperature

Heat is a type of energy, and temperature describes the concentration of that energy. A lake contains more heat than a cup of coffee. However, it has a lower temperature because the energy is spread out more thinly over its large area.

Heating and cooling

Usually, heating a solid substance causes it first to melt (or thaw) and then to turn into a gas (called boiling if the change is rapid or evaporation if it is slow). Cooling a gas usually causes it to condense and then freeze (left). But sometimes the liquid phase is missed out—frost in sunlight can sublime, changing directly to gas.

Heat transfer

Heat moves in three ways. It passes through solids by conduction (the metal bucket above would burn anyone who touched it). It moves through liquids and gases by convection (like the draft of hot air rising from the bucket). And it is transferred through gases or space by radiation (the molten metal is glowing with invisible infrared heat radiation as well as light).

Electricity and magnetism

Electricity and magnetism are vital to the way we live. Streetlights and phones are electrically powered, while motors and credit cards need magnets to work.

Both electricity and magnetism depend on the motion of electrons. Force fields around magnetic or electrically charged objects push or pull other similar objects.

Natural electricity

Our brains and nerves use tiny amounts of electricity in order to function and control our bodies. Much larger amounts of electricity can be seen when lightning strikes during a thunderstorm.

Electronics

Materials that allow electricity to pass through easily are called conductors, and those through which electricity cannot pass are insulators. Semiconductors allow a variable amount of electricity to pass and are used to control the flow of electricity in electronic circuits.

Electric circuits

A battery is a device that produces electricity. It has two "poles." If these are connected by a wire, electricity flows from the negative pole to the positive pole. A battery can be made to do work along the way, by powering a bulb or a motor.

Static and current electricity

When an object loses or gains electrons, it becomes electrically charged. This charge is called static electricity, because it stays where it is. When areas with different amounts of charge are connected by a metal wire, electricity flows along the wire and is called an electric current.

Magnets

Magnets attract other magnets. They also attract iron and some other metals. All magnets have a north and a south pole, and each pole attracts poles of the opposite type and repels poles of its own type.

Electromagnetism

A current-carrying conductor generates a magnetic field. If the conductor is wound around an iron core, the field can be very strong. Devices like this are called electromagnets and provide controllable magnetic fields.

EARTH EVIDENCE

THE EARTH AS A MAGNET

Movements of molten metal deep inside Earth generate a worldwide magnetic field. This magnetic field protects life on Earth from harmful radiation from space. In a compass, a small, thin magnet lines up with Earth's field, pointing the way to the North and South poles and helping people navigate.

FORCES AND MOTION

A MOVING OBJECT IS SAID TO HAVE KINETIC ENERGY—THE FASTER IT MOVES, OR THE MORE MASS IT HAS, THE HIGHER ITS KINETIC ENERGY. THE VELOCITY OF AN OBJECT IS ITS SPEED IN A PARTICULAR DIRECTION. ACCELERATION IS A CHANGE OF VELOCITY.

The wing profile makes air flow faster over upper wing surfaces, reducing the downward air pressure on them. The higher pressure under the wings pushes them upward.

The A380 can seat 525 people because it has 50 percent more floor space than any other passenger aircraft.

The upward force on the wings opposes the downward force of gravity.

FORCE AND PRESSURE

To start an object moving, slow it down, or change its direction, a force (a push or pull) is required. When air resistance or friction is present, a force is required in order to keep the object moving. Where there is no air resistance or friction—in space, for example—objects will continue to move with no force present. Pressure is the amount of force applied to a particular area.

WORK AND POWER

When an object is moved by a force, work is achieved. The higher the force, or the greater the distance, the more work is done. Power measures how quickly this happens. Whether you walk or run upstairs, you do the same amount of work, but running needs more power.

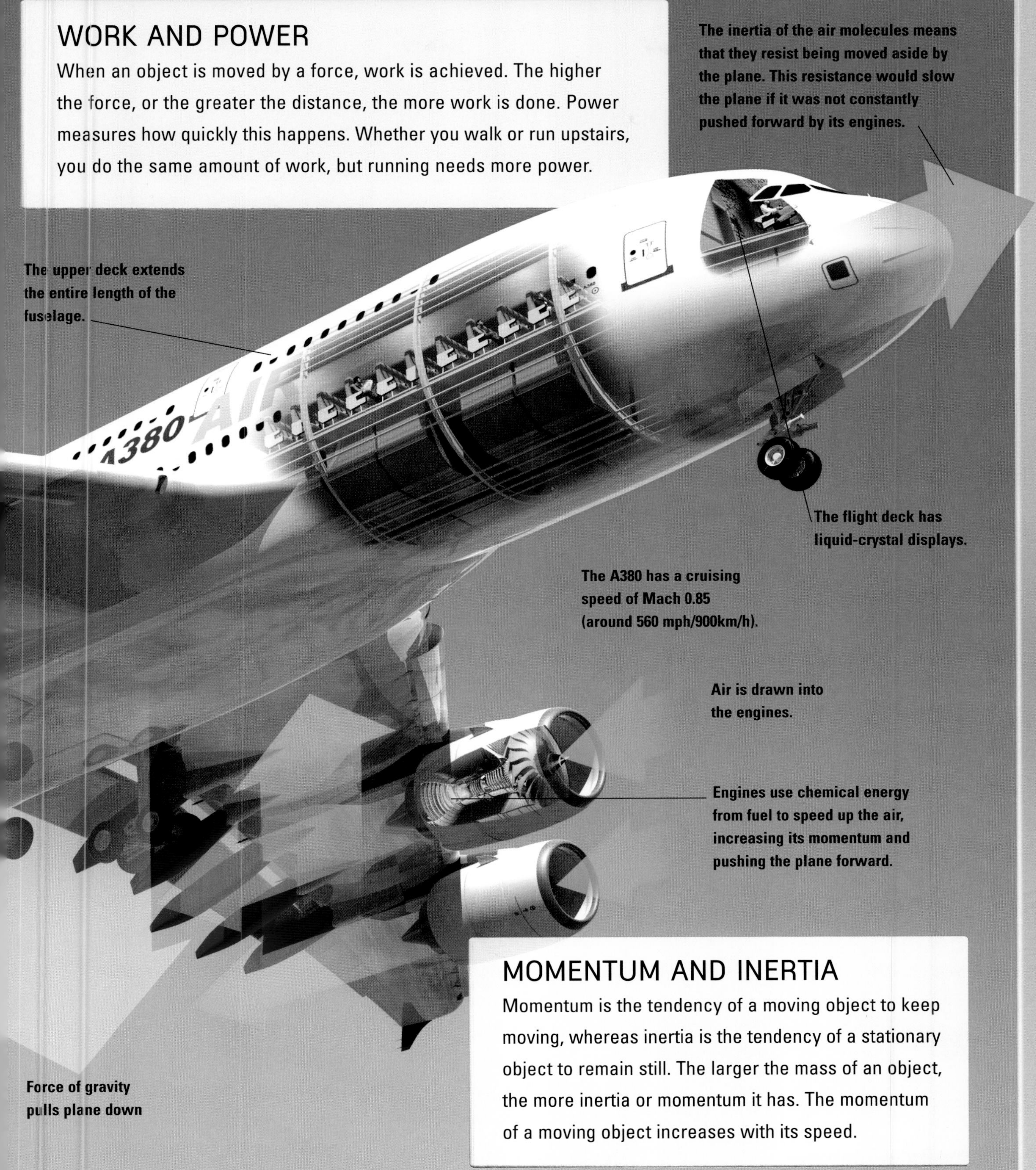

The inertia of the air molecules means that they resist being moved aside by the plane. This resistance would slow the plane if it was not constantly pushed forward by its engines.

The upper deck extends the entire length of the fuselage.

The flight deck has liquid-crystal displays.

The A380 has a cruising speed of Mach 0.85 (around 560 mph/900km/h).

Air is drawn into the engines.

Engines use chemical energy from fuel to speed up the air, increasing its momentum and pushing the plane forward.

Force of gravity pulls plane down

MOMENTUM AND INERTIA

Momentum is the tendency of a moving object to keep moving, whereas inertia is the tendency of a stationary object to remain still. The larger the mass of an object, the more inertia or momentum it has. The momentum of a moving object increases with its speed.

Engineering

Engineering is the application of science to the construction of the systems and structures we use.

DEVELOPMENT OF AIRCRAFT
Aircraft have developed rapidly over the past 100 years.

Biplanes were invented in the 1900s.

Monoplanes replaced them in the 1930s.

The first successful jet plane flew in 1939.

The first supersonic flight was in 1947.

Rocket planes reached the edge of space in 1963.

We live in an engineered world. Cities can be thought of as vast machines, containing many smaller machines and systems.

Civil engineering

Over thousands of years, civil engineers have gradually developed materials, designs, and methods to build roads, bridges, and buildings. Today, computer models are essential for all civil-engineering projects.

Mining

Mining engineers organize the extraction and transportation of minerals (such as coal or salt) and metal ores (such as iron) from mines. They are responsible for miners' safety, too.

Machines and vehicles

Mechanical engineers design, build, and test machines, from factory robots to trains. Cars, motorcycles, and trucks are designed by automotive engineers.

Electrical engineering

Electrical engineers develop electrical and electronic devices and systems. These include electricity-distribution systems, computer hardware, and telecommunication systems such as phone networks and television.

Aerospace

Aerospace engineers design and build aircraft and spacecraft, which are some of the most challenging and complex machines of all. They have to be able to keep passengers safe while they travel through environments that may change rapidly and unpredictably.

Software engineering

Software has to be engineered not only to perform a function—for example, transferring money between banks—but also to be fast, efficient, and reliable. It is often necessary for it to run properly on different types of computer systems.

AMAZING FACTS

RECORD-BREAKING TUNNEL

Almost 13,000 people, including mining, mechanical, civil, software, and electrical engineers, were needed to construct the 30-mi. (50-km) Channel Tunnel (above), which connects the United Kingdom and France. It is the longest undersea tunnel in the world, and it is air-conditioned by a system that is equivalent to 260,000 domestic refrigerators. Some of the tunnel-boring machines used were the length of two soccer fields.

Industry and manufacturing

Over the last few hundred years, the application of science through technology has transformed the world. It is used to produce all types of things, from foods to cars.

Almost every part of our lives depends on industry and manufacturing—the vehicles we travel in, the books and computers we use, and our homes, foods, and clothes. Many products are built where they can be made cheaply and are transported all over the world.

Food production

Industry affects every stage of the food-production process. Biological expertise is used to develop improved vegetables and fruit. Chemicals are used to fertilize seedlings and keep them free from weeds and pests. And the crops are harvested, processed, preserved, packaged, and transported by machinery.

Industrial chemistry

Many of the things you use every day, including plastics, fuel, and many fabrics, were made chemically in industrial plants. The increasing use of robots and computers in these plants has gradually reduced the numbers of human workers involved in the processes. Safety has been improved because machines have taken over work that was often unpleasant and dangerous.

Mass production

Most machines are made by other machines in large numbers and with very limited human involvement. Standard-size, accurate machine-made parts mean that different components of large machines can be made in different countries and will still work together correctly when assembled. This amazing storage facility for newly completed cars is in Wolfsburg, Germany. It is fully automated—a robot arm moves the cars up and down when needed.

Medicine

Medicine is one of the greatest triumphs of science, giving most of us many more years of life than our ancestors had.

TYPES OF MEDICINE
Medicine is a wide-ranging field of science and includes the skill areas below.

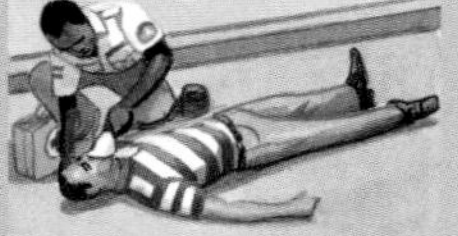

First aid delivers rapid help at the scene of an accident.

Surgery involves operating on the body, usually in a hospital.

Minor ailments are treated at a doctor's office.

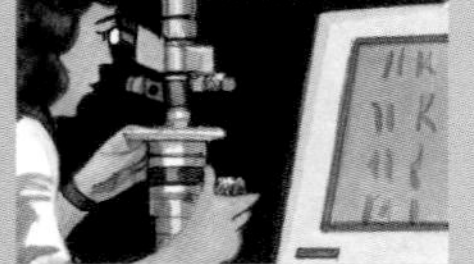

Medical research develops new cures and treatments.

Early doctors tried different cures to see what worked. Today, the discovery of germs and a greater understanding of the way the body works have led to much more effective treatments of illnesses.

Health and illness

Modern medicine recognizes that it is as important to encourage health through a good diet, exercise, and living conditions as it is to cure illnesses. Good health does not only mean a healthy body—the mind can also become unwell. Holistic medicine refers to care of all aspects of a person's health.

Injuries and healing

The body is capable of healing most injuries itself if it is protected while it recovers. Antiseptics stop wounds from becoming infected, and bandages support injuries. A good diet and a desire to get better are important.

Operations and antiseptics

To replace organs, remove tumors, and install artificial body parts, it is necessary to operate on the body. To avoid pain, local anesthetics numb body parts. For major surgery, general anesthetics cause unconsciousness.

Microbes

Diseases are spread by microbes (germs). Microbes include large molecules called prions, viruses, single-celled creatures called bacteria and protozoans, parasites, and fungi. The picture above is of MRSA bacteria, which are resistant to many common antibiotics.

Antibiotics and vaccines

Antibiotics are one of the most important weapons against diseases. "Broad-spectrum" antibiotics, such as penicillin, are capable of destroying almost any type of bacterium. In many cases, if a person is vaccinated with a weakened version of a virus, his or her body's immune system can adapt to fight the full-strength virus.

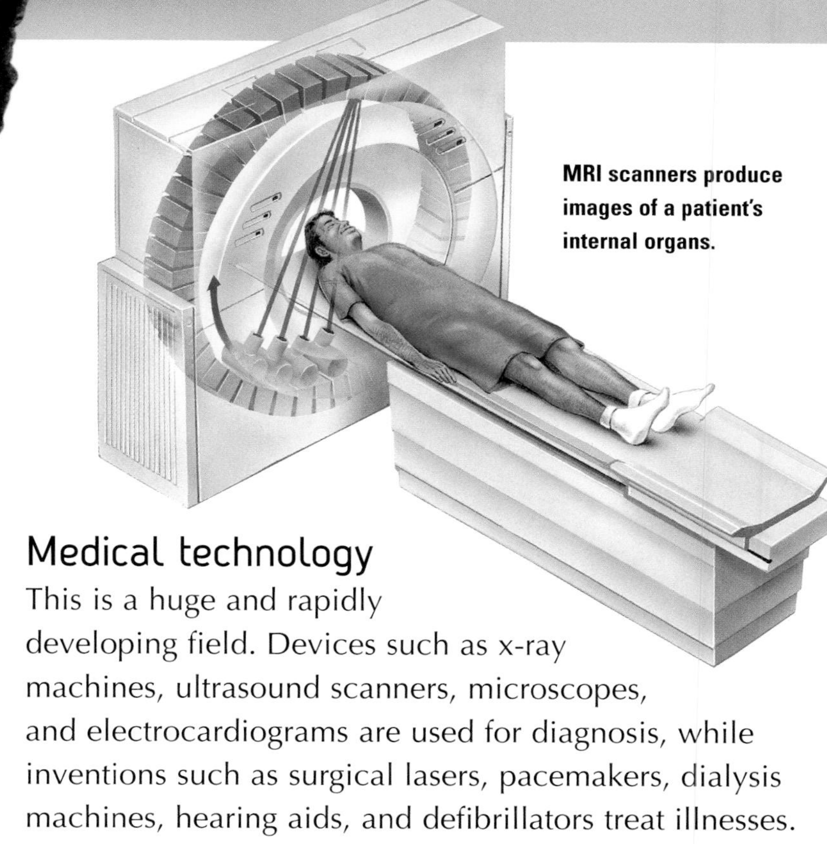

MRI scanners produce images of a patient's internal organs.

Medical technology

This is a huge and rapidly developing field. Devices such as x-ray machines, ultrasound scanners, microscopes, and electrocardiograms are used for diagnosis, while inventions such as surgical lasers, pacemakers, dialysis machines, hearing aids, and defibrillators treat illnesses.

HISTORICAL DATA

DISCOVERY OF GERMS

In the 1670s, Anthony van Leeuwenhoek used microscopes to discover nearly invisible living organisms, later called germs or microbes. In the 1860s, Louis Pasteur's experiments (above) proved that germs came only from other germs, not from rotting meat or other nonliving materials. In 1877, Robert Koch showed that particular types of germs cause particular diseases when he identified the type that causes anthrax.

Biotechnology

Biotechnology is the scientific design and alteration of living things to benefit human beings.

Farmers have been developing animals and plants for food and other uses for thousands of years. Today, research into the chemical basis of life has led to rapid developments.

Making medicine

Making medical drugs in laboratories is an important application of biotechnology. Today, insulin, which treats diabetes, can be produced from genetically modified bacteria cheaply and effectively.

Fermentation

Fermentation is the biological process that changes fruit juice into wine and flour dough into bread. To make wine, yeast (a type of fungus) is added to juice. If the temperature and other conditions are right, the yeast multiplies, feeding on sugar in the juice and producing alcohol as a waste product.

Genetic engineering

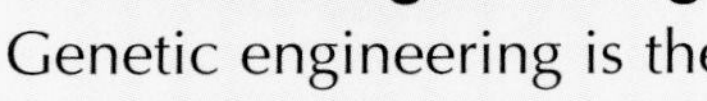

Genetic engineering is the modification of genes. It is used to improve food crops, develop drug-producing bacteria, and breed new types of experimental mice for research. Genetically modified crops may be designed to stay fresh or to resist pests and disease.

DNA and genes

Modern advances in biotechnology rely on modifying genes. Genes are structures that form parts of enormous molecules of DNA (deoxyribonucleic acid). Genes are the instructions, found in every cell, that tell cells how to grow and function.

DNA coils up, and then the coil is itself twisted into a structure called a chromosome.

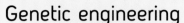

Identity cards in the future might carry DNA information.

Genetic fingerprinting

Every person's genes are unique. Because they are found in all of our cells, this means that each of us can be identified from a tiny trace of blood, skin, or even sweat. Since our genes resemble those of our relatives, family relationships can also be explored by our genetic fingerprints.

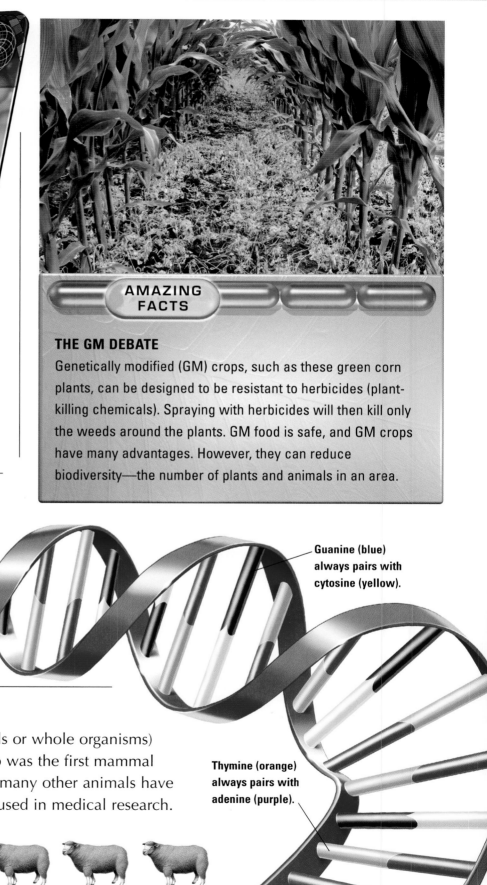

AMAZING FACTS

THE GM DEBATE

Genetically modified (GM) crops, such as these green corn plants, can be designed to be resistant to herbicides (plant-killing chemicals). Spraying with herbicides will then kill only the weeds around the plants. GM food is safe, and GM crops have many advantages. However, they can reduce biodiversity—the number of plants and animals in an area.

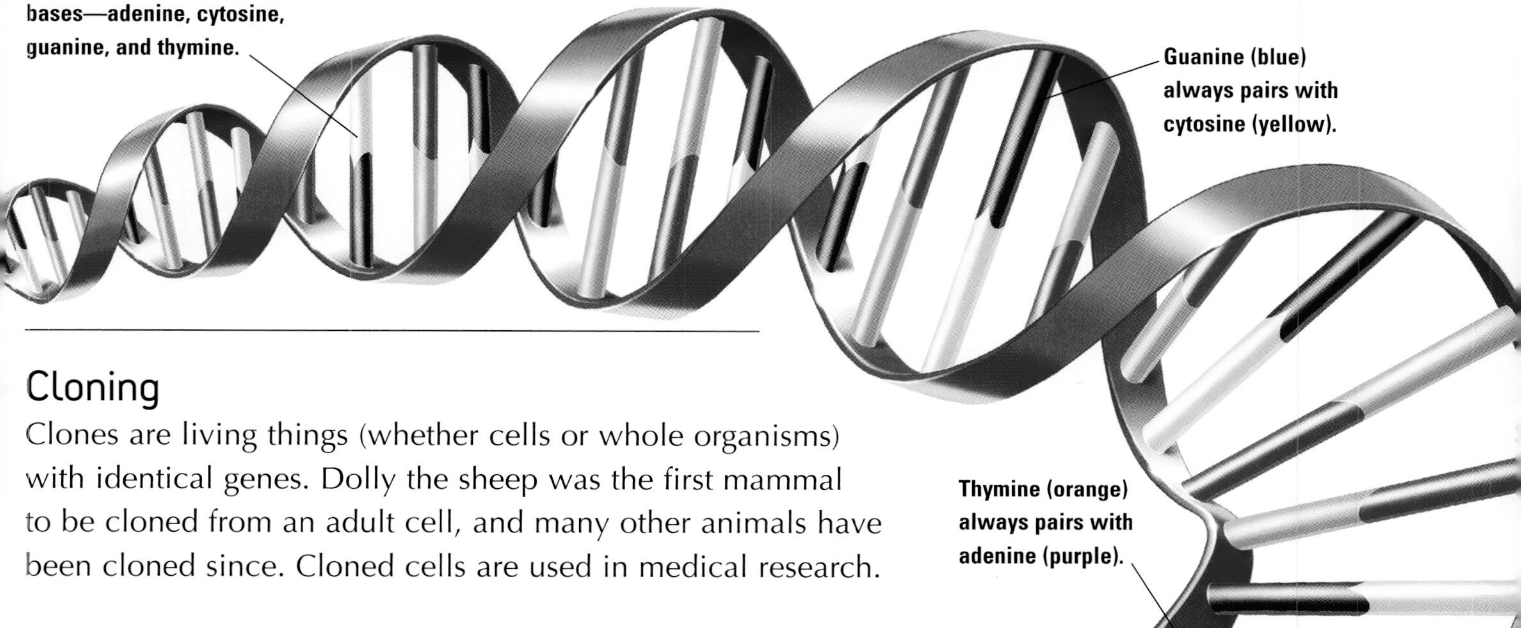

Each "rung" of DNA is made of two out of four bases—adenine, cytosine, guanine, and thymine.

Guanine (blue) always pairs with cytosine (yellow).

Thymine (orange) always pairs with adenine (purple).

Cloning

Clones are living things (whether cells or whole organisms) with identical genes. Dolly the sheep was the first mammal to be cloned from an adult cell, and many other animals have been cloned since. Cloned cells are used in medical research.

Science facts

People in different countries use different units to measure things—for example, inches, hands, yards, meters, fathoms, feet, and kilometers all measure length. But scientists always use the same set of units, some of which are given below.

UNITS OF MEASUREMENT

Base units

Mass: kilograms or pounds
Length: meters or feet
Time: seconds
Temperature: kelvins
Amount of substance: moles
Electric current: amperes
Luminous intensity: candelas

Units combining base units

Frequency: hertz (cycles per second)
Speed: meters per second (or feet)
Volume: cubic meters (or feet)
Energy: joules
Pressure: pascals
Force: newtons
Power: watts

VALUES

Speed of light: 983,571,056 ft. (299,792.458m) per second
Charge on electron or proton: 1.602×10^{-19} coulomb
Mass of an electron: 9.109×10^{-31}kg
Mass of a proton: 1,836 times more than an electron
At normal air pressure, pure water boils at 212°F/100°C (373.15 kelvin) and freezes at 32°F/0°C (273.15 kelvin).
Power of a teakettle: around 2,500 watts
Energy required to heat 1 qt. (1L) of water to boiling point: around 330,000 joules
Force with which an apple pushes down on a hand: around 1 newton
Piano notes range: 27.5–4,186 hertz
Normal air pressure: 101,323 pascals

ELECTROMAGNETIC SPECTRUM

In order of shortening wavelength and rising frequency

Radio waves
Microwaves
Infrared
Visible light:
red, orange, yellow, green, blue, and violet
Ultraviolet
X-rays
Gamma rays
Speed of light = wavelength x frequency

Pitcher of ice melting over a four-hour pe

USEFUL WEBSITES

www.sciencenewsforkids.org/ The latest science news geared toward kids, plus games.
www.physics4kids.com/ Kids' website full of information and facts about physics.
http://library.thinkquest.org/J001539/ Everything you need to know about chemistry.

Communication

Communication is the sharing of information, instructions, and ideas between people. It can happen face-to-face or using technology with people thousands of miles away. Today, there are more ways of communicating than ever before. They range from television and electronic media to improved transportation technologies that enable people to travel around the world.

Messages and the media

A message is the information that is to be communicated. The transmitter is the person or thing that is sending the message, and the audience is the person who receives the message.

ANIMAL COMMUNICATION

Creatures communicate with their own or other species using sound, scents, and displays.

Cranes perform an elaborate mating dance.

The bullfrog's loud call is heard far away.

Bees make patterns to guide each other to food.

Tigers transfer body scents by rubbing.

Methods of communicating, from sending an email to speaking over the telephone, are known as media.

Short or long

Messages can be short, for example, a stop sign or the blast of a whistle. Books contain several thousand words. The longest novel, by Frenchman Marcel Proust, has almost 1.5 million words.

Targeting an audience

Some messages are aimed at large numbers of people, for example, a neon sign in a city or a pop concert in front of a big audience. Here, a large crowd is at a rally to hear Archbishop Desmond Tutu speak.

Holospot is sprayed on belongings, for example a car, and can only be read in ultraviolet light.

Private messages

Some messages are private or only intended for a specific audience. Secret letters written in invisible ink are an example. This Holospot (above) is a tiny dot containing security information about an object, for example, a car

Mass media

Some forms of media reach many people in different places at the same time. They are called mass media. Television, newspapers, magazines, radio, films, and giant advertising billboards are all examples of this.

Without words

Many messages can be sent without language. Visual communication includes road signs, photographs, and posters. People can communicate without words by using signs and gestures. Here, a member of the U.S. Air Force uses hand signals to give messages to the pilot.

Sending a message

Messages carried by hand or by messengers on horseback used to take weeks to reach their audiences. Today, SMS text messages and emails are almost instantaneous. Around 25 billion emails alone are sent every day. The amount and major locations of Internet traffic (emails and other electronic information) are represented on this map.

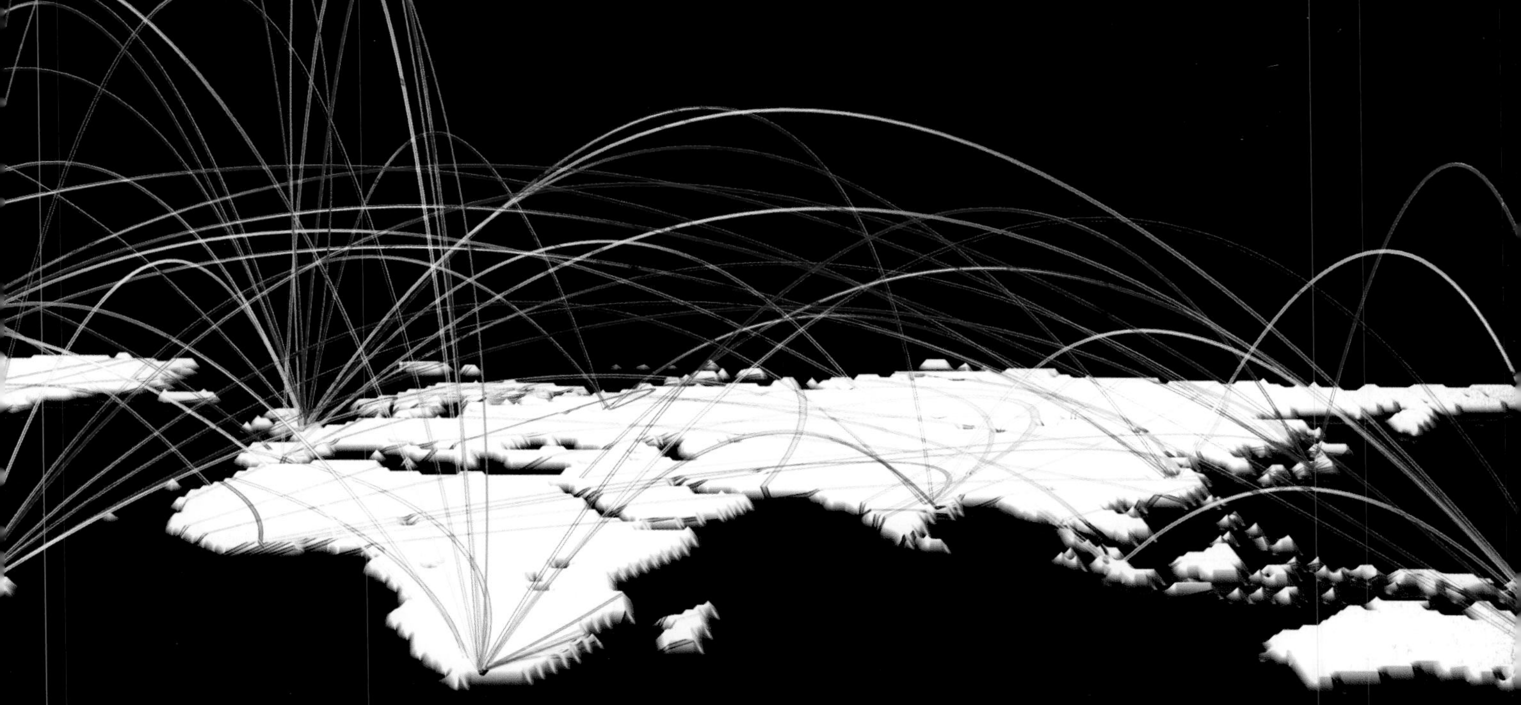

Why we communicate

Every time you choose to communicate, you do so for a reason. It may be for fun, for example, telling a story, or to give information to someone.

HAZARD SIGNS

There are several international symbols used to warn people about dangers.

Radioactivity—warns of harm to living things

Explosives—warns of dangerous materials

Fire—warns of flammable materials

Skull and crossbones—warns of poisons

People also communicate to express their feelings and to try to influence the feelings or decisions of other people.

Warning

One of the oldest forms of communication is to warn another person or creature. Warnings can be verbal (spoken) or nonverbal (using a sign). Here, a referee shows a soccer player a yellow card to warn him about his playing.

Instructions

Communication can be used to instruct someone how to perform a task or order them not to do something (above). Leaflets and frequently asked questions (FAQs) on websites also provide instructions.

Information and education

One of the most important uses of communication is to provide help and information to others. Land maps, for example, communicate vital details about the terrain that allow people to find their way.

Propaganda

Propaganda is information that influences people's beliefs. The propaganda materials above glorify a leader. Other propaganda may blame people for things that they did not do or contain lies or exaggerations.

Entertainment

From telling a joke to listening to music, communication often entertains an audience. This can be live—for example, going to the theater or a concert—or through recorded media such as a CD, book, or DVD.

Advertising

Advertising uses communication to promote the sale of a company's goods or services. Advertisers use many forms of media, from giant displays in cities (above) to TV, Internet, and newspaper advertisements to persuade people to buy their products.

SCIENTIFIC INPUT

CREATING AN ILLUSION

Special effects (FX) are techniques that are used in movies and television to create the illusion of something happening that is not real. This includes moving physical models and computer-generated imagery (CGI). This image of the Human Torch—a superhero covered in fire—was created using CGI graphics for the movie *Fantastic Four* (2005).

Long-distance communication

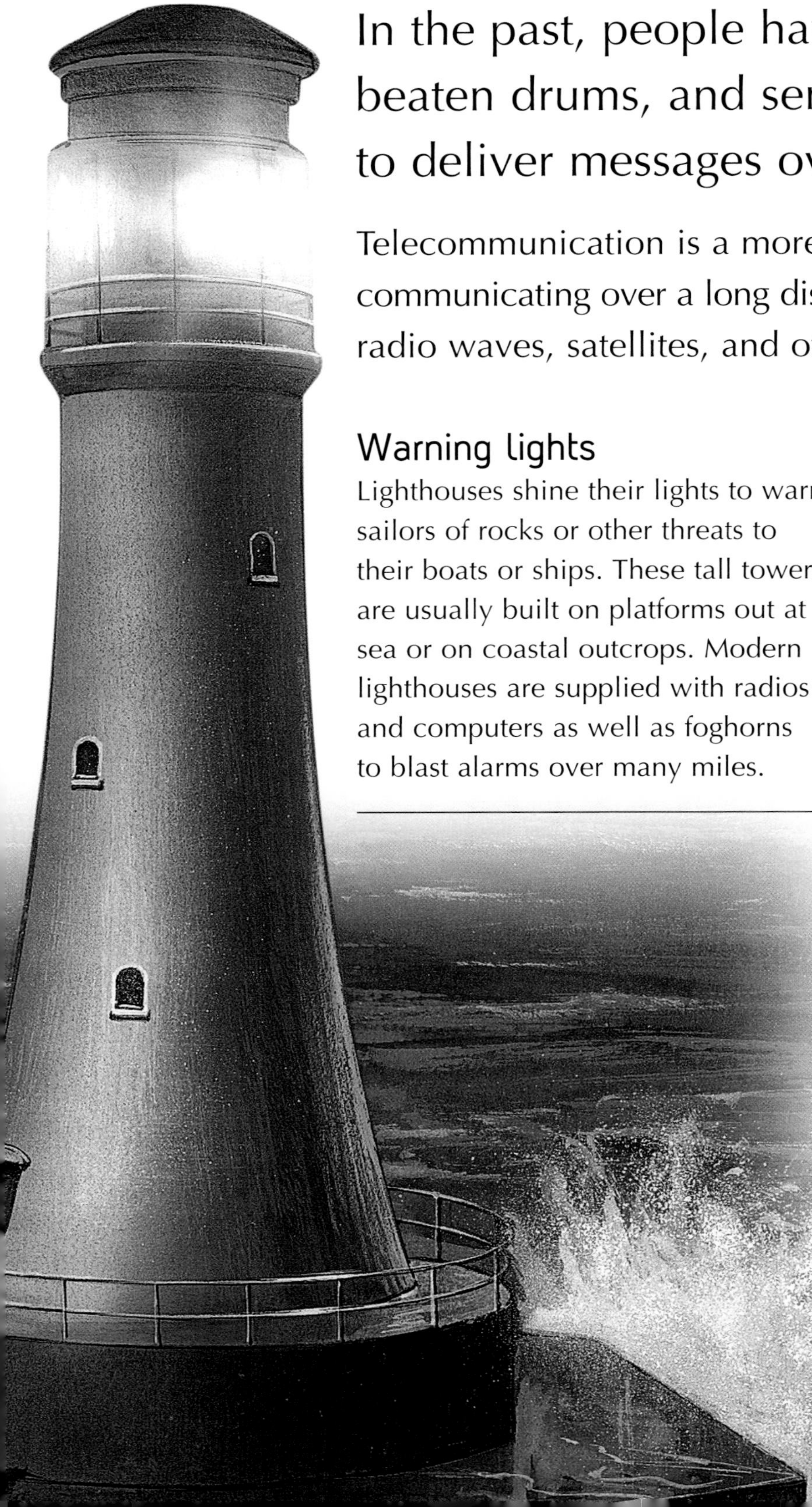

In the past, people have blown horns, beaten drums, and sent smoke signals to deliver messages over distances.

Telecommunication is a more modern way of communicating over a long distance using electrical signals, radio waves, satellites, and other electronic devices.

Warning lights

Lighthouses shine their lights to warn sailors of rocks or other threats to their boats or ships. These tall towers are usually built on platforms out at sea or on coastal outcrops. Modern lighthouses are supplied with radios and computers as well as foghorns to blast alarms over many miles.

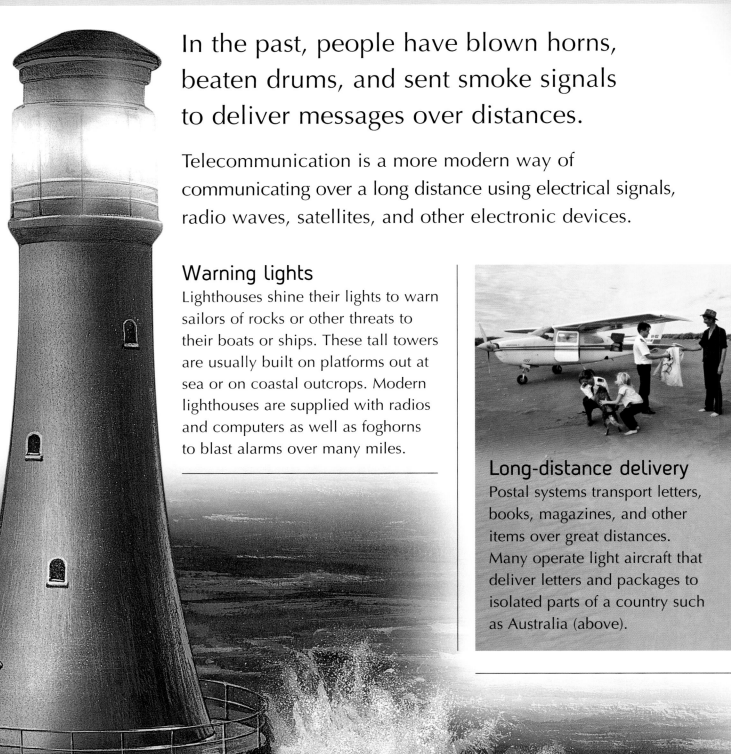

Long-distance delivery

Postal systems transport letters, books, magazines, and other items over great distances. Many operate light aircraft that deliver letters and packages to isolated parts of a country such as Australia (above).

Signal transmitted
from dish on Earth
Satellite relays signal
to receiving dish
Person using a
portable device to
read their emails.

Satellite communication

Most communication satellites orbit approximately 22,260 mi. (35,900km) above the equator. Telephone, radio, computer, and television signals can be beamed to and from the satellite in only fractions of a second.

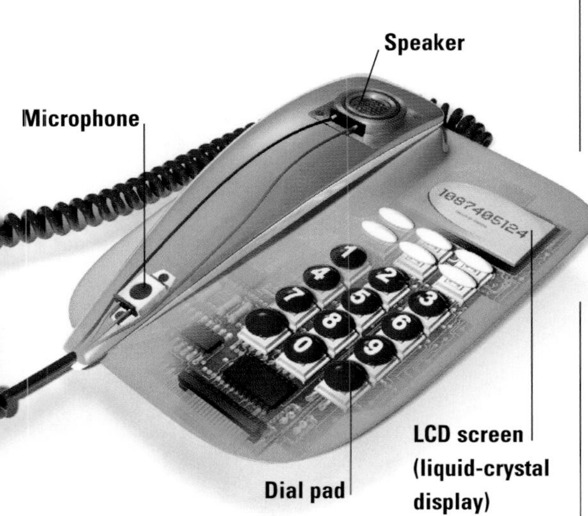
Speaker
Microphone
LCD screen
(liquid-crystal
display)
Dial pad

Telephone

Telephones convert sounds and speech into electrical signals that travel along wires to a telephone exchange. Computers direct a call along fast cables or use radio waves to beam the signal via a satellite.

Radio

Communication can be sent through the air as radio waves. Some radios are used by people on the move such as pilots, police, and truck drivers (right). Broadcasted speech, music, and computer data can be collected by a household radio receiver.

Cellular phones

Cellular phones transmit their signals wirelessly using radio waves. Users can make voice calls and send and receive SMS text messages, photos, and videos. Many cellular phones can now connect to the World Wide Web and send and receive emails.

TELEVISION

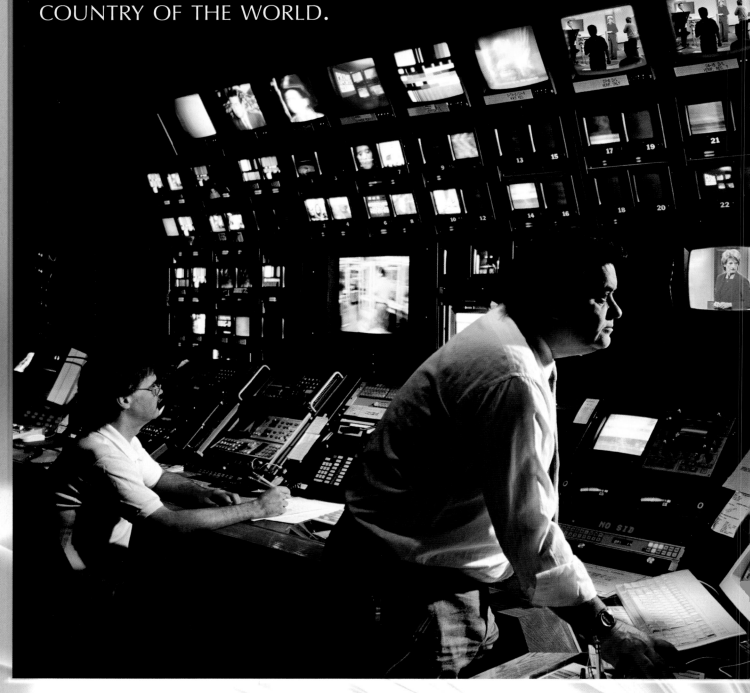

THE CAPTURING OF SOUND AND IMAGES WITH CAMERAS AND SOUND-RECORDING EQUIPMENT CHANGED EVERYBODY'S LIVES. TODAY, BROADCAST TELEVISION PROGRAMS REACH PEOPLE IN EVERY COUNTRY OF THE WORLD.

IN THE STUDIO

Programs are usually produced in television studios. A show may be recorded in advance or filmed as it happens. There may also be some outside broadcast—footage filmed outside the studio. The studio floor (below) is where TV cameras film the action. The images and sound are sent to a control room (left), where the different camera angles are displayed so that a director and their assistants can select the ones that they need to make the program.

TRANSMITTING AND RECEIVING

Television signals are broadcast using transmitters that send the signals via radio waves. Many long-distance broadcasts are made using communication satellites that orbit Earth to relay the signals. The signals are picked up by aerials or small satellite dishes or sent along a cable connection buried underground. Modern televisions are often the center of a complete home-entertainment sytem that can record, store, and even pause live television.

Languages

Languages are collections of sounds and symbols forming words that have meanings. Children learn at least one language as they grow up.

Most languages, such as French, Hindi, and German, have a spoken and a written form. Some spoken languages also include sighs, grunts, laughter, and other noises.

Body language

This is the collection of signals that is given out by people's facial expressions, gestures, and how they stand or sit. Some body language is obvious—for example, the angry faces and finger pointing of two people arguing.

Verbal language

Verbal communication has existed for tens of thousands of years. Before there were written or recorded languages, history, legends, and teachings were passed from parent to child through stories and speeches. Today, storytelling is still an important method of communication.

Languages of the world

Experts estimate that there are as many as 6,000 different spoken languages around the world. There are many more dialects (different versions of the same language). The most-used languages are English, Hindi, Mandarin Chinese, Spanish, and Arabic.

Other types of languages

Languages have been developed to make communication easier for people with special needs. Braille, for instance, uses raised dots on a page to represent letters for people who are blind or sight-impaired. This teacher is using sign language for people who are deaf and hard of hearing, where hand gestures represent letters, numbers, and entire words.

The written word

Writing is a way of recording information using signs or symbols to represent words and meanings.

Russian	Greek	Arabic
А а	Α α	ا
Б б	Β β	ب
В в	Γ γ	ت
Г г	Δ δ	ث
Д д	Ε ε	ج
Е е	Ζ ζ	ح
Ж ж	Η η	خ
З з	Θ θ	د
И и	Ι ι	ذ
Й й	Κ κ	ر
К к	Λ λ	ز
Л л	Μ μ	س
М м	Ν ν	ش
Н н	Ξ ξ	ص
О о	Ο ο	ض
П п	Π π	ط
Р р	Ρ ρ	ظ
С с	Σ σ	ع
Т т	Τ τ	غ
У у	Υ υ	ف
Ф ф	Φ φ	ق
Х х	Χ χ	ك
Ц ц	Ψ ψ	ل
Ч ч	Ω ω	م
Ш ш		ن
Щ щ		ه
Ъ ъ		و
Ы ы		ي
Ь ь		
Э э		
Ю ю		
Я я		

The Russian, Greek, and Arabic alphabets look very different.

The oldest example of writing to have been discovered is a 5,100-year-old clay tablet from the Sumerian city of Uruk.

Alphabets

An alphabet is a system of symbols or characters that allow the sounds in a language to be written down. Usually, each symbol represents one sound and can be combined with other symbols to form all of the words.

Books and publishing

Today, a book goes through many stages, including writing, editing, design, illustration, and production before its pages are printed and bound together. It is published when it is finally available for sale (above).

Printing presses

Printing presses were invented in China and first used in Europe by Johann Gutenberg around 1450. They originally featured metal letter shapes arranged in trays to form a page. This was then covered in ink and pressed onto sheets of paper. Modern printing presses use computers and can output tens of thousands of pages per hour.

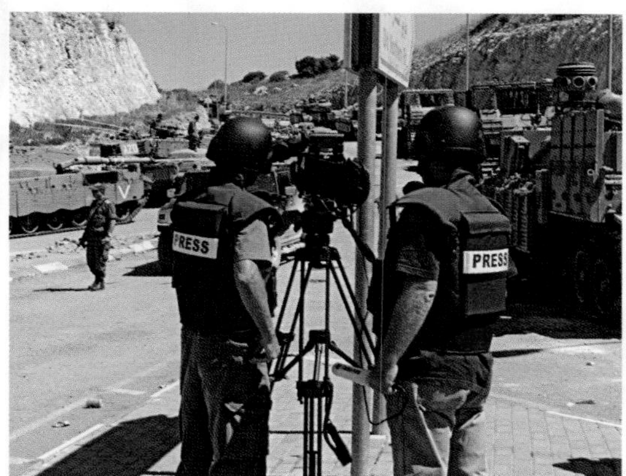

Journalism

Journalists collect information so that they can write news stories, which are published in newspapers or magazines or broadcast on radio, television, or the Internet. They interview people on location. Some risk harm working in war zones (above) to report the news.

Newspapers

Newspapers communicate news and features of interest to their readers. A newspaper earns money from selling space for advertisements. The circulation of a newspaper is the total number of copies of a newspaper to have sold.

Today's large industrial printing presses are powered by electricity and can produce the huge numbers of magazines, newspapers, or books that the public demand.

Electronic books

More and more books are being published in electronic formats in addition to, or instead of, on paper. Some of these can be read on the Internet or can be downloaded and viewed on a portable eBook reader. These electronic devices can hold several books at one time.

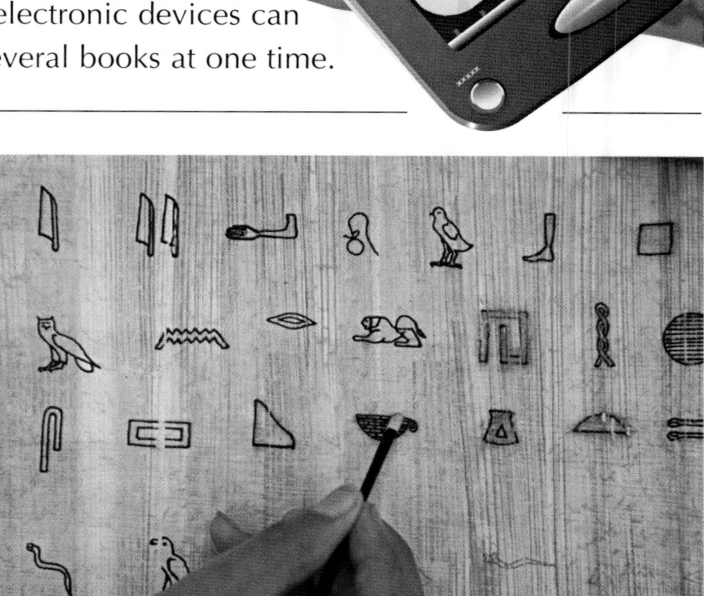

HISTORICAL DATA

THE WRITING SYSTEM OF ANCIENT EGYPT

Around 5,000 years ago, the ancient Egyptians developed one of the first writing systems. Each symbol or picture, called a hieroglyph, represented an object (such as "boat" or "bread") or an idea (such as "hot" or "powerful"). More than 2,000 symbols were developed. These symbols were carved into stone or painted with brushes on wood or on scrolls called papyrus. Papyrus was made of flattened fibers of reeds.

COMPUTERS

COMPUTERS ARE MACHINES THAT PERFORM HUNDREDS OF DIFFERENT JOBS. THEIR MICROPROCESSORS ALLOW THEM TO GATHER INFORMATION, PROCESS IT, AND THEN OUTPUT THE RESULTS.

PROGRAMS

Computers need instructions—computer programs or software—to perform tasks. The operating system (OS) is a collection of programs that control and organize the computer. Useful programs, known as applications, include word processing, graphics, and games.

A wireless mouse beams its instructions to a computer using an infrared light beam.

INPUT AND OUTPUT

A computer uses input devices, such as a keyboard, joystick, or mouse, and to allow users to enter information and commands. Once these have been processed, the results are usually displayed using an output device such as a monitor or a printer.

Each of a keyboard's keys powers a small switch. When the switch is pushed down, a tiny electric current tells the computer which key has been pressed.

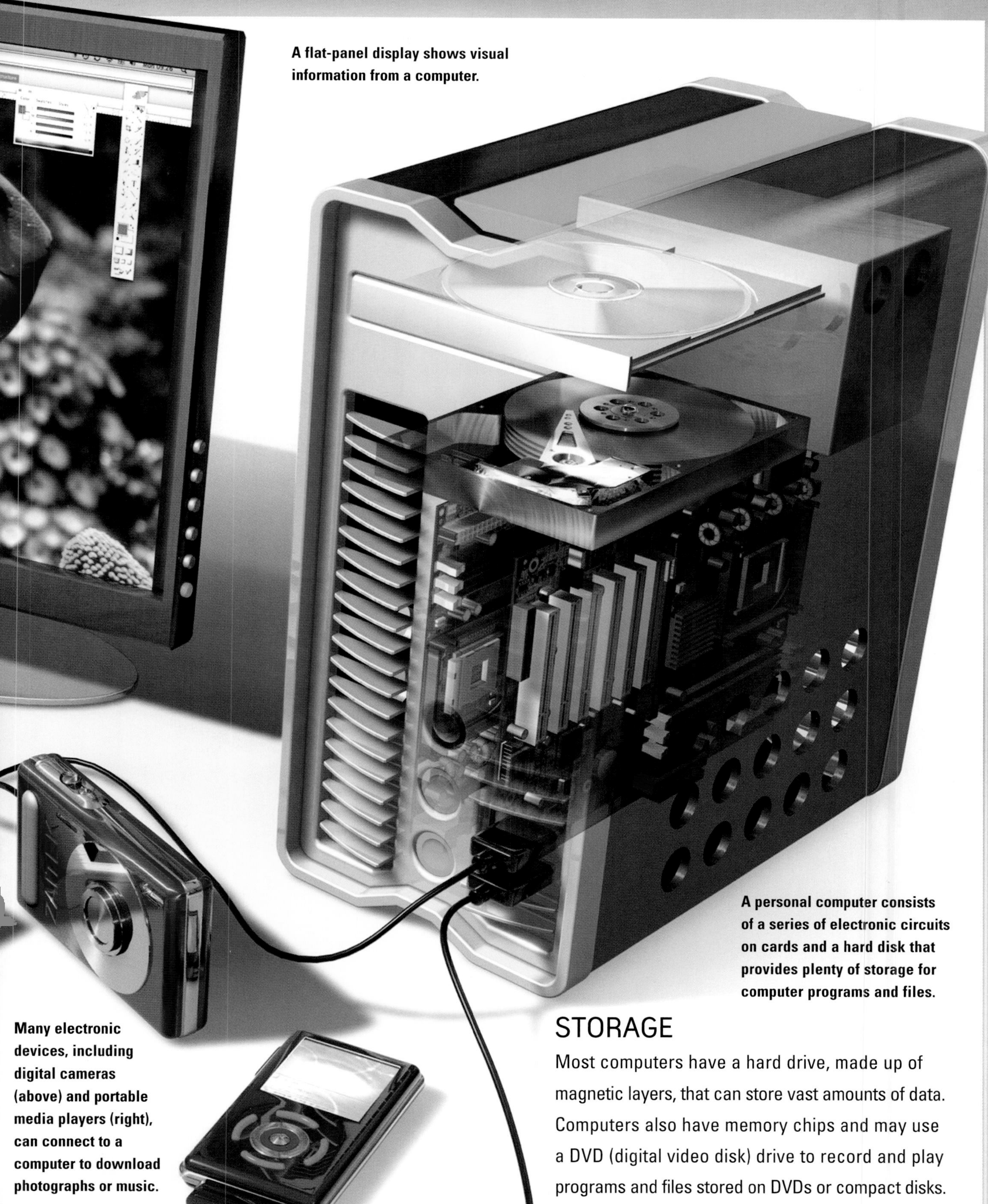

A flat-panel display shows visual information from a computer.

A personal computer consists of a series of electronic circuits on cards and a hard disk that provides plenty of storage for computer programs and files.

Many electronic devices, including digital cameras (above) and portable media players (right), can connect to a computer to download photographs or music.

STORAGE

Most computers have a hard drive, made up of magnetic layers, that can store vast amounts of data. Computers also have memory chips and may use a DVD (digital video disk) drive to record and play programs and files stored on DVDs or compact disks.

Land transportation

Land transportation is the most common way of moving people and goods from one place to another.

Today, there are more than 800 million trucks, buses, and cars on the world's roads. Railroads carry millions of passengers and huge quantities of freight such as coal and chemicals.

Moving goods

Milllions of tons of raw materials and finished goods are transported every day on roads. The freight is carried by vans, trucks, and giant semitrailer trucks.

Bicycles

Today, one of the most popular, healthy, and environmentally friendly methods of transportation is the bicycle. It has a rear wheel that is driven by a chain. The chain is connected to pedals that the cyclist turns.

Trains

Railroads are large networks of steel tracks on which trains run. Trains were first pulled by steam engines, but today they are mostly electric or powered by diesel engines. High-speed train systems, such as this Japanese JR500 train, can cruise at speeds of up to 185 mph (300km/h).

Special transportation

Some conditions on land require special vehicles. Off-road vehicles often have large, chunky tires for extra grip. This snowmobile runs on caterpillar tracks that are driven by an engine. It balances on two small skis.

AMAZING FACTS

LAND-SPEED RECORDS

In 1898, Gaston de Chasseloup-Laubat set the first land-speed world record of 39.15 mph (63.15km/h) in France. Advances in technology today have sent the record soaring. In 1997, Thrust SSC (above), driven by Andy Green, set a new land-speed world record by traveling at an incredible 761mph (1,228km/h).

Underground systems

Many large cities have transportation systems running deep under the ground. Known as metro, subway, or tube systems, they carry millions of commuters and tourists around.

Safety and modern vehicles

Modern cars, trains, and trucks are packed with safety features that are tested thoroughly. These cars are being crash tested to check that their bodies crumple on impact in the correct way, channeling the energy from the crash around the vehicle and away from the driver and passengers.

WATER TRANSPORTATION

PEOPLE HAVE BUILT BOATS FOR THOUSANDS OF YEARS. THEY USE THEM TO FERRY PASSENGERS FROM PLACE TO PLACE, TO CARRY HEAVY GOODS FROM CONTINENT TO CONTINENT, OR SIMPLY FOR THE JOY OF TRAVELING ON WATER.

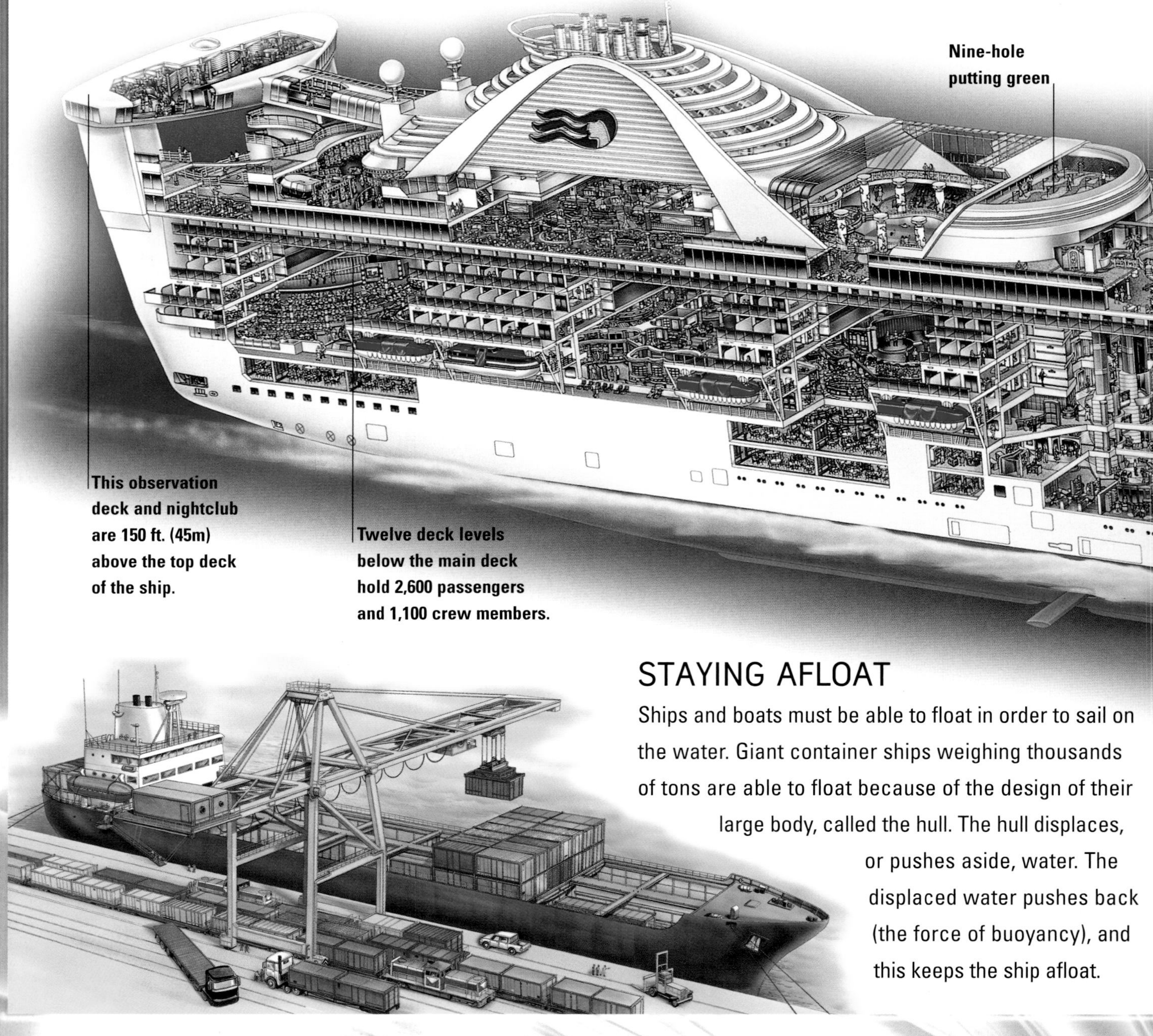

Nine-hole putting green
This observation deck and nightclub are 150 ft. (45m) above the top deck of the ship.
Twelve deck levels below the main deck hold 2,600 passengers and 1,100 crew members.

STAYING AFLOAT

Ships and boats must be able to float in order to sail on the water. Giant container ships weighing thousands of tons are able to float because of the design of their large body, called the hull. The hull displaces, or pushes aside, water. The displaced water pushes back (the force of buoyancy), and this keeps the ship afloat.

SMALL AND LARGE

Boats and ships vary in size, from the smallest one-person kayak or canoe to giant cruise liners and navy aircraft carriers that transport thousands of people. Whatever their size, boats and ships need some type of propulsion (power to move them forward). A kayak uses human effort to push a paddle through the water. Other boats use large sails to catch the wind. The fastest ships use engines that turn large propellers in the water. The propeller drives water backward, thrusting the vessel forward.

Paddle pushes back against water

Kayak moves forward

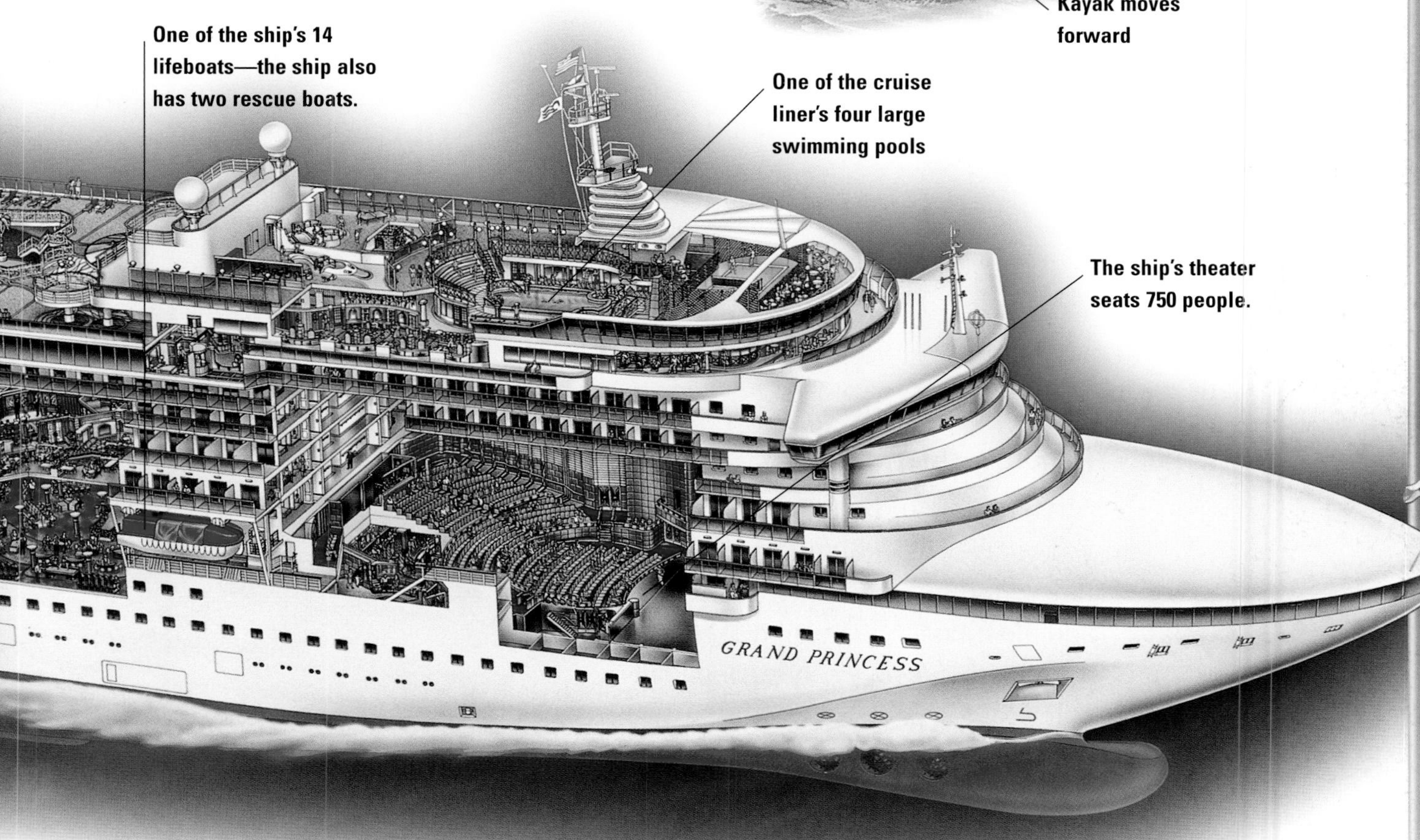
One of the ship's 14 lifeboats—the ship also has two rescue boats.
One of the cruise liner's four large swimming pools
The ship's theater seats 750 people.
GRAND PRINCESS

The ship is powered by six giant electrical generators. These generators power engines that turn two large propellers. The typical cruising speed of the ship is 25 mph (41km/h).

CRUISING THE SEAS

Millions of people travel on water using canal boats, ferries, and cruise ships. The Grand Princess (above) is one of the world's largest passenger ships. It is 950 ft. (290m) long and taller than the Statue of Liberty. At the same time, billions of tons of food, raw materials for industry (such as coal, oil, and metals), and finished goods are carried in tankers and container ships.

Air transportation

Aircraft can fly through the air. As an aircraft moves forward, its wings generate lift, which helps it rise.

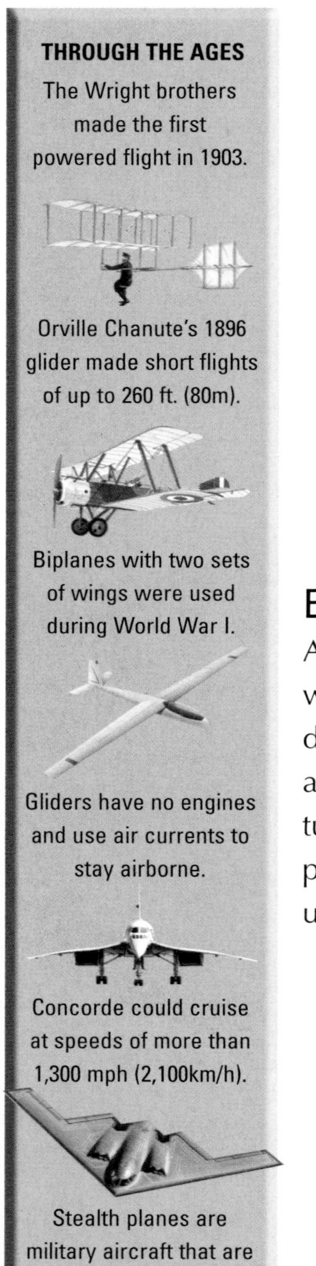

THROUGH THE AGES

The Wright brothers made the first powered flight in 1903.

Orville Chanute's 1896 glider made short flights of up to 260 ft. (80m).

Biplanes with two sets of wings were used during World War I.

Gliders have no engines and use air currents to stay airborne.

Concorde could cruise at speeds of more than 1,300 mph (2,100km/h).

Stealth planes are military aircraft that are are difficult to detect.

Most aircraft are either powered by jet engines or by engines that drive propellers around.

Helicopters

Helicopters have a set of rapidly spinning rotors. As these spin, they act like wings. They generate lift and allow the helicopter to fly, as well as hover in the air.

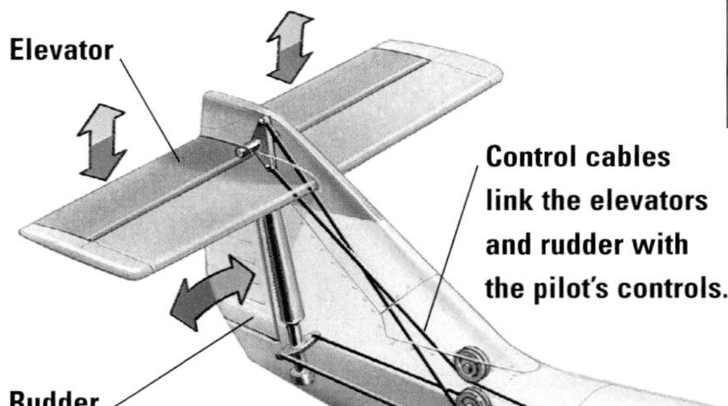

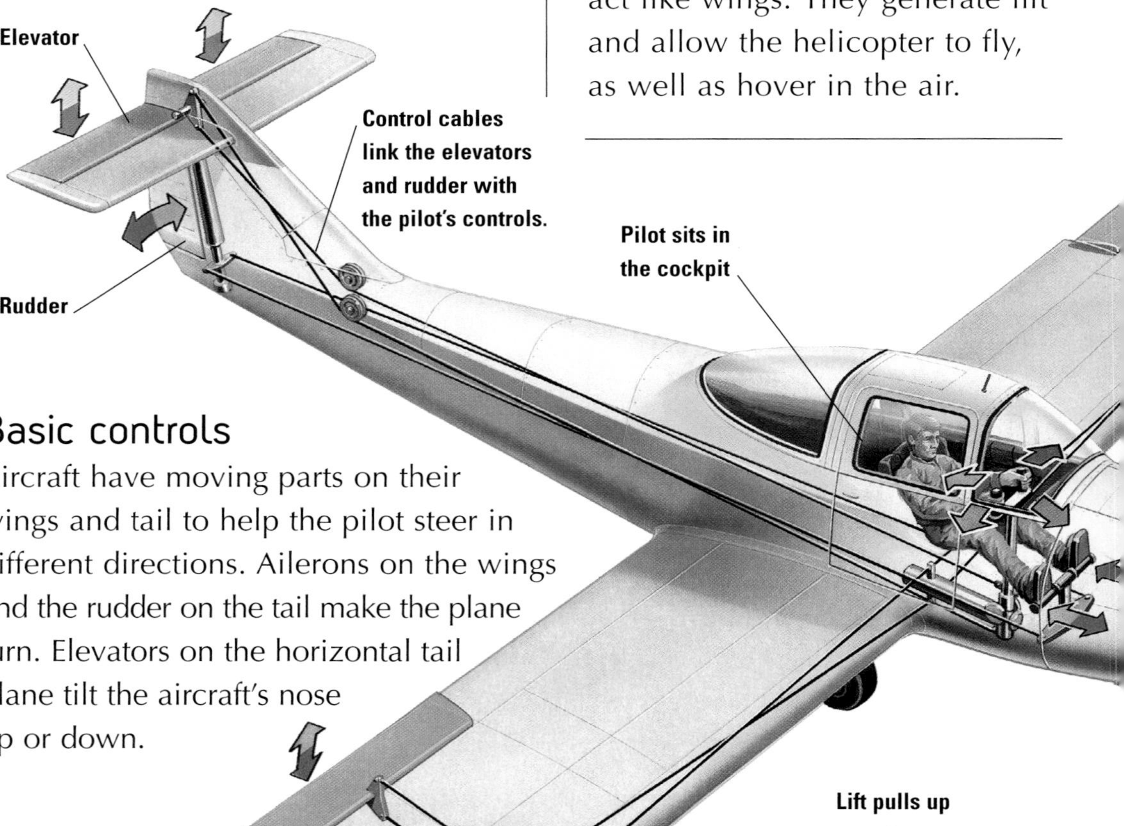

Control cables link the elevators and rudder with the pilot's controls.

Pilot sits in the cockpit

Basic controls

Aircraft have moving parts on their wings and tail to help the pilot steer in different directions. Ailerons on the wings and the rudder on the tail make the plane turn. Elevators on the horizontal tail plane tilt the aircraft's nose up or down.

Ailerons are controlled from the cockpit

Lift pulls up

Drag slows down

Gravity pulls down

Thrust pulls or pushes forward

Four forces act on an aircraft as it flies: lift, gravity, thrust, and drag.

Flying boats

Some aircraft are capable of floating in water. These "flying boats" have stabilizing floats attached to their wings. Some have been modified to fight forest fires. They skim the surface of a lake or sea to gather up water, which they then drop on the fire.

SCIENTIFIC INPUT

HOT AIR BALLOONS

Balloons consist of a giant bag, called an envelope, that is filled with gas and has a basket suspended underneath. Some balloons are filled with helium gas, but many are filled with hot air. A gas burner heats up the air inside to make the balloon lighter than the air around it. This makes it rise.

Jet propulsion

The development of jet engines in the 1930s allowed aircraft to fly faster. Jet engines pull in large amounts of air. This is mixed and burned with fuel to generate huge amounts of thrust, which propels the aircraft forward.

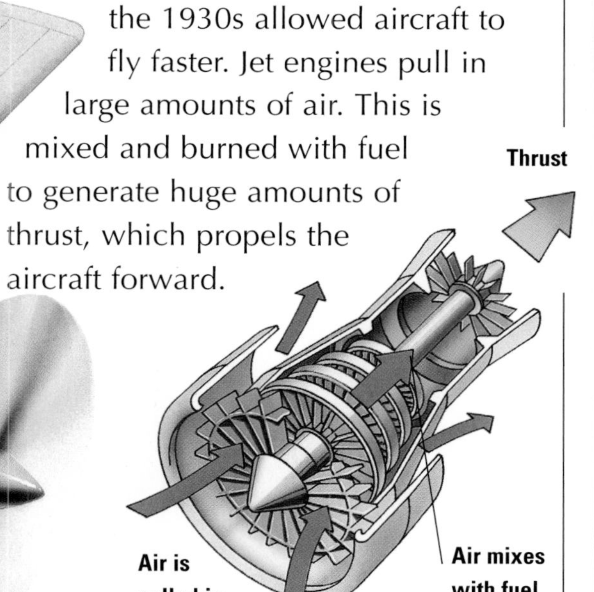

Airliners and airports

In 2007, more than 4.4 billion people flew on aircraft, mostly in giant airliners carrying up to 500 passengers. These airliners and smaller light aircraft take off and land at airports. The busiest airports have to handle hundreds of airliners every day.

Future communication

Over the last hundred years, there have been amazing advances with the arrival of television, computers, the Internet, cars, and aircraft.

Future advances in technology may see machines take an increasingly active role in the everyday lives of people around the world.

Newer technologies

Mobile communication will continue to develop. Wearable computers will shrink to the size of a tiny box, but they will have all the power of a home computer. They may work with voice and touch commands and project their display onto a tiny screen in front of the user.

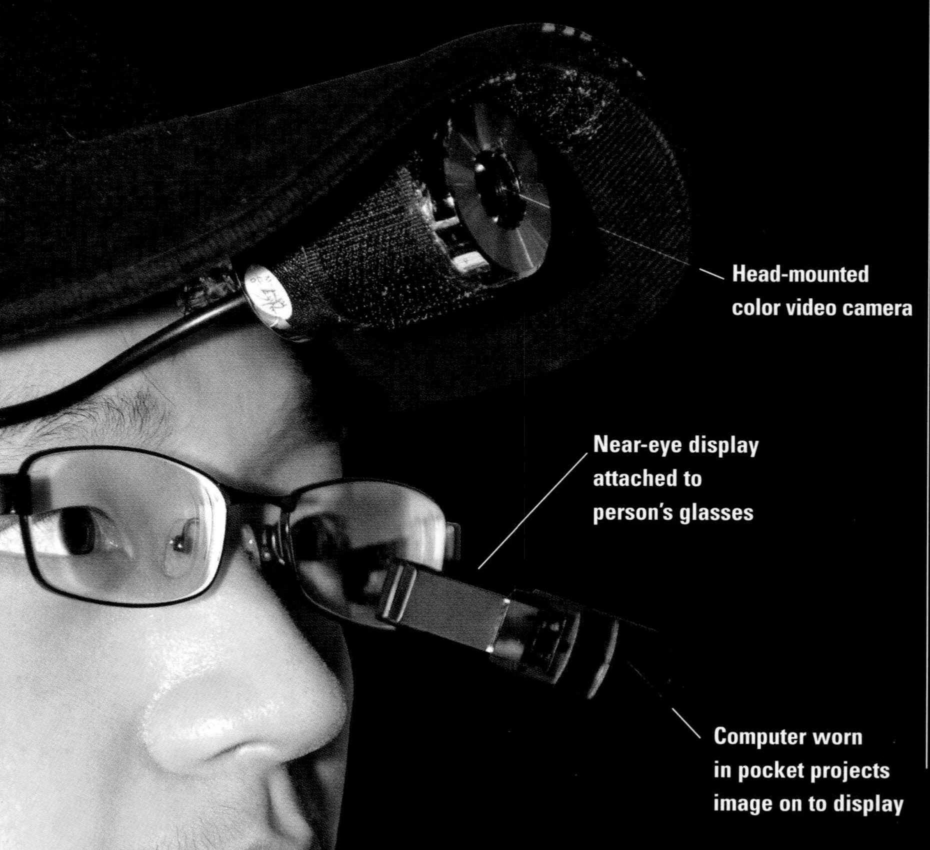

Cyborg implants

In the future, tiny microprocessors may be implanted in the human body (above). These will communicate directly with other computers, acting as identity devices and translating foreign languages instantaneously.

Robot workers

Robots will work alongside humans, performing tasks with perfect accuracy. They can be sent into danger areas to rescue people or act as war reporters, like this Afghan Explorer.

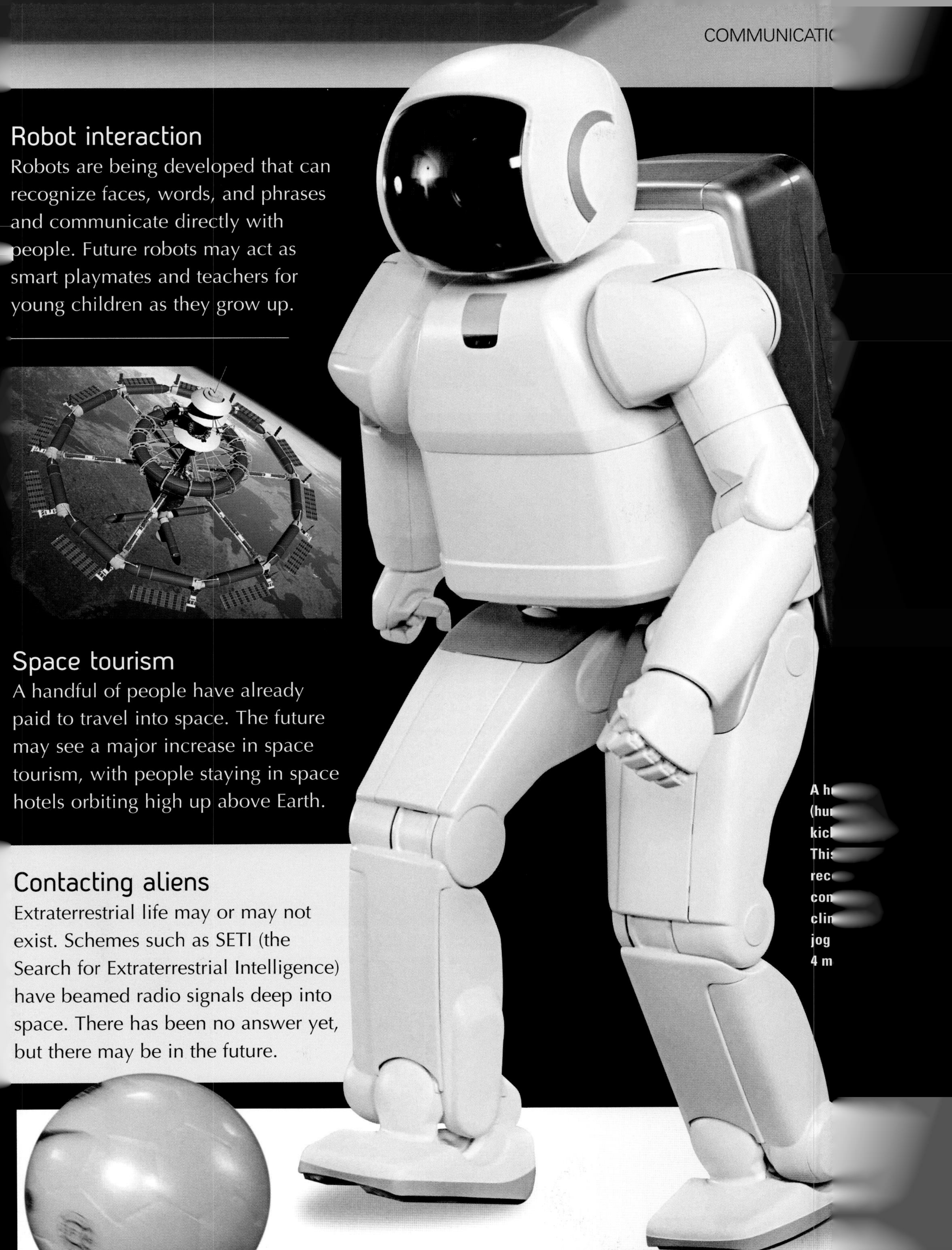

Robot interaction

Robots are being developed that can recognize faces, words, and phrases and communicate directly with people. Future robots may act as smart playmates and teachers for young children as they grow up.

Space tourism

A handful of people have already paid to travel into space. The future may see a major increase in space tourism, with people staying in space hotels orbiting high up above Earth.

Contacting aliens

Extraterrestrial life may or may not exist. Schemes such as SETI (the Search for Extraterrestrial Intelligence) have beamed radio signals deep into space. There has been no answer yet, but there may be in the future.

A h (hu kic Thi rec con clin jog 4 m

Communication facts

As populations have risen, transportation and communication systems have grown. The World Wide Web, which contained only a few hundred webpages in the early 1990s, is estimated in 2008 to consist of more than 45 billion webpages.

INTERNET GROWTH

Approximate number of regular Internet users

1995	16 million
1996	37 million
1997	70 million
1998	147 million
1999	248 million
2000	361 million
2001	513 million
2002	587 million
2003	719 million
2004	817 million
2005	1.02 billion
2006	1.09 billion
2007	1.26 billion

MOST TV STATIONS

7,306—Russia, 1998

LONGEST-RUNNING TV SHOWS

"Meet The Press," NBC, first broadcast November 1947, still on air 2008.

Children's TV: "Sesame Street," PBS, first broadcast 1969, still on air 2008.

BUSIEST INTERNATIONAL AIRPORTS

London Heathrow (U.K.) 61,348,340 passengers per year

Paris Charles de Gaulle (France) 51,888,936

Amsterdam (Netherlands) 45,940,939

Frankfurt (Germany) 45,697,160

Hong Kong (China) 43,274,765

Tokyo Narita (Japan) 33,860,094

Singapore Changi (Singapore) 33,368,099

London Gatwick (U.K.) 30,016,837

Bangkok Suvarnabhumi (Thailand) 29,587,773

Dubai (UAE) 27,925,522

LARGEST PASSENGER SHIP

RCI Freedom of the Seas: 1,112 ft. (339m) long and carries up to 4,375 passengers and 1,365 crew members

BIGGEST ROAD NETWORK

U.S.: a network of 4 million mi. (6.4 million km) of paved roads throughout

Japanese Shinkansen *Bullet* train speeding past Mount Fuji

USEFUL WEBSITES

www.gutenberg.org/wiki/Main_Page More than 20,000 e-Books to read for free.

www.fcc.gov/cgb/kidszone/ Information about every aspect of communication.

www.bbc.co.uk/worldservice/programmes/bbc_journalism/ Learn how to become a journalist.

www.meineke.com/stuff_about_cars/how_work.asp Animated site about how a car works.

Glossary

acid rain Rain containing toxins from factory and car fumes that falls and poisons trees and plants.

adaptation The way in which a plant or animal changes over generations to suit a different environment.

amoeba A tiny, single-celled animal with no fixed shape that lives in water.

amphibian A cold-blooded, smooth-skinned vertebrate that begins life in the water but can live on land when it is an adult. Frogs, toads, and salamanders are amphibians.

antibiotic A medicine used to kill the bacteria that cause diseases.

apartheid An official government policy previously practiced in South Africa involving discrimination against nonwhites.

arachnid An animal that has four pairs of segmented legs and a body divided into two parts. Spiders and scorpions are arachnids.

asteroid A rocky body that circles the Sun. Most asteroids are between Mars and Jupiter in the asteroid belt.

astronomer A person who studies the stars and planets, as well as other bodies in space.

atmosphere The layers of gases and clouds that surround a planet, star, or moon.

atoll A ring-shaped coral reef, or a ring of small coral islands, enclosing a shallow lagoon.

bacterium (pl. bacteria) A microscopic, single-celled organism. Some bacteria can cause diseases.

big bang The starting point of our universe, according to modern theory.

biodiversity The number and variety of animals found in a particular area.

biome A community of living organisms found in a particular ecological area such as a desert.

biotechnology The use of living organisms to generate useful products.

black hole The remains of a star that pulls in any object around it in space, even rays of light, so that it appears black from Earth.

blood pressure The pressure of the circulating blood against the inner walls of blood vessels.

camouflage The color, markings, or body shape that helps hide an animal in its surroundings.

carbohydrate An energy-giving substance made by green plants and found in starchy foods such as bread.

cartilage Gristly material that is found in some parts of the body such as the joints and outer ear.

cell The basic unit from which all living things—plants and animals—are made up.

cephalopod A mollusk with a beaked head and tentacles such as an octopus.

ceramics Objects made by firing clay or porcelain.

chemical Any substance that can change when joined or mixed with another substance.

chlorophyll The green pigment found in most plants that absorbs light and gives energy for photosynthesis.

chromosome A threadlike part of the nucleus of a cell that contains genetic information.

civilization A human society that has reached a high state of cultural, political, social, and intellectual development.

civil war A war fought between groups from and in the same country or region.

climate The meteorological conditions—for example rainfall and temperature—of a particular area.

comet A ball of frozen gas and dust that travels around the Sun. Some of the dust streams out behind the comet to make a "tail."

communism A political and economic movement that seeks to establish a system in which all property is held equally.

coniferous Describes trees or shrubs that bear cones and evergreen leaves.

conservation The preservation and careful management of natural resources and the environment.

cosmology The study of the structure and origin of the universe.

Crusades The European military campaigns to recover Palestine from Muslim rule that took place from 1095 to 1192.

crustacean A usually aquatic group of animals, with segmented bodies and paired, jointed limbs. Lobsters, crabs, and pill bugs (wood lice) are crustaceans.

culture The knowledge, values, and way of life of the people of a country or region.

deciduous Describes trees and shrubs that shed their leaves annually.

democracy Government based on rule by the people, usually through elected representatives.

digestion The process by which food is broken down so the nutrients can be absorbed.

DNA Deoxyribonucleic acid, a substance in cells that carries all the genetic information in the form of a chemical code.

dynasty Generations of rulers from the same family.

echolocation A way of finding objects by sending out sounds and then listening for the echo. Bats use echolocation to navigate.

ecosystem A self-contained community of plants and animals and their environment such as a rainforest.

election The selection of someone for public office by voting.

electron A tiny particle that has a negative electrical charge and that usually orbits the nucleus of an atom.

endangered Describes animals threatened with extinction.

epinephrine (adrenaline) A hormone released into the bloodstream in response to physical or mental stress.

equator An imaginary circle on the surface of a planet or star, at equal distances from the two poles.

erosion The wearing away of Earth's surface by water, wind, ice, or gravity.

ethnic Describes the cultural, racial, religious, or linguistic tradition of a group of people or society.

evolution A gradual process of change in the genetic makeup of a species over generations.

exile A person banished from his or her native land.

extinct No longer existing or living.

fossil The ancient remains, impression, or trace of an animal or plant, usually found in rocks.

fossil fuel An energy-containing substance—coal, oil, or gas—that is formed from the remains of prehistoric plants or animals.

galaxy A collection of millions or billions of stars, planets, gas, and dust, bound together by gravity.

gene A section of DNA in a chromosome that carries information about an inherited characteristic.

geological Relating to the scientific study of the origin, history, and structure of Earth.

geothermal Energy produced by harnessing the heat from inside Earth.

germination In plants, when seeds or spores sprout.

gland An organ or group of cells in the body that produces a specific substance such as a hormone.

gravity The force that pulls everything toward the center of Earth, making objects fall and giving them weight.

habitat The place where an animal or plant normally lives or grows.

hemoglobin An oxygen-carrying, iron-containing protein found in red blood cells.

hieroglyphs The ancient Egyptian writing system that used pictures to represent objects, ideas, and sounds.

hormone A chemical messenger produced in a gland to control processes of the body such as growth.

humidity Dampness in the air.

independence Freedom from control and influence.

invertebrate An animal that does not have a backbone.

larva The second stage in the life of an insect, between egg and adult.

law A system or collection of rules that people must obey.

literacy The ability to read and write.

magma Liquid molten rock found underneath Earth's crust.

magnetism Having the power to attract objects made of iron or steel or force them away.

mammals Warm-blooded vertebrates that have a covering of hair on the skin, give birth to live young, and nourish their young with milk.

marsupial A mammal that has a pouch on the outside of its body in which its young develop.

media The communication with and influence on people, by magazines, radio, television, and newspapers, etc.

metamorphosis The transformation of an animal during growth, for example, from a caterpillar to a butterfly.

meteorite A piece of rock or metal from space that manages to pass through a planet's atmosphere without burning up.

microwaves Radio waves of very short wavelength that are used for communication, radar, and cooking.

migration The movement of animals, birds, and some sea creatures from one place to another to find food, warm weather, or produce young.

mineral A natural substance that has not been formed from plant or animal life, for example, rocks, metals, and salt.

molecule The smallest unit of an element or chemical compound, made up of at least two atoms.

mollusk An animal with a soft body that usually lives in a shell, for example, a snail or a limpet.

monotreme One of a group of egg-laying animals that live in Australia and New Guinea, for example, the platypus or the echidna.

moraine An area covered by rocks and debris dropped by a glacier.

mummification To preserve a body by embalming and drying it, as practiced by the ancient Egyptians.

nebula A cloud of dust and gas found in space.

nocturnal Active at night.

nuclear Operated or powered by atomic energy.

nutrients The parts of a food that can be used by animals or plants for health and growth.

observatory A building or spacecraft that astronomers use to watch space.

orbit The path of one body around another, such as the Moon's path around Earth.

ozone A gas that absorbs harmful ultraviolet radiation from the Sun.

photosynthesis The chemical process in which plants use the energy in sunlight to turn carbon dioxide and water into food (glucose sugar).

pitch How high or low a musical note sounds to the ear.

plague A disease that causes high numbers of deaths.

pollination The transfer of pollen from one flower to another (for example, by an insect) to help make seeds.

pollution Substances such as chemicals from factories that poison the air, land, or water.

predator An animal that lives by hunting and eating other animals.

prehistory Human history in the period before recorded events.

prey An animal that is hunted or eaten by another animal.

propaganda News and information designed to persuade people to adopt a particular point of view.

radar A way of finding the position of an object using radio waves.

radiation Anything that radiates from its source. It could be waves, such as light or sound, or a beam of invisible particles such as neutrons.

revolution The overthrow of a government by the people.

ritual Ceremonial acts or rites used in an act of religious worship.

robot A machine that can do work automatically.

seismograph An instrument for measuring and recording earthquakes.

species A group of organisms that look alike and breed with each other.

superpower An enormously powerful state with influence around the world, for example, the U.S.

temperate Describes a climate that has mild summers and cool winters.

temperature The measure of how hot or cold something is.

vertebrate An animal with a bony skeleton and a backbone. Fish, reptiles, birds, amphibians, and mammals are all vertebrates.

virus A tiny microbe that can invade and take over living cells.

Index

U, V

W, Z

KINGFISHER
Published in the United States by Kingfisher, an imprint of Henry Holt and Company LLC,
175 Fifth Avenue, New York, New York 10010.
First published in Great Britain by Kingfisher Publications plc,
an imprint of Macmillan Children's Books, London.

Distributed in Canada by H. B. Fenn and Company Ltd.

Library of Congress Cataloging-in-Publication Data
Goldsmith, Mike, Dr.
Explore / Mike Goldsmith, Clive Gifford, Sean Callery.—1st American ed.
p. cm.
Includes index.
1. Children's encyclopedias and dictionaries. I. Gifford, Clive. II. Callery, Sean. III. Title.
AE6.G65 2008
031.02—dc22
2007047343

ISBN: 978-0-7534-6269-0

Kingfisher books are available for special promotions and premiums.
For details contact: Director of Special Markets, Holtzbrinck Publishers.

Printed in China
10 9 8 7 6 5 4 3 2 1
ITR/0808/SCHOY(SCHOY)/WKT/128MA/C

Note to readers: The website addresses listed in this book are correct at the time of publishing. However, due to the ever-changing nature of the Internet, website addresses and content can change. Websites can contain links that are unsuitable for children. The publisher cannot be held responsible for changes in website addresses or content or for information obtained through third-party websites. We strongly advise that Internet searches are supervised by an adult.

Acknowledgments

The Publisher would like to thank the following for permission to reproduce their material. Every care has been taken to trace copyright holders. However, if there have been unintentional omissions or failure to trace copyright holders, we apologize and will, if informed, endeavor to make corrections in any future edition.

Top = t; Bottom = b; Center = c; Left = l; Right = r

Pages 11tr Getty/National Geographic Society; 11cr Corbis/Sygma; 15tr Corbis/Reuters; 18tr Alamy/Mike Greenslade; 21cr Science Photo Library (SPL)/Adam Hart-Davies; 22-23 Getty/National Geographic Society; 31t Digital Vision; 32 Getty/Stone; 35tl SPL/Mark Garlick; 41cr Bridgeman Art Library(BAL)/National Gallery; 43cr SPL/Mark Garlick; 48 SPL/RIA Novosti; 51cr SPL/Julian Baum; 56 NASA/Wally Pacholka; 60cl NASA/Stanford University; 61cl Kobal Collection/Columbia Pictures; 63tl SPL/Larry Landolfi; 64 Getty/Panoramic Images; 69cr SPL/Dr. Keith Wheeler; 73tr Getty/Stone; 73cr Alamy/Scott Hortop; 74-75 Corbis/Scott Stulberg; 78bl Naturepl/Stephen David Miller; 83tr Corbis/Phil Schermeister; 86cr Corbis/Kazuyoshi Nomachi; 90-91 Corbis/Frans Lanting; 93tr Corbis/Keren Su; 93br Corbis/Wayne Lawler/Ecoscene; 94b Corbis/Du Huaju/Xinhua Press; 95cr Corbis/Paul A. Souders; 96 Corbis/Kazuyoshi Nomachi; 99cr Naturepl/Meul/ARCO; 106-107 Photolibrary/Michael Duva; 113cr Corbis/Daniel J. Cox; 117tr Corbis/Joe McDonald; 119c Getty/Jeff Lapore; 124-125 Corbis/Patricia Fogden; 127cr Corbis/Alexander Demianchuk; 128 NHPA/Stephen Dalton; 131tr SPL/Zephyr; 133 Alamy/Jupiter/Brand X; 137tr SPL/AJ Photo/Hop Americain; 137cl Alamy/Horizon International; 138-139 SPL/Philippe Psaila; 139tr BAL/Menil Collection /Giraudon; 140cl Corbis/Keren Su; 141tr Alamy/Eddie Linsson; 142cl Getty/Angelo Cavalli; 143cr Corbis/Mediscan; 145 SPL/Susumu Nishinaga; 147tr Alamy/Medical; 148br SPL/Steve Gschmeissner; 149tr Alamy/Sinibomb Images; 149cr SPL/Alfred Pasieka; 150c SPL/Robert Brocksmith; 150bl SPL/Tek Image; 151tr SPL/Dept of Clinical Cytogenetics, Addenbrookes Hospital; 151cr SPL/Dr. Jeremy Burgess; 153 SPL/Medi-mation; 155tl Corbis/Anna Peisl/zefa; 155bl Corbis/Don Hammond/Design Pics; 155tr SPL/Helen McCardle; 155br SPL/Helen McCardle; 156-157 SPL; 160 Corbis/Bo Bridges; 163 BAL/National Museum, Aleppo/Giraudon; 177cr AKG Images; 178l Corbis/Michael Nicholson; 178-179 Corbis/Gianni Dagli Orti; 181cl BAL/Charmet Archive; 181cr Corbis/Bettmann; 181b SPL/David Ducros; 182cl Alamy/Mary Evans Picture Library; 183 Getty/Edwin Levick/FPG; 186br Corbis/Hulton; 187tr Corbis/Hulton; 189t BAL; 189b Corbis/Wolfgang Kumm/dpa; 190tl Corbis/Reuters; 190br Getty/Courtney Kealy ; 191cl Getty/Jaafar Ashtiyeh/AFP; 191tr Corbis/Hubert Boesi/dpa; 191crl Corbis/Reuters; 192 Corbis/Jacques Langevin; 194b Alamy/Chad Ehlers; 195tr Haiduc; 195cr Corbis/Gideon Mendel; 195cl Alamy/Sebastian Green; 196 Getty/Christopher Pillitz/Reportage; 197 Alamy/Alan Gignoux; 198tr Corbis/Les Stone/Sygma; 198cr Corbis/Robert Garvey; 199l Corbis/Ajay Verma/Reuters; 199br Perrinpost; 200cl Sergio Luiz; 200bl Tomascastelazo; 200l Sengkang; 203cr Corbis/Jose Fuste Raga/zefa; 204b Corbis/Kazuyoshi Nomachi; 205 Corbis/Jon Hicks; 206cr Getty/Popperfoto; 207c Alamy/Richard Wareham; 208tl Corbis/Tim Wimbourne/Reuters; 208-209 Corbis/Gary Hershorn/Reuters; 209tr Corbis/Duomo; 210tr Corbis/Joe Travers/Reuters; 211tl Getty/David Rogers; 211tr Getty/Daniel Mihailescu/AFP; 212 Corbis/Claudia Daut/Reuters; 213t Photolibrary/Hisham F. Ibrahim; 213c Corbis/Peter Turnley; 214cl Alamy/Jim West; 214bl Alamy/Jupiter/Brand X; 215 Alamy/David R. Frazier; 217b Getty/Romeo Gacad/AFP; 218-219 Getty/Robert Harding; 219cr Alamy/John Sturrock; 220cl Alamy/Guatebrian; 220b Corbis/Kai Pfaffenbach/Reuters; 221tl Alamy/Jeff Gynane; 222cl Alamy/Jenny Matthews; 223 Alamy/Vario Images; 224 Corbis/Steve Terrill; 227 Pete Clayman; 229tr Corbis/Paue Seux/Hemis; 229cr Alamy/JoeFoxKrakow; 230tr Corbis/Randy M. Ury; 231 Corbis/Al Rod; 234tr Kobal Collection/Hal Roach/Pathe Exchange; 234-235 Kobal Collectio/Dreamworks/Aardman Animations; 235tr Corbis/Sharie Kennedy; 235cl Getty/Stewart Cohen; 235b Corbis/David Brabyn; 236cl Kobal Collection/Walt Disney Pictures/Elliot Marks; 236bl Corbis/Louie Psihoyos; 237t Corbis/Keith Hamshere/Paramount Pictures; 237b Corbis/Mark Dye/Star Ledger; 238c Alamy/Janine Weidel; 239tr Corbis/Robbie Jack; 239b Corbis/Eddy Risch/epa; 240tr Alamy/Redferns Music Picture Library; 240b Getty/Robert Mizono/Photonica; 241t Corbis/Jeff Albertson; 241cr Range Pictures; 242cl Alamy/Uppercut Images; 242br Art Archive/Musee du Louvre; 242-243t BAL/Musee National d'Art Moderne, Centre Pompidou/Giraudon; 234tc Alamy/The Print Collector; 243cr Art Archive/Claude Debussy Centre, St. Germain en Laye; 243b Alamy/Alex Segre; 244cl Alamy/Vario Images; 245 Pete Clayman; 246-247 Pete Clayman; 248c Corbis/Gideon Mendel; 249tr Corbis/VIP Production; 249cr Digital Vision; 249bl Pete Clayman; 250bl Getty/Koichi Kamoshida; 251tl Getty/Michel Boutefeu; 251tr Corbis/Gideon Mendel; 251cl Alamy/Jerome Yeats; 251cr Alamy/The Photolibrary Wales; 253tr Alamy/Vehbi Koca; 254cr Alamy/Barry Mason; 254bl Photolibrary/Robin Smith; 254b Alamy/Wildscape; 255tr Pete Clayman; 255cr Corbis/Elizabeth Kreutz/Newsport; 255b Alamy/Paul Broadbent; 256 Corbis/Gary Hershorn/Reuters; 258br Corbis/Louie Psihoyos; 259t Corbis/Julian Smith; 259br SPL/A.B. Dowsett; 261cr BAL/BL; 262tl Corbis/Kelley Mooney; 262cr Alamy/Ulrich Doering; 263c Alamy/David R. Frazier; 265cr SPL/Drs A. Yazdani & D.J. Hornbaker; 266cl Photolibrary/Imagesource; 267cr Nicky Studdart; 268tr SPL/Geoff Tompkinson; 268c Alamy/Ace Stock; 269t Corbis/Richard Cummins; 269bl SPL/Klaus Guldbransen; 270cl Corbis/Roger Ressmeyer; 272tr SPL/Robert Brook; 272-273 SPL/Lawrence Lawry; 273tr Digital Vision; 273cr SPL/Andrew Lambert; 275 Corbis/William Taufic; 276c Photolibrary; 277bl SPL/Peter Menzel; 280cr Alamy/Horizon International; 281bl SPL/Scott Bauer/Dept of Agriculture; 281cr Alamy/Roger Bamber; 283 Corbis/Christian Charisius/Reuters; 284-285t SPL/Dr. Kari Lounatmaa; 285cr Corbis/Hulton; 286cl Corbis/George Steinmetz; 286bl Alamy/AWPhoto; 287t SPL/AGS; 288 SPL/Ted Kinsman; 290tr Corbis/David Turnley; 291tl Pete Clayman; 282b Corbis/Brand X; 293tr Corbis/Image 100; 293cl Getty/Stephen Shaver/AFP; 293cr Corbis/Kerry Hayes/Twentieth Century Fox; 294c Alamy/Bill Bachman; 295tl Getty/DK Stock; 295tr Getty/Taxi; 295cr Alamy/Radius Images; 295br Digital Vision; 296 Getty/Science Faction; 297 MDR Kripo; 298b Alamy/Danita Delimont; 299 Corbis/Gabe Palmer; 300 Pete Clayman; 301tl Alamy/Eddie Gerald; 301cr Corbis/Richard T. Nowitz; 305tr Getty/David Taylor; 305cr Corbis/Yuriko Nakao/Reuters; 309cr Alamy/Buzz Pictures; 310bl Rex Pictures/Sipa Press; 310tr SPL/James King-Holmes; 312 Photolibrary/Vidler Vidler.

The Publishers would like to thank the following artists for original material commissioned for this book:
Mark Bergin; Peter Bull; Ray Bryant; Stuart Lafford, Patricia Ludlow, Sebastian Quigley, Sam Weston, Steve Weston (Linden Artists)